"An interesting book that combines reporting with hard-nosed thought about public policy and culture."

—*The Weekly Standard* survey of the best books of 2004

"Steven Rhoads has written an exceptionally brave book that uses a mountain of empirical evidence to show what all of us know intuitively but are usually afraid to say out loud: that men and women are different, and that these differences are in important respects rooted in nature rather than being socially constructed. This book demonstrates in a host of ways how awareness of these differences will have important implications for social policy."

—Francis Fukuyama, author of *The End of History and the Last Man* and *Our Posthuman Future*

"Provocative, compelling, entertaining. Rhoads weaves together the findings of hundreds of new research studies with personal anecdotes in a lively refutation of 40 years of feminist cant."

—*National Review*

"This is a great book. Feminists will hate it. Social engineers will detest it. But ordinary men and women will find it a breath of fresh air."

—*News Weekly* (Australia)

"Steven Rhoads has got balls.... Particularly when it comes to the sexual revolution championed by feminism and the battle over gender roles in the family and, more particularly, in child-rearing, Rhoads' aim at the androgyny project of feminism is withering. One could almost subtitle the book, 'The Misogyny of Feminism's Androgyny Project.'"

—*Virginia Quarterly Review*

"Scintillating and utterly persuasive. For several decades, gender ideologues have aggressively promoted the view that 'gender is a social construction.' Rhoads marshals massive amounts of evidence showing why they are wrong."

—Christina Hoff Sommers, author of *Who Stole Feminism?* and *The War Against Boys*

"Marriage is good for men and women, and children fare better in a home with both a mother and a biological father. And marriage would be better yet, Rhoads concludes, if in the process of negotiating the roles and the rules of marriage, husbands and wives would take sex differences seriously."

—*Academic Questions*

"*Taking Sex Differences Seriously* is a pleasure to read. The book is well written, well researched, and makes a strong contribution to disseminating what we understand about sex differences. The combination of an accessible and engaging writing style and solid footing in the scientific literature makes the work a good undergraduate text or adjunct text, in addition to a fun read for anyone interested in learning more about why men and women differ."

—David C. Geary, Ph.D., Professor and Chair, Department of Psychological Sciences, University of Missouri, and author of *Male, Female: The Evolution of Human Sex Differences*

"The Empress of Androgyny has no clothes. Steven Rhoads provides a responsible, clear, exhaustive, and convincing description of human sex differences and what they mean for social policy and personal life. While members of the academy rush to consume 'natural' foods and protect 'nature' they simultaneously ignore and even avoid 'human nature,' especially in the sexual sphere where political intensity is greatest. Rhoads offers a generous-minded but hard-headed corrective to ideological fatuities and concernocrat assertions which have polluted the intellectual air. And his scholarship is as punctilious as his writing is efficient."

—Lionel Tiger, Darwin Professor of Anthropology, Rutgers University

"Upon finishing Rhoads's work, many readers will discover that they have renewed respect for the nature of women, and, perhaps, unexpected esteem for the nature of men. Where Rhoads succeeds is through his presentation of all views and his relentless attempts to explain human behavior. He ignores nothing and shares with the reader many a citation which does not support his case."

—*Men's News Daily*

"Can we get out of the mess that decades of 'revolution' have left? . . . That would mean, for instance, recognizing that men and women need each other, but in different ways; and that children need mothers and fathers, but need different things from them. It would mean regaining the ability to talk intelligently about what girls and boys, men and women, are like and what they seek in life. This book is a major contribution toward enabling us to do that."

—*The American Spectator*

Taking Sex Differences Seriously

Taking Sex Differences Seriously

Steven E. Rhoads

ENCOUNTER BOOKS
NEW YORK · LONDON

First paperback edition published in 2005 by Encounter Books, an activity of Encounter for Culture and Education, Inc., a nonprofit corporation.

First edition published in 2004 by Encounter Books, an activity of Encounter for Culture and Education, Inc., a nonprofit corporation.

Encounter Books website address: www.encounterbooks.com

Manufactured in the United States and printed on acid-free paper.

The paper used in this publication meets the minimum requirements of ANSI/NISO Z39.48-1992 (R 1997)(Permanence of Paper).

Paperback edition ISBN 978-1-59403-091-8

Library of Congress Cataloging-in-Publication Data

Rhoads, Steven E.
Taking sex differences seriously / Steven E. Rhoads.
p. cm.
Includes bibliographical references and index.
ISBN 1-59403-091-X (alk. paper)
1. Sex roles. 2. Sex differences. 3. Child rearing. I. Title.
HQ1075.R48 2004
395.3—dc22

2004040495

10 9 8 7 6 5 4 3 2 1

for Diana,
the queen of our forest
and
the love of my life

"An interesting book that combines reporting with hard-nosed thought about public policy and culture."

—*The Weekly Standard* survey of the best books of 2004

"Steven Rhoads has written an exceptionally brave book that uses a mountain of empirical evidence to show what all of us know intuitively but are usually afraid to say out loud: that men and women are different, and that these differences are in important respects rooted in nature rather than being socially constructed. This book demonstrates in a host of ways how awareness of these differences will have important implications for social policy."

—Francis Fukuyama, author of *The End of History and the Last Man* and *Our Posthuman Future*

"Provocative, compelling, entertaining. Rhoads weaves together the findings of hundreds of new research studies with personal anecdotes in a lively refutation of 40 years of feminist cant."

—*National Review*

"This is a great book. Feminists will hate it. Social engineers will detest it. But ordinary men and women will find it a breath of fresh air."

—*News Weekly* (Australia)

"Steven Rhoads has got balls. . . . Particularly when it comes to the sexual revolution championed by feminism and the battle over gender roles in the family and, more particularly, in child-rearing, Rhoads' aim at the androgyny project of feminism is withering. One could almost subtitle the book, 'The Misogyny of Feminism's Androgyny Project.'"

—*Virginia Quarterly Review*

"Scintillating and utterly persuasive. For several decades, gender ideologues have aggressively promoted the view that 'gender is a social construction.' Rhoads marshals massive amounts of evidence showing why they are wrong."

—Christina Hoff Sommers, author of *Who Stole Feminism?* and *The War Against Boys*

"Marriage is good for men and women, and children fare better in a home with both a mother and a biological father. And marriage would be better yet, Rhoads concludes, if in the process of negotiating the roles and the rules of marriage, husbands and wives would take sex differences seriously."

—*Academic Questions*

CONTENTS

INTRODUCTION

In 1966, a botched circumcision left one of two male identical twins without a penis. A leading sex psychologist, Dr. John Money of Johns Hopkins University, persuaded the parents to raise the toddler as a female. When the child was twenty-two months old, surgeons castrated him and constructed what appeared from the outside to be female genitalia. Called *Brenda* and treated like a girl, the child was later prescribed female steroids to "facilitate and mimic female pubertal growth and feminization."[1]

When Brenda was twelve, Dr. Money reported that she and her parents had adjusted well.[2] The media loved the story of the "opposite-sex identical twins." In a long report, *Time* magazine called the case "strong support" for the view that "conventional patterns of masculine and feminine behavior can be altered." The 1979 *Textbook of Sexual Medicine* noted the girl's "remarkably feminine" development, which was taken as demonstrating the flexibility and "plasticity of human gender identity and the relative importance of social learning and conditioning in this process."[3]

In academia, numerous introductory psychology and sociology texts used the case to argue that sex roles are basically learned.[4] Theorists who believed that gender roles are socially constructed were ecstatic. In 1994, Judith Lorber described how the girl's parents "bent over backwards to feminize the girl and succeeded. Frilly dresses, hair ribbons, and jewelry created a pride in looks, neatness and 'daintiness.'" The social construction of gender, she concluded, "overrode any possibly inborn traits."[5]

In retrospect, one wonders whether it is fair to say that what happened to Brenda was simply "social construction." With the injection of female hormones and without the male hormones coming from testicles, Brenda was getting a bit more encouragement toward femininity than families and society usually administer. Nonetheless, when the facts became more accurately known, it was clear that neither the chemicals nor the socialization efforts had succeeded in making Brenda a girl. Some hardworking researchers and journalists were able to show that Dr. Money had completely misrepresented the results of his experiment. In the early 1990s, they located the grown-up Brenda and found that she was now named *David*, working in a slaughterhouse, married to a woman, and the adoptive father of three children.[6] At age fourteen, Brenda had decided to start living as a male, and at fifteen, she had been told the truth about her biological past. She then announced that she had always felt like a male and wanted to become one again. She was given a mastectomy, male hormones and a constructed penis.

The story that emerged revealed that David had always acted like a male even when everyone in his world had told him he was a female and should behave like one. The first time "Brenda" was put in a dress, she pulled it off. When given a jump rope, she tied people up or whipped them with it. At nine, she bought a toy machine gun when she was supposed to buy an umbrella. The toy sewing machine went untouched; she preferred to build forts and play with dump trucks. She rejected cosmetics and imitated her dad shaving. On a trip to New York, she found the Rockettes to be sexy. She wanted to urinate standing up. On the playground, her kindergarten and elementary school teachers were struck by her "pressing, aggressive need to dominate."[7]

As the real story of the reconstruction of David was made public, responsible researchers on the Johns Hopkins medical staff decided they should find out what had become of the many boys born without penises, most of whom had been castrated and subsequently raised as girls. Of twenty-five located (ranging in age from five to sixteen), every single one exhibited the rough-and-tumble play more characteristic of boys than girls. Fourteen had declared themselves to be boys, in one case as early as age five. Two children were found who were born without a penis but had not been castrated or sexually reassigned. Both these children, raised as boys, fit in well with their male peers and "were better adjusted psychologically than the reassigned children."[8]

On hearing this Johns Hopkins paper, Dr. Margaret Legato, a Columbia University professor of medicine and an expert on sexual differentiation, asserted: "When the brain has been masculinized by exposure to testosterone [in the womb], it is kind of useless to say to this individual, 'you're a girl.' It is this impact of testosterone that gives males the feelings that they are men."[9]

Scientists today would call this impact of testosterone on the developing brain a permanent "organizational effect," which cannot be altered in any substantial way.[10] When I was growing up, the science of the brain was in its infancy, but everyone assumed that boys and girls had different natures. These days, such a belief is quite controversial. The contrary view—that families and culture create notions of masculinity and femininity and establish gender-specific roles—has become commonplace. And if one looks at changes in male and female behavior over the last fifty years, those who believe in the fluidity of gender have evidence to point to.

My teenage years were in the 1950s, when men and women, boys and girls lived very different lives. Boys asked girls out on dates and made the sexual advances. After graduation, they scoured the "male help wanted" ads and tried to land the well-paid jobs that would impress girls and ultimately enable them to support a wife and children. Husbands were the breadwinners.

On dates, girls were coy and hard to get, at least at the beginning. After graduation, women scanned the "female help wanted" ads for jobs that almost always paid less than those the men sought. They would look to marry, and once they had children, they usually quit their jobs or worked part-time for low wages. Wives were the nurturers and homemakers.

In the few decades that have elapsed since then, the world has been breathtakingly transformed in important ways. Girls frequently ask boys out on dates and sometimes take the sexual initiative. The "his and hers" want ads have thankfully disappeared, and women now flock to the best-paid professions. One sign of the scale of change is the dramatic increase in relative numbers of women and men earning degrees in law and in medicine. In 1960, only 3 percent of law degrees and 6 percent of M.D. degrees were earned by women. In 2000, the equivalent percentages were 46 and 43, respectively.[11] Another sign is the current tendency of most women to remain employed even when they have very young children.

Now, Father's Day never passes without the national media highlighting Mr. Moms. In 2003, for example, Lisa Belkin of the *New York Times* described the life of Michael Zorek, whose only job was taking care of his fourteen-month-old son, Jeremy. Zorek felt that he had become "remarkably good" at shopping, at cooking, and at entertaining his energetic toddler. He was angry at the parents' magazine whose essay contest was open only to mothers. "I'm the one who does the shopping, and I'm the one who does the cooking," he reasoned. "Why is it only sexist when women are excluded?" Mr. Zorek could be a stay-at-home husband because his wife, Shelly Friedland, brought home a good salary as a corporate lawyer.[12]

A month before Belkin's article appeared, *Newsweek*'s cover story, entitled "She Works, He Doesn't," told of more Mr. Moms. The article described the marital tension that frequently accompanied the reversal of historic roles. It noted, as well, that wives of househusbands "have one universal regret: they spend too little time with their children." Still, the mood of this article, like most others on the topic, was upbeat. Marriage historian Stephanie Coontz opined that most couples in the twenty-first century would be taking turns being primary breadwinner and domestic caregiver. The nine women and two men who put the *Newsweek* cover story together concluded that in the future, career-oriented women might think the good catches were not the hard-charging businessmen but rather the laid-back guys with patience and interest in full-time parenting.[13]

Accompanying this sea change in cultural norms has been a telling shift in terminology. When discussing the lives of men and women, we now use the term *gender* far more often than *sex*. Thus, in most circles even the title of this book would be considered anachronistic. Instead of *sex differences,* contemporary observers now usually say *gender differences*. The term *gender difference* reflects the assumption that any distinctions between the sexes' traits, values, interests, skills and behaviors arise from society's rigid gender roles, which channel people's thoughts and actions in stereotypical directions.

This book goes against that grain. It argues that sex differences are large, deeply rooted and consequential. Men and women still have different natures and, generally speaking, different preferences, talents and interests. The book presents evidence that these differences can be explained in part by hormones and other physiological and chemical distinctions between men and women. Thus they won't disappear unless we tinker with our fundamental biological natures.

Though teenage girls may sometimes initiate sex, in time even the most sexually experienced women almost always find that they are emotionally unsuited for casual sex, and their interest in it fades. Similarly, though young girls may ask guys out on dates, when things get more serious, the old patterns of male initiative still hold. In 1952, 76 percent of the married couples polled said that the husband had proposed marriage; 12 percent said the wife had. In 1997, 82 percent said the husband proposed and 9 percent said the wife did. In this 1997 survey, couples under thirty proved to be the most traditional of all: 90 percent said the husband proposed and 4 percent said the wife did.[14]

To explain why traditional behaviors like these haven't changed, this book focuses on three of the most fundamental human passions or instincts—sex, nurturing, and aggression or competitiveness—and shows how differently they manifest themselves in men and women. It reveals why these differences are a part of male and female natures, and why, rather than try to wish or legislate them away, we should take them into account when we think about our culture and public policies.

Mixing modern careers with the often unexpected or inexplicable need to bond with their young, for instance, can bring heartbreaking torment to some of our most talented women. From the earliest ages, distinctions appear between boys' and girls' desire to nurture. Day-old infants cry when they hear recordings of other infants crying, but girls cry longer than boys. Girls between twelve and twenty months old display more empathy and comforting behavior than boys of the same age. A few hours after birth, mothers can recognize their own infant's cry, while fathers rarely can. Fathers are less attuned than mothers to infants' ways of conversing and usually don't enjoy taking care of them for extended periods.

The culture wars are really about the role of women. But women are split between a majority who are traditionally feminine and others who are more like men than their sisters are. The latter group, which on average has been exposed to higher levels of testosterone, is more interested in the physical side of sex, more independent, assertive and career-oriented, more competitive in sports and more conflicted about children. The tension between the two kinds of women will arise in all parts of the book.

I see my task as explaining why the sex differences discussed are profound and why they should affect the way we think about specific policies and cultural issues. Despite the unconventional nature of the argument, I do not think my burden of proof is high. I will not consider my argument disproved if some of my evidence is questioned. There is so much of it that what remains will be enough to challenge the dominant ideology of the last thirty years that sees men and women as having fundamentally equivalent natures and goals. Such an ideology, I believe, cannot withstand scrutiny. We need a new view of gender for a new century.

PART 1

NATURE MATTERS

1
ANDROGYNOUS PARENTING AT THE FRONTIER

If gender identities have changed dramatically, we would see it most clearly among the junior ranks of university faculties. A number of studies indicate that university faculty have less stereotypical understandings of gender roles than do most Americans. For example, though they may not always demonstrate common sense, most academics have been among the brightest students in their high schools, and research shows that intellectually gifted high school students, whether measured by IQ or academic achievement, have less stereotypical personalities, interests and behaviors than others of their sex.[1]

There is other evidence suggesting that academics should be more androgynous than the norm, possessing a mix of masculine and feminine traits. One study finds that both women with jobs and women with college degrees score lower on femininity (gender-related personality traits) than do other women. Moreover, their husbands score somewhat lower on masculinity scales.[2] Another study of women finds that younger age and advanced degrees are both associated with egalitarian gender role attitudes.[3] And still another study finds that "the *expression* of high intellectual ability is linked to the rejection of 'traditional' sex-role ideology."[4]

Attitudes aside, advanced degrees and professional status seem to be associated with a more equal parental distribution of baby care and of domestic work in general.[5] Professors, of course, have advanced degrees and professional status. Moreover, compared with most Americans, university faculty are much more likely to have spouses with advanced degrees and professional status. Thus we would expect men in academic families to do more child care than other men.

With this in mind, I initiated a nationwide study of how male and female faculty members use parental leave. Our research team conducted lengthy phone interviews with 184 assistant professors (109 men and 75 women) trying to obtain tenure—the holy grail of academic job security—while simultaneously raising a child under age two. We wanted to learn about differences in the frequency with which male and female faculty took advantage of paid leave opportunities after the birth of their babies, how much child care each did compared with the spouse, and how they felt about the baby care experience and about gender roles more generally.

More male child care might seem especially likely among those men married to the female professors in our study. These women are serious careerists. The schools that offer paid postbirth leave are generally the rich ones, those ranked among the top colleges and universities in the country. Female assistant professors who have gained appointments at such institutions are typically bright, hardworking and ambitious. If they do not have enough time to do research during their probationary period, they will not achieve tenure. Thus, as two scholars put it, "[If there is] any occupational group in which the ideology of gender equality would be expected to develop sooner than the general population, it would be female college faculty."[6] Husbands of female faculty are also aware of their wives' career requirements and should be more likely than most men to help with baby and toddler care.

In our study, we asked the professors how strongly they agreed or disagreed with the following statement: "Families usually do best if the husband and wife share equally in child care, household work, and paid work." Here is what we found:[7] Over 75 percent of female faculty agreed with this statement, and less than 10 percent disagreed. Male faculty were less supportive, 55 percent agreeing with the statement and 33 percent disagreeing. (Some respondents said they neither agreed nor disagreed.) Although there is a significant difference in responses, it is striking that majorities of both sexes agreed with a statement strongly in support of equal gender roles in child care.

The actual performance of child care tasks, however, did not reflect the professors' intellectual commitments. To start with, the men did not often take the offered leave that might have made equal care of their newborns possible. Whereas 67 percent of eligible female faculty took the paid leave available to them, only 12 percent of male faculty took postbirth leave.

Leave-taking aside, we measured child care effort by specifying twenty-five child care tasks and asking whether they were always or usually done by the respondent, always or usually done by the spouse, or done equally. The tasks encompassed items that assess the division of parental responsibility for basic care (e.g., care when sick, changing diapers); logistics (e.g., taking the child to paid day care or buying food or toys); consulting and planning (e.g., seeking and implementing advice about child care or managing the division of labor for child care); recreation (e.g., playing with the child, taking child for walk in stroller); and emotional involvement (e.g., comforting the child when he/she is upset).

Female academics, on average, did all twenty-five of the tasks far more often than male academics. Gender differences in the amount of child care performed remained extremely large when we compared separately the male and female leave takers on the one hand, and those who did not take leave on the other. While those males who took leave had ample opportunity to participate in child care and did so more than males who took no leave, they still did significantly less baby and toddler care on average than females in either group, those who took leave and those who did not.

If we look only at those faculty who say they believe that child care should be shared equally, we again find that women with this egalitarian attitude do more than half the care, whereas men with these beliefs do less that half. The sex differences in responses were again quite large. More specifically, by their own reports, none of the six men who took leave, had an egalitarian gender ideology and were married to women with full-time jobs did as much as half the baby and toddler care. In fact, taken as a whole, less than 3 percent of our male respondents said they did more child care than their spouses, whereas 96 percent of female faculty said they did more.

Why is there such a disconnect between gender role attitudes and gender role performance? I think that differences in innate male and female preferences are at least partly responsible. We asked our faculty how much they liked doing the twenty-five baby/toddler care tasks (*liked a lot; liked somewhat; neither liked nor disliked*; *disliked somewhat; disliked a lot*). The sex differences here were not as large as the differences in the amount of child care performed; nonetheless, the existence of sex differences was unmistakable. Female faculty liked doing 24 of the 25 tasks more than male faculty, and for 16 of the 25 tasks, this difference was large.

The one task that the men liked to do more than the women was managing the division of labor of parenting tasks. Except for getting up at night to care for the child, this was the task that women liked least, perhaps because taking on this task led to tension or arguments with their husbands.

The survey revealed other evidence that women like baby care very much. Of the 72 women who breastfed their child, 71 indicated that they enjoyed it. For the set of twenty-five questions measuring enjoyment of all the child care tasks, only 2 percent of the total female responses indicated a strong dislike for a task. Only 14 percent of the time did women indicate a moderate dislike for a task. In other words, to the extent that female responses varied on the appeal of child care, the variation was usually between indifference and great enjoyment. There was relatively little indication of actual dislike. Women often indicated liking what to most men seem disagreeable tasks, such as changing the child's diapers. More women liked than disliked this task, while two times as many men disliked it as liked it.

One reason that women may like baby and toddler care more than men do is that the children respond more favorably to a mother's care. We asked our respondents if the child seemed to have a preference about whom he played with and who comforted him. There were essentially no differences with respect to playing, but the children had an overwhelming preference for being comforted by their mothers. All in all, when the babies had a preference, the babies and toddlers preferred their mothers to their fathers by fourteen to one. Even among men who took leave, the children were twice as likely, by their father's report, to want to be comforted by their mother.

Academic women seem to enjoy baby and toddler care. Our survey shows that they also love their jobs and they care almost as much about getting tenure as the male faculty do. Yet these women are dramatically more likely to have thought about dropping off the tenure track or getting out of the academic world entirely because of the pressures of balancing work and family. Fully half of all female professors in the survey responded that they had considered leaving the tenure track, while only 27 percent of the male professors had thought of doing so. Additionally, academic women are nearly twice as likely as the men to report feeling overwhelmed by their responsibilities as a parent and are much more likely to report that the division of child care labor in the family is unfair to them.[8]

Paid postbirth leave originally appeared in academia as a way to help level the playing field for young women trying to get tenure while raising children. But the women's movement has insisted on policy that resists stereotypes and encourages men to take on a larger share of parenting. As a result, most of the professors in our survey were at institutions that allowed both fathers and mothers to take paid postbirth leave.

Despite what they said about the importance of sharing child-rearing, these male professors, who by all rights should be more egalitarian than most men, were not often taking leave, nor were they doing intensive baby care in the way that the female professors were. Indeed, there is reason to think that our formal results overstate how much of it the male faculty actually do. When we debriefed our phone interviewers, they said that the men often seemed embarrassed when they kept answering that their wives always or usually did the specific child care tasks we enumerated. Half way through the list, one guy joked, "I don't sound too good here, do I?" Another admitted, "If I were completely honest, I would look like a bad parent." Some men even interrupted their string of "she does it more" answers with editorials to the effect that their wives were more emotionally suited to baby care. The interviewers on the survey came to believe that many of the men were also defensive on the questions about enjoying baby care and were saying they liked it more than they really did because they were embarrassed to tell the truth.

We heard stories of male academics who took paid postbirth leave in order to advance their publishing agendas. One top university had to change its rules in an effort to minimize this behavior. Some assistant professors were taking leave even though their wives didn't have jobs. Another had taken leave while his child was in full-time day care. At my own university, a young female colleague has told me of similar instances of male abuse of the policy at the school where she received her Ph.D. She also recalls a revealing conversation with a male colleague upon her return from postbirth leave. He asked how the leave had gone, and she replied, "I used the time well." Then the man said, "So you got a lot of work done"—a statement that did not reflect what she meant at all.

One woman gave this answer to an open-ended request for further thoughts about tenure-track professors facing parenthood: "If women and men are both granted parental leaves and women recover/nurse/do primary care and men do some care and finish articles, there's a problem, though a problem with no clear solution."

Solutions would become clearer if we took sex differences seriously. Our study of parental leave in academia shows that despite egalitarian gender ideologies, almost none of our male faculty, including male leave takers, do half the baby care. Even the three men (out of 109) who say they *do* perform half the work are not simultaneously recovering from pregnancy and delivery as their female counterparts are. Moreover, none of them is breastfeeding, a task more time-consuming and physically draining than any of the other tasks in the survey.

Refusal to take sex differences seriously, rather than helping women, leads to a policy that could injure those seeking tenure by giving their male counterparts an unfair advantage. If men should begin to take leave in much larger numbers, far from leveling the playing field, gender-neutral postbirth leaves will tilt the field further in favor of men.

this must be a tiny fringe; but in fact it is cutting-edge theory. Anne Fausto-Sterling believes that labeling someone *male* or *female* is a "social decision." To bolster her case, she points to hermaphrodites and other instances of biological ambiguity.[8] Similarly, O. Muldoon and J. Reilly doubt there is a biological basis for the view that male and female are "dichotomous, mutually exclusive categories."[9] And a respected feminist literary theorist thinks that by realizing "we are not two sexes, but as many as there are humans in the world," we can liberate the "polymorphous creativity of nongendered minds."[10] Other feminists, however, warn that doing away with the category of *women* means "political paralysis, for no political program can be launched on behalf of a nonexistent subject."[11]

Almost all feminists are committed to some practical political goals that advance the interests of women. One might then wonder why so many of them subscribe to the view that neither sex nor gender is grounded in nature—a view that will seem outlandish to many who might otherwise have been brought to endorse feminist causes. The explanation rests in the unswerving commitment of most academic feminists to a world in which men and women share domestic and other kinds of work equally. Some of these feminists believe that even granting the existence of these two fundamental categories—men and women—could lessen the chances of achieving this goal.

A leading academic theorist, Susan Okin, asks us to imagine a "just future"—one without gender:

> In its social structures and practices, one's sex would have no more relevance than one's eye color or the length of one's toes. No assumptions would be made about "male" and "female" roles; childbearing would be so conceptually separate from child rearing and other family responsibilities that it would be a cause for surprise, and no little concern, if men and women were not equally responsible for domestic life or if children were to spend much more time with one parent than the other. It would be a future in which men and women participated in more or less equal numbers in every sphere of life, from infant care to different kinds of paid work to high-level politics.[12]

Another theorist, Judith Lorber, defends the same vision: "Unless women and men are seen as socially interchangeable, gender equality does not challenge the concept of sex differences that leads to separate spheres in the family and marketplace division of labor, which in turn results in women's lesser access to control of valued resources and positions of power."[13]

Child care would seem to be the greatest hurdle in the way of real-world implementation of this vision. As Simone de Beauvoir once famously proclaimed, children are the problem. If women stay home for the first year after a baby's birth, they will lag behind their husbands on the career "fast track." Since the husbands, on average, will be bringing home more money, it will consequently make monetary sense for the women to be the ones jeopardizing careers for the sake of the family. And if many women make these choices, all female careerists will lose because employers will assume that their female employees are less likely than their male employees to be fully committed to their jobs.

In view of this dilemma, Supreme Court justice Ruth Bader Ginsberg, a committed feminist, focuses on child care in some of her speeches. "Motherly love ain't everything it has been cracked up to be," she asserts. "To some extent it's a myth that men have created to make women think that they do this job to perfection." Ginsberg believes that women will not be truly liberated until men share child care with them equally.[14]

But most women do not share Ginsberg's ideal. Many want to spend lots of time with their children, and, as we will see in Chapters 8 and 9, most think husbands should concentrate on providing and wives on nurturing. Many feminists deal with these difficulties by suggesting that since gender differences are the product of a patriarchal culture, women's unequal status may lead them to have irrational "adaptive preferences" by which they come to validate their own unequal status.[15]

Other theorists have criticized this feminist approach, arguing that even if someone's identity and tastes are in large part socially given, that identity and those tastes are what count. Conforming to someone else's view of what one should be is unlikely to make a person happy, so it makes little sense to measure well-being on the basis of hypothetical desires.[16]

How to Assess the Debate over Sex Differences

Unlike feminists, researchers whose business it is to consider biological explanations for sex differences believe these differences are large and that social construction cannot explain them. Anne Campbell notes that among the human universals found in every known society are binary distinctions between men and women, division of labor by sex, more child care by women, more aggression by men and domination of the public sphere by men.[17] (Campbell remarks that she takes no pleasure in the latter fact and fervently hopes to see it altered.)

Psychologist Alice Eagly, who does not attach great consequence to biological distinctions between the sexes, may well be the most prolific researcher of sex differences in the whole country. Her articles are widely cited in the leading psychology texts on sex and gender. Yet in "The Science and Politics of Comparing Women and Men," she argues that these texts set forth an outdated consensus on the indefiniteness of sex differences. In Eagly's view, they draw on feminist research of the 1970s, which, in order to eliminate stereotypes hindering women from fulfilling their potential, highlighted the idea that sex differences were ephemeral. According to Eagly, however, new research indicates that women and men really do conform to some of these stereotypes: Women, for example, do "tend to manifest behaviors that can be described as socially sensitive, friendly, and concerned with others' welfare, whereas men tend to manifest behaviors that can be described as dominant, controlling and independent." In other words, ordinary people's gender stereotypes are, as Eagly says, "fairly accurate," and most people do recognize that men and women occupy "partially overlapping groups, possessing different average levels of various attributes." Eagly concludes that scientists currently studying men and women "have begun to realize" that they have shattered "not cultural stereotypes," but the "scientific consensus forged in the feminist movement of the 1970's."[18]

In a still more recent study, Lloyd Lueptow and his colleagues complain that most research on gender has "almost completely" ignored a "large and consistent body of empirical evidence" revealing differences between men and women; the result has been "a discrepancy between the empirical evidence and the assumptions current in the sex role literature."[19] As far as they are concerned, the results of their research and that of others are "very clear": gender stereotypes "are not decreasing, if anything they are intensifying."[20]

If explanations based on socialization were correct—that is, if changes in sex roles lead to changes in the characteristics of the two sexes—then sex differences should be decreasing at a rapid rate because of the dramatic changes in sex roles in recent decades. But in fact, the most notable change observed by Lueptow and colleagues was an *increase* in the femininity of females, a result completely opposite to that predicted by the socialization model. Other studies find that self-descriptions as well as stereotypes are unchanged over the last thirty-five years. Women, for example, are much more likely than previously to describe themselves as "tender-minded" and men to consider themselves "assertive."[21]

Other writers whose approach to gender has been influenced by biology have more directly blamed feminists for ignoring or belittling good science on sex differences.[22] But the other side replies that some of the sociobiological literature is filled with "sexism," "biased selection of examples" and "a social construction of gender that is relatively independent of the facts."[23] Mainstream feminists regularly charge that a hidden or not so hidden agenda meant to preserve male status lies behind the sex difference research.[24]

Feminists who make charges of this kind are often remarkably candid in declaring that their politics influence their scientific judgments. Thus Anne Fausto-Sterling admits to demanding "the highest standards of proof . . . on claims about biological inequality."[25] Sheila Tobias, author of *Overcoming Math Anxiety,* says she does research on girls and math to get the truth, but also to get the country to believe that girls have the potential to perform equally with boys.[26]

As Eagly suggests, academic feminists originally loved sex difference research because they were sure the results would show that such differences were either nonexistent or inconsequential. Then, the patriarchy would collapse. Naomi Weisstein remembers, "We really believed that pretty soon we could change the world."[27]

Instead, the new evidence has pointed to significant and enduring differences; so now many feminists say that gender differences are not "a relevant feminist concern." They argue that by focusing on those differences, we ignore the social forces that cause them and the ways in which society converts difference into female disadvantage.[28]

Many feminists outside academia are angry about research that supports the notion of fundamental differences between the sexes. Gloria Steinem accuses it of keeping women down and even of being anti-American. Gloria Allred asserts that the research is "harmful and dangerous to our daughters' lives, to our mothers' lives."[29]

Inside academia, feminists are every bit as angry. When Rachel Gur presented her research on differences in brain activity, she was approached afterward by a group of female medical students who asked her not to publicize her work.[30] When Alice Eagly presented her data calling into question the out-of-date consensus on sex differences, people in the audience began stomping their feet and glowering.[31] Camilla Benbow's early work on sex differences in cognition led the American Women in Science to cancel a half-day of their meetings in order to free up time to attack her research.[32]

Researchers who study sex differences seem convinced that it is hard to get this work funded and the results published. Diane McGuinness told me that her research in other areas was considered fine and publishable, but her work on sex differences was deemed unpublishable. She said publication difficulties became so tiresome that she dropped sex difference research in favor of safer topics.[33] J. Richard Udry, a chaired professor of sociology at the University of North Carolina and past president of the Population Association of America, has done substantial research on biological influences on gender roles. When he first proposed research revealing that the hormonal environment of fetuses in mothers' wombs could help explain gender role behavior of women later in life, reviewers were skeptical but thought the project worthy of support nonetheless. Indeed, the funding review panel ranked Udry's proposal in the top 2 percent of all applicants. When his data strongly supported his hypothesis, he applied three separate times for funding of a study seeking to replicate his findings using different data. All three applications were rejected. Professor Udry has told me that he has never before been rejected three times for any of his proposed projects.[34]

Feminist suspicions of sex difference research are based in part on the unscientific opinions that have made their way into this research in the past. Until quite recently, arguments about differences between the sexes were often linked to claims about the inferiority of women. A prominent nineteenth-century social psychologist declared that "all psychologists who have studied the intelligence of women ... recognize today that they represent the most inferior forms of human evolution and that they are closer to children and savages than to an adult civilized male."[35] Sometimes much was made of women's smaller head and brain size. Also in the nineteenth century, Dr. Edward Clarke of the Harvard medical school produced a text that went through seventeen printings arguing that women were physically and intellectually weaker than men and should not be educated in the same way. Horatio Storer, a nineteenth-century officer of the American Medical Association, focused especially on menstruation, calling it a form of "temporary insanity" that left women more in need of medical aid than able to furnish it to anyone else.[36]

Today, however, the majority of the sex difference researchers who focus on biology are women. In preparing his book on sex differences, Robert Pool read widely and spoke to many researchers in the field, and was struck by the fact that this research fraternity was "really a sorority. Most of the scientists doing the provocative, ground-breaking research into human sex preferences are women." This seems to be for two reasons: First, men are wary about publishing any findings that might bring charges of sexism. Second, some female researchers seem to have been suspicious about what their male colleagues were up to; these women say they got involved because they believed that male researchers were neglecting the serious study of women. Others did so because they were intrigued and troubled by some differences favoring men and they wanted to find out what could explain these results.[37] Pool finds that almost all of these female researchers "identify themselves as feminists or at least sympathize with feminist goals. . . . They are not fools or tools of male-dominated society, nor do they have any hidden agendas, and they uniformly resent such implications."[38]

Many of these female researchers also began their studies convinced that sex differences were minimal and that societal forces caused those that existed. John Williams and Deborah Best, for example, began their international comparison of stereotypes believing there was no basis for them, but concluded that they had "a substantial degree of behavioral validity" and were explained in part by biology.[39] Similarly, Diane Halpern intended to demonstrate that any gender differences in cognition were the result of "socialization practices, artifacts and mistakes in the research, and bias and prejudice."

> After reviewing a pile of journal articles that stood several feet high and numerous books and book chapters that dwarfed the stack of journal articles, I changed my mind. . . . [T]here are real, and in some cases sizable, sex differences with respect to some cognitive abilities. Socialization practices are undoubtedly important, [*sic*] there is also good evidence that biological sex differences play a role.[40]

It is not usually pleasant to change one's mind about core convictions, but these researchers say the data has forced them to do so.[41] Eleanor Maccoby's research has led her to give more emphasis to biology in her study of children. In a recent lecture, after noting the stereotypical pattern of young boys' and girls' fantasy stories (Batman and the like for boys, brides and ballet for girls), Maccoby told her audience of fellow academics, "I too want to say, 'ugh.'"[42] But the truth was the truth.

Two groups of well-educated female feminists are involved in this debate. One conducts the studies and has reluctantly come to believe that sex differences are significant and to a substantial degree biologically based. The other mainly critiques the studies and has little or no interest in seeing them conducted at all. This group's worldview would collapse if the research in question were universally accepted.

A Biological Basis for Sex Differences: Types of Evidence

If some female researchers reluctantly abandoned the view that socialization accounted for significant sex differences after seeing research evidence, others first began to doubt socialization theories when they had children of their own. Many educated, nonacademic feminists also became more open to the arguments for the centrality of sex differences after they became parents. This makes good sense because many sex differences become apparent at an astonishingly early age—well before society has had much of an opportunity to shape preferences, character and behavior. And they often occur in families that are determined to raise gender-neutral children.

The mother of one such family wrote in the 1980s of her Herculean efforts to bring up a peaceable male three-year-old in left-leaning Berkeley. The men in the area raised funds for the nuclear freeze movement; the women walked in anti-Reagan marches. At home, the only television her son watched was *Sesame Street.* There were no toy guns in his home or in the homes of his four closest friends. The local toy store didn't even carry toy guns.

Nevertheless, the boy seemed to be obsessed with guns. He quickly learned that Tinker Toys make wonderful guns, and one of his male friends found that even waffles could be used to shoot his dad at breakfast. As soon as the boy learned to switch TV channels, he turned from *Sesame Street* to what he called "shooting" cartoons.

The mother mused that surely the culture had introduced her son to guns. But on the other hand, it had also introduced him to "computers and ocean liners and farm animals" and a lot of other interesting things that had not become comparable obsessions. The boy knew that his mother strongly disapproved of guns; but the only effect this had was a touching concern on his part for her sensibilities. When he entered a big toy store, he ran straight for "a shelf that looked like the welcoming table at a Third World arms convention." When his mother caught up with him, he looked up at her and said kindly, "Mommy, don't look at this. These are guns. You don't like guns but I do. So I'm going to look at them."[43]

Feminist parents of daughters are no less frustrated. This Berkeley mother observed that the neighborhood was filled with female bus drivers and women in overalls and running shoes, but the little girls didn't seem to be getting the message. Devlin would not go to nursery school in anything but a dress and tights. Nicole, not yet two, insisted every morning that her mom pull out the dress and the "shoes with seat belts" (strap pumps) that she had worn to a wedding the previous summer. Even spunky Rachel, the best baseball player on the block and the daughter of a fierce-willed attorney, announced to the boys that she didn't want to play ball anymore, but instead would be the cheerleader.

Academics often cite their own kids as the impetus for their research on sex differences. Science writer Deborah Blum, who grew up with toy stoves *and* baseball gloves in what she calls a PC household, was taken aback when her sons displayed traditionally male personality traits from the day they were born.[44] Marc Breedlove, an expert on sex differences at the University of California at Berkeley, favored nurture over nature until he had a daughter. He observed that her older brothers' toys did not interest the girl. Before she could talk, the thing she most wanted to do was go into her mother's closet and put on her mother's shoes. Her mother wore a dress maybe three times a year, but by age six, Breedlove's daughter would wear only dresses. Breedlove now uses the term "childless" to describe people who think "society alone molds children into sex roles."[45]

Some feminist academics, of course, look at similar facts and draw opposite conclusions. Virginia Valian has studied young children and noticed that boys are quite different from girls by the age of two. The boys do more running around, and when looking at a picture book with passengers in vehicles, the boys focus on the vehicles while the girls focus on the people inside. Valian has been "astonished" by the depth of "passion" some boys have for vehicles. Before his second birthday, one child knew the difference by name between a front-end loader, a back-end loader, a dump truck, a cement mixer and other kinds of trucks. His parents said that when he was eight months old, he would periodically get excited for no apparent reason, but eventually the parents "connected the excitement with the sound of a neighbor's Volkswagen driving down the street."[46]

While noting the broad range of characteristics that separate boys and girls, however, Valian cautions against drawing broad conclusions from such observations. She reminds us that we are not really aware of the different ways we treat the sexes from the first moments of their lives. In the final paragraph of her book *Why So Slow? The Advancement of Women*, she assures her readers that egalitarian parents can "bring up their children so that both girls and boys play with dolls and trucks."[47]

But Valian's story about the truck-loving baby makes it clear that the parents were not responsible for that passion. Nor are parents responsible for the way girls focus on the passengers and not the trucks. In trying to encapsulate an important moment in her life, one *Washington Post* reader said,

> My 20-month-old son looks out the window and eagerly asks, "It coming?" He sees the cans on the corner and knows it is the day. He can hear the sounds from down the block. He reaches out for my hand and says, "Let go see!" We walk hand-in-hand, looking for the garbage truck. Each time we find it, it is as if we are seeing it for the first time. I look at his face, filled with joy, and realize that I look forward to that Friday morning more than he does.[48]

When new toys are introduced in nursery school, the boys drop what they are doing to go over and look. When new children are introduced, it is the girls who show more curiosity.[49] Young boys are interested in "machines, weapons and deeds"; they like "chasing, climbing, wrestling, cowboys and jumping." If given dolls, they sometimes put them in vehicles and drive them off a dollhouse or beat their heads against furniture. Young girls are interested in "people, clothes and words"; they like playing with dolls, whispering, drawing and dressing up.[50]

Many of these differences appear "from the very beginning of autonomous behavior"—too early to have been affected by much socialization.[51] Still, our expectations can certainly influence what we see. Feminists who like to focus on social construction frequently cite a study in which college students watched a nine-month-old sometimes called *Dana* and sometimes *David*. When watching the identical film, students watching *Dana* were more likely to see a timid and sensitive child; those watching *David* tended to see a strong and bold one.[52] But the gender texts tell us much less about an experiment that involved watching different babies, not identified by sex. On average, "the female babies were judged to be more sensitive, the males to be stronger."[53]

Compared with one-day-old male infants, one-day-old females respond more strongly to the sound of a human in distress. One-week-old baby girls can distinguish an infant's cry from other noise; boys usually cannot. Three-day-old girls maintain eye contact with a silent adult for twice as long as boys. Girls will look even longer if the adult talks; it makes no difference to boys. Four-month-old girls can distinguish photographs of those they know from people they do not; boys the same age generally cannot. On the other hand, five-month-old boys are more interested than girls in three-dimensional geometric forms and in blinking lights. They smile and babble at them as if they were animate—a mistake that girls rarely make.[54]

Young children, moreover, are quick to self-segregate by sex, a fact that puzzles researchers. Experiments conducted with infants suggest that nature must have something to do with it, since same-sex preferences are clearly present before playmates arrive on the scene. One-year-old infants will prefer to look at same-sex children even if the girl is shown in dark dungarees banging on a drum and the boy in a frilly dress holding a doll. When shown movies with infants of both sexes in them, the boys will look at the boy babies more and the girls at the girl babies. If you attach lights to the joints of the infant models and show movies of just the lights moving, the babies have little trouble identifying the gender of each model, and they prefer looking at one of their own sex.[55]

Studies Comparing Cultures

Social science is about generalizing; we try to find patterns that hold across time and/or space. As political scientists, for instance, we think we are on to something important if we find that for several elections in a row, an increasing proportion of women are voting Democratic while more men vote Republican. We talk about "gender gaps" even though the split in each party may be only about 60/40. Moreover, no one protests if we talk about such a gap, even if it does not hold across time or place—if it has not always been present, and if in many other countries women do not vote disproportionately for the "liberal" party. How then can we ignore gender gaps like those that Eagly talks about—women showing more friendliness and sensitivity, and men more dominance and independence—when they are apparently universal and timeless?

Alan Feingold did a sophisticated and extensive survey of gender differences in personality across cultures and came to conclusions similar to Eagly's. Moreover, Feingold found that the "differences in personality traits [such as independence and friendliness] were generally constant across ages, years of data collection, educational levels and nations."[56] Williams and Best wrote one book comparing cross-national stereotypes and another looking at cross-national personality traits. As noted above, they were surprised to find substantial likenesses across cultures. They were also surprised to find that "men are not appreciably more masculine, nor women more feminine, in traditional countries than in egalitarian countries."[57] Similarly, Gallup international opinion surveys find very substantial cross-national agreement about sex differences in many personality traits.[58]

Cross-nationally, girls show more interest in babies and are preferred as babysitters.[59] Neither Israeli kibbutzim nor U.S. communes have had any success in abolishing such sex roles, although many have made doing so their highest priority.[60] In the United States there are predictable differences as to what activities are found enjoyable. Women, for example, enjoy activities such as decorating a room with flowers and reading the family pages in newspapers, while men enjoy tinkering with small hand tools and reading the sports section. Moreover, the sex differences on these sorts of measures were essentially unchanged from the 1930s to the 1980s.[61]

Evolutionary Psychology

Evolutionary psychology presents a coherent account of why sex differences exist. This discipline is increasingly influential, but also controversial.[62] One area of evolutionary psychology studies sexual selection, which concerns characteristics that enable one to beat out intrasexual competitors so as to be preferred as a mate by the opposite sex. The following chapter presents evidence that men and women prefer somewhat different traits in mates. Indeed, these differences, which include differences in personality and temperament, are large enough so that evolutionary psychologists often treat men and women as subspecies.[63] Evolutionary psychologists look to sexual selection to explain how male and female roles in reproduction and subsequently in the nurturing of the child would induce contrasting psychological predispositions in men and women. For example, in a wide range of societies, West and East, developed and underdeveloped, men have stronger libidos and a greater taste for a variety of sexual partners than women do.

In the earliest epochs of human existence, males who procreated with many fertile, healthy mates were more likely to produce surviving offspring than males who did not, while women, who had to carry and nurse their children, did not have this option in passing on their genes. In contrast, those most apt to reproduce successfully were choosy women who favored partners with traits that would enhance the survival of their children. As a result of this evolutionary mechanism, women care more about a mate's status and resources than men do. A woman who chose to mate only with unusually strong men or men with resources and a willingness to commit them to her children's needs would increase her children's likelihood of survival, and thus through the ages women with such tastes would be more apt to reproduce successfully.

Most of human genetic inheritance developed while people were hunters and gatherers, their condition during 99 percent of hominid existence. Evolutionists call this state of affairs the "environment of evolutionary adaptation (EEA)."[64] During this time, males and females passed on their genes only if they could survive long enough to mate and if their offspring survived long enough to mate, and so on.

Evolutionary psychologists think that because women did the foraging, they developed a better memory than men for where things exist in space. Women who could remember where edible plants were located "within complex arrays of vegetation" were more likely to find foods in later growing seasons.[65]

Evolutionists point out that our adaptations are suited "more to life in the EEA than to life in the present."[66] A common contemporary scenario provides evidence for this position. Husbands (including this one) regularly lose things and have to ask their wives to find household objects. Studies show that women really are better at remembering the location of objects in general. In one of many experiments that have demonstrated this, students were asked to sit in a room for a bit until an experiment was ready for them. After three minutes, they were called into another room and asked to remember the location of objects in the waiting room. The women did 60 to 70 percent better at this task.[67]

Brain Research: Structure and Hormones

Brain research also reveals inherent sex differences. For example, neuroscientists have determined that men have fewer neurons connecting the left and right hemispheres of the brain.[68] This difference may help to explain why women are better at talking about their emotions. (The left brain controls talking; the right brain controls emotions.)[69]

More important than physical differences between the male and female brains are differences in the way the sexes use their brains and in the effect of their brains' hormones. Positron emission tomography (PET) scans show that women seem to use more neurons for almost every activity tested.[70] The typical woman's brain seems to be "networked," the typical man's compartmentalized. The woman's way seems to be better for many verbal tasks and for recovery from strokes, the man's for spatial tasks.[71]

The popular press focuses on testosterone, the most important of the masculinizing androgens, when referring to the effect of hormones on sex-differentiated preferences and behavior.[72] Women have testosterone, but men have much more, typically at least ten times as much.[73] Later we'll explore the consequences of this disparity in detail. For the time, it is worth noting that researchers attuned to biology are convinced that men's higher testosterone levels explain in large part their greater desire to dominate. Mainstream feminists ask how one can be so sure. They postulate that successful dominance in a patriarchal society could give men a testosterone high—that is, causation may run from the behavior to the high testosterone, instead of the reverse.

There is no question but that competitive success—in games such as tennis, wrestling and chess, for example—can give one a testosterone boost.[74] So causation can indeed go from environmental or behavioral factors to biological ones, in this case a change in hormone levels because of competition and achievement. But in many cases, high testosterone clearly causes aggressive or dominating behavior rather than the other way around. First, studies have shown that prenatal levels of testosterone are more important than adult levels in explaining later preferences and behavior.[75] Prenatal levels cannot be explained by the kind of environmental factors that social-constructionist feminists focus on. Second, forty years of animal research has clearly established that "the same hormones which cause between-sex differences in a behavior cause within-sex variance in the same behavior."[76] And researchers who study women exposed to unusually high doses of testosterone find that they are much more masculine than most women. Similarly, women who do not produce any testosterone "are exaggeratedly feminine in their behavior, with typically a special interest in babies, clothes, housekeeping and romantic stories."[77]

Two Kinds of Females, One Kind of Male

Academic feminists sometimes charge that scientists spend all their time studying men, but scientists doing research on hormonal sex difference certainly cannot be accused of this bias. They spend most of their time studying women. There are some significant testosterone-related differences in men's attitudes and behavior, and these will be discussed in a moment. But the scientists usually study women because the more interesting and consequential differences are among women. Those with below-average levels of testosterone seem more feminine; those with high testosterone often seem to mix the feminine and masculine. In short, while there is one basic type of man in civil society, there appear to be two types of women.

The women exposed prenatally to very high levels of testosterone have been studied most extensively. Most of these have a condition known as congenital adrenal hyperplasia (CAH). With optimal therapy, the hormone levels of these women can be returned to normal postnatally. But the prenatal and neonatal exposure to high levels of testosterone has dramatic and persistent effects on girls. They "prefer boys' toys which are more mechanical than girls' toys. They like transportation and construction toys, including helicopters, cars, fire engines, blocks, and Lincoln Logs better than dolls, kitchen supplies, toy telephones, and crayons and paper."[78] These girls are more aggressive than most girls, including their unaffected sisters. They like rough-and-tumble play. They are more competitive and self-assured.[79] They are much more likely than most girls to be long-term tomboys and are less interested than most in clothes, cosmetics, infant care and keeping a diary.[80] Looking to the future, CAH girls age eleven and older have less of a wish "to have their own children" and more of a wish for "having a career versus staying at home."[81] The CAH girls also have better spatial skills than most girls. (In men, a relatively low testosterone level is most regularly associated with spatial talent, but girls with a relatively high level of testosterone approach this male talent level more closely.)[82]

Supporting these findings are studies of pregnant women who have ingested masculinizing hormones to help prevent miscarriage. Girls born to such women have preferences and behaviors like those of CAH girls.[83] Recent studies comparing female identical twins to the female half of mixed-sex twins have also been informative. Female twins born as part of a mixed-sex pair are more likely to enjoy taking risks and to do better on spatial tests.[84]

J. Richard Udry of the University of North Carolina provides the most convincing evidence for the importance of hormones in explaining differences among women. Udry managed to find a group of 163 adult women whose mothers had given blood samples while they were pregnant thirty years earlier. These samples had been preserved, and testosterone levels in the mothers' blood could thus be analyzed. There was also information on the presence of a hormone-binding globulin that prevents testosterone from passing through the mother's membranes to reach the fetus.

The mothers had also been interviewed about their childrearing practices when their children were young and again when they were adolescents. Udry did further interviews and took blood samples from the children, now fully grown. He then developed a "gendered" scale including factors relating to the importance of home (e.g., domestic division of labor), feminine interests (e.g., likes baby care), job status (e.g., proportion female in current or last job) and masculine/feminine self-image (e.g., adjective checklist).

There were some limitations in the thirty-year-old data: Only one second-trimester blood sample, when testosterone levels are the most decisive, had been taken from each of the mothers. And no blood samples had been taken from the fetuses, where testosterone levels would have been even more informative. Even so, after controlling for socialization variables, Udry found that testosterone exposure levels *in utero* and, to a lesser degree, adult testosterone levels thirty years later predicted gendered behavior to a statistically significant degree.[85] In other words, women exposed to more testosterone were less stereotypically feminine. For example, higher-testosterone women had stronger career ambitions and weaker interests in caring for babies than did women exposed to less testosterone.

In further research, Udry attempted to sort out the degree to which socialization can override physiological factors such as androgen exposure. Trying to determine if parents can steer girls toward the feminine, Udry questioned the adult women whose behavior had been predicted in part by their prenatal exposure to androgens: "Did your parents encourage you to defend yourself physically, to repair things around the house, to be athletic, to have an interest in math?" Such encouragements counted as efforts to produce more masculine behavior. Udry also asked, "Did your parents encourage you to wear jewelry, to wear dresses, to have an interest in sewing, to plan to have children?" Those mothers who had encouraged the most feminine behaviors as against the masculine ones were considered to have done the most to promote femininity in their daughters.

Udry found that parents' ability to create a more feminine daughter is dependent on their daughter's prenatal androgen exposure. Women with low exposure to androgens were strongly affected by their mother's encouragement to take on the trappings of femininity. But when mothers tried to encourage femininity in women with high androgen exposure, their efforts had little effect. Indeed, Udry concluded, "The more the parents worked to improve below average femininity, the less successful they were; the more they tried, the less feminine the daughters were as adults."[86]

Elizabeth Cashdan's work further supports the idea that there are two kinds of women. Testing the amount of testosterone and other masculinizing hormones in the blood of thirty-two Utah college women, she found that young women with high levels of these hormones were the most interested in casual sex, had the highest self-regard, and seemed the most assertive. These students' high levels of self-regard, however, did not reflect the views of their social peers. These women were not popular with their female peers, and in fact they overrated their popularity with same-sex peers more than the other women did.[87]

Other research also clearly links high testosterone in women to more typically masculine characteristics. A 1985 study found that the women with high testosterone were full of confidence and energy (and perhaps full of themselves), much as Cashdan's and the CAH research did. These women saw themselves as impulsive but also robust, resourceful, sharp-witted and enterprising. By contrast, low-testosterone women saw themselves as civilized, rational, helpful, practical and worrying.[88]

Again, as with Cashdan, other studies link high testosterone in women to a greater interest in sex, though also to arguing more with partners.[89] High-testosterone women are more assertive, more career-oriented, and more likely to have high-status and traditionally male-dominated careers.[90] Such women are also more likely to have a male-typical brain pattern. Like the CAH children discussed earlier, high-testosterone women have superior spatial skills as compared with low-testosterone women. (Women in general do better in spatial skills when tested during the time in their cycles when their estrogen levels are lowest—a result hard to explain by recourse to socialization theory.)[91] High-testosterone women are infertile in higher proportions than low-testosterone women. They are also more likely to be balding, but with large amounts of body hair, and to have high blood pressure.[92]

The research described here does not indicate that high-testosterone women look or act like men. Instead, it suggests that compared with other women they are more likely to mix typically feminine with typically masculine traits and behaviors.

One study, for example, found that female scientists tend to have better spatial ability than other female careerists, though less than male scientists. This study did not measure testosterone, but other research described above associates high testosterone with female spatial ability (helpful in many scientific fields) and with an interest in stereotypically male careers such as science. Female scientists on average are found to have a lower need for approval than most female careerists, but a greater need than male scientists. They have narrower interests than other female careerists, but broader interests than male scientists.[93] Another study finds that very bright seventeen-year-old women who seek a time-intensive career, a preference associated in other studies with high testosterone, spend less time than equally bright noncareerist women in thinking about the age to marry and start a family, but that equally bright careerist boys spend even less time thinking about marriage and family.[94]

Testosterone and Men

It should go without saying that there are noticeable and important differences among males as well as among females. In high school, boys tend to settle into different groups—for example, the jocks and the nerds—based on mutual interests such as athletics or computers. But this male variation is more superficial than fundamental. Responsible men everywhere have the same role: protectors and providers for their wives and families.[95] The real issue among men is whether they have enough testosterone or too much—whether they are masculine or hypermasculine.

High-testosterone men are more likely to be big-boned and muscular, rambunctious and self-confident, always seeking to dominate. Perhaps ironically, the very high-testosterone man does not do as well in the contemporary world as the low-testosterone man. The latter, on average, has better spatial abilities, does better in school in all subjects and holds a higher-status occupation. He has closer friends and a happier marriage.[96]

But the low-testosterone man is, nonetheless, almost always

masculine.[97] As a boy, he may not like to play rough sports, but he does not share the interests of girls his age. He doesn't like to dress up dolls, share confidences in long self-revealing conversations with one or two special male friends, spend hours reading romantic fiction or play board games about dating and girls. While there are lots of "tomboys," there are few "bettygirls." When the boys grow up, they may become cads or dads, but even the dads do not generally dote on young children as so many women do. They may be good family men, but they do not usually do much domestic work. Males, like high-testosterone females, tend to be more stubborn and intractable about this and other matters.[98] Thus, mainstream academic feminists talk of the "stalled revolution"[99] in which men refuse to combine career and family in the way that many women would like them to do.[100]

Even the low-testosterone man is usually competitive with his male peers. For instance, we would expect below-average testosterone levels among advanced male mathematicians, where spatial abilities are helpful. But in *A Beautiful Mind,* Sylvia Nasar describes top mathematicians who are "wildly competitive." One luminary, G. H. Hardy, always wanted to be a mathematician but couldn't remember feeling a real passion for math when young. Rather, he said, "I wanted to beat other boys, and this seemed to be the way in which I could do so most decisively."[101]

Like mathematicians, computer aces do not usually have the muscular build suggesting high testosterone; yet Bill Gates and the teenage computer game enthusiast both love to compete.[102] Those computer games include plenty of violence, something that turns off the game buff's girlfriend.[103] The computer nerd often loves science fiction, another genre tinged with violence.[104] He may watch pro football games or reality shows like *World's Wildest Police Videos* or "shockumentaries" such as *When Good Pets Go Bad*—the types of programs most popular among young men in general.[105]

The latest male hobby for technonerds is Battlebots. Contestants assemble robots the size of pets, and place two of them together in a ring. Only one of the robots will emerge after ramming, hammering, crushing or sawing the other into pieces. The current champ, the Mauler, was built by engineers, physicists and machinists who live near Silicon Valley.

The Bot community is almost entirely male. One of them describes the Battlebot philosophy: "Our ideas go out on the floor and kick [butt]." The man behind the Mauler lives next to a high-tech millionaire who reputedly has the country's largest private collection of military vehicles. This honcho says Battlebot appeals to men "because it's raw doses of adrenaline and testosterone plus techno music plus smashing stuff to PIECES." Battlebots is surely a guys' activity, with cool new machines, violent competitions, statistics, standings, prize money, even "bodacious babes" who interview the winners on TV.[106]

Many other male hobbyists, like the Battlebot community of technonerds, have interests that focus on machines or war. There are the car enthusiasts, the model train lovers, the war board-game connoisseurs, the Civil War buffs. These hobbyists are single-minded about what they love; and studies have found single-mindedness and a highly focused brain to be more characteristic of men than women.[107]

In short, the nerds aren't so very different from the jocks as it appears. Likewise, the hormonal studies that found sharp differences among women corresponding to prenatal testosterone levels find no such differences among men. Reports on the effects of CAH and other hormonal abnormalities on boys use phrases such as "do not support a clear conclusion" and "subtler effects if any."[108] The studies finding that a male twin masculinizes the female partner also show that the female twin has no feminizing effect on the male partner.[109]

These studies that find little to separate the high-testosterone males from others are mirrored by the cross-country studies of self-concepts. Asking women and men across cultures how they see themselves and how they would like to see themselves, Williams and Best find that the self-descriptions and ideal self-descriptions of men tend to be more uniform than those of women.[110]

The War among Women

What we have already learned from hormonal studies might lead us to predict that, on average, women with a very strong desire for careers equal to those of their husbands are likely to have been exposed to more testosterone than is typical for their sex. One might also predict that women who are relatively uninterested in baby care will have been exposed to more testosterone. To my knowledge there have been no studies that attempt to link testosterone levels directly with feminism or other political beliefs, and any natural tendencies, of course, would be modulated by cultural forces and by an individual's attempts to formulate a reasoned response to the tension between career and family. We do, however, have evidence suggesting that feminists may be like female careerists in their attitudes toward work and children. A June 2000 NBC/*Wall Street Journal* poll found that only among women making more than $100,000 a year was there a majority who considered themselves feminists.[111] And a 1997 study found that in six western European countries "progressive attitudes toward women's work and family roles are negatively associated with favorable attitudes toward the centrality of children."[112]

That being the case, it is understandable that careerist or feminist wives with social-constructionist worldviews might look at their husbands and say, "Look: I want a career; you want a career. I want children; you want children. But children take time, and care of a young child is often boring and tedious. So why shouldn't we share equally on the home front?"[113] What they want in their own lives, most feminist women assume other women want as well—or *would* want if they were not socialized to want something else.

This argument would make good sense if there were no fundamental differences between the sexes or among women. But the evidence presented above suggests that even the relatively androgynous, career-oriented women seem less single-mindedly focused on career than their male counterparts are. My parental leave study also indicates that young female professors like to care for babies more than young male professors do. So feminists are incorrect if they think that the men they marry are likely to have the same preferences that they do about dividing time between career and child care or homemaking. Moreover, the scientific studies summarized above provide evidence that these sex differences are not just a result of the way men are socialized.[114]

Most feminists don't understand more traditional women who want their husbands to be the principal breadwinners while they are the primary homemakers.[115] A study in the Netherlands surveyed subscribers to a feminist magazine and to a more conventional women's magazine. The Dutch feminists had a division of household labor approaching equality, but they were unhappy with it nevertheless, because getting their husbands to do nearly half the housework required conflict and regular pressure on the men. The feminists were more likely than traditional women to think that most Dutch women did virtually all the housework, and also more likely to think that a higher percentage of women were discontent with the division of labor in their homes.[116] In the United States, feminists studying marriage often acknowledge that most wives are content with the division of labor in their marriage even though they do substantially more child care and housework.[117]

Carolyn Graglia gives a powerful explanation of why traditional women are not discontent. A top-ranking graduate of Columbia University's law school, Graglia gave up her promising legal career because she preferred the unique role of mother to her children over the fungible one of writing briefs for clients. She is grateful that her husband's income spared her from market work, "which would have required an unbearably constricted maternal role." To her, raising young children was an "everyday epiphany of exquisite happiness."[118]

Most feminists would be baffled by Graglia's lyrical praise of a mother's job with a description of its most salient characteristic as "cheerful responsiveness to constant interruptions."[119] Powerful careers require organizing life in blocks of time. Cultural anthropologist Robbie Davis-Floyd finds that pregnant professionals in positions of real power tend "to see the body as an imperfect tool that the more perfect self should control. They tend to experience pregnancy and birth as unpleasant because they are so out of control."[120] Their "conscious choice to dissociate themselves from their biology" is very unlike the worldview of homebirthers who *"see the self and body as One"* and who, while pregnant, see themselves as *"actively growing the baby,"* with mother and baby forming "one 'energy field.' " In contrast, many of the professionals in this study see the baby as a "separate entity," a "foreign body growing inside my body." They see the holism of the homebirthers as "frightening, irresponsible, limiting and disempowering."[121]

There are certainly more women with powerful careers than women giving birth at home, but another study finds that with respect to pregnancy, most American women seem to have more in common with homebirthers. When reflecting on past pregnancies, the majority of mothers said either that they were both good and bad or that they were different with different children. But of those who gave pregnancy a clear verdict, 13 percent remember pregnancy as "easy, no problems," and 23 percent as "rapturous, wonderful." Only 8 percent remember their pregnancy as "awful."[122]

I don't mean to take sides here, but simply to point out that most academic and work-oriented feminists still have trouble making sense of their more traditional sisters. Most feminists are more tolerant than they were in the 1970s, when so many of their leaders called housewives "parasites."[123] But two recent and much-praised feminist books reveal that they still don't fully understand traditional women.

In *Why So Slow? The Advancement of Women,* Virginia Valian asserts that "most men aspire to high-level professional success." Then, turning to women, she argues that "one way to accommodate a lower than hoped for level of achievement is to accept the superiority of those who are powerful and align oneself with them. People commonly see heterosexual women" doing this through marriage; *"unable to achieve their own goals* [emphasis added], they obtain gratification from being married to someone who can."[124]

In an even more widely praised book, *Woman: An Intimate Geography,* Natalie Angier acknowledges that feminists of the 1970s were wrong to assume that all women shared the same goals. Nonetheless, she maintains that "fine, free day care" is as close as any objective "to being of universal benefit to women." In defending this view, she asks women without children to consider that "Anything that keeps women in the world, visible and unrelenting, that neutralizes the acidic effect of mother guilt and its corollary presumption that women are not up to the task of professional tenacity, buoys all women, raises all our madly paddling canoes."[125]

In speaking only to female careerists without children, Angier does not see the need to address the larger group of more traditional women who stay at home with children or who work part-time till their children are in school. These women may have less "mother guilt" to neutralize. And they are not "buoy[ed]" by free day care for female careerists financed with higher taxes on the incomes of their husbands.

Feminists deal with the fact that large numbers of women do not share their worldview[126] by assuming they have been cloistered or not fully exposed to liberative achievement in the larger world. They like to cite statistical studies that conclude, after seeming to control for all relevant social and economic variables, that women whose mothers had careers are much more likely to be careerists themselves or that most top female executives played a competitive sport in college.

Some feminists conclude from such studies that they are pioneers.[127] They expect that as more and more women have mothers with jobs or play sports in school, the serious careerists will become the vast majority and the traditional women will disappear.[128] But hormonal research reveals that serious careerists have higher testosterone than most women,[129] and that mothers with high testosterone are more likely to bear girls with high testosterone.[130] So maybe it's the testosterone that best explains the desire for a serious career in both mother *and* daughter. We do know that high testosterone is associated both with strong interest in competitive sports *and* with interest in demanding careers.[131]

At a time when few women played sports or pursued demanding careers, a high proportion of women athletes and careerists probably had higher testosterone than most other women. In an era when young women more routinely play school sports, girls with closer to average levels of testosterone will predominate in sports and careers, but they may be less passionate about both. They are likely, in turn, to give birth to girls with average testosterone who likewise will be less committed to sports or careers than the feminist pioneers.

In any case, Carolyn Graglia is not far off when she says that feminist careerists and home-centered women are engaged in a war. Graglia thinks the sides are unevenly matched in that the war pits "the best educated, most sophisticated, most aggressive, and most masculinized portion of the female population against women who generally possess less education and less worldly experience, who are more likely to be docile than aggressive, feminine than masculine."[132] The careerists used to define the home-based mom as boring, "idle and self-indulgent"; but these days the traditional woman may give as good as she gets, responding that the working mom is "neglectful and egotistical."[133]

There are few physical casualties in this war, but the anger is palpable. Moreover, the stakes are very high. The economist's concept of *externality* or *spillover* can help us understand why. (These terms describe the effects of a person's behavior on others' well-being—effects not captured by the usual economic indicators.) Earlier we saw how homemakers hurt female careerists by dropping out of the workforce when they have children, thereby telling employers that they should favor men in training and promotions if they want a more reliable workforce. Thus when the top manager of Pepsi-Cola for North America resigned to spend time with her family, Susan Estrich called it a "selfish decision from the collective perspective of feminism."[134] Many years before, Simone de Beauvoir remarked that a woman at home with social status, living as a "parasite," demoralizes "the woman who aims at self-sufficiency."[135]

Traditional women thwart careerist feminists in other ways. When traditionalists seem pleased with husbands who do far less than half the housework, they make it harder for feminists to bring their husbands around. There are issues of symbolic importance as well. For instance, when the vote was called on President Clinton's removal from office, every married female senator was called "Mrs." while every unmarried female senator was called "Ms." As long as the married senators insist on being "Mrs.," then "Ms." cannot become the neutral equivalent of "Mr.," and the feminist goal of encouraging society to make no more of women's marital status than men's is frustrated.

For their part, the traditionalists can also complain about the ways feminists may hurt them. I had a research assistant who refused to go through doors opened for her by men because she believed that doing so would reinforce the view that women need help in opening doors. In addition, she saw no reason why women should be denied an equal opportunity to extend courtesy, so she would often insist that men go ahead of her. Traditional women, however, often like to be shown such courtesies and see no reason why men, generally the more selfish sex,[136] should not be encouraged to show them. But if enough women scorn men who open doors for them, men will cease to do so.

Feminist causes such as subsidized day care, paid maternity leave and an end to alimony also harm traditional women. And in the wake of the sexual revolution, female careerists who act on their stronger libidos threaten adult traditionalists of all ages. Wives have to worry more about husbands tempted by women at the office.[137] Would-be wives—women who want most of all to marry and start a family—are harmed by the large supply of single women willing to sleep with men without demanding commitment in return.[138] And traditional teenage girls and young women wonder why they can't live in a world where men expect less at the end of a date. A student once sat in my office sadly noting that while she had no difficulty attracting men's interest, she could not keep it for more than a date or two because she refused to meet the sexual competition.

In the war among women, mainstream feminists have an enormous advantage because of their influence in the media. Twice as many women think the Christian Coalition serves women's interests as consider it a threat; yet as liberal Democrat Jeffrey Berry's well-researched book *The New Liberalism* says, conservative groups like that have little effect on legislation because liberal lobbies, in alliance with the press, dominate Washington opinion.[139] A mere 2 percent of Washington reporters consider themselves "conservative."

The striking power of feminist careerists in the media is evidenced in reporting on day care. In the summer of 2000, many major newspapers, including the *New York Times* and the *Washington Post,* prominently featured articles with headlines such as "Day Care, for Keeping Asthma at Bay." David Murray, research director of a media watchdog organization, was struck by this unusual press attention and checked out the medical study behind the story. It was a good study in a prominent journal, but Murray noted that there were a host of equally good studies warning of health *dangers* from day care that had received almost no attention at all. As Murray remarked, "The dramatic rise in the number of children attending early day care exactly coincides with the epidemic rise of childhood asthma."

A cultural anthropologist who sent his daughter to day care when she was three years old, Murray thinks that the good day care news is played up "because it helps reassure journalists [who are likely to use day care] that they're personally doing the right thing for their children."[140] These journalists also assume that everyone is like them, and are predisposed to ignore how many traditional women are still out there and proud of what they do. One humorous piece of evidence on this point comes from the style manual of the *New York Times,* which instructs writers not to identify women as housewives or homemakers, as this would be "belittling." A few lines after this edict comes a warning against writing stories that describe the occupation of a famous person's father but not the situation of the mother. Dan Seligman, who called this to his readers' attention, wondered what a poor writer is to do if the famous person's mother was a homemaker.[141]

Elementary and secondary school textbooks are even more biased than the media in the way they treat the differences among women. They search far and wide for nontraditional female achievements to celebrate. Indeed, they have to. In California the state education code demands that wherever reading presents achievements in science, history or other fields, "the achievements of women and men should be represented in approximately equal numbers." As a result, one widely used history text gives more attention to Maria Mitchell, a nineteenth-century astronomer who discovered a comet, than to Albert Einstein; another has three pictures of Civil War nurses but none of General Sherman or General Grant.[142] During the 1980s, the most popular American history texts increased the representation of women important to the feminist movement on average from fewer than 10 to 35.

Some feminists might argue that these textbooks must correct history in this way so as to fight stereotypes and expand the horizons of young women. But after examining social science texts, Paul Vitz, a psychology professor at New York University, says that they never mention that being a homemaker or a volunteer can be a worthy goal, never celebrate motherhood "as a rich and meaningful way of life" and never show "any woman or girl with a positive relationship to a baby or young child."[143]

The same deficits occur as well in textbooks that teach students to read. Diane Ravitch explains how the National Organization for Women and other feminist groups worked successfully to change textbooks across the country. They testified at state hearings against books they found unacceptable, pressured state and local school boards to reject these books, and lobbied publishers to revise books with language the feminist groups considered sexist or with illustrations of women baking cookies or sewing.[144]

In 1975, the California Department of Education went so far as to reject reading texts with any portrayal of women in a household role. The publisher Open Court appealed the rejection of its reading texts, which had already been revised to meet standards of gender equality. (The publisher noted that California bureaucrats had even complained about a brief reference to Mother Hubbard.)[145] Open Court made little headway. In later editions of the text, for example, The Little Engine That Could became female.

It may be time to start questioning the assumption that society pressures young women to be homemakers. My observations of bright University of Virginia students suggest that they feel pressured in other directions entirely. I remember one young woman with a 3.8 grade point average in economics who told me how furious she was at her economics professors. When she told them she loved children and wanted to be an elementary school teacher, they let her know they were disappointed—she could do so much more.

I encounter feminist students who seem to have absorbed all of their teachers' opinions but whose hearts appear to be at war with their opinions. In class they are sure that women would be physicists and engineers—or, at the very least, have demanding careers of some kind—if it were not for discriminatory socialization. I remember one of my students who openly declared that she was looking for a husband who would be the "wife" so she could quickly advance in her career. But when our discussion meandered into the popularity of romance novels, she said she read them all the time. When I expressed surprise and asked why she would purchase so many books filled with powerful and worldly heroes and spirited but traditional heroines, she said, "Lots of things I do have nothing to do with what I spout around campus all day."

Another student who in class vigorously agreed with mainstream feminists on every issue we had been discussing seemed to have strong domestic interests in all our discussions out of class. I suggested that her ideology was at war with her nature, and she replied: "Totally. I have an earth mother side."

Finally, I remember an extremely bright, extremely feminine woman who throughout the class would give variants of the same speech whenever work/family issues arose: "I grew up in Norway, and it was very unfair how my mother was pressured to use day care. I believe parental care is very important, and when I get married, either my husband or I will stay home with the children." The "either/or" seemed to be a way of proclaiming that she was both traditional and progressive at the same time. Near the end of the term I posed the following hypothetical situation: You meet a wonderful guy. He agrees completely with your views on parental care and says, "Let's get married. I love kids, and I'll stay home with them." After hesitating a moment, she said, "Well, that would be a problem; I was thinking that I would be the one to stay home with the children." Until she was asked to really look into her heart, she had acted as if her concern were only with good *parental* care and not with *her* desire to give *maternal* care.

Many bright young women are a little ashamed of who they are. Their shame comes in part from school texts that completely ignore the worth, even the existence, of a large proportion of women who put home and children and often volunteer activity at the center of their lives. The texts treat this group as an embarrassment—we all know they are out there, but we will be happier if our conversation never brings them up.[146]

Why Sex Differences Have Policy Implications

One point unites many feminists who believe in the social construction of sex roles with the researchers who emphasize the importance of biology. They all believe that the existence of sex differences should not affect our public policy. The more sophisticated feminists will grant some sex differences on average, emphasize the many exceptions and say, "So what. If there are sex differences in the brain, they have nothing to do with struggles over fair pay, economic security and who does the dishes."[147] For their part, the scientists who see differences as partly biological, and are eager to do their research but not to be mislabeled as "conservative," often make the same point even more strongly: "Biological data can only be used politically when it is being misinterpreted,"[148] one of them says. And another asserts that the theories have "no implications for what one should do.... There is an unbridgeable gulf between is and ought."[149]

I certainly have no quarrel with the view that we should not encourage everything we may be inclined by nature to do. Of course, men's tendencies toward violence and predatory sex should be combated, not condoned. But there are some inclinations that seem civilizing and well worth encouraging. We have already seen, for instance, that on average women may naturally be more nurturing than men with small babies, and that far more men than women are inclined to enjoy and be good at jobs and hobbies that require spatial abilities. Are these differences acceptable? Is it acceptable, even desirable, for natural tendencies to play out in these arenas? Or must we push against these tendencies in the interest of seeking a world in which both sexes are on average equally interested in and equally good at all worthy endeavors?

Given their belief that sexual equality requires equal sharing of domestic and other work, it is not surprising that most politically active feminists think we should aim for an androgynous world. What is more surprising is that some scholars who find biological causes for human behavior also think we should be combating the nature whose operations they document in their research. In their work one sometimes finds acknowledgment that men have a biological advantage in math-related areas coupled with calls for society to intervene so as to achieve equality between the sexes in math-related jobs. Similarly, there are proposals to expose boys more than girls to nurturing situations.[150]

These sorts of proposals might leave one with the impression that no one is to be held back. Boys can still play spatially oriented computer games, and girls can still play with dolls, but each will also be encouraged in endeavors that come naturally to the other sex. As we have already seen, however, the sexes' opposite inclinations appear early, are strongly held and change little through time. Udry's research explains how attempts to make unfeminine women more feminine can possibly have the opposite effect. Christina Hoff Sommers' *The War Against Boys* illustrates how repeated attempts to make boys more nurturing have not only failed, but backfired.[151]

It isn't clear how society is meant to change people's predispositions. Are parents supposed to say to their boys, "No more computer games until you play for three days with the dollhouse?" Or imagine a parent with a bright older boy who is unathletic and timid compared with his peers. He gets picked on a lot at school, and his self-esteem is low. But his parents are pleased that he has gotten interested in the physics and chess clubs. Are his teachers supposed to say, "No more physics club until you catch up on your dancing"? Or will this be required only of the more stereotypically masculine boys as a prerequisite for trying out for the football team? Is the chess club to be only for girls or at least to be disproportionately female on the assumption that the boys will play more chess on their own? Are day care centers to require that the boys play with dolls at least as much as the girls do? If so, as Sommers documents in her book, doll carnage is likely to result.

There is a certain unworldly quality to the suggestions that a just world would be one in which men and women do all things equally. This understanding would require that parents who are trying to tease out their children's natural abilities should instead do their part to help achieve a society in which a higher percentage of people do things they are not interested in and not very good at.

In the real world, any society will and should want to encourage people to do worthwhile things that they enjoy and do well. This means that natural inclinations will have policy and normative relevance, although they will not always be conclusive.

We saw above that professional and traditional women can adversely affect each other through their tastes and behavior. We might say that each group is fully entitled to pursue a life course without having to answer to the complaints of the other. But we have to make a collective decision about how women's lives are presented in civics and history textbooks. Currently, traditional women's choices are ignored in these books. If focusing primarily on one's family can have beneficial consequences and if such choices seem to flow genuinely from these women's especially feminine and nurturing natures, these facts, demonstrated by good science, are also relevant to policy questions.

PART 2

MEN DON'T GET HEADACHES

3

SEX

Your daddy's rich and your momma's good looking,
So hush little baby, don't you cry.
—George Gershwin, Porgy and Bess

Evolutionary psychologists attend to sex more than any other topic. But their subject does not make them popular because, as one of them acknowledges, "the theory is obnoxious."[1] The theory is particularly obnoxious on the question of sex differences in mating behavior.

When seeking a long-term mate, both men and women look for considerate, honest, interesting and loyal partners;[2] but women care more about a mate's status and resources, men about a mate's youth and beauty.[3] Most readers will not find these differences surprising, but they might object to evolutionary psychologists' explanations for them.

As already noted, evolutionary theory holds that natural selection will favor individual traits that enhance survival and reproduction. But the costs of reproduction can be much less for men than for women, who must undergo pregnancy and nursing. Men can have sex and then go off to impregnate other women, while a woman is busy with a single child. As the noted evolutionary psychologist Steven Pinker puts it,

> A prehistoric man who slept with fifty women could have sired fifty children, and would have been more likely to have descendents who inherited his tastes. A woman who slept with fifty men would have no more descendents than a woman who slept with one.[4]

In hunter-gatherer societies today, the closest we have to prehistoric societies, very few women bear and nurse more than eight children in a lifetime, whereas some men sire dozens by different women.[5]

Thus evolutionary psychology predicts that men will be more eager for sex than women are because eons ago those men who mated more frequently usually produced more heirs. Men with powerful sexual urges passed on their genes in greater numbers than men with a moderate or low inclination for sex. As compared with women, men would also have a greater inclination for sex with lots of mates, because more mates would mean more offspring; but a woman who took advantage of any sexual opportunity that came along would not produce children who thrived as well as choosier women. A woman who chose to mate with only unusually strong men or men willing to commit ample resources to her children's needs would increase her children's likelihood of survival, and thus, through the ages, women with such tastes would be more apt to reproduce successfully.

This theory does not suggest that women are necessarily loyal to a single man. If they can get away with such behavior, they may do better by secretly mating with a big, handsome man with good genes and tricking some other man—perhaps wealthier or more responsible—into raising children he mistakenly believes are his. Or they may provide men with sexual favors in exchange for resources to increase their children's likelihood of survival and successful reproduction.

Likewise, men are not necessarily promiscuous. Insofar as women may require commitment and resources in order to bear and raise a man's children, those men who are "dads" rather than "cads" may reproduce successfully by providing resources that will ultimately enable their children to reproduce competitively in turn. But men who cheat a lot on the side might do better still. And men with extensive resources might outdo the loyal mate by providing for more than one family through divorce and "serial monogamy."

In societies where paternal investment is common, men will choose carefully when settling on a long-term mate or marrying. Here men's preference for youth and beauty helps reproduction because, as explained later, both beauty and youth are signs of fecundity.

All these tastes and preferences which enhanced the survival of our distant ancestors' genes in the environment of evolutionary adaptation, the time period when our basic genetic constitution was established, may appear to make less or even no sense now. Nonetheless, according to evolutionary psychology, they are part of our genetically inherited psychological makeup and will affect decisions even when we are unaware of them and feel confident we have moved past the elemental urges of the first men and women.

Libido Strength and the Taste for Sexual Variety

Both evolutionists and social-construction feminists argue that the frequent threat of male violence makes it difficult to tell what women's true sexuality might look like in a nonpatriarchal context. Indeed, in many cultures women endure sanctioned beatings for adultery, immodest dress or talking to strangers.[6] Even in places where female sexuality is less constrained, social pressures tell women that they are odd and foolish if they seem inordinately interested in sex in the way that many men are. Though weakened, the double standard still exists.[7] The man who sleeps with many partners is often called a *stud,* while the woman who does so is usually called a *slut.*

Most evolutionists, however, think there is a deep and substantial gender difference in libido and taste for sexual variety. In fact, evolutionary psychologists have repeatedly concluded that "not only do men report that casual, low-investment sex is more desirable, permissible, and arousing than women do, men also report that they behaviourally seek and engage in short-term mateships more than women do."[8]

One sign of men's greater interest in sex appears in studies that simply ask respondents how often they think about sex. On average men say three to five times a day. Women say several times a week or several times a month.[9] Another study asked young Americans to rate twenty wishes. There was not a lot of difference between men's and women's responses except in one respect: men had a much stronger wish "to have sex with anyone I choose."[10]

In 2003, 118 collaborators in 52 nations, on 6 continents and 13 islands reported on a study testing the desire for sexual variety. Over 16,000 men and women, mainly college students, were asked through anonymous questionnaires about their desired number of sex partners over the next month and over the next thirty years. In all nations men wanted more partners, on average just under three times more (5.95 vs. 2.17) over the thirty-year period. Over the thirty-day period, 25 percent of men on average wanted more than one sexual partner, compared with between 3 and 7 percent of women. Among those who said they were strongly seeking a short-term sex partner over the next thirty days, a majority of the men desired more than one in that period, whereas fewer than 20 percent of women did.[11]

As men and women age, many differences between the sexes diminish. Standard social science observes that grandfathers are kinder and more lovable than fathers, and that mothers become more independent as they grow older. Researchers who look for biological causes think this convergence can be explained in part by the fact that men lose testosterone over time, while women lose estrogen faster than they lose testosterone.[12] With regard to sexual drive, however, the differences remain great as we age. One survey of men and women over 45 asked how often they felt sexual desire. More than seven times as many men as women (18.4 percent vs. 2.6 percent) said more than once a day, and more than four times as many women as men (32.5 percent vs. 7.5 percent) said "not at all."[13]

It takes very little to get men to move from thought to action. About 6 out of 7 men report masturbating more often than the average woman.[14] And in one highly publicized study, men and women on a college campus were assigned to approach members of the opposite sex and say, "I have been noticing you around campus. I find you very attractive. Would you go to bed with me tonight?" Three-quarters of the men approached said yes; none of the 48 women did.[15] Even factoring in a fear element, similar studies produce striking results.[16]

Differences exist even after the diploma is in hand. One recent survey of American adults explored the importance of a host of things from marriage and parenthood to career, religion and sex. By far the greatest difference between the sexes was in the men's higher ranking for the importance of "an active sex life."[17]

Those who think differences in libido are the result of differences in socialization believe society teaches a woman that she should not have sex except with "her husband or at least her committed lover. . . . But modern sexual expectations call on her, once she is in bed with an approved mate, to turn into a passionate, uninhibited lover."[18] Surveys show, however, that men, despite their greater taste for variety in sex partners, also surpass women in their taste for sex with a long-term partner. For example, for men more than for women, good and frequent sex is closely associated with marital happiness.[19] In marriage, women often get more pleasure out of kissing and cuddling than out of intercourse.[20] In and out of marriage, women say they engage in sex to share emotions and love.[21] Men give reasons that are more narrowly physical, such as need, sexual gratification and sexual release.[22] And when deprived of sex, men are much more likely than women to become morose and irritable.[23]

As noted in the previous chapter, testosterone is implicated in the strengths of the male and the female libidos, and men have far more testosterone than women.[24] But this difference does not conclusively show that men have higher sex drives than women. Each unit of testosterone seems to have more effect on a woman's libido than a unit has on a man's.[25]

The best evidence for the importance of testosterone in helping to explain libidinal differences between the sexes is the effect of incremental testosterone differences among females. Whatever the circumstances of their socialization, high-testosterone women think and behave more like men than low-testosterone women do. They are more interested in sex, have far more sex partners and are much more likely to masturbate. They focus more on orgasms and genital sex than on cuddling. Women with medical conditions producing extremely high levels of male hormone have male-like sexual arousal patterns and they desire sex with strangers. When they voluntarily have their condition treated, they retain an interest in sex but are pleased to be "relieved of clitoral hypersensitivity."[26]

Testosterone level also correlates with a taste for sexual variety and an aversion to commitment. Theresa Crenshaw, coauthor of a leading text on sexual pharmacology, has said the

> "loner profile" of testosterone is absolutely crucial to understanding what men are all about. Just as testosterone separates the sexes physically at birth, it separates them emotionally as adults. Testosterone motivates the male to strive for separateness in ways a woman is not designed to comprehend. He wants to be alone! ... [Testosterone] wants novelty, shuns commitment.... It is fair to say that [testosterone] causes a compelling sexual urge that spurns relationships, unless they represent a conquest or acquisition of power.... It makes you want sex, but it also makes you want to be alone, or thoroughly in control of sexual situations—so it specifically promotes masturbation or one night stands.[27]

Pornography offers a parade of new women and no commitment—thus its popularity with males, many of whom use it for masturbation even when they have a willing partner in the home.[28] The appeal of prostitutes is the same. As one handsome actor puts it, "I don't pay them to come over.... I pay them to leave."[29]

Married men sometimes try to reconcile a taste for novelty with marital vows by changing the look of their mates.

> The novelty factor can be seen at work every Christmas in the lingerie department of the stores. The men sheepishly rummage through the sheer and exotic nightwear.... Come the new year and the same lingerie counters are thronged with women returning the love tokens.... They find them embarrassing and perhaps a little silly.[30]

If the husbands are less disciplined, they will stray. Even happily married men sometimes have affairs for sexual variety and excitement. Women are more likely to have affairs for emotional intimacy that they find lacking with their husbands.[31]

Evolutionists find it instructive to examine the differences between heterosexual and homosexual men and women. One study suggests that for all their obvious differences, homosexual and heterosexual men have the same desire for uncommitted sex.[32] Heterosexual men, however, must negotiate with women who have very different preferences. The resulting patterns in actual activity are striking. Among married men, 7 percent have had sex with more than twenty partners. Among male homosexual couples, 43 percent have had sex with more than twenty partners. Among lesbian couples, only 1 percent have had sex with more than twenty partners. Lesbians have slightly less desire for uncommitted sex than do heterosexual women, and they have sex with a slightly lower number of partners. They seek permanent partnerships based on fidelity, affection and intimacy.[33]

Partnered sex is often a compromise between what you would like and what you can get. No such constraints exist for sexual fantasies. Studies show that women are twice as likely as men to fantasize about a current romantic partner; men are three times as likely as women to fantasize about someone they are not involved with and have no intention of becoming involved with. For men, the heroine is frequently a stranger, and often there are multiple partners. Women are two and one half times as likely to focus on the personal and emotional characteristics of a partner; men four times as likely to focus on the physical characteristics. Women are twice as likely as men to find "the idea of anonymous sex 'not at all appealing.'"[34]

Women's fantasies are full of "details about the partner and the environment." The pace of an imagined sexual encounter is usually "slow and sensual" with "lots of caressing and emotional exchange."[35] For men, fantasized sex "is sheer lust and physical gratification, devoid of encumbering relationships, emotional elaboration, complicated plot lines, flirtation, courtship, and extended foreplay."[36]

These are also the characteristics of pornography, almost all of which is consumed by men. Women prefer romance novels, which constitute about 40 percent of all mass-market paperback sales in the country. In any given year, one in three U.S. women reads a romance novel.[37] These days, the heroine is often a working woman. The hero, though, is still a powerful older man, sometimes a "bad boy who actually commits." The plot? "It's all love. All the time. Getting love, keeping love, making love."[38]

One interesting experiment made members of each sex sit through the other's sexual turn-ons. Scientists read to college students stories that combined romance with steamy sex. When the students were asked what they remembered, "women recalled lines such as 'They looked deeply into each others' eyes.' Men, on the other hand, accurately recited lines such as: 'She clutched his back and wrapped her legs around him.'"[39]

I do not think that most people who come to the issue without ideological agendas believe women's libidos and desire for sexual variety are as great as men's. The differences reflect nature, not just nurture. Could the seemingly self-destructive behaviors of a Bill Clinton or a Gary Condit have been avoided if only they had received the same messages about sex that today's women do? It is interesting that the occasional female politician brought down by a sexual partner—for example, Senator Carol Mosley-Braun of Illinois and Congresswoman Enid Waldholtz of Utah—are not undone by a passion for multiple trysts, but instead by their entanglement and partnership with *one* good-for-nothing man.[40]

Looking carefully at the doubts about the standard evolutionist argument on libido and taste for sexual variety, one has to wonder if there really is any substantial debate. Helen Fisher is one of the few evolutionists who believe that men may not have a significantly greater interest in sex and sexual variety. She mentions a study finding that male students are consistently more likely than women to tell a researcher that they would sleep with an anonymous student of the opposite sex if there were no danger of pregnancy, discovery or disease. But she believes this finding is not persuasive because it does not cater to the primary motive for women to sleep around:

> This study takes into consideration the primary genetic motive for male philandering (to fertilize young women). But it does not take into account the primary motive for female philandering—the acquisition of resources.... Evolutionary logic holds that women sleep around for goods and services.[41]

Fisher recommends asking the young women a different question: "Would you be willing to have a one-night stand with Robert Redford if he gives you a brand new Porsche?" She thinks this question would reveal that women as well as men are willing to pursue adultery as a complement to monogamy.[42]

But no one has ever doubted that some women will sleep with many partners in order to gain resources; this is what prostitution—and "gold-digging"—is all about. On the other hand, before AIDS intervened, many male homosexuals flocked to bathhouses to find partners willing to have free sex with them just because they *liked sex* with strangers, not because they expected to get resources out of it. Many straight men also would have flocked to bathhouses for free sex with women, but there was not a supply to meet the demand.

Carol Tavris also believes that the sexes do not each have a distinct sexual nature or sexual essence.[43] Her book *The Mismeasure of Women* is one of the most influential arguments against the importance of sex differences. But soon after stating her position, Tavris launches into an extended complaint about the treatment of sexual dysfunction in the *Diagnostic and Statistical Manual of Mental Disorders* (DSM). As she sees it, the DSM *tries* to treat men's and women's sexuality equally, but to do so it must discuss body parts and genitals as entities separate from a whole, human, sexual encounter. Approvingly quoting psychologist Leonore Tiefer, Tavris notes that "women's actual sexual *experiences* are absent. There's nothing ... about emotion or communication ... about commitment." In a later paragraph she remarks that there is also nothing about "affection."[44]

After reading Tavris, the evolutionist is sure to think, "What are we arguing about? I say that women will be less interested in sex with multiple partners because to enjoy sex, most will need emotion, communication and affection. These will be seen as signs of commitment—signs that the man will stay around and help support any resulting children. All these things take time to develop and make sex with strangers relatively unappealing for women and thus less likely."

Most men need none of these extras to be interested in sex. They just need a willing, reasonably attractive woman. They desire only the sex, the physical release. Since the male physical requirements are so much simpler than the additional requirements women have, many men will always be searching in vain for women as "easy" as they are.

It is surprising that many feminists and some others think the stakes are so high in the debate over the libido and promiscuity.[45] Deborah Blum is a feminist but also an evolutionist. She thinks it obvious that there are a lot more "females patiently accommodating excited males than vice versa."[46] And she is "not insulted by the idea that men are more sexually driven than women overall, which seems to carry a definite plus and minus factor. If we want only to one-up each other in terms of quick sexual hits, we might as well evolve into rabbits."[47]

Or as the women of *Ally McBeal* used to put it, females simply don't have the male "dumb stick."

Beauty

Both sexes care about a potential partner's appearance, and both care more now than they did a half-century ago. In 1939, U.S. men ranked physical attractiveness 14th out of 18 desirable mate characteristics; in 1996, they ranked it 8th. In 1939, women ranked attractiveness 17th out of 18; in 1996, they ranked it 13th.[48]

The movement in these rankings presumably reflects cultural change, but what has not changed is the greater importance that men give to attractiveness. This is true cross-culturally.[49] In personal advertisements, men are as much as three times more likely than women to mention a desire for a good-looking date and over nine times more likely to mention body shape.[50] An attractive woman is more likely to be sought after than other women, while a man's good looks seem less important than a good job. Additionally, good-looking women marry men with more education than do less good-looking women.[51] In one in-depth study of twenty male and twenty female medical students, "85 percent of the men mentioned physical attractiveness as the trait most important to them in choosing a partner for serious relationships. Only 10 percent of the women gave this response."[52]

In experiments in which the same man is *described* as studying to be a doctor or *pictured* as a doctor as opposed to being associated with less prestigious professions, women not only prefer average looks and a higher profession to good looks and a less prestigious profession, but they actually think the *appearance* of the man improves when he is associated with a prestigious profession.[53]

Feminists may be skeptical about the idea that men naturally care more about a mate's appearance than women do, but they often

cater to what men care about as much as do traditional women. The readers of the original feminist magazine, *Ms.*, bought cosmetics and toiletries at a higher rate than the readers of any other women's magazine. *Ms.* readers ranked first among "heavy users" of lipstick and lip gloss, second among "heavy users" of eye shadow.[54]

Susan Estrich—a prominent feminist, the first woman president of the *Harvard Law Review,* and the first woman to run a presidential campaign—wrote a diet book in which she described her feelings when she went from a size 14 down to a size 6:

> Nothing I do now or have done in the past (other than falling in love with the right guy, and having our children, which I consider blessings, not accomplishments) has made me prouder, happier or more fulfilled than losing weight and getting in shape.[55]

Estrich's book brought "shrieks of betrayal" from some other feminists.[56]

Six years earlier, Gloria Steinem wrote a book of "self-esteem" in which she confessed to having fallen in love with a man the opposite of everything she stood for and believed in politically and socially, but who had great personal and occupational power. She thought she was drawn to his power because our society does not value or permit such power in a woman. What society teaches men and women to value in females is their beauty, Steinem said, the standards of which are *"really about what society wants us to do or not to do"* [italics in original]—a way of "getting rid of women" as they age and begin to attain authority and power:

> Though we are supposed to think that standards of beauty conform to an objective aesthetic handed down from history or the heavens—which is how society shirks the blame for creating them and makes us feel intrinsically wrong for not conforming to them—they are capricious, perishable standards that people made and people can unmake.[57]

A large contingent of feminists join Steinem in condemning "lookism" and in arguing both that society *teaches* women that they should care about their looks and that standards of beauty have no objective, cross-cultural basis.[58] Nonetheless, a body of research shows not only that a male emphasis on female beauty probably makes reproductive sense, but also that there are certain cross-cultural standards of beauty that seem to be deeply rooted in nature.

When shown photographs of women of various races—mostly Chinese, Indian, U.S. and South African—men agree on which women are the most and least attractive.[59] Also, psychologists have found that "even three-month-old infants prefer to gaze at faces that adults find attractive, including faces of people from races they had not been previously exposed to."[60]

Humans are attracted to what is reproductively useful—or rather what would have been reproductively useful in the environment of evolutionary adaptation, the Pleistocene Era, when most of the basic wiring of our brain was established. Men acknowledged to be good-looking are also tall and strong. Such men were usually most able to protect ancestral women and their offspring. In tribal life, big men dominate politically and have more sex with more women.[61] In China, as in the United States, women rate stature as highly desirable in a potential mate. Even in American politics, physical stature apparently helps give one "stature": Washington and Lincoln towered over most men of their day, and in the last century all but three American presidential elections were won by the taller candidate. In business it's not much different. Half the chief executives of Fortune 500 companies are at least six feet tall, whereas the average height of an American man is five feet nine.[62]

Not only does a man's size correlate with his professional stature, but his professional stature also affects how he is perceived. In one extraordinary experiment, an Australian psychologist had the same man visit different groups of students. In one class he was introduced as a student, in another as a lecturer, in still another as a professor. Once the visitor had left the room, the students were asked how tall they thought he was. The "lecturer" was thought to be about an inch taller than the "student," and the "professor" more than two inches taller.[63]

Women care about a man's strength as well as his height. In one survey, the three characteristics of a man's body thought to be the most sexy were "imposing body proportions," "muscular, athletic body" and "broad shoulders."[64] Men report that when they go to the gym, they spend most of their time on activities that increase upper-body strength. Women, who on average bench-press about one-third of what men do, nonetheless "specifically avoid activities which add bulk to the upper body and torso."[65]

As for the face, women prefer men with angular features, deep-set eyes and prominent chins,[66] features that have been associated with dominance and high testosterone. Men can, however, look too masculine, seeming "Neanderthal," cold and unfriendly. Men with such faces have especially high testosterone. And men with high testosterone are more likely to cheat on, leave and hit their wives. When shown pictures, women go for very manly looks for a one-night stand, but prefer a less masculine look for a long-term mate, when commitment and a willingness to provide resources would be more important.[67]

Though a man's face can look too masculine, a woman's can rarely appear too feminine.[68] The especially feminine face exaggerates the features that make women look different from men—for example, high cheekbones, plump lips, more delicate lower jaw, large eyes relative to the rest of the face. If one uses a computer to alter a picture of a female face so as to exaggerate these characteristics, one creates a face perceived as more and more beautiful.[69]

If testosterone levels are reflected in the face of the handsome male, the same holds true of estrogen in the attractive female.[70]

Estrogen levels directly correspond to both fertility and beauty. Men think women are most beautiful when their estrogen levels are highest—at about age twenty-two,[71] and mature women seem younger than their age when they have above-average levels of estrogen.[72] Social constructionists usually say that men find younger women more attractive only because they are taught to do so. But a teenage male is more attracted to a woman in her early twenties than to one his age or younger.[73]

Turning from the female face to the female form, one finds a clearer influence of culture. The ample, full-bodied Rubens look is clearly passé in the United States these days; and the super-thin models presented as ideal types of female beauty lead some girls to develop life-threatening eating disorders such as anorexia. It might help if more young women knew that most men prefer somewhat plumper women than women themselves think men do.[74]

Within a given culture, some men prefer a shape like Marilyn Monroe's, while others favor the Audrey Hepburn type. But Monroe and Hepburn both had a waist-to-hip ratio of about 0.7.[75] A number of studies have argued that this ratio signifies health and fertility, and thus is most attractive to men.[76]

The hourglass figure may be highly valued because women with hourglass figures seem to get pregnant more easily. For example, in one study of five hundred women, an hourglass fat distribution affected fertility more than either obesity or age. At least one other study also showed that women with waist-to-hip ratios above 0.8 (thicker waist and more tubular shape) had a harder time getting pregnant.[77]

An attractive body and an attractive face go together. Men who rank female bodies without seeing faces and faces without seeing bodies come up with very similar rankings for the same females. Symmetrical faces and bodies are both seen as more attractive than asymmetrical ones, and they are better able to fight exposure to pollutants, parasites or pathogens—all of which can cause a lack of symmetry.[78] People with high body symmetry have higher IQs and fewer minor ills such as headaches and stomach pains.[79] Even their voices are rated as more appealing.[80]

Women with symmetrical breasts are consistently rated more attractive than women with asymmetrical breasts, a condition associated with infertility.[81] The more symmetrical a man's body is, the more sex and the more partners he has, and the more pleasing he is to his lovers. Women even find the body odor of symmetrical men more attractive.[82]

A few years ago, trying to get my students to reflect on the microeconomist's worldview, which treats consumer sovereignty as almost the only relevant value, I asked whether any students had tastes they wished they did not have. An appealing, big-hearted and politically liberal student said yes, he wished that he "did not care so much about women's looks." The same year, at a convention, I happened to mention to a senior professor that I was planning to attend a talk by a female scholar who was bright and would speak on an interesting topic. I suggested he join me. Torn between that session and another, he asked, "What does she look like?"

Telling men not to become aroused by signs of beauty, youth and health is, as David Buss has noted, like "telling them not to experience sugar as sweet."[83] Using MRIs to examine young men's brains as they look at beautiful women, researchers found that feminine beauty affects a man's brain at a very primal level—similar to what a hungry man gets from a meal or an addict gets from a fix. One of the scientists involved said, "This is hard core circuitry. This is not a conditioned response."[84] Women of almost all political persuasions and parents of both sexes probably wish that males were more reasonable about female beauty. But though they can be held responsible for what actions they undertake in the presence of a beauty, men apparently cannot do anything about their pleasurable feelings.

When the beauty is not fully clothed, men may have a harder time keeping actions from following thought. In author and psychologist Sharon Lamb's observations of high schoolers, the teenage girls dress provocatively, but find the sexual responses of their male peers aggravating: "Girls are saying, 'Why can't he learn to control himself? I want you to look at me and say I'm sexy but not have sex with me.'"[85]

Evolutionary psychologists contend that the modern media weaken marriages by constantly reminding men of the extraordinary beauty that is available elsewhere. His brain may tell the man that the beautiful movie star is one in a thousand, air-brushed besides and surely unavailable to him. But the pictures still affect him. In one experiment, some men were shown pictures of beautiful women, while others were shown pictures of older and less attractive women. Each group was then asked questions about how sexually attracted they were and how committed to their current partners. Those shown pictures of the beautiful women said they were less attracted and less committed to their current partners than the other group did.[86]

Spending a lot of time around young, attractive women apparently leads to a higher divorce rate for men. Two sociologists report:

> While men in general are less likely to be divorced than women, and secondary school teachers and college professors in general are less likely to be divorced than others, simultaneously being male and being a secondary school teacher or college professor statistically increases the likelihood of being divorced.[87]

But male infidelity could be worse. Men who are in an exclusive dating relationship rate "babes" as less attractive than do uncommitted men; they also pay less attention to photos of the "babes" than do the uncommitted men.[88] As psychologist R. S. Miller puts it, "Even if the grass is greener on the other side of the fence, happy gardeners will be less likely to notice!"[89]

It is not surprising, though, that women everywhere seem to care very much about how they look. In Syrian universities, women attending classes with men spend as much time dressing for classes as American women spend dressing for a dinner party. On the streets, demure Muslim girls in head scarves practice a "below the knees exhibitionism" with sheer stockings and sling-back heels beneath their skirts.[90] A student who spent a summer in a small Jordanian city confirms that when Islamic women are not allowed to show hair or ears and when they wear their skirts to their ankles, they use more makeup than Western women do and spend more time on pedicures. A recent study examining the self-images of Iranian-born women living in Los Angeles and Tehran found that the latter group, largely unexposed to Western media and required to wear body-encasing clothes, were nonetheless *more* concerned about their weight and *more* dissatisfied with their bodies, on average, than were the women living in Los Angeles.[91]

We will see in the next section that men also have to compete, in those areas that women care about. Still, it seems unfair, in some cosmic sense, that men can attract women in different ways—through success in politics, business, sports or music, for instance—whereas for women so much depends on how they look. As a thoughtful author of a book on beauty puts it, "Every woman finds herself, without her consent, entered into a beauty contest with every other woman."[92]

As long as men love female beauty, women will care about their appearance. And the "male gaze" so often attacked by mainstream feminists will continue to please as well as annoy. As a younger woman, writer Anne Roche Muggeridge hated the street taunts and the "horrid, cold-faced girl-watching in school corridors and pubs." But, like most women, she enjoyed being "approvingly noticed." She even liked—"very much" liked—the clearest sign of such notice, the wolf-whistle:

> Girls don't know whether they are pretty or not. They stand in despair in front of their mirrors and wail to their mothers: I look so ugly! [Mothers reassure,] and the daughters don't believe it. But when a group of young, handsome male strangers spontaneously burst into a chorus of admiring notes, a girl must, even in her confusion and diffidence, experience a glow of pleasure and a dawning self-confidence.

Muggeridge wishes she were still in "the being-whistled-at age bracket."[93] Other women approaching their fifties also feel a loss because men no longer gaze at them in "that safe but sexual kind of way."[94] Indeed, feminists such as Germaine Greer are among those who have complained about becoming invisible to men as they grow older.[95]

Resources, Power and Status

If men care more than women about a partner's beauty, women care more than men about a partner's resources and status. Several studies have found that women divorce men who are not ambitious and do not work steadily at good jobs. An increase in male income increases the likelihood of marriage for cohabiting couples and decreases the likelihood of divorce for married couples. In contrast, couples with ambitious wives or wives with increasing income are more likely to divorce. And while women seldom divorce men based on a failure to do enough housework, men do seek divorce on that ground.[96]

A cross-cultural anthropological study examining reasons for conjugal dissolution in 160 modern and primitive societies finds this pattern everywhere. Since many of these societies are poor, one might have guessed that men would divorce women who did not help bring home the bacon. But as Laura Betzig reports, the economic reasons for divorce are "clearly segregated according to sex. Husbands are

In addition to resources, hundreds of studies have found that women care intensely about men's status.[109] In traditional, less modern societies, high-status men provide not just resources but also protection to their mates and offspring. In the mating market of the industrialized world, wealth, high income, professional degrees, education and greater intelligence are all signs of status, and all help men more than women. As with money, well-off women care even more about status in mates than do less well-off women. And unlike high-status men, they frequently prefer someone who is better educated and smarter than they are.[110]

If the goal were simply living in comfort, millionaires should do as well as multimillionaires or billionaires. But multimillionaires and billionaires have more power, and for women (but not for men), power is an aphrodisiac.[111] A relatively poor but prominent male politician is often considered a better catch than a wealthier but unknown vice president of some large company.

A female author honest enough to acknowledge that women love wealth believes that women see far more than what all that money might buy. They "see what created the wealth in the first place: genius, vision, daring, and an indomitable spirit.... What woman would not want to be moved by the men who move the world?"[112]

Fabio is a handsome male model with enormous shoulders and a rugged face. Men can see why women would find him attractive. What men don't understand is how his money and the power it brings can add to his *physical* attractiveness. But one columnist covering a Fabio appearance tells her female readers—"Lest the sex appeal of Fabio escape you, repeat 'multimillionaire' to yourself."[113] Similarly, Pamela Harriman, U.S. ambassador to France during the Clinton years and a woman who had affairs with some of the most powerful men in the world, famously said, "Well, of course I wanted a powerful man. What could be sexier?"[114] And fans of *Sex and the City* know that Mr. Big is so named because of his money and power; creator Candace Bushnell recognizes that for women, money is tied to power, which is tied to sexiness.[115]

For men, on the other hand, there is nothing particularly sexy about a powerful woman. Power does not increase the sex appeal of former attorney general Janet Reno or of Senator Dianne Feinstein. Indeed, as political insider Zandra Kayden says, power can threaten "a woman's sense of femininity." Power makes a man more manly, but it does not make a woman more womanly.[116] Some men today dislike women who are completely dependent on them financially,[117] but this attitude does not extend to desiring a mate who seriously competes with them or has a higher status than they have.[118] Women can find it *sexually* exciting to have their partners better them in an intellectual argument.[119] I doubt that many men do.

In her book *Marital Equality*, the feminist psychologist Janice Steil reports, unhappily, that almost all men and women in one study of dual-career professionals say it is easier for the marriage when the wife's career is less successful than her husband's. The women hold this view because they believe that the husband's work is more important to his sense of self, but also because *they* need their husbands to be successful.[120] Steil quotes other research showing that "Couples will go to great lengths to conceal a high-earning wife's income to protect the husband's status as primary provider." Moreover, married women in managerial and professional positions are more likely than women in less prestigious jobs to leave the labor force or move to a lower status position than are women in traditionally female employment. This pattern is more common when "the wife's position is similar in status to her husband's than when it is of lower status."[121] And, finally, Steil reports that a husband beginning to make more money feels better about himself as a spouse; "but the greater a wife's earnings relative to her husband, the worse she feels about herself as a spouse."[122]

Women are simply much more commonly attracted to social status than men are, as various studies indicate. For example,

> Using a rating scale from irrelevant or unimportant to indispensable, American women from Massachusetts, Michigan, Texas, and California rate social status as between important and indispensable, whereas men rate it as merely desirable but not very important. In one study of 5,000 college students, women list status, prestige, rank, position, power, standing, station, and high place as important considerably more frequently than men do.[123]

A survey of medical students found that half the men preferred a spouse with a lower income or occupational status, while none of the women did. No man desired a spouse with higher income or occupational prestige, but one-third of women did.[124] And just as men frequently exposed to very beautiful women tend to value their own partner less highly, women frequently exposed to socially valuable men also tend to devalue their partners.[125]

Some upper-middle-class husbands have lower self-esteem if their wives have jobs, but this effect is minimized if the husbands make significantly more money than their wives. Occupationally successful husbands in dual-career couples often feel that their wives work for their own benefit—to realize and express themselves. While most are proud of their wives' accomplishments, they worry about the associated costs, especially the "diminished attention to child care and home management." A 1986 study found that "young, highly educated, and occupationally successful fathers in dual career marriages are less satisfied with their work, marriages, and personal lives than similar men who are sole providers for their families."[126]

Perhaps evolution helps explain these apparently deep-seated sex differences in preferences for social status in a mate. Evolutionist Bobbi Low explains:

> For men, having power in and of itself can be reproductively rewarding. Straightforward status can set a man apart reproductively. It doesn't work quite that way for women. In the few societies where women wield substantial public power, as opposed to informal influence, they show no clear reproductive gain from doing so.

In fact, Low thinks there is often a direct conflict between political power and reproduction for women—if only in time and energy.[127]

In an important review article, Elizabeth Cashdan notes that women seeking both economic success and involvement with investing long-term mates may face dilemmas. If they compete successfully with men and make considerable money, their men may not stick around because the women can raise the children without the men's financial contributions and also because the wives' successes may threaten the husbands' positions in the male hierarchy—a result that would please neither husbands nor wives.[128]

What Women Don't Like to Talk About

Women like strong men, powerful men—men with status who can dominate their male competitors and protect and provide for their mates. If this finding is provocative, the sexual, intimate side of women's desire for dominant men is even more so.

We saw above that women like tall, physically powerful men with big shoulders, attributes that indicate an ability to offer protection. But why, when Fabio makes his appearances, do so many

female admirers, some decked out in business suits, ask him to sweep them up into his arms? Why do so many women still like to be carried over the threshold on their wedding night? And why do so many swoon when Rhett Butler ignores the protests of Scarlett O'Hara and swoops her up into his arms on the way upstairs in Atlanta?[129]

Women are three times more likely than men to say they want "someone to look up to."[130] They want to look up physically as well as intellectually. Men prefer a woman shorter than they are, and women a man who is taller. But on average men prefer her to be 4.5 inches shorter, while women want him a full 6 inches taller.[131] One *ABC News* experiment gauging the willingness of women to date short, albeit successful men revealed that regardless of their accomplishments, shorter men were far less appealing to women than men of average or above-average height.[132]

In a Victorian novel by Anthony Trollope, one of the author's more androgynous and independent young women declines to marry a duke because she "could never feel him to be my superior. That is what in truth a wife ought to feel."[133] Similarly, I know an attractive, bright Ph.D. student with an independent spirit who tells me, "I must think the man I marry is more intelligent than I am. He may not be, but I have to think he is."

In the Bridget Jones books, Bridget is especially attracted to both the cad Daniel and the worthy Mark Darcy when they seem particularly "authoritative." Darcy, when he seeks to get Bridget's mother out of a jam, is "thrillingly" so:

> "Where is your mother now, what is being done to find her," he started to pace around the room like a top barrister. "What are the sums involved, how did the matter come to light, what is the police's involvement, who knows about it, where is your father now, would you like to go to him? Will you allow me to take you?" It was pretty damn sexy I can tell you.[134]

Bridget also thinks it is "sexy" when "handsome Jed" lectures her for leaving her money in a hut in Thailand.[135]

A similar but real-life story is told by an independent, female professional who had a fire in her apartment and soon saw four firemen taking control, pulling wires and being helpful, reassuring and masculine. Her friend says she sounded "a little giddy" as she described her reaction to a houseful of firemen. "They're just so ... God, this is a terrible word, *manly*. There's something very rugged and sexy [about them]."[136]

The literature on sex differences shows that women like men who are "confident," "independent," "trendsetters," "interpersonally dominant (assertive)."[137] But there is a subtext: all these traits make a man sexy as well as useful. A hip female columnist who gives advice to the "under 30 crowd" responds to a woman who writes asking why men are such selfish idiots: "People act all surprised when they're treated like dirt, but then if you look at the qualities they find attractive (nice looking, rich, successful, charismatic, confident) you see a recipe for one self-absorbed SOB."[138] One strongly feminist academic admits that she enjoys going out with men who are "totally sexist.... Let's face it a lot of sexiness emerges from their being comfortable with their privilege and power."[139]

A man who is comfortable with his privilege and power is, of course, the typical hero in the romance novel. He is often a hard-edged, dangerous man of honor who is "strong enough to dominate everything in [the] world except the heroine." She makes him earn her love. He comes to cherish her. She is the only woman in the world "capable of making him happy, of making his life complete."[140] The hero in the romance novel may come to cherish the heroine, but he is also forceful with her, and sexually he often dominates her.

A few years ago, a student brought me a romance novel, Laura Taylor's *Anticipation,* that was used in her course on women's literature. She said the climactic scene appeared to her to be a rape. In it Spence declares that Viva and he will marry, and Viva asserts they will not. Her blue eyes flash as she walks out of the room toward her bedroom. He follows, relieves her of her wine glass, and smiles at the outraged expression on her face. He scoops her up and deposits her on the bed while shedding his clothes in record time. She glares at him and says, "Are you deaf?" He gently topples her on her back.

> Leaning over her, he efficiently jerked the front of her caftan apart, sending dozens of buttons flying every which way, then stripped it off her body.
>
> "What do you think you are doing?" she demanded as she glared at him.
>
> He watched her nipples tighten into mauve nuggets that invited his mouth. "Easing your tension," he announced in a matter of fact tone, despite the heat flooding his loins and engorging his sex. He came down over her, his hips lodging between her thighs, his upper body weight braced by his arms. "As sexist as that probably sounds."
>
> She squirmed, trying to free herself, and a sound of fury burst out of her when she failed to budge him.

Spence abruptly says their children should have names. She asks what children; they are not getting married. He declares his love. She asks if he is sure. He's " 'never been more sure of anything in my life.' " He asks if she will make babies and grow old with him. " 'Yes, Yes, Yes!' " Then they make love "as their bodies, hearts and souls mated forever."[141]

This is very rough sex, in which consent comes only after the man has forcefully and matter-of-factly stripped off the woman's clothes and placed his nude and aroused body between her legs. It comes as the high point in a fantasy aimed at women.

There have been many academic studies of sexual fantasies. One of the most interesting has found that pornographic films can be classified by theme. Of the nine themes reported by psychologist Roy Baumeister, the one that was by far the most sexually arousing for women

> involved a woman who was initially reluctant to have sex but changed her mind during the scene and became an active willing participant in sexual activity.[142] [This study and another] suggest that the woman's transition from no to yes, as an idea, increases sexual excitement.
>
> A review of the literature on sexual fantasies found that fantasies

of being overpowered and forced to have sex were far more common among women than men. In some studies, over half the female sample reported fantasies of being overpowered, and other research found a third of women endorsing such specific fantasies as being a slave who must obey a man's every wish. When women are given lists of sexual fantasies to choose among, that of being forced sexually is sometimes the first or second most frequently chosen one.[143]

Baumeister, like the author of similar reviews,[144] is quick to point out that these studies do not mean that women have any genuine desire to be raped.[145] Likewise, Theresa Crenshaw, a therapist and author of academic work on sexuality, describes one of her patient's favorite fantasies not as rape but as a "desirability" fantasy: A handsome neighbor who has frequently seen her undress at night through her window rushes over, prevents her scream with his lips, and in a frenzy of passion throws her down, overcomes her protests and does whatever he wants with her, "being alternately rough and tender." She is so irresistible that he loses all reason and ravishes her. "Control? She has it. He lost it."[146]

Confronted with findings of this kind, one skeptical journalist says, "So they are being forced into sex, but they're in perfect control?"[147] However we might interpret fantasies like the one just related, Crenshaw reports that her patient, a strong feminist, was appalled that she herself had such thoughts.

Robin West is a radical feminist theorist, but an unusual one in that she believes there are deep differences between the sexes. One of the most important, she thinks, concerns sexuality. West sees the conflict "between felt pleasure and stated ideal" as being a real dilemma for most feminists:

> Women report—with increasing frequency and as often as not in consciousness-raising sessions—that equality in sexuality is not what we find pleasurable or desirable. Rather, the experience of dominance and submission that go with the controlled, but fantastic, "expropriation" of our sexuality is precisely what is sexually desirable, exciting and pleasurable—in fantasy for many; in reality for some.... [An important item on any feminist agenda ought to be] to facilitate the exploration of women's sources of pleasure. Women take pleasure—and often, intense pleasure—in eroticized submission. Whatever causes women pleasure without causing attendant pain is something we should celebrate, not censure.[148]

Helen Fisher, an evolutionary anthropologist, notes that psychologists imagine that submission fantasies are women's attempts to avoid guilt about their sexual drive or to shed the responsibility of initiating sex. But according to Fisher, "women's daydreams of surrender may arise from primitive parts of the female brain—because feminine sexual surrender is exceptionally common in the animal kingdom."[149]

The authors of one study of female sexual desire were puzzled to find that women with high sexual satisfaction in marriage also reported low initial interest in sex; their subsequent high arousal and satisfaction appeared to be attributable to the ability of their husbands to overcome their wives' initial reluctance.[150] This experience is common enough for marital therapist Michele Weiner Davis to counsel wives to go ahead with sex even when they "might not have been thinking sexual thoughts or feeling particularly sexy." She reports that many clients have been thrilled with the results of this strategy.[151]

We do not know how the wives' initial reluctance is overcome, but it is not through rape. Only 0.5 percent of men find it appealing to force a woman into sex, and fewer than 0.5 percent of women say they want to be forced.[152] But these wives did apparently get a particular sexual charge when their husbands did something to turn a "no" or at least a "why bother?" into a "yes."

As novelist Mary Gaitskill notes, while disrespect for women is unacceptable, "the pleasure of sexual violence is not something only men like."[153] And *some* people, men and women, do consider a good fight to be excellent foreplay.[154] Eddie Fisher and Debbie Reynolds both tell of a dinner party at their house where Mike Todd and Elizabeth Taylor started belting each other. Todd ended up dragging Taylor across the floor by her hair as she kicked and scratched. When Reynolds became alarmed and jumped on Todd's back to get him to stop, Todd and Taylor both turned on her. According to Fisher, Taylor said,

> "Oh Debbie ... Don't be such a Girl Scout. Really, Debbie, you're so square."
>
> What Debbie didn't realize was that ... they loved a huge fracas as prelude to a heavenly roll in the hay.[155]

Taylor herself has said of her relationship with Richard Burton, "We had a ball fighting."[156]

Though the sex may have been "heavenly," the Taylor marriages were not. So, too, in the study described above, the women most satisfied with their marriage report high initial sexual interest and arousal, but only moderate sexual satisfaction.[157]

At any rate, there is some evidence that, despite all the hoopla, women do not particularly like the much-heralded, gentler "new men." Statements that incorporate feminine (expressive) characteristics and masculine (instrumental) characteristics were tried out on 160 college-age students from the United Kingdom—80 of each sex, and of both Asian and Caucasian ethnicity. The goal was to discover what were considered desirable traits in a peer group member of a respondent's own and of the opposite sex. Examples of the statements used to test reactions: "I am a warm and friendly person" and "I really like to do things for other people" on the one hand, and "I enjoy trying to win games and contests" and "I feel sure I can do most of the things I try" on the other.

Both Caucasian and Asian males thought the feminine characteristics were *more* desirable than the masculine ones for women, but both also thought the masculine characteristics were desirable for women. Women, on the other hand, did not at all like feminine characteristics in men and strongly liked the masculine characteristics in them. Traditional women and Asian women disliked feminine traits in men more than liberal and Caucasian women did, but the latter also disliked them. These results could not be explained by a generally contemptuous view of feminine characteristics because both women and men liked the feminine dimension in women.[158]

Surveys of mature married couples also find that women dislike men who regularly give way, even when it is their husbands giving way to them! One well-researched topic compares marital power to marital happiness, which can be measured by subjective scales. Marital power is trickier to measure, but social scientists try by asking questions (who makes up first after a quarrel? who decides where you will live?) and by observing couples debating something (who gives commands, interrupts and conciliates). One survey of over twenty such studies found only one constant: Wife-dominant couples were the least happy, and the wives in wife-dominated unions were less happy than their husbands.[159] (When male dominance helps marriages, it is moderate, not autocratic, dominance; marriages do not work where wives cannot influence husbands.)[160]

Liz Gallese's 1985 study of women in business offers in-depth analysis of six female graduates of the Harvard Business School class of 1975. Gallese considers one of the women, "Martha," to be typical of many women in her class who were surveyed more briefly. Martha does not want to outshine her husband; in particular, she will not relocate to another city to further her career. Her doctor husband explains his wife's attitude in the following way:

> [S]he doesn't want to lose esteem for me, to become the "man" in the family. I think she's worried that if she went to Boston she would flourish and star, and I would be kind of lost, and eventually that would lead to the loss of respect for me and the end of our marriage.

This is precisely what happened to "Tess," another of Gallese's subjects, whose business career shot past that of her husband, Kevin. So Kevin took on most of the child care; and while she was writing her book, Gallese believed this case demonstrated that role reversal could work. Tess seemed proud of her job, proud of her son, proud of her husband. She said she was much more ambitious than her husband, but that Kevin was interested in supporting her in her career. Gallese spent long evenings with Tess, but did not begin to see the truth until she spent time alone with Kevin, who was dissatisfied because he and his wife had almost no sex life.

Tess began to seduce other businessmen. She eventually came clean with Gallese, saying she would love to have another child someday but not with Kevin. She stayed with her husband because he was "a wife." But she declared, "I absolutely refuse to sleep with that man.... I'll never have sex with him again."[161]

Psychologists—and divorce lawyers—see a recurring pattern in this type of relationship: "First, the wife starts to lose respect for her husband, then he begins to feel emasculated, and then sex dwindles to a full stop."[162] Divorce rates are much higher when the wife's career is more successful. These higher rates appear even in a country such as Finland, where the androgyny project is more advanced than in the United States.[163]

Most feminists will no doubt say they want neither Martha's typical marriage nor Tess and Kevin's unorthodox one, but rather a more equal "partnership" in which promotions and raises come in tandem or sequentially and each relocation for her career is followed by one for his. Family researchers avidly seek out androgynous marriages. In her study of "peer marriages" Pepper Schwartz did not insist on a Solomonic 50/50 split of child care, housework and control of discretionary funds; a 60/40 split was good enough to fulfill her criteria for an "equal" relationship. Still, she encountered many couples who were praised by others as egalitarian but who did not meet her requirements. Many of these turned out to include wives whose domain centered on the children but who neither had nor wanted "equal status" with their husbands.

But what were the rare, genuinely "peer" marriages like—those where there was a close to 50/50 split of all kinds of work? Schwartz found that the couples in these marriages thought they had a stronger marital relationship with more intimacy, mutual respect and mutual interest. But there were a number of serious problems. Many husbands were not happy when their careers suffered. There was a constant need for negotiation and compromise. Co-parenting often meant economic sacrifices, and even more frequently it led to very serious conflicts over childrearing.

And many of the men and women in these marriages had a bit of the Tess-and-Kevin problem. Schwartz notes that their intimacy and familiarity made them feel more like siblings than lovers. They were more likely than other couples to "forget to include sex in their daily lives." "Women had fantasies of being 'taken' or mildly dominated," and one complained of a husband who began treating her "too darn respectfully." Many of the peer couples, however, thought they had terrific sex lives, often through adopting different personas in the bedroom. Schwartz recommended this adaptation and advised against preconceived notions of "egalitarian sex." She suggested therapy for those who could not "transcend their identities in everyday life" by finding a way to separate their days from their nights.[164]

Feminists who insist on minimizing sex differences will not read with sympathy discussions of gendered dominance and submission in sexuality. Some of them simply assume that the contempt for feminine traits in men—traits they find theoretically appealing—comes from traditional women.[165] And there may be something in this belief: we saw above that traditional women do have the *strongest* dislike of feminine qualities in men. But liberal women also dislike them. Moreover, some feminists have fantasies about being dominated sexually, and some females in "equal marriages" would prefer their husbands to be much more dominant in the sexual arena.

Some feminists openly admit that power is an aphrodisiac. After the Clinton/Lewinsky affair, former *Time* magazine White House correspondent Nina Burleigh described how she had felt one evening when she noticed President Clinton admiring her legs. Burleigh confessed that she would gladly have been his Monica for the evening if the President had suggested that they slip off to a nearby motel.[166] Later, on the television news show *Hardball,* she did not recant when she told host Chris Matthews that having the most powerful man in the world look at her in a certain way was "seductive and flattering. Any woman would feel that way."[167]

In the wake of Burleigh's confessions, other feminists outdid themselves in volunteering to outdo Monica.[168] The liberal *New York Times* columnist Maureen Dowd decided that President Clinton had been responsible for a new genre of "feminist erotic journalism": "After decades spent trying to dissuade powerful men from thinking they can have their way with less powerful women, feminists now have a terrible confession: they pant for power. They crave droit du seigneur. *Take me! Take me!*"[169]

Perhaps Dowd is being sardonic; but often, to the dismay of other feminists, such a desire for being dominated—even if latent or unspoken—does seem to exist in a number of feminists. Carolyn Graglia has called our attention to *Remaking Love,* a book coauthored by Barbara Ehrenreich and other feminists, that would substitute for what it calls the "great," "presumedly natural" "[sexual] drama of domination and submission" a "consciously chosen and deliberately scripted ritual" of domination and submission that begins by tying up the woman. While acknowledging the importance that the "feeling akin to surrender plays in achieving women's sexual gratification in genital intercourse," Graglia wonders why it should be necessary or desirable to resort to sadomasochism in order to bring it about.[170]

In the course of my research, it was remarkable to me how often I encountered examples of prominent feminists choosing, in some sense, to "submit" in their intimate relationships. When she married Ted Turner, Jane Fonda called herself the luckiest woman alive as she quit acting and moved to Atlanta so she could devote more time to her then-husband—a man her friends called "strong, domineering."[171] And Barbra Streisand told a TV critic, "Even though my feminist side says people should be independent and not need to be taken care of by another person, that doesn't necessarily work that way. There's the human factor, you know."[172]

When one looks to some of the greatest figures in feminist thought, Mary Wollstonecraft and Simone de Beauvoir, one finds a similar situation. Wollstonecraft sent a letter to her emotionally abusive lover in which she expressed her wish that he take her to North

America, where they would settle on a farm, and she would bear him six children.[173] Simone de Beauvoir's story is even sadder. She fell in love with Jean-Paul Sartre, a man she considered her intellectual superior. Their friendship lasted fifty years, but they had sexual relations for only sixteen of these. Carolyn Graglia, quoting historian Paul Johnson and others, explains that Beauvoir was Sartre's " 'cook and manager, female bodyguard and nurse' [though] she never held 'legal or financial status in his life.' " She became " 'like a eunuch in charge of a harem,' inspecting the women who wished to have affairs with Sartre and 'disposing of past sexual partners of his who became troublesome in their continued affection for him.' " Sartre pursued "innumerable affairs with ever younger mistresses, one of whom, in his ultimate humiliation of de Beauvoir, he legally adopted so that she was his sole heir and literary executor."[174]

Women often accuse men of incredible inconsistency: men want a woman who is a sexy, youthful temptress, but simultaneously a mature, loyal and reliable mate, homemaker and mother of their children. Women's tastes appear to be similarly contradictory: they say they want a kind, gentle, thoughtful mate who is emotionally available and deeply involved with the children, but in fact are not physically attracted to such men.

It seems likely that there are evolutionary reasons for what attracts women. The big, strong, confident man was—and, for that matter, often still is—best able to protect his mate from physical danger. Similarly, the man with high status, a good education and material resources is often well placed to protect his mate from financial dangers. And, of course, wealth can often buy physical security.

When John Townsend asked female medical students what they wanted in a mate,

> one third said that they wanted a man who made them feel "protected." When I asked what they needed protection from, they were vague and said it was not a rational desire. They knew they would have sufficient money and resources themselves, and they did not actually expect a man would ever have to protect them from physical danger. Nevertheless, having a man they truly respected would make them feel more secure. In answer to the same questions no man offered responses remotely similar to these.[175]

In the blockbuster novel *I Don't Know How She Does It,* the heroine Kate Reddy's separation from her husband Rich is painful always but especially when she locks up at night. She says the bolts don't seem as safe then.[176] In *The Edge of Reason,* the sequel to *Bridget Jones' Diary,* Bridget feels safe and cozy when cuddling with Mark Darcy after a "shag."[177] Following the September 11 terrorist attack on the World Trade Center, the ex-boyfriend of a shaken Chelsea Clinton gave her the "greatest gift" by agreeing to fly from California to New York to give her the "good, long hugs" she "craved."[178]

One researcher on sexuality has noted that the

> intense desire for contact and cuddling seems so much stronger in women than in men.... [When being held by your mate] you feel completely content, safe and sound.... There is submission and dependence, born of trust. Allowing yourself to be held requires dropping all pretense, relaxing, and becoming vulnerable.[179]

The radical feminist theorist Robin West says that "placing trust in one who is stronger is felt by some [women] to be intensely pleasurable."[180] Similarly, Alice Rossi, a prominent feminist and sociologist, says she suspects that

> even the most ardent feminist, in her innermost heart, would feel more positive about being comforted with her head on the shoulder

> of a male than she would about comforting a man whose head was on her shoulder. These deeper emotional responses may be at odds with what our cerebral cortex prompts us to espouse, and, if so, such discordance may trigger inner intellectual conflict and emotional turmoil.[181]

Whether desiring roughness or gentle cuddling, women are signaling a desire for dependence on a stronger male. One female author believes that "women don't want to be dependent on men considered as a group," but they "feel it is sexy to be dependent on the particular man they have chosen."[182] This dependence probably makes sense to most women only if the man is *at least* as powerful as they are.

Theresa Crenshaw wonders if we do not overdo our disparagement of women who seek dominating men:

> What if it is *healthy,* not *sick,* for an estrogen-laden woman to be attracted to a high-testosterone male—the dominant leader of the pack who maintains his position of authority harshly when necessary? Such is the ordinary case among lower primates.[183]

Power, on the other hand, is not all that women want in men. They regularly divorce men who behave like dictators and who make them feel devalued.[184] Women seem to like a strong man in the outside world and in the bedroom, but they could often do with men who are a little less lordly in the rest of the house.

One study of mating found that women want a romantic partner who is dynamic, charismatic and interpersonally warm.[185] This is, of course, the formula presented in the romance novel. It is also what one of Townsend's talented female medical students wanted: "a strong man with one weak spot—me and our family, and we're so dear to him he'll do anything for us. But with everyone outside the family he'll be able to walk over them if he has to."[186]

Just as it is hard for a man to find that beautiful, sexy, youthful free spirit who is also loyal and great with the kids, so it is hard for a woman to find the strong guy with high status who is completely devoted to his wife and family. Not long ago, Melinda Ledden Sidak wrote an article entitled "Why Paul McCartney Is the Sexiest Man Alive." Ledden argued that to be really sexy a man must demonstrate not just the falling "madly in love with her" love but also the "happily ever after" love. McCartney and now-deceased wife Linda were together for three decades, hated being apart and were separated for only a few nights during their whole marriage.

4

FATHERLESS FAMILIES

In the last fifty years, the family has changed dramatically. From 1960 to 1998, the percentage of women ages 35 to 44 who were married dropped from 87 to 72.[1] Declining and less stable marriages have meant more fatherless families. At the same time, evidence has accumulated that two-parent families produce healthier children than alternative arrangements. While recognizing that two-parent families are not always possible, policy and cultural analysis must focus on innate male/female differences in sexuality if the number of fatherless families is to be reduced.

The research on the effects of father-absence on children almost universally shows it to be deleterious in a host of important areas. Linda Waite and Maggie Gallagher recently reviewed the evidence and concluded that

> Children raised in single-parent households are, on average, more likely to be poor, to have health problems and psychological disorders, to commit crimes and exhibit other conduct disorders, have somewhat poorer relationships with both family and peers, and as adults eventually get fewer years of education and enjoy less stable marriages and lower occupational statuses than children whose parents got and stayed married. This "marriage gap" in children's well-being remains true even after researchers control for important family characteristics, including parents' race, income, and socioeconomic status.[2]

It should be emphasized that the pervasive effects of fatherlessness are substantial in magnitude. For example, daughters growing up in divorced households are fully three times as likely to become unwed mothers, which dramatically increases their chances of being poor. In addition, because children of divorced parents are themselves twice as likely to divorce in adulthood, fatherlessness resulting from divorce will often be perpetuated in the next generation.[3]

Children living in families without the biological father are less healthy than those living with intact biological families,[4] and in the last half-century suicide rates among teens and young adults have tripled, with two-thirds of this increase occurring among people living in homes with divorced parents.[5] In this, the United States is not alone. Recent Swedish studies find that children of single parents are twice as likely or more to develop psychiatric disease, to attempt suicide, or to have an alcohol-related disease.[6] Swedish boys in single-parent families are four times as likely to develop a narcotics-related disease, and girls are three times as likely. The risk of dying in youth is more than 50 percent greater for boys in Swedish single-parent families than for boys living with both parents.[7]

Fathers have special expertise in teaching young children how to deal with novelty and frustration, perhaps because they are more likely than mothers to encourage children to work out problems and address challenges themselves—from putting on their shoes to operating a new toy. As Brad Wilcox points out in a report for the U.S. Department of Health and Human Services, fathers are especially important to children as guides to the outside world. They introduce their children to work, sports and civil society. In general, fathers more than mothers help their children "to develop confidence in their ability to explore and excel in the world around them" and give them "the knowledge and the skills they need to make a mark in the world."[8]

Though father-absence hurts both girls and boys, the latter are particularly at risk. Boys raised in families without a biological father are more likely to exhibit delinquent and criminal behavior. Boys raised in single-parent families are twice as likely to have committed a crime, and boys raised in stepfamilies are three times as likely to have done so.[9]

Clearly, many of these results affect all of us, not just those families with the problem children. As one review notes, "time and again in the literature" family structure explains more about crime than does race or low income.[10] The effects start early—with two-year-olds in single-parent families showing more emotional and behavioral problems than those in married families,[11] and with preadolescents lying and destroying property more frequently.[12] And the effects last. A study following a sample of academically gifted children for seventy years finds that—even after controlling for childhood health status, family background, and personality characteristics such as impulsivity and emotional instability—parental divorce reduces a child's life expectancy by four years.[13] Forty-year-olds who grew up in divorced but otherwise advantaged homes are three times as likely to die prematurely from all causes as are their peers.[14]

Of course, some fatherless children might fare worse because some people with difficult personalities don't marry or can't stay married. As Andrew Cherlin of Johns Hopkins University puts it, "troubled parents often raise troubled children."[15] Alternatively, difficult kids may cause family tension that leads to divorce. In other words, for some children it may only appear to be divorce or the absence of marriage that is causing their emotional problems, when in fact something else altogether is responsible.

Divorce, however, seems to hurt kids of parents who have no significant psychological or emotional problems before the separation. Moreover, one recent study attempted to control for a hereditary predisposition to psychological problems by comparing the effects of divorce on children in biological and in adoptive families. It found that the "connections between divorce and children's psychopathology may be attributed to environmentally mediated processes."[16] Thus, while some traits such as a child's social competence can be attributed to genetics, it is primarily the environment—specifically, the cumulative experience of divorce—that has been shown to be responsible for the decline in children's well-being after a divorce. Another study, this one observing fraternal and identical twins after their parents' divorce, controlled for genetic factors and relatedness and still found a 42 percent greater risk of major depression in children of divorced parents than in children of two-parent families. Andrew Cherlin interprets these results as an indication that "divorce indeed has an effect on mental health—the variation is not due only to genes."[17]

Although most studies show that offspring of divorced parents are significantly less well off than offspring of continuously married parents, most children who grow up in single-parent homes do all right.[18] On some measures the differences between single-parent and two-parent families are small. But one of the most cited studies points out that such risks rarely seem small to parents: "While the chance that a middle-class child will drop out of high school or become a teen parent is very low, it is higher than the likelihood that he or she will be severely injured or killed in a car accident. Yet parents take the latter [risk] very seriously."[19] And five different national surveys reveal that, compared with a girl from a two-parent family, a girl in a single-parent family has twice the risk of giving birth as a teenager or of dropping out of high school.[20]

The greatest impact of single parenthood is on children's psychological distress. There is only a modest increase in serious mental health problems, but "despite their competent functioning, children from divorced families report a number of painful feelings, unhappy memories, and ongoing distress."[21] One study comparing college students from divorced and two-parent families found that 49 percent from the divorced families, compared with 14 percent from the married families, "reported that they had a 'harder childhood than most people.' " Forty-eight percent of those from the divorced families also said they "really missed dad."[22]

What do fathers do that is so important? In part, they do what mothers do: provide food, shelter, comfort, discipline, instruction.[23] The presence of two parents means there is more time to do these things. In two-parent homes, even mothers spend more time with their children than mothers in single-parent homes do.[24] Having two people also means that talents and interests are more abundant, providing more expertise in a wider variety of activities and in performing different parenting functions. Fathers are twice as likely as mothers to help their child build or repair something. They play more sports with their children than mothers do.[25] They find it easier to control unruly boys.[26]

Fathers who are not married to their children's mothers spend very little time with their offspring.[27] Children in single-parent homes with a strong attachment to the custodial parent become delinquents more often than do children from two-parent families with a strong attachment to both parents.[28] Even when a mother and a grandmother both live with and love the child, the results are the same as for children in a single-parent family; having a father thus seems very important in this equation.

The Importance of Biology

Children need not only a father, but a biological father living in the home. Studies show that even vigilant mothers, or vigilant mothers and grandmothers, do not prevent young girls from engaging in sex (and too often becoming unwed mothers) in the way that fathers do.[29] It helps very little for the child to see an unmarried biological father outside the home.[30] And although stepfathers can raise family income considerably, they do not help prevent childhood and adolescent problems.[31] Large numbers of stepfathers become disengaged from parenting and compete with the child for the mother's time.[32] Stepfathers praise and hug their children significantly less than biological fathers do.[33] They are less likely to have intense conversations with them.[34] Even worse, child abuse goes way up when stepfathers are present. Stepfathers commit most of this abuse, but even biological mothers are more abusive when they remarry than when they remain single. The rate of infanticide increases by 6,000 percent, and sexual abuse increases by a multiple of eight in stepfamilies as compared with traditional families.[35]

The stench emanating from these depressing statistics should not attach itself to the legions of fathers who do right by their nonbiological children. But surely it is not accidental that fathers, on average, treat their own flesh and blood better than their biologically unrelated children.

Biology—which at first might seem less significant than culture in the panorama of abuse and dysfunction sketched above—plays a surprising if less remarked upon role. It is well known, for instance, that unwed mothers often raise daughters who become unwed mothers. But it is less well known that this occurs in part because unwed mothers produce daughters who mature earlier sexually. Signs of early development put these very young girls at risk of taunts from their peers and sexual propositions from older boys. More importantly, early female sexual development is associated with a greater incidence of unplanned pregnancy; it is also associated with other significant problems such as sexual promiscuity, sexually transmitted diseases, depression, anxiety and alcohol consumption.

One mid-1990s study showed that by age eight, "48 percent of black girls and nearly 15 percent of white girls had begun to develop" sexually. Doctors used to routinely suggest testing for abnormalities when girls under eight showed signs of breast development or pubic hair or other signs of "precocious puberty." Now, pediatric endocrinologists say that such development in African American girls as young as six and white girls as young as seven should no longer be considered abnormal.[36]

The proportion of girls with early sexual development parallels an increase in fatherless families. From 1960 to 1998, the proportion of children living apart from their biological fathers rose from 17 to 35 percent.[37] Studies conducted by the Child Development Project show a "significant relation between single-mother family and [earlier] pubertal timing" in adolescent girls.[38]

Evolutionists explain differences in female maturation by suggesting that the environment is all-important in determining which of two biological forks a woman's sexual development takes. Early development seems to be associated with two interconnected phenomena: troubled environments, and girls living with single mothers or mothers living with men not related to their children. A troubled environment, they note, causes stress, which leads to an elevated level of cortisol, a hormone that if constantly present contributes to an impaired immune system, slower cognitive development and psychological distress.[39]

Single mothers face stresses of various kinds. They often have economic problems; boyfriends may come and go. Mothers are consequently less attentive to their daughters. Poor housing and diet do not greatly affect a child's cortisol level, but family stressors—conflict and change—have a very significant impact. Father-absence increases chronic stress, and the presence of stepfathers increases it even more. When stress goes up, girls develop more quickly.[40]

Studies suggest that stepfathers accelerate a girl's development, not only because they often cause stress, but also because they emit pheromones, chemical secretions that influence behavior.[41] There is evidence that humans unknowingly communicate with pheromones. And in other animals there is clear evidence that the presence of biological fathers' pheromones inhibits puberty while the presence of unrelated males' pheromones hastens it.[42]

A study published in 2000 finds that the presence of a stepfather produces early pubertal maturation in girls living apart from their biological fathers.[43] The longer the stepfather is present, the earlier pubertal development occurs. A more recent (2003) longitudinal study of 762 girls by Bruce Ellis and his collaborators concludes that absence of a biological father increases significantly the risk of sexual activity and adolescent pregnancy, and that the presence of a biological father is a major protective factor against early sex even when other risk factors are present.[44]

Evolutionists relate this phenomenon to strategies that are likely to enhance survival. While girls are growing up, they observe their surroundings, and especially their family surroundings. If a biological father is present and invested in their well-being, "their mating and dating strategy is to take their time and wait for 'Mr. Nice Guy'; they expect a stable relationship and, because of their behavior (cautious, confident, and faithful), they are likely to get it."[45]

If, on the other hand, female children grow up amidst stress, with fathers absent and maternal boyfriends present, they usually do not expect male support. They are more apt to take an opportunistic, short-term mating strategy, getting what support they can by providing sexual access to a series of men. They show more problem behavior when young and are more likely to divorce later on.[46]

For boys, the mating environment sends some parallel signals. In unstable environments, interpersonal manipulation, risk taking and striving to fill the vacuum of dominance may lead to more copulation with more women and thus more progeny. On the other hand, when they are born into an environment where women take investing mates for granted, boys learn that investing in wife and children will be the best route to successful reproduction. A study of at least one group of students has found that contrasting expectations about male investment can explain contrasting mate attraction strategies of both men and women.[47]

The view that developing girls pick up and act on environmental mating signals can explain demonstrable facts—for example, that girls growing up in single-parent or stepparent homes enter puberty and begin to have sexual relations earlier while being more aggressive in their sexual display. Sociological variables such as amount of adult supervision do not explain these phenomena.[48] The evidence is not as surprising as it may seem. Nature is often adaptable so that humans can function in varying environments. We develop calluses through a biological process, but they emerge only if the environment provides the friction that suggests calluses would be helpful.

Sex Codes and Babies among Underclass Youth

In his study of "Sex Codes among Inner City Youth," Elijah Anderson, a sociologist at the University of Pennsylvania, presents a rich portrait of sex in an underclass community. Anderson was struck by the differences in the mating goals of these young men and women. These differences would not be surprising to evolutionists.

Anderson entitles one crucial section of his explication "Sex: the Game and the Dream." The girls

> dream of being carried off by a Prince Charming who will love them, provide for them, and give them a family.... In accepting a boy's advances, a girl may think she is maneuvering him toward a commitment or that her getting pregnant is the nudge he needs to marry her and give her the life she wants.[49]

Perhaps this phenomenon that Anderson sees among American teenage girls applies universally. In her study of British youth, Anne Campbell finds that even girls in street gangs describe their "perfect future" as life with a man who will provide protection and "unconditional love."[50] Elizabeth Cashdan describes a similar pattern among young women in several African countries and concludes that "a period of mating optimism among young adult women may be a regular feature of female psychology."[51]

Boys, on the other hand, want to play a game and avoid marriage. Anderson observes that inner-city male peer groups place a high value on getting as much of what they call "pussy" as possible.

> Sex is the prize, and sexual conquests are a game whose goal is to make a fool of the young woman.... Some boys want babies to demonstrate their ability to control a girl's mind and body.... [For many, though,] the object is to hit and run while maintaining personal freedom and independence from conjugal ties.... [If a boy admits paternity,] his peer group likely will label him a chump, a square or a fool.... A certain regard is given to men who father children out of wedlock as long as they are not "caught" and made financially responsible to support a family.

The boys succeed most easily when they target younger girls. The young men's age, "at times four or five years older" than the girls, gives them "an authoritative edge" and makes their fictional readiness to settle down more credible.* The young men play elaborate

---

*One-third of girls who have sex when they are 15 or younger do it with boys over 18; 13 percent have male partners who are over 20. Seventy percent of the men who get teenage girls pregnant or who give them venereal diseases are over 20, with 15 percent of them over 25. "A man over 25 is as likely to cause a 'teenage' pregnancy, birth, or STD case as a [boy under 18]." [Males, 1992; National Survey of Family Growth.]

games, presenting themselves as the type they know the young women want to see. As an aid to conquest, they may go to church with the girls' families or go house hunting and shop for furniture.

What does Anderson find helps thwart the boys? Ministers, teachers, upwardly mobile peers and—perhaps most important of all—fathers in the girls' homes. Though some single mothers with domineering personalities also "'sit the boy down' and have a ritual talk," the fathers, or sometimes older brothers or uncles, are more likely to possess a combination of "moral authority" and "the believable threat of violence." When there are only single mothers and teenage daughters, "the dwelling may be viewed ... as an unprotected nest."

As the young mothers with babies become older, they will deride the "nothin" men who shun commitment. At the same time, they often accommodate these men.[52] And perhaps inconsistently, the "good man" willing to provide for mother and child "runs the risk of being seen as a pussy by the women as well as by his peer group." In a tough environment, the man who dominates women as well as his male peers has a certain attraction even if he cannot be tamed as easily as the hero in the romance novel.

As they grow older, Anderson's inner-city men often seek a "'main squeeze'—a steady and reliable female partner who mimics the role their mothers played, a woman who will cook, clean and generally serve them, with few questions about the 'ladies' they may be seeing" and even fewer about their male friends.[53]

In this world, the men's game trumps the women's dream. The result, Anderson says, is "profound hostility between young men and women."[54] It is easy to see why the women might come to hate men, but the feeling seems to be mutual. The men distrust women to whom they are not related. They assume that those they sleep with have multiple sexual partners, and they often doubt that their putative children are in fact theirs.[55]

This hostility is manifest in the world of hip hop. A recent biography of Tupac Shakur echoes much of Anderson's story, and the music itself is full of "rhetorical violence." Tupac and others are "playas" and bedding women is the game. They "seek promiscuous sex while resenting the women with whom they share it"; they love their own mamas while dissing their babies' mamas. The biography's author thinks these themes of the rap artists have broad currency among poor blacks generally.[56]

Inner-city culture among young whites is less often studied. But one recent report on the working-class young in Milton,

Massachusetts, echoed Anderson's main finding: "The girls have sex for love and the boys establish status through sexual conquest." One difference is that peer pressure in Milton prods young males to take some responsibility for pregnant partners even if it is only helping to pay for an abortion or providing some money for the child.[57] Other studies show that in the longer run, unmarried fathers forget about financial support and tend to disappear.[58]

Nearly a decade before Anderson wrote about inner-city youth, Bill Moyers produced a riveting CBS special on the family crisis in black America. The most memorable character was a twenty-six-year-old by the name of Timothy McSeed, who had been brought up by an unwed mother who was sixteen when he was born. McSeed, in turn, had six children by four different women, one of whom told Moyers that Timothy charmed her by talking of his desire "to have a home, have children, take care of them." At the time Moyers spoke to him, McSeed had not held a steady job in two and a half years. He saw only some of his children, and these only sporadically. Speaking of his kids, he told Moyers,

> You say, "This is something that I've done." Just like the carpentry, it's something that you've done.... like they might grow up to be doctors or actors, you know, and you can say, "look, that's my boy" or "that's my girl," you know. Where there's, you know, some people that can't have children at all.[59]

McSeed does not explicitly mention passing his genes through to later generations, but the message of his behavior and his defense of it is clear nonetheless.

To proliferate their genes, our male ancestors either mated with many women or promoted their offspring's survival by supporting and defending the mother and children. In a subculture where it is possible to take either the quantity or the quality approach to siring the next generation, McSeed, with less of what social scientists call "embodied capital" than more mainstream males, is better able to succeed with the quantity approach.[60] A white version of McSeed was more recently in the news when the Wisconsin Supreme Court affirmed a judgment forbidding a man named David Oakley from having any more children until he supported those he already had. Oakley, an unemployed factory worker, had nine children by four different women.

The quantity/quality trade-off is present throughout contemporary America. Men who cease to live with one or more of their children have "higher fertility rates than those who fully parent all of their children."[61] And men seem to be more likely to "graze" among female mates when alternative resources will keep the children they serially sire from slipping into poverty.[62]

One of these alternative resources is often welfare. The *New York Times* recently reported a rise in two-parent families after welfare laws were overhauled to reduce funding to single mothers. The "dovetailing of positive trends" included a higher marriage rate "particularly among lower-income blacks," and, according to a similar upbeat *Washington Post* article, a decrease in birth and high school dropout rates for "high risk" teenage girls. [63] Since every year 19 percent of all teenage girls who have sexual intercourse become pregnant, these trends could have positive effects on a large number of lives.

But as one study shows, welfare and wages have similar effects for low-income women. As these women begin to earn more money, marriage rates, marital births and the percentage of children living in two-parent families all go down. One explanation for the direct correlation of increased female income with higher divorce rates is that the women are getting out of bad marriages once they can afford to.[64] But this correlation can also reflect men's perception that they can effectively spread their seed while relying on their female partners to support their children.

This same process may be at work in nations other than the United States. In several underdeveloped countries, men reduce their parental investment and begin to father children with other women as their wives begin to earn more money.[65]

Implications

In this cold war between the sexes, civilization takes sides. If the young women can get the loving, loyal, providing and permanent mates they seek, the children they bear and the society they inhabit will be healthier. At the same time, if men fail in their inclination toward irresponsible promiscuity, most of them will fare far better as well. The men Anderson studied are in competition for sexual access to multiple women. Only a small minority of them will end up with a "main squeeze" and some "ladies on the side." While some may produce lots of babies and have multiple women "sick with love for [them],"[66] many will end up with no children and no ladies. Or they may end up dead because the competition they have entered makes plenty of room for violence.

Theory and evidence suggest to Elizabeth Cashdan that high expectations of paternal investment and the associated female mating strategies will most likely occur

> a) when the ratio of men to women is high, creating from the female perspective a "buyer's market"; b) other women are restricted in their sexuality so that a man cannot obtain sexual access without investment; c) males are able to provide significant investment; and d) male investment significantly enhances the survival of offspring.[67]

While almost everyone would prefer a society in which males invest in their young, the conditions Cashdan has outlined as favoring this outcome suggest how daunting is the task of influencing underclass culture in that direction. Most males there are not able to provide significant investment. And one study found that black men had a much lower desire to marry than did white or Hispanic men—in large part because they did not expect marriage to improve "their sex lives and personal friendships" in the way that white and Hispanic men did.[68]

The sex ratios among blacks relative to those among whites, moreover, make it much harder for black women to be able to demand investment as a condition of sexual access.[69] At ages 20 to 24 there are 105 white males for every 100 white females, but only 97 black males per 100 black females. And young black urban men are more likely than whites to be unemployed, imprisoned or addicted—"bad bets as potential husbands."[70]

Only the ability of male investment to enhance significantly the survival of offspring gives much cause for optimism. At least by the standards of developed countries, the United States government support available to single mothers is not great these days, and even when inner-city single mothers find employment, it does not usually pay very well. Adding a father's wages can significantly increase family income.

The key to unlocking male investment seems to be marriage. Married men earn more than single men. Even men in shotgun weddings (where there was a premarital conception), who are younger and have less education on average than other marrying men, also earn more once they are married.

So how might women in poor neighborhoods get males to marry? First, understand that large numbers of men lie to get sex. *Washington Post* columnist Richard Cohen has written about a guy called Max, a jeweler in Manhattan's Diamond District. For Max,

Fridays were especially good for business because on that day young men would come in with young women to put deposits down on engagement rings. Then the couples would go off for an intimate weekend, and Max would never hear from them again. If a man tells a girl he loves her, as with those Elijah Anderson studied, he may be lying. If he really loves her, she'll know for sure in time. He will propose. But Max's story suggests that even then she'd better wait, at least till she gets the ring, before she completely lowers her guard.[71]

Like Timothy McSeed, many of the men that underclass women meet will be delighted to father a child they do not plan to support. By fooling women, they achieve status with their peers and remain free to sire more kids elsewhere. The woman gets nothing she really wants. These days, having a man's baby is a poor matrimonial strategy.[72] The paternal shotgun has all but disappeared.

Having another man's baby, moreover, makes a woman far less attractive to other prospective husbands. The chances that "a woman of a given age, race and socioeconomic status will be married is 40 percent lower for those who first had a child out of wedlock.... By age 35 only 70 percent of all unwed mothers are married, in contrast to 88 percent among those who have not had a child before marriage."[73] In addition, "Not only are unwed mothers less likely to marry than those without children, but when they do marry, they do not marry as well. Their partners are more likely to be high school dropouts or unemployed than the partners of women who have similarly disadvantaged backgrounds but no children."[74]

Men often prize promiscuous sex in the short term, but they want faithful wives.[75] Through the ages, men with faithful mates have sired more children, and a taste for faithfulness will thus have been "naturally selected" for. If a man finds a woman hard to get, he will sense that she is more likely to be faithful after marriage. Cross-culturally, men provide more for their young when paternal confidence increases and less when it decreases.[76]*

---

*Technology today allows researchers to morph the faces of undergraduate students with the faces of toddlers. When asked to choose the face of the most attractive baby and the baby they would be most likely to adopt or pay child support for, males, unlike females, consistently picked the child with the greatest resemblance to themselves. This unconscious mechanism (when asked about their choices, "none identified resemblance as a factor in how they chose which child to support ... nor did they even realize that their faces had been morphed with the child") is probably a throwback to evolutionary strategy to deter women from seeking parental investment from nonpaternal males. [Platek, Burch et al., 2002.]

Studies have shown that men can and will change their behavior in response to what they think women require for sex. Anthropologist Elizabeth Cashdan found that men who thought "high levels of male parental investment were the norm were significantly more likely to attract mates by displaying both their ability and willingness to invest."[77] Essayist Stanley Crouch insists that the bad-boy, predatory male will fade "once black females decide they're tired of that.... If the real brother can't get no date, the real brother is going to become another kind of real brother."[78]

The irony is that although marriage has become an endangered institution among underclass males, men seem to gain the most from marriage, although almost all studies conclude that women gain some. Married people live longer and feel healthier. This is true in studies conducted in the United States and in other countries. A study in the United Kingdom reveals that from 1970 onward, the relationship between marriage and improved health has become progressively stronger for both males and females. In 1991, for example, only 10 percent of hospital beds were occupied by married people.[79] Moreover, married men can handle workplace stress much better than divorced men. For married men, turmoil at work does not correlate with a significant increase in death, but for divorced men it does.[80]

Married men and women are much more likely to say they are very happy than are the single, divorced or cohabiting. They are less depressed and anxious. Their use of drugs and alcohol decreases.[81] They enjoy more and better sex than their single peers. One recent study finds that unmarried adults have 63 percent less total wealth than married adults.[82] A report by the Center for Data Analysis even "confirms other research that shows that 80 percent of poor single-parent families would escape from poverty if the single parents were married."[83] These findings hold for blacks and Mexican Americans as well as for whites. Indeed, one study of these minority groups shows that being married is more strongly linked to personal happiness than is income or education.[84]

But does marriage deserve the credit, or are happy and healthy people simply more likely to get married? Research indicates that marriage deserves a lot of the credit. The sick, after they marry, become healthier than the equally sick who do not marry. The happy become even happier than the single (and equivalently happy) when they marry.[85]

Encouraging marriage will help little if divorce remains pervasive. The evidence presented earlier on the benefits of marriage for children and partners could well cause reconsideration of divorce among many couples where violence is not an issue. So too could myth-shattering research conducted by Linda Waite and Ye Luo of the University of Chicago. Using data that canvassed for changes in measures of emotional well-being over a five-year period, Waite and Luo find that dissolving a marriage seen as unhappy does not usually lead to an increase in emotional well-being and by some measures lowers it. Moreover,

> Marital unhappiness shows little stability over time, and much less stability than marital happiness. About two-thirds of those who rated their marriage as unhappy, and who remained married, rated that same marriage as happy five years later.[86]

"Just the facts" messages like this should have an effect on some young men and women. But pointing out the benefits of long-term commitment and marriage will be less fruitful with men than with women. Explaining to men how much they have to gain from marriage will not reliably lead to the altar males with a wandering eye and a passion for freedom. More than calculating reason is at work. Those who believe that utilitarian considerations are determinative should consider whether young, inexperienced male drivers, having sat through driver's education, motor cautiously since the risks of an accident are so demonstrably high for them.

Affecting men's behavior will be a harder task than affecting women's because men desire multiple mates to a greater extent than most women do. Moreover, in many communities, and not just poor ones, studs have high status. Like the young men in Anderson's underclass community, boys at good private schools have also competed via sexual conquests, in one case with "point systems and statistics."[87]

But boys don't need to be egged on by their peers to desire sex. In both sexes, testosterone "is responsible for the 'active' libido—the drive associated with sexual appetite, attention, motivation and action."[88] While prepubescent girls and boys have the same amount of testosterone, girls' levels only double during puberty while boys' levels increase by a factor of ten to twenty.[89] Studies find that peers and family have much less affect than these biological changes do on adolescent male sexual motivation and behavior. For girls, on the other hand, "differential involvement in coitus is controlled by social processes not by hormones."[90] Thus, a young, white female virgin whose best friend is a nonvirgin is six times as likely to lose her virginity over the next two years as is a virgin whose best friend is also a virgin. There is no such effect for boys.[91]

Perhaps in time the men who hit and run with women can be stigmatized; but we are now a long way from Victorian England. A more promising approach would appeal to men's sense of self-importance. John Gray must have gotten something right since his *Men Are from Mars, Women Are from Venus* sold six million copies. One of his themes is that men have to feel needed.

Young men might feel more needed if they could be introduced to Jonetta Rose Barras, whose poignant book *Whatever Happened to Daddy's Little Girl?* describes how she (and others she interviewed) felt when the men who lived with her and whom she came to love and who seemed to love her suddenly disappeared as they parted from her unmarried mother. Barras painfully relates the typical desire of fatherless daughters to both seek and resist intimacy. Knowing that "to love is a dangerous thing," these women repeatedly try to create "a sense of belonging, of being loved," through physical intimacy. "Too often, women who are wounded by the loss of their fathers . . . go from man to man, from bed to bed, calling sex 'love' and hoping to be healed by the physical closeness."

After her own husband abandoned their daughter, Barras watched her child go through a pattern of experience nearly identical to her own, from hair loss, to anger and depression, to engaging in destructive relationships. Barras began to recognize the universal effects of losing a father and concluded that

> A girl abandoned by the first man in her life forever entertains powerful feelings of being unworthy or incapable of receiving any man's love. Even when she receives love from another, she is constantly and intensely fearful of losing it. This is the anxiety, the pain, of losing one's father.

Without a father, a girl has a hard time reading men. She lacks "a daily resource from which to draw to interpret a boy's flirtations, advances or conversations." But if her father loves her, a girl will see herself as worthy of genuine affection and respect and will be able to demand the same from the other men in her life.[92]

Men are capable of a high-mindedness not hinted at by the sobering sociological evidence discussed above. At the end of any work week, for instance, poor immigrant laborers can be seen lining up to wire most of their paychecks to their families in the mother country. And sociologist Steve Nock has found that husbands are actually more likely than wives to avoid divorce because they believe their mate is committed to the marriage and would be seriously harmed by a divorce.[93] A man's sense of duty and capacity for sacrifice will be brought forth more readily if women will say "no" to casual sex and give them time and motive to turn their lust into love.[94]

5

THE SEXUAL REVOLUTION

A variety of factors incited the sexual revolution of the 1960s. The birth control pill was crucial.[1] For the first time, women could reliably control pregnancy and thus could regard sex as recreational rather than as solely procreative. Another cause was the rise of a counterculture that espoused a philosophy of "if it feels good, do it" and "make love, not war." Perhaps most important was the growth of feminism. For women, free sex became a declaration of independence.[2] The emotion and romantic love that had always been associated with female sexuality began to be seen as merely a way to keep women devoted to—and thus dependent on and subordinate to—their husbands.[3] In a recent article for the *Washington Post,* Lynn Darling remembers the heady days of 1969, her freshman year at Harvard, when she and other virgin women listened to doctors matter-of-factly discussing birth control and certain exercises that would enhance the pleasure of both partners.[4]

Women are still told by sex educators and some feminists that healthy, enjoyable sex is relaxed, comfortable and pleasurable, light-hearted, devoid of high emotion and dependency.[5] Young girls, in this view, should "condition consent on pleasure and desire ... rather than on love."[6] Partners should not risk opening their hearts "in hopes of joyful union," but instead be negotiators who demand and accept conditions for their mutual pleasure.[7]

Echoes of the sexual revolution are prominent in the work of younger, contemporary feminists. Naomi Wolf, for example, insists that a girl's sex drive is "at least as intense" as a boy's and encourages women to appreciate their "slut" side.[8] Leora Tanenbaum thinks that "sexually active 'sluts'" are "independent sexual agents" with "a healthy attitude" about their sexuality and their futures.[9] Katie Roiphe would fight the stereotypes that say men want sex and women don't. Following this line, gender textbooks say that socially constructed stereotypes—"sexual scripts"—are still entrenched despite the sexual revolution and still serve to explain the sexuality differences we see around us.[10] In her influential book *The Mismeasure of Women,* Carol Tavris concludes the chapter on sex by suggesting that both men and women should have "sex for the sheer pleasure of it." She quotes an English writer, Wendy Faulkner: "'Sex is about enjoying ourselves. Let us get on with it.'"[11]

Though the "let's get on with it" attitude remains prominent among many feminists, there have been some defections over the last forty years. Germaine Greer, for instance, talks about the "lie of the sexual revolution"—an era she describes as liberating male sexuality by giving women a false sense of sexual equality.[12] Sally Cline argues that the sexual revolution did not work to women's benefit:

> What the Genital Appropriation Era actually permitted was more access to women's bodies by more men; what it actually achieved was not a great deal of liberation for women but a great deal of legitimacy for male promiscuity; what it actually passed on to women was the male fragmentation of emotion from body.[13]

This skeptical view of sexual liberation is most visible in the movement to combat sexual harassment, which is in conflict with an androgynous outlook on sexuality. If someone in the office asked to have sex, more than 62 percent of women say they would feel insulted, while only 15 percent of men would. Indeed, over 67 percent of men say they would be flattered by such a proposition, compared with less than 17 percent of women.[14]

Since some conduct that would offend most women is thus clearly unobjectionable and even desirable to most men, some U.S. courts have decided that sexual harassment law should seek to determine whether a "reasonable woman" would find any given behavior offensive. But many jurists, including Supreme Court justice Ruth Bader Ginsberg, prefer a "reasonable person" to the "reasonable woman" standard, which they consider dangerous in that it reinforces the notion that women are different from men. In the words of the Michigan Supreme Court,

> Standard stereotypic assumptions of women . . . [imply that] women are sensitive, fragile and in need of a more protective standard. Such paternalism degrades women and is repugnant to the very ideals of equality that the [law] is intended to protect.[15]

The Double Standard: Sluts and Studs

The one thing most women can probably agree upon is their strong opposition to the double standard. Why is it that good girls don't and good boys can? Why are promiscuous men called *experienced* or *studs* and women who are far less promiscuous *sluts?* Whole books rail about this phenomenon, and gender textbooks interpret these labels as just another sign that socially constructed patriarchy still rules.[16]

As noted earlier, however, the double standard in one form or another seems nearly universal.[17] It is especially strong in societies where male investment in offspring is important for children's well-being. Sexually permissive women who require no investment might give men pleasure without cost, but evolution has not been kind to the genes of men who raised other men's children. Thus the male psychology that has developed over time makes *both* sexually permissive women *and* faithful wives appealing. Indeed, of sixty-seven traits enumerated in a survey, American men "regard infidelity as the least desirable characteristic in a wife." (Wives also abhor sexual infidelity in husbands, but believe that "several other factors, such as sexual aggressiveness, exceed infidelity in the grief they cause women.")[18]

As long as men more than women abhor promiscuity in potential spouses, some sort of double standard will exist. And society will reinforce these attitudes because parents want their children to be able to attract good mates; and parents will know that female promiscuity affects long-term prospects far more than male promiscuity does. Sexual reputation aside, the effects of pregnancy and other factors discussed below also reinforce parents' inclination to be more concerned about their daughters' sex lives than those of their sons.

Amid the swirl of conflicting advice, what message comes through to college women these days? A systematic look at what recent issues of *Cosmopolitan,* the best-selling magazine in college bookstores, has to say about relationships and sex within relationships is a good place to start. Recently I examined all the issues of *Cosmo* for an entire year. The magazine clearly assumes that its female readers are deeply concerned about and involved in sex, although there is nothing that would suggest they prefer sexual pleasure with lots of different men. One article explains how to have an orgasm with your partner. *Cosmo,* however, also prints a letter from a woman craving the "closeness of sex" without an orgasm but fearing she will bruise guys' egos if she doesn't fake it; and one from a women who complains about a "sexaholic" partner.

The magazine seems to focus at least as much on pleasing the male partner sexually as on what will please the female readers sexually. The lead article in the February 2002 issue was "Cosmo's Map to Male Pleasure." Another cover article in that issue dealt with the sexual pleasure of women, and emphasized the need for female surrender:

> [The] one essential element of ultimate lovin: the ability to surrender completely to the erotic experience. . . . The rewards of absolutely losing it are *sooo* worth it. . . . let your limbs go limp, lie back, and enjoy everything you have coming to you.

The interests of evolutionary psychologists might be piqued by this article and others in the magazine on a man's need to take charge and to "assert his inner alpha male."

In addition, one letter writer had a question about how to greet a guy she had hooked up with who never called again, and another asked whether the guy she slept with on the first date will think she is a total slut. The "advice guy" responded that it depends on the guy. A poll in another issue, however, found that 76 percent of male respondents said they would not date again any girl they slept with on the first date.

There are many articles on the desire for intimacy and commitment and on emotional differences between men and women. There are articles on how to rope a man in: "How to be a guy's girl." "How to be his dream girlfriend." About how not to lose him: "Should you try to hurry love?" "Top 10 Girlfriend Mistakes." "How to stay blissfully bonded." And about getting to and succeeding in marriage: "How to get a man to propose." "Marriage Skills to Master Now: Even if you're a few years away from walking down the aisle, you can start honing your happily ever after expertise this minute."[19] *Cosmo*'s view of young women and their sexual anxieties may not be the whole picture, but it is certainly different from the image conveyed by those who propose a strictly egalitarian approach to male and female sexuality.

When I was in high school and college in the mid-fifties to early sixties, men and women had dates in which the man asked the woman out and paid for the evening. There was no particular expectation of any physical intimacy. Rather, dates were a chance to get to know each other one on one. If the dates continued, increasing emotional attachment, though not always equivalent for both sexes, was usually paralleled by increased physical intimacy. Both sexes often dated more than one person. People dated for fun and often ended up, in time, with a "steady" whom they might someday marry. With steadies, in time, some heavy petting above and below the waist often occurred, but intercourse was not likely.

How extensive is dating in college today? Norval Glenn and Elizabeth Marquardt recently produced an extensive study that surveyed one thousand randomly selected college women and sponsored long interviews with sixty-two others. They found that dating—in which the man asks a woman out, picks her up and pays for the evening—is no longer a weekly occasion. In fact, dating of this kind rarely occurs. Only 50 percent of the seniors surveyed had been on more than six such dates while in college, and even these were often for prearranged special occasions such as a fraternity-sorority event.[20] There is still some of the fifties-style "going steady." Of the women surveyed, 48 percent had a boyfriend, and 24 percent of those with boyfriends had never had intercourse. (Of the whole sample, 31 percent were virgins.) But the boyfriends came without much "shopping around" beforehand, since the relationships often developed from hanging out with a group of friends in an apartment or a dorm. When these established couples have intercourse, they often end up "joined at the hip." Joined-at-the-hip couples see each other every day and sometimes find it awkward to break up because they may be living in the same dorm.

Apart from these relationships, there is a considerable amount of casual sex, typically at a social occasion known as the *hookup*. Hooking up can mean anything from kissing to having intercourse, but it usually entails a sexual interaction with a stranger or an acquaintance "without commitment or even affection."[21] Forty percent of college women say they have participated in a hookup; 10 percent have done so more than six times.[22]

Why do they do it? The women gave a long list of reasons to Glenn and Marquardt. Heavy drinking is usually a part of the picture.[23] Some simply want short-term physical intimacy. Some, especially first-year students, think the hookup will lead to a relationship.[24] Others hook up because, they say, they *don't* want a relationship. Some women, particularly those at good schools, don't want to make the time commitment that a joined-at-the-hip partnership would require. A number are protecting their emotions—avoiding the "hurt and rejection" they may have experienced in the breakup of a previous sexual relationship. With the hookup you can "pretend like it didn't mean anything to you." And besides, "you were drunk."[25]

Many women who hook up like the feeling of power they get from being desired. "'I would say we go out looking to kiss somebody or to dance with somebody ... to feel sexual.'"[26] The girl can see herself as "the irresistible erotic lure who drives men wild."[27] At parties there can be competition to see who can attract the most desirable men. "It's the ultimate ego boost to have a bunch of guys come up to you and want to be with you, even if it is only for one night."[28] One sign that the double standard still has legs can be seen in the fact that the big catches for hookups are the men who have had their way with other women, not the less experienced "nice guys."[29]

Swinging Bachelorettes?

Are women, then, becoming more sexually liberated? Are there signs that with the "liberation" of the sexual revolution, women are beginning to develop a taste for sex with multiple men? One national survey found that while teenage girls are much more likely to be sexually active than they were a generation ago, they are also much less likely than boys to say that they "really feel good about their sexual experiences so far."[30] Two other surveys have found that girls are more likely than boys to say they wish they had waited longer to have sex.[31] More than two-thirds of sexually active teenage girls say they regret not waiting longer.[32]

What about college women specifically? Are they enjoying hookups? None of my sources concludes that women who hook up are getting much out of it.* The Glenn/Marquardt study, which

*What I will report is based mainly on the work of Glenn and Marquardt; on several studies by John Marshall Townsend interviewing over 350 students in varying depth; and on detective work by two of my female research assistants. One of these research assistants was a female dorm resident advisor for two years and wrote me a long

notes that only 40 percent of college women ever hook up, gives the most favorable presentation. Their phone poll asked the female college students how they felt a day or two after the hookup. Those questioned were given eight words, three positive and five negative, and were asked which fit. Of the four words that drew the most agreement, all between 52 and 62 percent, two are favorable—*adventurous* and *desirable*—and two negative—*awkward* and *confused.* After that, the negative emotions dominate, with 44 percent of respondents saying they were *disappointed,* about a quarter feeling *empty* or *exploited,* and only 18 percent feeling *triumphant.*

The authors found the same sort of ambivalence during in-depth, on-campus interviews. A number of women said that afterward they felt strong, desirable and sexy, while others said they felt awkward, hurt and confused. A dominant theme was the wish that something more would happen with the guy, but they never knew if it would, and it was entirely up to him. Sometimes the guy would call back, and the girl would think it was serious and might lead to a relationship. But often the guy just wanted to hook up once again. A number of women blamed their "unusually" emotional or sensitive natures for the fact that hookups did not work for them.[33] John Townsend's research reveals that the progression from excited experimentation to disappointment is common even among women who have no moral qualms about casual sex and who have frequently participated in it.

A Woman's Casual Sex Cycle

Townsend is an evolutionary anthropologist who believes that we possess unconscious emotional-motivational mechanisms that warn women via bad feelings when they engage in sexual behavior that would have been maladaptive in earlier evolutionary eras. Casual sex with men unwilling to invest in them or their offspring is a prime instigator of such negative feelings.[34]

Townsend's multiple studies include two sets of in-depth interviews, one with forty medical students and one with fifty undergrad-

memo on her impressions and recollections of conversations. I have since had half a dozen women of varying gender ideologies read her memo, and all have thought it was right on the mark.

uates who were culled from a much larger number because they were unusually open to casual sex.[35] Townsend finds that women, in time, want investment from their sexual partners, whether the investment is in terms of "attention, affection, time, energy, money [or] material resources."[36] But before insisting on investment, women may go through a "coming out" stage when they view casual sex as an opportunity to test their attractiveness. Women at this stage do not find that emotions intrude unduly on their physical flings, though they do wonder if sex was "all he was after."

Women who have progressed to stage two are more experienced with casual sex. They engage in a pattern of "awareness and denial." They *say* that sex without emotion is okay, but they worry about the guy's intentions after intercourse because previous sexual encounters have not evolved into the desired relationships.

Women at this stage try to hold back their feelings, which might otherwise get in the way of a sexual relationship. But their desire for "intimacy and signs of caring and their feelings of vulnerability" intrude in "involuntary, disturbing and compelling" ways.[37] Stage-two women try to avoid the discrepancy between desired and offered investment by attempting to suppress emotions either consciously (trying not to think about the partner) or by getting drunk.

In stage three, women reject casual sex as a result of the powerful negative emotions they experience when they cannot get the desired investment from a sexual partner. Men they sleep with might subsequently act as if they were strangers, while for the women, "intercourse itself produced feelings of bonding and vulnerability."[38]

After canvassing female friends and acquaintances, my research assistants report the same patterns. Their anecdotes reveal that women find it nearly impossible to avoid these recriminatory emotions, even when they deliberately try to keep the sex low-key by sleeping with a friend in whom they have no long-term interest. Below is one of several stories related by students who came to my assistant for advice:

> I started sleeping with this guy whom I have been good friends with for years. Having just gotten out of a serious relationship, I wanted to try a casual, non-emotional and purely physical one. It was working for a while. We would hook up, not make a big deal about it, and remain friends and nothing more. Then as I was getting myself together one evening after a rendezvous at his place, he shared that he disliked the fact that we hooked up in his room. "After all, my girlfriend lives across the way, and people might gossip, she might find out." At that

> point I was furious. I had tried my best to not care, let this be only physical. And it was. I didn't want a "relationship" with him really. But . . . it was over! He didn't see what the problem was. It makes me so mad at myself. Why can guys do that and I can't?! I tried but I couldn't. I somehow got emotionally involved, despite promising myself that I wouldn't.[39]

Townsend asked his fifty students who were very sexually active to react to the following statement: "Even if I think I don't want to be emotionally involved with a person, if I have sex with her/him a few times, I begin to feel vulnerable and would at least like to know she/he cares for me." Fifty percent of the males disagreed with that statement, while only 4 percent of the females did.[40]

Townsend gives a full description of the answers of the five most sexually active women. Four of the five said they did not *think* they should have to be emotionally involved before having sex, and the other one used to think that way but had changed. Despite these sexually liberated *attitudes*, each of the five had found that her *emotions* interfered with casual sex. The most active said that many one-night stands had "broken my heart." The second most active wondered if those she slept with wanted only sex, and she broke off with those who seemed to take her for granted. The third "used to have a guy's point of view that I could sleep around with whomever I wanted," but now felt used and demeaned when she did so; sex, she explained, "is like giving a part of yourself to a guy." The fourth said she used to be promiscuous, but she began to feel used and "it was not fun anymore": "I didn't like waking up with strange guys in strange places. It was time to settle down and start getting serious about finding a husband." The fifth had trouble not getting emotionally involved when she had sex; she had marital yearnings and wondered how her partner would treat her in the morning.[41]

The sexually active men had quite different reactions to casual sex. Many of them regularly engaged in pleasurable sex with women they didn't know and sometimes didn't like. One, Mark, thought sex without emotions was not justifiable, but he had nonetheless slept with six women whom he did not want to get emotionally involved with. "They were available," he explained. "If a girl wants to put out, I won't turn her down. . . . I usually prefer to date girls that are younger than me because they are easier to screw."[42]

Another guy, Aaron, one of the medical students who described himself as sympathetic to feminist causes, would hang out for an hour and then have sex several times a week with an undergrad he met at a political rally. She wanted more from him, and he sometimes felt "a little guilty," like he was "using her." But he didn't feel too guilty because he thought she was pretty good at protecting her emotions. Besides, he rationalized, "She's young and doesn't really know what she wants. She has lots of time to settle down." Aaron wanted to meet some new women, but because of the easy availability of sex, he also wanted desperately to keep the relationship with the undergrad going for the time being.[43]

To keep the sex going, other men surveyed also stayed in relationships with women they had no desire to marry but who hoped to marry them. On the other hand, there were men whose consciences induced them to limit the number of partners they might have. These men felt guilty because of "their partners' reactions to casual relations rather than because of their own reactions: really hurting a woman by just 'screwing and dumping her' makes some of the men 'feel like shit.'" Rob explained: "If a woman wanted just sex, it would be cool, but they always get involved. That's why I usually only sleep with girls that I really like. I really hate hurting girls. It makes me feel guilty."[44]

Generally speaking, the female medical students' sexual experiences led them to avoid transitory relations because they "were damaging to their mental balance, their marital goals and their careers." The male medical students' sexual experiences, by contrast, typically "led them to seek and enjoy more transitory relationships in the future, because such a course would be less damaging to their mental balance and career aspirations than would more involved relationships."[45] The most sexually active women were just as likely as other women to think about love, commitment and marriage with the men they slept with. Sexually active men thought less about love, commitment and marriage as they had more casual sex. The men's feelings about casual sex were often very positive. The women's were more often negative. Townsend believes that "thoughts about marriage, honeymoons, and romance direct women toward relationships that can offer high-quality investment."[46]

The Big Chill

Feelings about casual sex seem to be among the most stubborn of sex differences. Women who are not traditionally feminine in any other way feel "sexual vulnerability and remorse" when they cannot obtain the desired level of male investment.[47] Townsend continues:

> Most of the women [with substantial casual sex experience] are assertive, ambitious, and successful in their careers. Two of the women medical students competed in what were traditionally male sports and stated that they were always "tomboys," were good in math and science, and had always identified more with their fathers than their mothers. They reported that they had never accepted a traditional female role and did not plan to do so in the future. Most of the women quoted rejected traditional sexual morality and traditional sex differences. They found sex outside of marriage totally acceptable.... Because they did not accept traditional sex differences in sexuality, they were surprised and shocked by their intense emotional reactions to their experiences. They honestly believed that they could enjoy sexual relations that involved little investment from their partners. They did not expect these emotions, could not understand them, and were surprised and disturbed by their inability to control them. These feelings were not part of their sex-role ideology and that is why the women were caught off guard.[48]

Somewhere along the way, even the young female authors who have experimented with casual sex and often say nice things about the sexual revolution tell the same story. Katie Roiphe speaks of feeling "a peculiar chill" when a date told her he had slept with five Katies. She was "almost sick with the accumulated anonymity of it, the haphazardness, the months and months of toweled men."[49] In *Lip Service,* Kate Fillion recounts how she retroactively decided she was in love with every man she had sex with, and how the power she got from sex "was the power to cause myself emotional pain."[50] In *Unzipped,* Courtney Weaver describes her fury when a man she liked a lot suggested she was "high maintenance." Nevertheless, she would phone fruitlessly and wonder why he wouldn't behave like a normal boyfriend and give her "flowers and presents."[51]

My wife teaches at Hampden-Sydney College, one of the few remaining all-male schools in the country. She reports that her students' most common complaint about the women they see is that they are nags. My wife does not think that women who went to college with her in the early 1960s nagged men. So what has changed? Townsend would say that women today nag because they sleep with the men, and something deep inside them wants a sign of investment in return; but they often get none at all. In the past, the lucky woman got a man who would marry her, share his income and help raise their children. The less lucky would barter with a series of men for money and resources in exchange for sex. In the era of the hookup, today's woman doesn't get even a phone call.

Townsend gives an evolutionary explanation of the reasons for sex differences in reactions to casual intercourse. In time, the evolutionary explanation may be buttressed by hormonal evidence on proximate causes. Animal studies already find that the "tremendous increase in oxytocin at puberty drives both sexual behavior and attachment in females, [but] it increases sexual drive without increasing the drive for pair bonding in males." Remember the "loner profile" of testosterone discussed in Chapter 3—a profile that gives men "a compelling sexual urge that spurns relationships." At puberty, boys begin to spend more time alone; girls begin to spend less time alone.[52]

The scientists who call attention to the special role of oxytocin in females going through puberty are looking for an explanation for the precipitous rise in depression rates in females between the ages of ten and fifteen. They find that in the depressed girls studied, a stressful interpersonal event occurred within six months of the onset of depression 68 percent of the time, but such an event preceded depression in only 14 percent of the depressed boys. They believe that

> if and when the increasingly intense affiliative bonds (and closely linked sexual needs) of the adolescent girl are frustrated through real or symbolic breaches in affiliative bonds, the hormonal changes of puberty can interact with the common interpersonal and romantic disappointments of adolescence in such a way as to produce depressive symptoms and, in many cases, syndromal depression.[53]

Girls have presumably faced such added depression risks on account of adverse interpersonal events from time immemorial. But until the sexual revolution this has *not* meant that girls and women became much more depressed than boys and men. Studies do show that since 1970, women are more than twice as likely to be depressed as men. But throughout their lives, women born before 1945 have been only slightly more likely to be depressed than men of comparable age. Almost all the higher incidence of depression in adult women has occurred among women who "spent their impressionable years of growing up or becoming young adults in the 1970s and 1980s."[54] Similarly, if one looks at trends in a "happiness index" of high school seniors, one finds that since 1976, the happiness of young women has been trending downward, whereas for young men it has risen slightly. The two greatest concerns expressed by the young women are men and their own bodies (they wish they were thinner).[55]

STDs Are Not Gender-Neutral

The discussion to this point has offered three principal reasons why women would be wise to realize that they have a different sexual makeup than men and that they should be slower to give men sex than the men and their own hormones seem to want: (1) From the last chapter, the risk of pregnancy; (2) Men fall in love with and prefer to marry women who are slower to give men the sex they ask for; and (3) In time, most women who hook up or otherwise give sex without receiving investments find that their behavior brings them great emotional pain.

A fourth reason is the disparity in the spread of sexually transmitted diseases (STDs). Women exposed to an STD are biologically more susceptible to becoming infected than are men exposed to an STD. From one act of intercourse, for example, a woman is more than eight times as likely to get HIV and about four times as likely to get gonorrhea as her male partner. Only one-quarter of men know about women's greater vulnerability, and only one-third of women do.[56] Since an infected partner is often symptomless, it is very hard to control or protect against these diseases. Having multiple partners is, of course, a big risk factor, but so is having *one* partner who has had multiple partners. Greater awareness of this fact certainly could affect the pleasure felt by women who land the most popular and experienced guy in the fraternity for their weekend hookup.[57]

The STD *consequences* for women are also far greater. "Once infected, women are more susceptible to reproductive cancers and infertility."[58] About 20 percent of female infertility is the result of the scarring of pelvic inflammatory disease caused by untreated STDs. Untreated STDs are also estimated to be the cause of 9 percent of entopic pregnancies and 18 percent of cases of chronic pelvic pain.[59] Forty-five million Americans have the human papillomavirus (HPV), which can cause both genital warts and cervical cancer.[60]

Attention is rarely given to women's greater risk of contracting an STD from an infected partner and to the more serious consequences if they should become infected. My last two female research assistants, both "A" students, were not aware of these facts. In my community at least, this information is not a part of sex education curricula or of Planned Parenthood's literature on STDs.[61]

A recent *Manifesta* from new-generation feminists waxes eloquent about female sexual pleasure. It briefly mentions STDs, but not the greater risks for women. One of the authors does acknowledge her own herpes as a way of helping to end the "ethic of silence" surrounding STDs and trying to build sisterly solidarity.[62] But however much sympathy one may feel for those with incurable STDs, sisters without them are likely to attract more-desired men and to live more pain-free lives.

The Birth Control Pill: Preventing Pleasure and Successful Partnership

Today, over forty years after its conception, the birth control pill continues to have consequences unanticipated at the outset. Young, unmarried women assume that it is crucial to their sexual freedom, but if women are not enjoying the casual sex facilitated by the Pill's use, its benefits diminish. They would diminish further if it were better known that the Pill might actually block sexual pleasure and make finding the right marital partner less likely.

Research indicates that the birth control pill may interfere with a deep, unconscious mechanism involving the sense of smell by which women have ensured that the partners they choose can help them produce healthy offspring. Studies that ask women to smell T-shirts worn by men find that women disagree about which smell best. The tested women, however, do regularly prefer the smell of men whose immune system is unlike theirs in terms of key proteins that detect and attack invaders. This is significant because in all animal species, immune systems of offspring are stronger when the female mates with a male who has an immune system makeup unlike hers. In humans, some couples who endure repeated miscarriages have been found to share immune system genes to an unusual degree.[63] Moreover, a woman's sense of smell is most keen around the time that she ovulates and is most fertile.[64]

The birth control pill changes all this. Women on the Pill do not have a heightened sense of smell at any part of their cycle. And as science writer Deborah Blum explains in *Sex on the Brain,* when on the Pill, women have smell preferences that are "reversed ... almost completely." Women taking oral contraceptives prefer the smell of men with immune systems similar to theirs.[65]

Scientists are beginning to wonder if the birth control pill has led to a whole generation of marriages that have had more difficulty producing offspring, or that have produced more vulnerable offspring. The "scrambling of sensory messages" during courtship may also explain why "some women complain about a husband's odor—which they'd never noticed before—after they go off the Pill."[66]

The extent to which males pick up on these chemical olfactory signals, known as pheromones, is "as yet, an entirely open question." Because less is at stake for a male in any given copulation, one would guess that pheromones might not influence men's preferences or behavior—a result suggested by preliminary studies.[67]

The Pill has another unfortunate and underreported effect: the dampening of female sexual interest. Blum reports that studies of other primates and at least one study of women have found that females on the Pill "see the world as a far more platonic place" than other females. As argued above and in Chapter 3, men seem to get more pleasure from the physical act of sex itself than women do, and the Pill, by suppressing the desire of women, accentuates this physical pleasure gap.[68]

Let's Get Physical

Birth control pills aside, if one thinks about what we know of the sexual act itself, it is hard to imagine how anyone would predict that women would enjoy casual sex as much as men do. Young men's orgasms usually come easily; women's often require a partner who is skilled and considerate. As some young women have learned the hard way, "a steady sexual partner has a far better idea of what she likes and a far bigger investment in pleasing her than a man she's just met and is only planning to sleep with once."[69]

The hookup partner is often drunk and in a hurry. Foreplay may go by the wayside. And if the male enters the woman before she is ready, he can hurt her. Of course, this near-stranger may come inside her against her will as well as at the wrong time. Men, on the other hand, don't have to worry about being raped on a date.

Sex experts say that for a woman to really enjoy herself, she must relax completely—let her limbs go limp and, as some have put it, "surrender." In casual sex there is often a much larger, unfamiliar man lying on top of her and quite capable of hurting her. Her eyes are often closed. To say she is physically vulnerable would be an understatement. Trust in the partner would seem essential if the woman is to have a pleasurable experience. But she has little reason to trust the one-night stand partner.

I have had female students, determined to bring me into the modern world, explain that college women have sex these days—that's just the way it is. After saying as much in class one day, a senior continued in an angry voice: "But men have to understand that we have needs and want to have pleasure too." Why would casual sex partners pay attention to such pleas?

Carolyn Graglia, a sexual traditionalist, was surprised at how accurately the radical feminist Andrea Dworkin's book *Intercourse* describes the sex act from the woman's point of view. Dworkin depicts sexual intercourse as a much more momentous experience for a woman than for a man, because it is

> an act of possession in which . . . a man inhabits a woman, physically covering her and overwhelming her and at the same time penetrating her. . . . By thrusting into her, he takes her over. His thrusting into her is taken to be her capitulation to him as a conqueror; it is a physical surrender of herself to him; he occupies and rules her, expresses his elemental dominance over her. . . . [During intercourse, says Dworkin, a woman] "is occupied—physically, internally, in her privacy."[70]

Graglia agrees with Dworkin's description, but thinks that sex can be an "incomparably gratifying experience" when it occurs with a loving man and in the context of marriage.[71] But that act is "an overwhelmingly personal, a truly awe-inspiring, event in which a woman should shrink in horror from participating on any basis even remotely casual."[72]

The best-selling—albeit controversial—dating guide called *The Rules* aims for a compromise between Graglia-like tradition and the modern hookup scene. *The Rules* says no to sex until the woman has waited at least a few weeks or months. After this probationary period, when the couple has had sex, the authors try to head off the behavior that Townsend predicts will follow. The woman should not "try to exploit the physical closeness of sex to gain emotional closeness, security, and assurances about the future." She should "stay emotionally cool no matter how hot the sex gets." And the next morning she should "be casual and unmoved about the fact that the date is over."[73]

The Rules wants its readers to avoid clinginess with men who have given no sign that they see themselves as part of a couple. But would a woman wanting to land a husband—and that is the goal of *The Rules*—really want to act so nonchalant after she and a potential prince charming have given each other great sexual pleasure? Might not the man wonder how often she has had similar nights with other men if their wonderful night together seemed so routine? It is hard to see how a woman becomes coy again after surrendering in such an intimate way.

The Rules tries to make the most of a "relationship culture" that treats casual sex as the ante allowing one to be part of the game, simultaneously stacking the odds against any woman hoping for marriage or for emotional fulfillment. Maybe playing her hand close will keep a woman in the game a little longer; but without a context in which sex is presumed to involve commitment, the man will almost always have the upper hand. Many college men do see sex as simply an enjoyable game. A student in my wife's class at all-male Hampden-Sydney College illustrates this attitude in a comment inspired by a discussion of Tom Wolfe's essay "Hooking Up": "Sleeping with a woman who has already submitted is like playing a computer game you have already won."

In any case, a few weeks' acquaintance is usually not long enough for a woman to enjoy sex. According to sociologists Linda Waite and Kara Joyner, only 7 percent of women who see their sex partners as "relatively short-term propositions" say that they are "extremely satisfied physically" with the sex. Not an impressive number. Even among women who expect their relationship to be a long one, only 11 percent say the sex is extremely satisfying physically. On the other hand, 39 percent of cohabiting and 41 percent of married women find sex with their partner extremely satisfying physically.[74]

Cohabitation is the modern solution for assessing marriage suitability. A substantial proportion of cohabiting couples have definite plans to marry, and in such couples the sex may be as good for the women as if they were married.[75] But as multiple studies have shown, married women on the whole are "significantly more likely than cohabiting women to report *emotional* satisfaction with sex [emphasis added]."[76] Moreover, when resurveyed, women much more than men say that the sex is better two years after marriage than it was in the first months.[77] And a 2002 study of two thousand British women reports that two-thirds think the best sex they ever had was within marriage.[78] It seems that for women, the "prospect of a lifetime commitment" is what really boosts sexual satisfaction.[79]

And many women suspect that their cohabiting partner is less committed to the relationship than they are.[80]

The live-in girlfriend seeking commitment is essentially auditioning to be a bride.[81] Auditioning for months or years on end can be draining and demeaning but rarely relaxing. Moreover, studies show that in both cohabiting and marital relationships, men do less housework than they used to when living alone, and women do more. But since the cohabiting couple is less likely to pool income, the women in this situation are frequently worse off and more vulnerable than in marriage.[82]

Often in cohabiting relationships, women confidently expect a marriage that never occurs. As one study concludesd, "men living with women they are not engaged to have very low levels of commitment to their partners and the relationships."[83] Or as yet another study reveals, "women tend to see [living together] as a step toward marriage, while men regard it more as a sexual opportunity without the ties of long-term commitment."[84] One researcher recommends that unmarried cohabiting women "should be very particular about how aligned they are with a particular man if he does not show any strong sense of marriage and a future together."[85]

What Men Don't Like to Talk About

Tyrants of old were in a position to act on their preferences. The evolutionary psychology texts delight in describing the hundreds, sometimes thousands of young women living in the despots' harems.[86] (Harems still exist in Brunei, where the sultan has 75 to 100 women, including some previously featured as *Penthouse* centerfolds.)[87]

Some U.S. men are still rich and powerful enough to be able to discuss their sexual passions openly without adversely affecting their success with women. Donald Trump reports that he and fellow mogul Ronald Perelman spend 5 percent of their time talking deals and 95 percent talking women.[88] Artists like Truffaut and Picasso were major womanizers.[89] Rock and sports stars probably lead the pack these days. Basketball great Wilt Chamberlain claimed to have slept with over twenty thousand women. Chamberlain said the women he was "the most attracted to, the most in love with," he "pushed away the strongest." There were "about five women" he cared for a lot, "but not enough to make a commitment."[90]

Even boys who are not famous or powerful but simply popular use their social status in schools today to get a leg up on the sexual competition. Whereas being a leader of a preadolescent male group once led to "comfortable dating, or perhaps early marriage," the same social position "now leads to lessened sexual restraint in adolescence and a greater readiness to exploit sexual opportunities and display sexual prowess."[91]

As Norman Podhoretz argues, the self-assured women parading around in revealing clothes drive men, especially young men, crazy. At almost any time or place, a girl can suddenly "plunge him into a fever of lust," but he has "no comparable power" over women.[92] I have already quoted *Ally McBeal*'s Ling, who puts it most succinctly: men have a "dumb stick." Evolutionists point out that to be reproductively successful, a man doesn't need much more than an attractive partner to get the stick ready to go.[93]

Men do not like to talk about the problems they have controlling their dumb sticks. They are often embarrassed by their lack of control. I used to have trouble getting good class discussions going on pornography; it seemed that none of my students used it. Things loosen up when I tell the guys that I know *they* don't use it, but ask them to tell us why their roommates do and why the roommates would defend its continued legality.

When I mention the experiments finding that about 75 percent of college men would have sex with an unknown and rather ordinary female coed who suddenly approached and asked them, the women look around the room at their male classmates with wide eyes.[94] And the men look embarrassed.

When discussing sexuality, feminist women in my classes often say that men and women have identical or nearly identical sexual natures, though because of the double standard, women can't show that they are equally interested in casual sex. But when we talk about the fact that college men seem to want sex with strangers, and about male sexual fantasies and the like, the very same women do not say, "We're like that too." Instead, they say defensively, "My boyfriend is not like that" or "My father is not like that."

The libidos of perfectly ordinary men, when fully understood by women, seem deformed and disreputable to them. Many women strongly resist an accurate presentation of male sexuality because they believe it "degrades men."[95] The women give those they love the benefit of the doubt and assume either that the average, easily aroused man is atypical or that those they love have more respectable libidos.

I have had one ex-student tell me that if her fiancé should ever want another woman, it would not matter what he *did;* the desire alone would destroy their bond. With a resigned smile but also with a touch of sadness and anger, another ex-student said of her boyfriend, "I fantasize about him, and he fantasizes about Britney Spears." I suspect her initial reaction was that of the wide-eyed wife in the *For Better or Worse* cartoon whose husband ends up sleeping alone.

What man would want to spill the beans? If he is unmarried and trying to bed some woman, he would like her to think he finds her remarkably beautiful and charming. And of course, if he is mar-

ried or engaged, he wants his wife or fiancée to think him totally smitten with her. Besides, as far as he is concerned, in most important ways and for all practical purposes he probably is.

There is one group of men willing to let the cat out of the bag. They make outrageous statements such as "the paramount dream of most men everywhere [is to] have the nubile years of more than one young woman."[96] And "all men are to one degree or another, natural predators when it comes to sex."[97] Who are these jaded sorts? Aging conservatives—George Gilder and Irving Kristol in the cases quoted above—who have been married to their first wives for decades. This love and stability give them room to tell the truth. Perhaps they brought their wives flowers to mitigate their disclosures. Gilder and Kristol must know that their wives believe their husbands have better characters than most men because they are able to love without straying, while admitting to the truth of man's nature.

Women's idealism and high expectations help goad men toward fidelity. They can help keep men faithful because men know the extent of the disappointment and anger they could otherwise bring to the women they love.[98] But the idealism can also be very dangerous to young women. When a loving father says to his teenage daughter, "All men are after just one thing," she cannot really believe it as she looks into the eyes of this loyal and wonderful man. She may even say, "But Daddy, I love him because he reminds me a lot of you." The dad has a hard time saying what he may be thinking—"He may end up like me. But he hasn't proposed yet. And I'll bet he's a damned sexual scoundrel just like I was before I met your mother."

The idea that women can transform men for the better is out of fashion, but as the social science on the effect of marriage makes clear, it is undeniably true. In one of my classes I had my students read Gilder on men, sex and marriage. One female student made her presentation complete with a cartoon showing a naked man in an aroused state in frame one, who ended up clothed with briefcase in hand, dashing to work in the final frame—all because he fell in love, married and produced an heir in the intervening frames. The story seemed amusing and preposterous to her.

I was lucky that year. In our class of sixteen, there were two male students who could report on just such a progression. The first told about his father, once a legendary rake, who now spent his weekends raking leaves. The guy could not believe the stories he heard about his premarital father. The second story was more powerful because it was self-testimony. The student was a big, strong-looking guy, noticeably older than most students and with the look of someone who had survived a war or two. The Gilder discussion induced him to tell his life story. He had been a heavy drinker, in and out of trouble and rehab. He had a girlfriend who insisted they marry or it was over. He did not want to lose her. They married and had a child. He got his life together. He had just finished junior college and worked full-time while going to school. Marriage had been great for him; he had never been happier in his life.

To these stories I am always able to add that of my father, who married at thirty after a dissolute life of high-stakes gambling and the proverbial wine, women and song. One summer he and his chums toured Europe and, in accord with their vow that water would never touch their lips, they brushed their teeth with liquor. I heard of this earlier life from my mother and from my father's male friends. (I saw only a tiny remnant of it—his insistence that any of his boys' playground bets were to be treated as anything but casual: "A gentleman always pays his debts." When we lost the backyard bet, we went to our room immediately and got the money to pay up.) The father I knew was completely devoted to my mother and a good family man. Like many other men of his generation, he was transformed because he fell in love.

This scenario seems to be less and less a part of young women's expectations. Since the sexual revolution began, women have been thinking worse of men. In 1970, 32 percent of American women said that "most men are basically selfish and self-centered"; in 1989, 42 percent believed that. In 1970, 67 percent of women said that "men are basically kind, gentle and thoughtful"; in 1989, only 51 percent of women believed that.[99] A 1993 Gallup poll reported that 40 percent of women were often or very often resentful of men because of "irritating and just typically male" behavior. Only 20 percent of men felt the same way about "typically female" behavior.[100] In 1970, 41 percent of women thought "most men look at a woman and immediately think how it would be to go to bed with her"; by 1990 that figure had risen to 56 percent.[101]

Stefan Bechtel, coauthor of a book on men and sex, collected data from over two thousand women before writing on women and sex. When asked what surprised him most in his research, Bechtel answered, "Rage": "Lots of women feel rage toward men. It was a revelation to me that you may be the nicest guy in the world and the women you encounter may have had bad experiences with men, and that will affect their dealings with you." In his earlier research on men, Bechtel had found "virtually no rage in the men's responses."[102]

The rage probably starts among teenage girls, where 71 percent report that they were in love with their latest sexual partner, but only 45 percent of boys say the same.[103] Then women get to college, where a substantial minority try a hookup or two, and many of them ultimately feel hurt and used.[104] They complain to magazines such as *Glamour,* which in turn lecture men, who unfortunately are not regular readers of those publications. *Glamour* says that too many men "are using feminism as an excuse to slack off on courtesy." Even if the one-night stand was consensual, "would it kill him to make one quick 'Thanks, that was great' call?"[105]

But the guy wanted a one-night stand precisely so it could be over after one night. If the girl had hopes for more, either before the sex or now that some bonding has taken place, the "quick" call would not really be short and painless. *Glamour*'s suggested courtesy would only falsely raise a girl's hopes.

After college comes cohabitation, where, as we have seen, men and women can have very different expectations. Only about one-sixth of cohabiting relationships last as long as three years.[106] Throw in a couple of cohabitation breakups, and women can end up where therapist Patricia Dalton says too many of her thirtyish female clients are: unmarried and very unhappy. (In 1999, 29 percent of 35-to-44-year-old females were unmarried; in 1960, fewer than 13 percent were.) They tell her that they have tried everything—"new clothes, new haircuts, and regular trips to the gym"—and think there must be something the matter with them. But they also think men are "jerks." Dalton believes that many of them are "acting like a wife" while their partners are "acting like a boyfriend."

Dalton is convinced that sex makes the breakup much harder. She knows that, though she can perhaps help these women in some ways, "the emotional costs of breaking up over and over ... are hard to calculate." She "can't magically restore the hope, optimism and innocence that these world-weary women have lost."[107]

By contrast, my wife's all-male classes seem jaded, but hardly world-weary. She thinks the young men are much less romantic than they used to be: "They used to idealize their girlfriends. Now they talk of 'compromise' and 'nagging.' They have no interest in imagining an ideal woman. Instead, most want only to sleep with plenty of women." In a post–sexual revolution era, it becomes more difficult for my wife to make her male students sympathetic to Shakespeare's tributes to romantic love. Recently, when she asked her class what sort of woman they would fall in love with, one guy said he had no idea and no interest in love at this point. He hadn't "slept with enough women yet."[108]

Getting Even or Getting Engaged?

Cultural chroniclers have begun to notice a new literary phenomenon: the growth of "dump literature." The genre contains both fiction and nonfiction, with much of the latter in the form of self-help books. Barbara Dafoe Whitehead lists some typical titles: *Dumped*; *He Loved Me, He Loves Me Not; The Heartbreak Handbook; Getting Over Him; Exorcising Your Ex; How to Heal the Heart by Hating;* and *The Woman's Book of Revenge*. The advice is often to get even: "In these books the functional equivalent of romantic passion is revenge.... The best therapy, many of them advise, is to work through your grief on his property ... [by] destroying or defacing his stuff."[109]

But other self-help books tell us that despite the pain and pitfalls, women are still desperately seeking marriage, not vengeance: *How Not to Stay Single; Marrying Smart! A Practical Guide for Attracting Your Mate; Finding True Love: The Essential Keys to Discovering the Love of Your Life; Were You Born for Each Other? Finding, Catching and Keeping the Love of Your Life; Beating the Marriage Odds: When You Are Smart, Single, and Over Thirty-Five.*[110] And this mating-game literature is almost exclusively aimed at women. In an informal Harvard Co-op bookstore survey, Sylvia Hewlett found only 3 of 62 books on the subject directed exclusively at men, while "three entire shelves of books were devoted to teaching women how to flatter, tease, dupe, and otherwise manipulate a man into marriage."[111]

In Manhattan, desperate professional women pay $9,600 for a marriage-centered beauty and personality makeover that ends by trying on a wedding dress.[112] *Glamour* prints articles on "ring anxiety."[113] Bridget Jones and Ally McBeal continue their quests for the perfect mate.[114] And a survey of female students in one college classroom reveals their belief that "finding and keeping a loving partner" is the single greatest obstacle facing women today.[115]

One of the pleasures of my occupation is getting the chance to see many newly engaged young people. If a creature came from Jupiter and asked me to show him a happy human being, I would point out a newly engaged woman. The elation typically lights up a room. Newly engaged men are happy too, but they mainly look more serious. Linda Waite and Maggie Gallagher report that in high school, 81 percent of girls say that having a good marriage is extremely important to them, whereas only 72 percent of boys say this.[116]

Of course, most men want to marry someday, but these days it takes longer for them to commit. I believe this reluctance is a result of the sexual revolution. If sex were not so easily available, young men would undoubtedly be more focused on relationships and on finding and attracting "the one."[117] As political scientist James Q. Wilson has said, it should be no surprise that men won't commit "if they can get sex, cooking and companionship on a trial basis, all the while keeping their eyes peeled for a better opportunity elsewhere."[118]

Men want more space than women do. In the workplace, men have a much stronger desire than women for jobs with no close supervision. Studies show that women like to be alone within the confines of a bedroom or an office, whereas men are more likely to need real isolation—a long drive or a trip to the mountains. Think also of those frequently solitary and overwhelmingly male pastimes, hunting and fishing. No matter how good their relationships, men are far more likely than women to report that they need free time to relax and pursue hobbies away from their mates.[119]

Boys do travel in large groups, bonded by a mutual interest in the same activities; but they are relatively more attached to things, less to people. From childhood, girls but not boys focus on close relationships and, especially, a best friend.[120] When female college students tell stories about themselves, they speak of friends and community; they are often giving or receiving advice, and if they act alone, something bad happens. Men's stories are very frequently about acting alone in contests, and they have happy outcomes.[121]

Harvard psychologist Carol Gilligan was "shocked by the violence and suspicion she found in men's reactions to materials that suggested intimacy and emotional attachment."[122] She thinks this reaction stems from society's efforts to teach men to withhold their emotions. But maybe the male taste for separation and standing alone is instead a result of what Theresa Crenshaw calls the "loner profile" of testosterone.

For men, marriage means giving up freedom and giving up the chance, however unlikely, for tomorrow's sex with a beautiful stranger. It also means taking on new obligations to provide and protect; 67 percent of men, but only 43 percent of women think that being married as opposed to being single imposes extra responsibilities and worries.[123] Trollope put it this way in *The Eustace Diamonds:*

> To be alone with the girl to whom he is not engaged is a man's delight; to be alone with the man to whom she is engaged is the woman's. When the thing is settled there is always present to the man something of a feeling of clipped wings; whereas the woman is conscious of a new power of expanding her pinions. The certainty of the thing is to him repressive. He has done his work, and gained his victory, and by conquering has become a slave.

"Why Men Won't Commit," a June 2002 report based on a Gallup poll and focus group discussions, presents some more specific reasons why men won't marry. Pointing out that the median age of first marriage for men has reached 27, the oldest age ever in America, the report explains that men rather than women are most often called "commitment phobic." The main reason for their failure to commit is their ability, in the post–sexual revolution world, to get sex without marriage. In fact, men say that once they have casual sex, they are "less respectful and interested in pursuing a relationship with a woman." Of single men age 25 to 33, 74 percent agree that if they meet someone they want a long-term relationship with, they try to postpone sex.[124]

Prime Time: Why Women Shouldn't Delay Marriage

Most women are not mistaken to focus on getting married. Married women, with and without children, are much more likely than unmarried women to say they are very satisfied with their lives. Ninety percent of married women say their marriage makes them happy all or most of the time; only 60 percent say the same about their job.[125]

Yet everyone seems to be telling young women these days that it is best to wait—to avoid marrying right out of college. Even parents often counsel their children thus: "Divorce is so prevalent. You should first get your career established. And maybe live with the guy for a while to be sure."[126]

Given current alimony and child support laws, a woman who abandons a career or career preparation to have children does take some risks. But if she wants children, she takes fewer financial risks with marital births than with extramarital ones.[127] In addition, as we saw in the previous chapter, a woman's husband is more likely to stay around if she is *not* making a large income.

No one should rush into anything, and women who marry young and have children will be economically more vulnerable in the wake of divorce. But if women took sex differences seriously, they would balance the possible emotional and economic costs of divorce with the emotional costs of multiple hookups and/or nonmarital breakups. Most marriages still last a lifetime. As noted above, only one-sixth of cohabiting relationships last even three years.

Few of the people encouraging young women to establish their careers before getting married consider that this strategy can lead to many years of unrequited sexual desire or to heartbreaking sexual relationships. The advice also takes no account of the best time for a young woman to find a desirable husband and start a family. Men care about looks, and they think women never look better than they do in their early twenties.[128] Although the marriages of teenagers break up more frequently than the marriages of older couples, there is no evidence that delaying marriage past the early twenties provides more marital permanence.[129] To the contrary, women who marry at 22 and 23 are actually more likely to report "very happy" marriages while experiencing lower divorce rates than women who marry at any other age.[130]

Babies born to young women are healthier than babies born to older women.[131] Because of a greater likelihood that mothers over age 35 will have gestational diabetes or pregnancy-induced hypertension, their risk of giving birth to a preterm baby is significantly increased. And according to Jerold Lucey, editor of the journal *Pediatrics,* "there's always some sort of biological penalty for premature birth," no matter how small.[132] Babies born to women over 35 are 11 percent more likely than babies born to younger women to have low birth weight.[133] In addition, the risk of fetal death nearly doubles for women over 35 in comparison with those under 30.[134]

Moreover, it is a massive risk to rely on modern medicine to help reset the biological clock and make late childbirth safer. Recent studies have revealed increased rates of major birth defects in infants born through intracytoplasmic sperm injection and *in vitro* fertilization over those conceived naturally. Even after controlling for the age of the mother and other factors, a child conceived by either IVF or ICSI is still more than twice as likely to be diagnosed with a major birth defect than is a naturally conceived child.[135]

Meanwhile, the benefits of giving birth at a young age are truly wide-ranging. In his book *The Mating Mind,* Geoffrey Miller explains that "females tend to be more fertile in youth, produce fewer birth defects, are in better shape to care for offspring, and are more likely to have living sisters and mothers to help with childcare."[136] Some researchers report that, after controlling for marital status, younger mothers have healthier children; those born to mothers age 18 to 19 have a significantly lower risk of being labeled "learning-disabled."[137]

Babies first and careers later, the approach taken by Supreme Court justice Sandra Day O'Connor and by former U.N. ambassador Jeane Kirkpatrick, can be much less stressful than the frantic combinations women who marry later often invent. Sylvia Hewlett's national survey found that this chronology—babies in early to mid-twenties and careers later—was the most common one among high-achieving women (the top 10 percent of female earners) who had children.[138] Her study found only 1 percent of these high-achieving women age 41 to 55 had a first child after age 39, and among "ultra-achievers," (women earning more than $100,000 a year), none had given birth to a first child after age 36. Of high-achieving women who married, only 8 percent did so after age 30; most did so before age 24.

Women in their late twenties are, with reason, much more pessimistic today about *ever* marrying.[139] Studies show that "the older she gets, the harder it is for a college-educated woman to find a husband." College-educated women "tend to seek husbands who are slightly older and have even higher levels of education and achievement than they do,"[140] but the number of men in this already limited pool declines as women age. So it is not surprising that 63 percent of women hope to meet their future husband in college. They will never again be surrounded by so many eligible men who share their interests and aspirations.

There is much to be said for women marrying younger than they now do. But the men are not usually interested, in part because, as my wife's male college student said, they "haven't slept with enough women yet." Only women can change that kind of calculation.

The Rules is a good starting place for women to learn how to "train men." This manual would have women insist on respect in relationships:

> After the end of a date three months into a relationship, one guy said, "'I'll call ya. I'll let you know what's a good night for *me* next week.'"
>
> Jody [took] an extreme but necessary *Rules* action. She didn't answer her phone the night he usually called. She just listened to it

> ring and ring. When he finally reached her the next day at work, he was a little less cocky and somewhat nervous. He asked her what night would be a good night for *her.*[141]

Modern women wonder why they must wait for men to call in the first place. They've taken charge of their careers, learned to "make things happen" on the job. The career breakthroughs, however, have not led to fundamental changes in the mating game. Men and women at one college were recently asked whether a man typically asks a woman for a first date or vice versa; 83 percent of the men and 68 percent of the women said the man typically does the asking, whereas 2 percent of the men and 1 percent of the women said the woman typically does the asking. The rest answered "either" or "both."[142] And at the end of the courting process, Americans are becoming more, not less traditional. Men were more likely in 1997 than in 1952 to be the ones proposing marriage.[143]

Feminists typically object when *The Rules* says that the man must be the first one to say "I love you" or "I miss you."[144] They hate that the book warns against chattering on the phone with men as if they were your girlfriends or that it tells women always to get off the phone first.

Ellen Goodman says women should instead take her friend's advice for his daughters: "Be yourself. The only man you will scare off is your future ex-husband." Goodman adds,

> The old games were based on mistrust. This ancient hostility skids unhappily across the pages of this modern manual.
>
> "Remember, early on in a relationship," the [*Rules*] authors warn, "the man is the adversary (if he is someone you really like). He has the power to hurt you. . . ." But if friendship is against the rules, why play?[145]

The old rules were indeed based on "mistrust"—women's mistrust of men's intentions based on centuries of experience. But the "ancient hostility" pales compared with the rage that has accompanied the current phase of the battle of the sexes.

The Rules are to be used, most of all, on the men you really care about.

> Your job . . . is to treat the man you are really, really crazy about like the man you're not that interested in. . . . Keep thinking, "How would I behave if I weren't that interested in him?"[146]

You do this because

> He has the power to hurt you by never calling again, by treating you badly, or by being around but indifferent.... The best way to protect yourself from pain is to not get emotionally involved too quickly.[147]

Women in a new relationship wonder if he will be The One. Men might wonder too. But *The Rules* is right. Men could just as well be wondering whether they can get this one to go to bed with them too. A man in this state is, indeed, an adversary. Early in the relationship a woman can't know what he is thinking.[148]

So *The Rules* says to slow down the process and force your dates to get to know you. "*The Rules* will make you harder to get so that a man who doesn't really like you won't waste his or your time."[149]

Slowing down the process with a man you are "really, really crazy about" can be "excruciating,"[150] but there are no good alternatives. Once women give men sex, women are emotionally drawn in, even if against their will. A recent study shows that on college campuses the men have almost all the power after sex. The man usually determines if he and the woman will continue to see each other, and it is almost always the man who determines if they are "a public, committed couple."[151] Even if they are such a couple, for the man this relationship may mean just good "sex, cooking and companionship ... while keeping his eyes peeled for a better opportunity elsewhere."

The deeper reason for women playing hard-to-get is that this strategy builds a foundation for a strong marriage. Writer Mary Elizabeth Podles explains this well:

> In serious courtship, a man conveys to a woman that if she is worth all this trouble to court, she must be worth more than any other mate in the world, and shall henceforth be The One Woman. On her part, the woman promises that if she was this hard for him to get, surely she will, as his wife, be impossible for others to get. The courtship dance is the unspoken pledge of future fidelity—the best of all bases for a happy marriage.[152]

Even if women have a real relationship with a man they love, they don't necessarily have the life-time partner they seek. There is still the hurdle of male commitment. My female students say, "Well, I certainly will not want to marry anyone who does not want to marry me." But many of these students know older women living with men they would love to marry, and the men are not asking. *The Rules* again gets it right:

> Many woman tell us that their husbands proposed after they *moved away from, not toward,* the relationship. One woman booked a trip to Club Med with a girlfriend after dating her boyfriend for a year, another started getting very busy and unavailable on weekends, and a third talked about taking a job in another city. Then their husbands proposed.
>
> Remember, men don't necessarily propose when you're cuddled up on the couch watching a rented video, but do so when they are afraid of losing you.[153]

This is true. In my courting days, my soon-to-be-wife lived in another city, and once cooked me dinner when I came to visit. I wrote and told her maybe we should cool it just a little. She didn't answer my letter. Six weeks later I proposed, though it took bushels of tulips to clinch the deal. My best friend in college proposed when his soon-to-be-wife said she was moving to another state. It happens all the time. Men sometimes need to be faced with life without a beloved before they can know for sure that they don't want to live without her. Women should not feel guilty if they set powerful, albeit tender traps. Civilization cheers them on. An end to fatherless families and mitigation of female rage and depression probably depends on reacquainting women with what, in less "enlightened" times, they were regularly taught.

Conclusion

No woman is an island. With respect to sexuality, this formulation is far more true than the familiar refrain about men. We have seen that women's eroticism is more malleable than men's. Women's sexual behavior, for example, is more influenced by same-sex peers' experience or lack thereof than men's sexual behavior is.

Teenage girls want to fit in.[154] There is always pressure toward the middle. On the one hand, women who hook up much more than the average are called "sluts" and "whores" by men and by other women.[155] On the other hand, women who are sexually inexperienced are often called "prudes" by men and by other women. Those who want to remain virgins until marriage face ridicule, and even hostility and ostracism.[156] Something about the virgins' reserve seems to infuriate women who are sexually active.[157] One middle school virgin had a boyfriend who did not pressure her for sex. Female rivals who resented her self-possession broke up the relationship by offering her boyfriend oral sex—an offer he accepted.[158]

Evolutionary psychologists might say that those women who call sexual outliers *sluts* resent the unfair competition for male companionship from easy women;[159] those who ridicule and badger the virgin outliers sense unfair competition for husbands. What has changed since the sixties is the sort of behavior that makes someone an outlier. Today it usually takes repeated random hookups to earn the *slut* label. And many of my students do not think the term is as pervasive or as cutting as it used to be. The "no sex till marriage" women used to be common and now *they* can be shunned outliers.

The old standard led to more happy young women than today's does. This observation seems clear from the self-testimony of women who have engaged frequently in casual sex. The overwhelming majority of women come to dislike uncommitted sex. The overwhelming majority of women want to find a husband with whom to settle down. Women who hook up undermine their own long-term interests. They also profoundly undermine the interests of other heterosexual women by making men less interested in relationships and by giving them the leverage to pressure women to agree to intercourse much more quickly than they would like. And the common "easy sex" mores can make for lonely year after lonely year among the resolute virgins.

The root of the problem is the assumption that the sexuality differences we see around us are not natural, but created by society. Consider the appalling sexual scene in one Montgomery County middle school in the affluent suburbs of Washington, D.C., a scene which apparently is not at all uncommon.[160] At this school, thirteen-year-old girls find that "morning brings the invitations," casual, routine invitations to have sex: "When are you going to give me head?" or some variation. The article reports that most of the boys ask. When the oral sex does take place, it is the girls servicing the boys, who do not reciprocate. The girls say they get no pleasure from giving the oral sex, but "it's not that bad once you do it." They do it to please a boy they like. One girl resisted mainly because acquiescing would mean her day would become "one endless stream of requests. 'They would ask me, and ask me, even more than they do now.'"

Some requests go beyond mere words. One girl, asked by a reporter to keep a diary, told how she bent to get books from her low locker "when a boy just came up from behind and was trying to hump me." On another occasion when she kneeled to get books from her locker, "a boy stands in front of me and puts his [crotch] in my face and says, 'Oh yes, you're the best.'"[161]

What does one say to a boy who continually badgers a girl for oral sex? Or who sticks his crotch in the girl's face? The answer is that we can't say much if we assume that there are no differences between males and females. We often can get young people to be more considerate by saying, "How would you feel if someone did that to you?" That might work if a boy took a girl's book bag. If we say, "How would you feel if she did that to you" about the crotch-in-the-face stunt, the boy is likely to say, "That would be *great*."

Most boys don't find this sort of behavior degrading or obnoxious. Why should they believe that girls do? If sex is recreational, why is it degrading?

The way to stop degrading horseplay is to try convincing the boys that they may not feel degraded by such actions, but girls will, because they are put together differently. They are more vulnerable, more sensitive.

Before the feminist movement began attacking the notion that men and women are different, this was universally assumed to be true. When I grew up, everybody assumed that girls were different. Early on we were told, "Don't play so rough around the girls" or "Don't be so loud around the girls." We now know in a scientific way that girls do not like rough-and-tumble play as boys do, and that girls do find sounds to be uncomfortably loud when they are at a volume that boys still find quite tolerable.[162] Similarly, in the 1950s we all knew that girls would find offensive certain sexual comments and behavior that boys would not.[163]

Since the 1970s, in the outside world, women have made dramatic strides in their access to and advancement in well-paid and traditionally male occupations. But in their intimate world, their desire for sex with emotional involvement and leading to permanence is much more difficult to achieve than it used to be. It is unclear that the career gains have compensated for the losses in intimacy and in emotional security. As noted above, starting in 1970 women have been more depressed and unhappy than they used to be. Women feel rage toward men, but men don't feel rage toward women. The sexual revolution gave men, not women, what they wanted. Writer

Danielle Crittenden notes that all women are now equal in their relative powerlessness to get the committed men they want:

> The woman who holds back from sex, waiting for the right man to come along, will find that no right man does—because he can get what he wants elsewhere—just as the woman who gives herself freely discovers that she holds no firmer grip over him, either. The sexual revolution, from a male point of view, could be summed up as, "You mean I get to do whatever I want—and then leave? Great!"[164]

The world of sexual come-ons is not androgynous: "Sex educators report that the question most often asked by teenage girls is how to say no to their boyfriends without hurting their feelings."[165] It is remarkable what many women will do to avoid this unceasing pressure. Psychoanalyst Mary Pipher reports what I have also seen evidence of: some women intentionally become overweight so that "guys will leave me alone."[166] One woman on MTV said she was "'sort of glad' she had gotten herpes because now she 'had an excuse to say no.'"[167] And I have heard the father of an attractive blonde at an Ivy League college explain in the following way the initial impetus behind his daughter's newfound dedication to Christ: "Men were constantly asking her for sex. She noticed that the women in the Campus Crusade for Christ didn't get bothered as much. She began going to the meetings and became more religious."

Women get little help these days in resisting predatory males. As opposed to the virgin-next-door film icons of the 1950s, the Doris Days who led *über*-bachelors into marriage with their chaste allure, today's stars gyrate and bare their way into men's consciousness. One father explains that he wants his daughter "to see herself as somebody who's worthy of being courted.... There's not enough that shows her that's what she should have—and that's what her mother and grandmother did have."[168]

Writer Wendy Shalit recalls this old-fashioned courtship as depicted in the popular 1948 duet, "But Baby It's Cold Outside." The lyrics give the male singer numerous reasons why it would be dangerous and wrong for his girl to venture out into the cold. She has as many—worrying mother, pacing father, angry brother, gossipy neighbors—as to why she must go. Today such a girl is all alone, asked only to "take responsibility" for her sexuality.[169] She is asked to do so without being given a clue that, unless she is very unusual indeed, she will not like uncommitted sex.

In the wildly popular novel *The Nanny Diaries,* the heroine describes the incorrigibly adolescent males produced by the easy-sex culture. The Harvard guy she has her eye on has suggested she meet him at one of three places that his college friends plan to drop in on later that evening. After later failing to track him down at any of the three, she muses:

> It's the whole Buffet Syndrome ... it's all you can eat. Why commit to one place when there *might* be a cooler one around the corner? Why commit to one model when a better/taller/thinner one *could* walk in the door at any moment?
>
> So, in order to avoid having to make a choice, a *decision,* these boys make a religion of chaos. Their lives become governed by this bizarre need for serendipity. It's a whole lot of "we'll just see what happens." ...
>
> So, if I "happen" to run into him three weekends in a row then I *might* end up a girlfriend. The problem, then, is that their reverence for anarchy forces those of us lucky enough to "happen into" relationships with them to become the planners—or *nothing* would happen. We become their mothers, their cruise directors—their nannies.[170]

A serious sex education begins by emphasizing the reasons why female sexuality is dramatically unlike male sexuality; it explains the natural reasons for female vulnerability. It explains to women why they like to be courted and how their sexual restraint can encourage a courting culture. It makes possible an education that does much more to rein in male sexuality. Writer Kay Hymowitz gets it right:

> The feminist view of the myth of love contained a curious, counterproductive misreading of history. For if love served to subjugate women, it did no less to men. In many countries where romantic love has not been institutionalized, men's philandering is winked at while respectable women are kept veiled and hidden. In its first institutional flowering in the guise of medieval courtly love, stylized passion turned the wandering, brutish young men of the day—who might literally rape an unprotected woman as easily as stay the night's dinner—into sensitive, pining poets. The important point altogether ignored by early progressive reformers and feminists was that it was precisely as a powerful way of sublimating the passions that romantic love was a civilizing force. A man in love was a man subdued.[171]

PART 3

MEN WANT THEIR WAY

6

AGGRESSION, DOMINANCE AND COMPETITION

We have already discussed boys' fascination with violent computer games and Battlebots, and the gun fetish that left one poor Berkeley mother in such a quandary. Like the Berkeley mom, founders of "intentional communities" devoted to peace and love also observe that their young boys are preoccupied with guns and war games.[1] Young girls like family role playing, but their brothers fantasize about "danger and righteous combat."[2] Men and boys can play at war with board games or paintball guns, or join the forty thousand Americans, mainly men, who gather regularly to reenact Civil War battles.[3]

Sex differences appear even in preferred forms of humor. As Ann and Bill Moir report in *Why Men Don't Iron,* women like to "laugh with other people and use jokes as a way of making others feel comfortable." In contrast, men communicate through "insult, jest and innuendo."[4]

Women are rarely fans of male aggression, but bridal magazines have noted that prospective brides are cheering on the trend for bachelor parties to revolve around "adventure and athletics" rather than strippers and lap dancing. In the late 1990s the *New York Times* visited a paintball outing—one of the most popular of the new bachelor party forms. Reporter Jane Gross describes the scene:

> Dressed in camouflage gear and war paint, reeking of bug spray and perspiration and armed with rifles and ammo, [thirty-year-old] Dan Furlong and his buddies were having the time of their lives.... The rowdy day of mock warfare [was] a cross between a "Die Hard" movie and a game of capture the flag.

The reporter located a Harvard anthropologist who linked this "aggressive coalitionary behavior" to the "evolutionary necessity for the male of the species" to hunt and wage war. She also quoted MIT psychologist Steven Pinker's opinion that " 'aiming and chasing' is inherently pleasurable to men."[5]

Unfortunately, aggression is not usually as harmless as paintball. But at all ages, in all societies, in every era, it is predominantly male.[6] There is much more violence in most preindustrial societies than in contemporary Western ones, but in all societies men are far more physically aggressive than women. Even in some tribes that are known for sexual equality, males commit almost all the homicides.[7]

Homicide is a form of aggression likely to be noticed, remembered and, at least in industrial societies, recorded. In the United States, females are arrested for about 10 percent of all homicides; their victims are almost always husbands or lovers killed because of jealousy or abuse. Evolutionists are especially interested in same-sex murder, which often involves removing competitors for a mate. Here the sex difference is even greater than for homicides as a whole: across cultures there are 25 to 30 men who kill another man for every woman who kills another woman.[8]

Since violence often begets violence, aggressors must be tolerant of risk. Males tolerate most kinds of risk, and especially physical risk, far more readily than females do. Studies of children as young as six months old find that boys are generally less fearful than girls and that fearlessness is connected to levels of testosterone.[9] In addition, an observational study of children at a San Antonio zoo found that preschool boys were about twice as likely as preschool girls to pet a burro, ride an elephant or climb a steep embankment and walk on a narrow ledge above it.[10]

This pattern continues in teenagers and adults. Males make up the overwhelming majority of those who engage in extreme sports like deep-sea diving, ice climbing, parachuting and downhill mountain bike racing.[11] Women who do participate in extreme sports approach them differently, and often consider their male peers to be reckless. Female mountain climbers, for instance, observe that men are much more inclined to climb in the wind, an extremely dangerous practice.[12]

As drivers, men are less likely than women to fasten seat belts and more likely to speed, tailgate and refuse to yield.[13] This kind of risk taking has a price. Not surprisingly, men are nearly three times more likely than women to die from accidental injury.[14] Nationally, males are three times more likely than females to drown, four times more likely to suffer a serious spinal cord injury, and over five times more likely to be killed by lightning.[15]

Most of the reckless behavior that results in these statistics might make little sense to those of us who don't participate in it. But the willingness to tolerate risk is related to fearlessness, a trait that can be an asset in some settings. And men generally are less fearful than women.[16] In one Harvard study, for instance, men and women were asked to evaluate twenty-five health risks, and the women ranked all twenty-five as riskier than the men did.[17] A willingness to accept risk can produce benefits. For example, men are more likely than women to volunteer for clinical trials,[18] go into combat, or risk their lives to rescue others. One study found that over a seven-year period, forty North American men—and one woman—died attempting to rescue people they did not know.[19]

Not only do men exhibit fearlessness in the face of danger, they seem to seek out dangerous situations and glory in their ability to bring others to safety. In the summer of 1998, firefighters, overwhelmingly male, came from all over the country to fight the blazes raging in Florida. The letters of gratitude from Floridians included expressions of amazement that people would leave their homes and travel from as far away as Los Angeles to rescue strangers. Some of the firefighters showed remarkable kindness—apologizing for damaging someone's fence or taking up a collection to help replace a child's wagon.[20]

Soldiers can also revel in the chance to face danger in a good cause: Many write home delighted when they get a chance to do what they've been training for. One U.S. soldier who died in Afghanistan left his wife a letter to be opened only after his death; it asked her to remember, "I died doing what I love to do."[21]

Why the Sex Differences in Aggression?

Differences in aggression take us right back to differences in sexuality, at least according to the theory of evolutionary psychologists. In traditional polygamous societies, the most "reproductively successful" women have about fourteen children over a lifetime. Reproductively successful men have far more, but they often have to fight for the opportunity to sire them.[22] Until the second half of the twentieth century, they joined with fellow tribal men in raiding other societies to capture women and resources.[23] And they still fight other men within their society to acquire new wives.

Polygamous men then need to fight to keep what they have; they may even need to use physical aggression against the women to ensure that they stay around. And they may need to fight rivals in order to keep their wives and protect their children. If they are successful in fighting male rivals, they need to use less coercion to keep their wives. Success in combat gives men resources and status, which in turn attract women. Among the preindustrial Yanomano Indians of Venezuela, the men who have killed "have a higher social status than men who have not killed, and two and one-half times as many wives, and about three times as many children, on average."[24] More generally, the fact that females tend to be "attracted to males who exhibit dominance displays has been confirmed by observational and questionnaire research."[25]

The anthropologist David Gilmore finds that in the vast majority of societies, men are under pressure.

> Manhood "is a triumph over the impulse to run from danger." The "Ubiquitous Male" is an "Impregnator-Protector-Provider." In most societies these three male imperatives are either dangerous or highly competitive. They place men at risk on the battlefield, in the hunt, or in confrontation with their fellows.... They stand to lose their reputations or their lives; yet their prescribed tasks must be done if the group is to survive and prosper.[26]

In most cultures "bigness—as measured by musculature, accomplishments, or numbers of possessions—" is associated with masculinity.[27] In the industrialized world, men can now attain bigness through lawful accumulation of honors or income. A man does not need to be physically aggressive if he is an aggressive businessman or a hard-charging professional. But even middle-class males who play by the rules may first have to navigate their way through physically aggressive toughs in middle school and high school.[28] Coming to terms with such toughs can be the equivalent of a rite of passage.

It is no surprise that young men from poor neighborhoods are the most violent. They do not usually have substantial lawful income or good prospects for the future. But their physical strength or refusal to be *dissed* "causes other men to back-off and [this] fearful respect provides evidence to women of their dominance."[29]

In tough neighborhoods, robbery is prevalent and, according to Anne Campbell's *A Mind of Her Own,* "a distinctly male crime" that mixes resource acquisition and violence.

> Only 18 percent of robbers say that they need the money for themselves or their families. A core concern for robbers is the lavish and conspicuous disbursement of money. As one street woman described it: "With money comes power, with money comes respect. You are a big dope man, you know what I'm saying, one of the best. And you had to kill a few people to get there, you had to rob a few people to get there. That even gives you more respect out there." The spending of surplus cash both impresses and indebts others.[30]

The problem of aggression is compounded as males in groups often try to outdo each other, and thus it can be a big mistake to try to change delinquents in a group setting. One well- designed study looked at the effectiveness of programs that brought troubled teens together to emphasize "prosocial goals and self-regulation, using peer reinforcement as one means to promote completion of home exercises, as well as compliance with session activities." It found that such programs caused participants significant *harm* as measured by later tobacco use, delinquency and the like. Participants in one such twelve-week program did significantly *worse* than equally troubled youngsters who were simply given free access to videotapes and written materials. The researchers thought it likely that "high risk peers will support one another's deviant behavior, so group affiliations should be avoided during retraining periods."[31]

Men usually fight each other, and the fights are frequently over women.[32] When men fight with women, it is usually in order to control their sexual behavior.[33] Though men these days very rarely raid other societies to carry off their women, they do rape women captured when territories are conquered. In the 1992 Bosnian conflict, Chetnik soldiers often raped Muslim women and threatened to keep them captive until it was too late for an abortion. "When we let you go home," they said, "you'll have to give birth to a Chetnik."[34]

Divorced, separated and never-married women are victims of violence four or more times as often as married women.[35] But when married women are victims of violence, it is often at the hands of their spouses. The leading cause of male spousal homicide is male sexual jealousy.[36] Not coincidentally, young women, who are more attractive to other males, are more likely to be victims of spousal homicide than older women.[37] Often the jealousy leads to extreme attempts to limit the wife's freedom of association, with the husband insisting that his wife not leave the house for any reason or that she cut off all her other friendships.[38]

Though intense jealousy can be dangerous and despicable, a capacity for jealousy may be, in the words of evolutionary psychologist David Buss, "an inevitable part of love. Those who show no concern about their partner's interest in another are unlikely to be very committed to the partner."[39] And "a study that gathered data on dating couples and followed them up over time found that those pairs who expressed greater jealousy about their partner were more likely to marry them subsequently."[40]

When asked to choose, most men say they would be more upset if their spouse formed a sexual but not a deep emotional relationship with another man than if she formed a deep emotional but not a sexual relationship. Most studies show that a woman, by contrast, is more likely to be upset if her spouse forms a deep emotional relationship with another woman than if he has a sexual relationship—presumably because she is concerned that his emotional connection elsewhere might lead to her loss of his financial support.[41]

Male jealousy has deep roots because the men whose genes were passed on to future generations were probably those who were deeply upset at the prospect of raising children who were not theirs and were vigilant in ensuring that this did not happen.[42] A fear of unwittingly raising other men's children is not completely baseless, as it still occurs in both industrial and preindustrial societies. Thus evolutionist Laura Betzig reports that "blood tests for misassigned paternity in human societies yield rates ranging from a low of 1.4 percent in rural Michigan, to 2 percent among the Kalahari !Kung, to 2.3 percent in Hawaii, to 6 percent in West Middlesex, England, to 9 percent among the Venezuelan Yanomamo, to 20 to 30 percent in the 'Liverpool Flats.'"[43]

Men seem to use resemblance as a way of assessing paternity. One study of men in a domestic violence treatment program asked the offenders how much they thought their children looked like them. Those who thought their kids resembled them were more likely to say they had a good relationship with their children and less likely to inflict the severest sorts of injury on their mates.[44]

At some level, women must sense that men make judgments of this kind: Another study found that mothers of newborns usually ascribed resemblance to the father rather than to themselves, and were especially likely to do so when the father was present. But unrelated judges shown pictures of the mother, father and newborn were significantly more likely to say the baby resembled the mother.[45]

Sexual jealousy can provoke aggression by women also; in fact, it is the most common cause of physical fights among girls and women. Typically a young woman attacks someone who has called her a slut—to her face or behind her back—or she attacks another girl who is moving in on her boyfriend.[46] Women get as angry as men,[47] but they get into physical fights much less often and with far less damage to those they attack. They are more likely to practice indirect relational aggression—they shun, stigmatize, gossip and spread false rumors.[48]

Evolutionists think this difference is rooted in female fear of physical aggression,[49] a survival mechanism that prevents women from fighting with men, who on average are far stronger.[50] Men have a greater incentive to overcome fear, because if successful in fights, they are likely to achieve more mating opportunities. A woman who fights can rarely gain much, and if she loses, serious injuries may jeopardize her ability to raise her offspring.

Scholars discuss our "fight-or-flight" response that kicks in under conditions of great stress. Such a response is often presented as an essential mechanism in our evolved survival process. But the physiological and behavioral research establishing the existence of such a response was done on men. Fighting as an evolved stress response seems much less likely for females because it puts them and their offspring in jeopardy. And flight is usually not a tenable option because women are slower than most men and because their ability to flee might be hindered by pregnancy or the need to protect young children.

The latest research suggests that women react to great stress through a "tend-and-befriend" process rather than through "fight-or-flight." Tending involves trying to protect one's self and offspring from physical harm and from mental distress. Befriending extends the protective element to groups who provide mutual aid and who can step in when a woman becomes unable to care for herself or her children. One of the most striking gender differences in all of adult human behavior is women's greater tendency to seek and use social support under conditions of stress.[51] In male prisons, for instance, subcultures often develop based on "hierarchies of power and coercion," while in female prisons, subcultures "revolve around make-believe families and intense friendships."[52]

Though individually weak, women can find strength in numbers. The tendency to befriend can create numbers. Female primates in general coalesce not for offensive purposes as men do, but for defense.[53] Women in particular are especially apt to gather together to help one another. In my community, women have organized the Shelter for Help in Emergency; the Sexual Assault Resource Agency; FOCUS, a group that aids women facing difficulties from divorce to joblessness; Take Back the Night rallies, which raise awareness of sexual abuse; and the Woman"s Center, which provides self-defense classes, sexual harassment seminars and a variety of other services.

Most battered women, however, turn to family or friends for help. Psychologist Anne Campbell notes that friends

> can provide sympathy, confrontation with the aggressor, referrals to agencies and shelter. But perhaps the main help from friends is preventative. Friends join a woman to a wider community and close friends are those with whom a woman can share her most private experiences. They can render semi-public, events that would otherwise be private. In this way they can act as an effective deterrent to abuse.[54]

The Biology of Aggression

Another explanation for males' greater aggressiveness focuses on demonstrable, biological differences. One study exploring interactions between adolescents and their families suggests that males are more aggressive than females not because they have a greater propensity to become angered, but because they are less able to control behavior resulting from that anger.[55] As they are growing, many young men also have a particular problem with impulsive violence. They lash out in an "overprimed, uninhibited" way that seems pointless to others and often to the young men themselves after they have had time to reflect on their actions. This behavior has been linked to reduced serotonin activity in the frontal cortex in aggressive men compared with other men, and in men as a whole compared with women. Spinal fluid levels of serotonin have also been "negatively correlated with a history of aggression."[56]

Numerous studies find a connection between testosterone and aggression. As with serotonin, testosterone has been linked to impulsivity and spontaneous aggression in both males and females.[57] In one case study, two Swedish girls became unusually aggressive and violent because of "a surge in their male hormones as they entered puberty." This behavior ceased when they were given medication to reduce these hormones.[58] Female-to-male transsexuals who are administered testosterone become more physically aggressive within three months. Correspondingly, male-to-female transsexuals who are administered anti-androgens and estrogens become less physically aggressive within three months.[59] Similarly, the testosterone-lowering drugs given to men with prostrate cancer make them less "aggressive and brusque" and more sociable.[60] On the other hand, body builders frequently take testosterone, which makes them more muscular as intended, but also more violent, which is probably unintended.

James Dabbs has spent a lifetime studying the effects of testosterone on human behavior. In one of his studies he compared the testosterone levels of 4,462 male Army veterans and found that the 10 percent with the highest testosterone levels had different life histories from the other 90 percent. In particular, they were more than twice as likely to be both delinquents and hard drug users as adults. Dabbs has also studied prison populations. In both male and female prisons he has found that those who were convicted of violent crimes and who were aggressive in prison had higher testosterone levels than those convicted of nonviolent crimes who were not aggressive in prison.[61] Among the general population, Dabbs has found that men with high testosterone are more likely to beat their wives.[62]

In addition to the testosterone differences that exist in adults, male and female brain differences in the hypothalmic preoptic area have been linked with greater male aggression. Specifically, men's brains show greater activity than women's brains in the "old limbic system," a portion of the brain associated with aggression. Women, on the other hand, show greater activity than men in the cingulated gyrus, a part of the brain that is associated with anxiety and which would thus be likely to suppress aggression.[63]

A recent study has shown that the orbital frontal cortices, brain regions known to be connected with aggressive behavior, are larger in men than in women.[64] It is thought that these brain differences are the result of male exposure to testosterone *in utero*.

There is more evidence indicating that testosterone helps explain why men are more violent than women.[65] Some good biologists, however, are not persuaded that testosterone causes aggression. In one careful review of the literature on biology and aggression, D. J. Albert and colleagues cite a number of studies that do not find testosterone levels to distinguish violent from nonviolent criminals. This review also notes that when males with underactive sex glands are treated with testosterone, they do have gains in sexuality but do not show increases in anger or aggression.[66] Others have pointed out that young boys who are very aggressive do not have high testosterone levels.[67]

Biologist Robert Sapolsky does not think the evidence shows that men with levels of testosterone on the high end of the normal range are more aggressive than those with levels on the low end of normal. On the other hand, he thinks that without a certain amount of testosterone, a man is likely to be very unaggressive indeed. Moreover, he thinks testosterone increases the degree of aggression, exaggerating "the response to environmental triggers of aggression."[68] Dabbs says more or less the same thing when he remarks that victims of high-testosterone murderers are "very dead."

> High-testosterone killers seemed to do more than necessary to kill their victims, like stabbing them twenty-eight times, or shooting them twice in the front and five ties in the back, or killing the victim and then burning the body. Their behavior seemed especially calculated and ruthless.[69]

There seems to be general agreement that behavior can influence testosterone levels as well as the reverse. When men win a fight or a sports competition, their testosterone levels rise.[70] We inherit our basic testosterone level, but Dabbs believes that, "like our blood pressure, it is subject to short-term fluctuations that follow our physical and emotional ups and downs."[71]

Socialization and Aggression

Earlier I argued that some feminists seem determined to show that women's sexuality is "naturally" as wild and unfocused as men's. Some seem almost as determined to show that women have the potential to be as violent as men.

These feminists think that socialization explains most of the sex differences in aggression that we all see around us. One popular gender text claims that boys are taught to be aggressive and are rewarded for displays of aggression , so they come to believe "they have a *right* to get their way through aggression."[72] In the same vein, psychologist Carol Gilligan believes that the "patriarchal social order" teaches boys and men "to hurt without feeling hurt." The process begins with toys that encourage aggression, such as superhero action figures.[73]

Feminists who focus on gender see a powerful and far different socialization process at work for girls and women. In *Reviving*

Ophelia, Mary Pipher says that girls "are not permitted to fight physically with their enemies."[74] The gender text quoted above claims that girls are taught passivity but "under the right conditions . . . it is likely that women have as much potential as men do to be aggressive."[75]

In such works, it is remarkable how little is said about the weighty evolutionary and biological literature surveyed earlier in this chapter. For example, little attention is paid to the possible effects on aggression of differing levels of serotonin and testosterone within and between the sexes. One recent article by two Danish academics is a partial exception. It explicitly seeks to join the debate with the evolutionists and show that the socialization explanation for differences in aggression is the more persuasive one. The article notes that men see aggression as functional, while women see it as problematic. For women the relationship costs seem too high, and they are more likely to fear retaliation. Moreover, men's aggression stems not from a desire to secure women's attention, but from a yearning to acquire respect and status among their fellow men. Those men who have avoided being corrupted by society's emphasis on male status and tough masculinity are less likely to be aggressive.[76]

But in fact, such arguments do not dent the evolutionists' case at all, for men who gain the respect and fear of other men will also get the attention of women without having to seek that attention directly. Men who are less masculine and more androgynous may not rank high in the male hierarchy; they may have less testosterone, a less muscular body and less to gain through physical aggression.

Women, being physically weaker than men generally, have less to gain from fighting and more to fear from retaliation; and sex differences in fear of physical danger are pervasive. Women do worry about how aggression may affect their relationships; but as noted earlier, there are also biological reasons why eons ago a tend-and-befriend approach to risk made more sense than the fight-or-flight option, just as it probably does today.

Some feminists have devoted entire books to the claim that women will close the strength gap with men once they train as men do,[77] but the best evidence shows otherwise. At West Point, intensive weight training for both sexes leads to an *increase* in strength differentials rather than a decrease. After eight weeks of training, male cadets demonstrate 270 percent more power on the bench press than do women who have gone through the same training. Only 5 to 7 percent of women are as strong as the average male.[78] One series of experiments found that "fit" men's greater hemoglobin concentrations and lower body fat gave them an edge over "fit" women in all sports except long-distance swimming.[79]

If parents have a boy who is unusually weak physically, they may try to teach him alternatives to physical conflict as means to protect himself.[80] But parents will usually be more likely to do so for daughters, since at least half the humans a girl encounters will probably be stronger than she.

It is true that men are more likely than women to be taught that they should be brave and willing to fight when necessary—for their family, for their community, for their country. A woman wants a mate who is willing to protect her and her children when protection is necessary. As long as women don't like men who are physical cowards and as long as parents desire grandchildren, most parents will worry more about their cowardly boys than their cowardly girls. But in teaching their sons to be assertive and courageous, they are not so much socializing them into aggression as channeling the male impulses that already exist.

In fact, sex differences in aggression "appear by the second year of life, well before girls and boys are capable of reliably discriminating [between] the sexes or knowing which behaviors are more characteristic of one than the other."[81] In preschool, boys tell stories with "aggressive violent themes" 87 percent of the time; girls tell such stories 17 percent of the time (76 percent of the girls' stories deal with family themes).[82]

Over 90 percent of both boys and girls agree that teachers punish boys more than girls,[83] and the punishments are often for aggression. Parents and other social institutions also spend much time teaching boys to be less aggressive. In fact, though men cross-culturally are encouraged to be aggressive more than women are, some studies in the United States find no difference in the way parents socialize boys and girls with respect to aggression.[84] As with sexuality, however, this type of socialization has less effect on boys than on girls. Punishments for boys who are aggressive are far less likely to influence future behavior than punishments for girls who are aggressive.[85]

If socialization explained most of the gender differences in aggression, one might expect males to become more aggressive as they age, since the sexes would become more and more socialized to their gender roles through time. But in fact, the reverse occurs: the sex differences diminish with age.[86]

If socialization were the cause, one would expect that the differences between the sexes in aggression would have been substantially reduced over the last twenty or thirty years with the dramatic increase in the percentage of women who have powerful jobs. While it is true that there has been a 288 percent increase in the number of violent crimes committed yearly by women and only a 115 percent increase in the number of violent crimes committed per year by men, in absolute terms the growth of male violent crime has been far greater. Between 1970 and 1997, the number of female violent crimes increased by 60,131 per year; over the same period, male violent crimes increased 225,028 per year.[87]

Culture and Aggression

Aggression is predominantly a male trait for biological as well as societal reasons, but some communities produce a little male aggression and almost no female aggression, whereas others produce a great deal of male aggression and a significant amount of female aggression.

Within a culture such as ours, the best way to make men more peaceable would be to encourage monogamous marriage and discourage divorce. Monogamy is preferable to polygamy, which leaves many more men without a woman, thus promoting violence among men competing for women.[88] It is also preferable to serial monogamy, which raises the possibility of violence by jealous former partners.

Monogamous societies such as the United States benefit from less violence within the first year of marriage and again within the first year of fatherhood because getting married and becoming a father both reduce male tendencies to be violent. Sociological studies that follow the same men through time show a "gradual and cumulative" decrease in criminal behavior as a result of the development of "quality marital bonds."[89] Similarly, in the first years of fatherhood men who previously emphasized their independence, aggressiveness and self-concern now find room for more caring and empathy.[90]

Men themselves often report that they gave up deviant lives when they got married and had children. Marriage and fatherhood meant they had to be good providers and set positive examples for their children.[91]

Additionally, David Courtwright's book *Violent Land* shows how violence and violent death follow groups of unmarried men in all locales throughout American history. The most dramatic evidence includes trends in criminal activity among the Chinese community in America. Passage of the Chinese Exclusion Act in 1890 meant Chinese women could not move to America. Soon afterward, Chinese men outnumbered Chinese women by more than 25 to 1, and the Chinese made up a disproportionate number of felons in U.S. prisons. By comparison, in 1965, when sex ratios had been much better equalized, there were only five persons of Chinese ancestry committed to prison in the entire state of California.[92]

The culture of marriage and fatherhood civilizes males, and in the wake of either marriage or fatherhood a man's testosterone level falls.[93] Marriage typically means less time spent with single men competing for women; both the companionship of single males and the competition itself probably serve to keep testosterone levels higher.[94] By changing the men's lifestyle and thus lowering testosterone levels, marriage and fatherhood most likely make men slower to "fly off the handle."

Marriage creates more peaceful men, and these men in turn create more law-abiding sons. When I earlier discussed the importance of biological fathers, the emphasis was on their benefits for girls. The benefits for boys are even greater.[95] Here the evidence is very strong.

After researchers control for race, income, parents' education and other societal variables, they find that family structure determines a large proportion of crime leading to incarceration. Teenagers and young men who grow up in single-parent homes are twice as likely to commit such crimes as males who grow up in two-parent homes. It doesn't matter if the single mom has never been married or if she is divorced. It matters little whether the boy was a child or a teenager when the divorce occurred. If his mother marries again, the impact on a boy is likely to be worse, not better; young men growing up in stepfamilies are three times as likely to end up in prison as those growing up in their biological families.[96] These stunning findings are supported by a study of adolescents convicted of homicide, which finds that only 19 percent of the adolescents' parents were married at the time of the murder.[97] Though genes may help explain these results, as indicated in Chapter 4, family structure must also bear some responsibility

Single-parent families are more likely to produce boys who commit violent crimes, and communities filled with single-parent families are more likely to be filled with male criminals.[98] In the absence of fathers, males are socialized by their peers on the street.[99]

A British study found that the presence of "unsupervised peer groups" resulting from family disruption is the strongest predictor of crime in an area.[100]

Single mothers have a hard time controlling their sons. Single fathers do too. One study shows that both kinds of homes have lower supervision of their adolescents, and that puts male children at risk for delinquency.[101]

One study found that female social ties help to combat crime. In neighborhoods where women borrow food from each other, lunch together and help each other with problems, crime rates are lower. But there is a catch: the women's support networks are major deterrents to crime only if fathers are around. In communities with high proportions of female-headed families, the ties between women are far less effective in combating crime.[102]

Substitutes for biological fathers do not seem to be very effective in raising male aspirations, education and job commitment—all of which reduce crime. As we've already mentioned, stepfathers hurt more often than they help. Male role models outside the family do not seem to help much either. Indeed, one study reports that inner-city kids in grades two through eight say they have more role models than children in more affluent areas say they do; the role models are not "unconventional" or "otherwise diverting children from mainstream norms." But still the aspirations of inner-city kids for white-collar careers were less than half as high as those of kids elsewhere, despite their contact with these role models. While many factors affect career aspirations, the study did note that children who live with their biological fathers are more likely to prefer higher-quality jobs. The authors suggest that "biological fathers are likely to be particularly conscientious mentors and models."[103]

Starting education early might be expected to improve the school performance of inner-city children; and this does hold true for girls. Those who went through Head Start are only one-third as likely as girls of similar socioeconomic backgrounds to drop out of high school years later. But for boys, Head Start seems to have no effect on high school completion rates.[104]

In rural areas and small cities and towns the same patterns appear. Perhaps surprisingly, one study finds that poverty rates are not associated with levels of crime in nonmetropolitan areas. On the other hand, "higher levels of family disruption ... were strongly and consistently associated with higher rates of arrest for violent offenses other than homicide."[105]

Failure of families to remain intact also has an indirect impact on violent crime. Trying to determine the causes of youth unemployment, one study of youths not in school discovered that parental divorce was a major factor while formal education had surprisingly little effect. Because unemployment is associated with violent crime, this relationship is significant for our discussion of aggression.[106]

Although family structure is of paramount importance in explaining variations in rates of violence in our country, other aspects of culture are also important. One interesting line of research distinguishes between honor cultures and other types. In the latter, upper-class men are taught to show strength through restraint and to resolve conflicts without violence. In honor cultures, on the other hand, upper-class men are taught even more often than lower-class men to use force if necessary in order to make a social statement and to maintain face.

Honor cultures have predominated in New World countries conquered by Spain and in much of the American South. In these cultures, a man often commits or threatens aggression if he is challenged or shown disrespect. Even today, homicide rates in the southern United States are significantly higher than in the North. This is because "argument-related" murders—those caused by a man thinking he has been insulted, by escalation of a barroom brawl, or by fighting over a woman—occur two and one half times as often in small southern cities as in small northern cities. If one compares larger cities in the South and the North, however, there is little difference in the rate of argument-based murders, while murder in the course of a robbery or a burglary in the larger cities is less common in the South than elsewhere. So there seems to be something about the culture of smaller southern communities that leads to short tempers and more violence when men are involved personally in a dispute.

Some researchers have set up an elaborate series of experiments to see if southern and northern college students respond differently to confrontations in various settings. In one of these experiments, students were deliberately bumped and insulted in a narrow hallway. The northerners tended to shrug this off, but the southerners became angry. Blood tests taken afterward showed elevated levels of testosterone and cortisol in the southerners but not in the northerners, suggesting that the southerners were stressed and prepared for aggression. In a subsequent experiment, a very large experimental accomplice came barreling down the middle of a hallway; the southerners who had become angry and insulted in the previous experiment were much slower to clear the way for him than were northerners *or* southerners who had not been insulted.[107] These experiments demonstrate the subtle interaction of male culture and biology.

Dominance

Studies give conflicting evidence about the existence of a link between testosterone and male aggression; but evolutionists think these findings make sense if aggression is viewed as a means to an end. What men really want is access to women. To get it, they seek high status through dominance over other men. (Observational and questionnaire research validate females' tendency to be attracted to males who exhibit dominance displays.)[108] Sometimes physical aggression helps one achieve dominance, but in developed societies it often does not.

Studies do indeed show that testosterone is more consistently related to the male attempt to achieve dominance than to acts of physical aggression.[109] If one seeks dominance—in the sense of power or influence over others[110]—it may be better to be an aggressive businessman or a trial lawyer than a bruiser.[111] Trial lawyers are usually high- testosterone men, and they can be alternately tough

with prosecutors and charming with jurors. More generally, the high-testosterone man seems able to move easily between smiles and toughness. The low-testosterone man finds it harder to be overtly aggressive.[112] He even looks different—more friendly and less strong.[113]

Men generally, and high-testosterone men in particular, want to be in charge. As James and Mary Dabbs say in their book on testosterone, men want to "drive the car, pick the topic, run the war." Confident men have high testosterone. So too do rodeo cowboys.[114] Some prisons have found they can tame young men by setting them to work taming horses—in other words, by finding a productive way for the men to fulfill their wish to be in charge.[115]

Men in prison—in contrast to women in prison, who miss relationships and intimacy—say they miss their lost power and sense of masculinity.[116] Prisoners are in a situation where they are dominated, but men both in and out of prison hate to be dominated. Men attempt to climb workplace hierarchies in part because of their strong desire for a job with no close supervision.[117]

Women and Dominance

Women in large companies disproportionately work in staff positions assisting men with more authority.[118] And women's dramatic advances in business have occurred disproportionately in small and medium-sized businesses.[119] Evolutionary anthropologist Helen Fisher says,

> Men more regularly sacrifice their health, safety and precious time with family and friends to win status, money, and prestige. Men and women exhibit no difference in what psychologists call "internal competitiveness," the desire to meet personal goals and display excellence. But men score much higher in "external competitiveness," the willingness to elbow others aside to get ahead.[120]

Matriarchies—societies where women have more political, economic and social power than men—do not exist; in fact, there is no evidence that they have ever existed. Even matrilineal societies, where kinship structures are determined by the female line, are rare.[121] Israeli kibbutzim tried to inculcate gender equality, but always found that men were more active politically, especially at the top levels. In the contemporary United States, women's political advances have been impressive, but achievements have been far more evident in the legislative branches than in the executive branches. As of 2001 there were still only twelve women who had ever been elected governor of an American state.[122]

There has, of course, never been a female U.S. President. Moreover, the voters have usually chosen men who seem stronger than their rivals.[123] A recent systematic canvassing of presidential biographers found that the most successful Presidents were "unusually assertive, dominant and forceful.... Presidents who succeed set ambitious goals for themselves and move heaven and earth to meet them."[124] Though female heads of state in Asia are not uncommon, their route to power has been almost exclusively dynastic, as in the case of India's Indira Ghandi.[125]

Even female executives in business wonder if they really want power as much as men do.[126] In a retrospective study of the women of the Harvard Business School class of 1975, Liz Roman Gallese found that two-fifths of these intelligent and highly trained women "were ambivalent or frankly not ambitious for their careers." Even those women who seemed the most ambitious appeared to "pull back from whatever one has to do or be" to make it to the top, a tendency that Gallese attributes to their "reluctance to forfeit what is uniquely theirs, their femininity."[127] Women's ideal self-image rarely includes possessing power. When men and women in six cultures were asked what kind of person they would most like to be, women used adjectives like *loving, sympathetic* and *generous,* whereas men used *assertive, dominating, competitive.*[128]

Women are less concerned about power in the broader society because it doesn't do as much for them as it does for men. Though dominance in traditional societies can mean greater access to food for females, the overall gains from fighting are so much less for females that they rarely fight in order to dominate. Moreover, for females, dominance tends to be temporary since in traditional human societies—and probably during the Environment of Evolutionary Adaptation—the females usually transfer from their own home groups to their husband's home group.

More important still, males are not attracted to dominant females, so the mating gains from achieving dominance do not exist for women as they do for men.[129] A number of studies show that men don't care about or even positively dislike dominant tendencies in a female mate. Sylvia Hewlett's book *Creating a Life* is filled with women who say that the men they have been with could not tolerate their success or ambition.[130] One of these men explains why he fits this pattern:

> I look around at my friends and I tell you, when a high-flying man marries a high-flying woman the strain is intense, especially if they have children.... It's also true that I don't have much to offer these women. They have everything already. I mean, I want my success in the world and my earning power to matter—to be appreciated.
>
> One final thing, and this is important. I'm money-driven enough and would want my wife to bring something different to the relationship—tenderness, expressiveness, and even a little silliness. I need someone who will help me wind down and smell the roses.[131]

Recall that there is evidence that highly dominant women are no better liked by women than by men.[132] Indeed, a number of studies have found that women particularly dislike members of their sex who seem to be putting on airs—at work as well as among friends. But in business, at least as presently constituted, it is the women who use the stereotypically male style—decisive, assertive, ambitious—who advance in their careers.[133] Since this style is not usually attractive to other women, or socially to men, females displaying these characteristics face difficult choices.

Some women, of course, are inherently more decisive, assertive and ambitious than most men. Such women have a high dominance tendency. They are inclined to be bolder, more confident and more competitive than other women, and to seek out traditionally masculine careers. It appears that they have, on average, higher levels of testosterone than other women do. For example, female trial lawyers have higher levels of testosterone than other female lawyers. For reasons as yet undetermined, such high-testosterone women have also been found to produce more sons than daughters. (Curvaceous beauty queens, thought to be low in testosterone, produce many more girls than boys.)[134]

Part of a male's biological makeup encourages him to attempt to dominate. When he is successful, he achieves a pleasurable testosterone high; but when he fails, loses, or is demeaned, he experiences a testosterone low. For example, when hazed by a drill sergeant, army officer candidates' testosterone levels and moods sink measurably. On the other hand, when officer candidates graduate, both testosterone and mood soar. Similarly, frightened novice parachutists have depressed testosterone levels, which then climb along with their mood when they become experienced and accomplished. When a man wins a tennis match or graduates from medical school, his testosterone and mood both rise.[135] Though the evidence is less clear, it seems that women do not get enjoyable hormonal testosterone, serotonin and dopamine surges when they win or achieve rank.[136]

Women seek influence with others, but they are more likely to "value the development of reciprocal relationships."[137] They "view group-oriented and group-facilitating acts" as more desirable than men do.[138] Their groups are more cohesive, but less structured and less hierarchal than men's.[139]

Helen Fisher believes that the female taste for egalitarian, harmonious connections is associated with estrogen.[140] We do know that in many cultures, women assume more leadership roles after menopause. There are, of course, social reasons for this trend; at this stage of life, children no longer claim women's attention so strongly. But it is also true that after menopause, women's estrogen no longer masks the dominance-motivating effects of testosterone.[141]

There are other reasons to think women's taste for group-oriented, egalitarian relationships is deep-seated. For one, this taste exists in women living in a wide variety of cultures. In Kenya, Ethiopia and Cameroon, for example, women's conversations in tribes emphasize "cooperation and connection," whereas men's speech more regularly reflects "competition and the pursuit of rank."[142] Second, this taste is observable in other primates. Both female humans and female chimpanzees form closer and more stable friendships than males do.[143] As discussed earlier, these patterns are also congruent with the female inclination to "tend and befriend."

Socialization and Dominance

Gloria Steinem thinks our "male dominated culture" is what convinces men that dominance is their "natural right."[144] But as with aggression, the case for deeper, more fundamental causes seems compelling.

As we've already noted, high testosterone in females seems to increase their dominance-seeking behavior. Moreover, boys are more assertive than girls at thirteen months of age.[145] By the time boys and girls reach preschool, boys are attacking people, fighting and destroying things much more than girls. They won't listen when girls give them instructions. Boys clearly dominate mixed-sex groups of children age thirty-three months.[146] Understandably, most girls prefer to play in their more civilized groups.[147] Those who do play with the boys play boy games and call themselves *tomboys* when they get older.[148]

Young girls often seem wary of boys and will withdraw rather than confront them. Until age ten, there is little difference in size or strength between the sexes. But girls will not test boys to see which ones they can dominate, and then withdraw only from those who are stronger. When teachers don't intervene, boys completely monopolize toys popular with both sexes, such as tricycles and trampolines.[149]

Eleanor Maccoby's extensive research on children leads her to believe that "certain aspects of male play, such as dominance struggles and themes of heroic combat, may be cross-culturally universal, or nearly so."[150] School-age females try to mitigate conflict, whereas school-age boys love it. Their play is often rough, but Maccoby emphasizes "how much fun boys have together."[151] In their speech also, boys have the same kind of fun:

> When boys issue dares, shout at each other, boast, and refuse to listen or yield the floor, they are doing the same thing they are doing in their rough play and physical confrontations: they are defending their turf, and vying for dominance—for recognition of status from other boys. This is the element in the male agenda that most distinguishes their interactions from those of girls.[152]

Among boys, toughness, a refusal to back down and athletic ability take one to the top of the strong-male hierarchies. Boys who are dominant at age six are generally dominant at age fifteen as well. Even in a university laboratory school, populated largely by children of professors, it is toughness and athleticism, not brains, that best predict social rank among fifteen-year-old boys. When the boys get closer to completing high school, among the college-bound, academic achievement begins to have more influence on rank.[153]

Judith Harris believes that this constant male striving for dominance best explains why girls' self-esteem goes down in early adolescence:

> By forming their own separate groups in childhood, they were able to avoid being dominated by boys. Then their biological clocks strike thirteen and suddenly they find themselves wanting to interact with a bunch of people who have been practicing the art of domination ever since they let go of Mommy's hand. It was bad enough when these people—the boys—were the same size or, for a brief time, a bit smaller. Now, to top it off, they are rapidly getting *bigger.*
>
> For a teenage girl to have any sort of status in a group whose dominant members are boys, either she must be good at something they value or she must be pretty. If she has neither of these assets, chances are she will be ignored. These are not things she can acquire just by trying hard: she has no control over them.[154]

Since the 1970s, women have flooded into traditionally male jobs such as law and medicine, have dramatically increased their participation in school athletics, have had smaller families and have become much more attached to the labor market. Yet as we discussed earlier, surveys show no decrease in sex stereotyping. The general public still sees men as more authoritative, ambitious, domineering and competitive than women. Moreover, these results are not just the products of inaccurate stereotypes. If women and men are simply asked to pick adjectives that describe themselves, not only do the sex differences remain, but differences in responses have not been closing. Men see themselves as more assertive; women see themselves as more tender-minded.[155]

Competitiveness

Since men care more about dominance, it is no surprise that they also like competition more than women do. The way that this difference manifests itself in games and sports will be discussed in the following chapter. But the sex difference in competition and dominance also appears in areas unrelated to sports.

A large body of research finds that males are more competitive and females more cooperative.[156] In school from second through twelfth grades, boys have more favorable attitudes toward competition, girls toward cooperation.[157] Even in law school, many women pursuing this adversarial profession are put off by the competitive style of most classrooms.[158] They are disproportionately attracted to courses in mediation. And after graduation, they are more likely than men to become judges or corporate counsels and less likely to become "criminal defense attorneys, the gladiators of the profession."[159]

Males don't just like competition more; they also do better when a situation is seen as competitive. In one study of medical students, men did better the more competitive the atmosphere was perceived to be; women did worse.[160]A different scholar explains a sex difference in scientific inquiry in the following way:

> Men often feel comfortable with a communication style that seeks to reduce one of the protagonists to rubble in the course of a scientific discussion. After the storm is over, they quickly forget about the incident. For many women this style of interaction is unacceptable, either as giver or receiver. A woman student may take weeks or months to recover from such an interchange, and it may contribute to a perma-

> nent loss of self-esteem. Women report that a process in which points are won at the expense of putting someone else down is to them an unacceptable mode of scientific debate.[161]

Many women in the military also see as unacceptable the combative, "barking orders" male style of communication.[162] But the Marines play on the male zest for competitive challenges, and they are the only service to meet their recruiting goals regularly. They ask television viewers if they want to be a part of "the few, the proud." One of their magazine ads says, "Running won't kill you—you'll pass out first."[163] These military mottos support a more general research finding: on average, men respond better to difficult challenges than women do.[164]

Eons ago our male ancestor knew that if he seemed competitive and cocky, he might get rivals to back off and leave him better able to climb the male hierarchy.[165] A man might avoid the need for violence and its contingent risks altogether if he appeared fearless and strong. Moreover, he would be likely to attract females by indicating his ability to protect. In contrast, a woman displaying similar behavior would be likely to lose the peer support that was so important to her own and her family's protection, a poor strategy for evolutionary success. A predisposition toward competitive and cocky display is thus more likely to have been passed on to today's men than to today's women.

Indeed, studies show that males are more confident and females more anxious when facing competitive situations.[166] It used to be thought that boys were simply more easily aroused than girls. But careful skin-test studies found that girls are more aroused by a sympathy-inducing film, while boys prove to be "more aroused by threats, challenges, and competition."[167] Boys like challenges from their peers and seek them out.[168]

Although boys do not generally like sitting for the SAT and similar tests, such experiences are another competitive challenge to which males respond well. An important study of eighteen-year-old Finnish youth taking national exams found far greater increases in the adrenaline of boys than of girls. Moreover, increases in adrenaline helped male achievement (beyond what intelligence tests would have predicted), but increased adrenaline had no such effect for the Finnish girls.[169]

As with sex, dominance and other traits, some girls do like to compete as much as most boys do. These girls seem to relish the special test of competing with boys, and they perform at their highest level in mixed-sex competitions. Such girls "tend to be those characterized by masculine or androgynous temperaments."[170]

More characteristically, girls want to compete for men by emphasizing good looks and denigrating the looks and sexual behavior of rivals.[171] But they cannot compete too openly—especially within their group—without alienating friends. They want a desirable man with good genes and a dependable character, but overt competition for men may undermine the tend-and-befriend strategy for gaining female support.[172] So competition is usually more subtle than among boys. Often women strive to achieve personal goals while avoiding direct competition with others.[173]

After pubertal development is completed and the "soothing effects"[174] of estrogen are fully available, the worst of the female "'backbiting, bickering and cattiness'" fades away. There is then a "marked rise" in the female preference for cooperation over competition.[175] The characteristic female superiority in reading emotions, responding to social cues and cultivating intimate relationships is further developed.[176]

7
SPORTS, AGGRESSION AND TITLE IX

Men's proclivity to compete and dominate can be dangerous to society when it is not constrained within the boundaries of a career or tamed by a loving relationship. During the teenage years and even later, though, perhaps the most effective way to channel the aggressive tendencies of males is via participation in sports. While we must sometimes prompt men into marriage, their own internal makeup often drives them toward athletics. But this important means of socializing males has been seriously damaged by Title IX of the Education Amendments of 1972. This law arose as a way to involve more girls and women in sports, but in effect it has also greatly constricted opportunities for boys and men. An examination of the history and interpretation of this law can illustrate how confusion over whether sex differences are inbred or socially constructed leads to confusion in public policy.

Contentious from its inception, the 1972 law to stop sex discrimination in publicly funded schools has become a political hot potato because of its effect on intercollegiate athletics. Since the passage of Title IX, there has been a fourfold increase in the number of women partaking in intercollegiate sports.[1] But Title IX regulations have also led to the dismantling of men's athletic teams in a variety of sports at a number of colleges and universities.

Reformers were convinced that sensible changes in the law could preserve the gains for women without further decimating men's teams, and they were cautiously optimistic that at least some changes were in the offing. Title IX reform was in the 2000 Republican Party platform.[2] The Department of Education's assistant secretary for civil rights, Gerald Reynolds, had put his own appointment at risk by appearing to support revision of the law during his confirmation hearings.[3] In 2002, the department had appointed a prestigious "Commission on Opportunity in Athletics," whose recommended changes in the law garnered the support of most of the women members, including a coach, a college athletic director and a WNBA All-Star.[4] But the letter issued by Reynolds in 2003 adopted none of the changes, and instead promised aggressive enforcement of the regulations set forth during the Carter and Clinton administrations.

These regulations essentially rely on quotas. Institutions can comply in one of three ways. The first and safest is to ensure that the ratio of males to females participating in sports is the same as the male/female ratio on campus. The second does not require quotas as long as the school has a "history and continuing practice" of expanding opportunities for the underrepresented sex and can demonstrate that its athletic programs are on a trajectory toward equal proportional representation. The third way to be in compliance is to ensure that the interests and abilities of female athletes have been "fully and effectively accommodated."[5] As interpreted, this test stipulates that in effect a school need not meet quotas or be on its way to meeting them as long as no female athletes wish the school had an intercollegiate team in a sport not currently offered.

Not surprisingly, most universities have decided that the only way to avoid trouble is to aim for an athlete gender ratio identical to the male/female student ratio. Given tight budgets, they make progress toward this goal by cutting male teams or trimming male squads while adding new teams for women.

The Bush administration's decision to continue the existing Title IX regulatory policy may calm the political waters a little, but the issue won't go away. The inevitable cutting of more men's teams to meet the law's requirements will continue to stir bitter resentment, and Education Department regulations are still being challenged in court by the National Wrestling Coaches' Association and others.

Meanwhile, the defenders of current Title IX regulations will also be stirring the waters. Washington-based Title IX advocates are not satisfied with the current results of the law and want much more vigorous enforcement. They note that statistical equality of participation has yet to be achieved—women represent 56 percent of the national collegiate student body but only 42 percent of intercollegiate athletes.[6] On the day that Reynolds made his announcement,

Senator Edward Kennedy warned against "a premature declaration of victory" and remarked that work remained to be done.[7]

But the progress that Senator Kennedy wants will come at the expense of lost opportunities for still more male athletes. From 1985 to 1997, over 21,000 collegiate spots for male athletes disappeared. Over 359 teams for men have disappeared just since 1992.[8] Christine Stolba of the Independent Women's Forum commented to the Title IX commission that "Between 1993 and 1999 alone 53 men's golf teams, 39 men's track teams, 43 wrestling teams, and 16 baseball teams have been eliminated. The University of Miami's diving team, which has produced 15 Olympic athletes, is gone."[9]

Certain male sports, such as wrestling, have been particularly hard hit. With athletes in many different weight classes, eliminating the wrestling team or reducing the number of slots on the team can bring sports participation proportions much closer to student enrollment ratios. But the wrestlers and other critics of these regulations insist that men, on average, are more eager to participate in intercollegiate sports than women. Thus, a policy providing men and women with proportionally equal numbers of spots on intercollegiate teams means, in effect, that men who desire to participate in intercollegiate sports have fewer opportunities than women with the same desire. Wrestling coaches argue that equal opportunity requires that colleges provide athletic opportunities based on relative interest levels of the sexes rather than relative enrollment,[10] but most supporters of current policy resist any change that would focus on interest levels. They insist that the mushrooming of female sports participation over the last two decades proves that women will participate in intercollegiate sports if sufficient opportunities are created.

Title IX proponents also oppose interest testing because they believe that it "may prevent future progress in providing opportunities for women because offering opportunities regardless of interest may encourage participation even where none currently exists."[11] Thus Title IX, originally an antidiscrimination law, is transformed into a federal endeavor to manipulate women's behavior in ways favored by certain women's groups.

A *Village Voice* essayist recently explained some other reasons to reject the commission's recommendation for interest testing:

> [Reformers] insist that universities conduct surveys to determine student interest in sports and use *those* numbers as the basis for determining proportional spending, but that misses the *substantive* work of Title IX, which aims, among other things, to redress a culture that

> consistently applauds boys for athletic achievement and pours resources in their direction. Is it any wonder that they would express more interest?[12]

Title IX, by this interpretation, should be part of a broad feminist campaign to "redress a culture"—American society—that is diseased with sexism and committed to discouraging girls and women from playing sports. Valerie Bonnette, head of the Title IX consulting firm Good Sports Inc., articulates a typical view: "Women aren't born less interested in sports. Society conditions them."[13] Other critics have been less theoretical; actress and amateur archer Geena Davis pretended (one hopes) to threaten the commission: "I am here to take you on a short ride in Thelma and Louise's car if you think it's fair and just to limit a girl's opportunity to play sports based on her response to an interest survey."[14]

Both the critics and the proponents of current Title IX enforcement argue that they are protecting Title IX's central guarantee that "no person in the United States shall, on the basis of sex, be excluded from participation in, be denied the benefits of, or be subjected to discrimination under any education program or activity receiving Federal financial assistance." One single issue is thus at the center of the controversy over Title IX. Are men more interested than women in competitive sports, and, if they are, is their greater interest rooted in natural differences or is it socially constructed?

Interest in sports can mean interest in following and viewing sports competitions or actually participating in sports. Title IX's focus is on participation. Still, the evidence on following and viewing is relevant. College students who like to act or dance will probably be more interested than other students in watching plays or dance performances. Similarly, those interested in playing competitive sports are likely to be more interested in following or watching them.

According to multiple tests and surveys, one of the greatest differences between the sexes is their level of interest in sports. Young men are much bigger sports fans than young women are. One academic concludes that 20 percent of men and 4 to 5 percent of women can be classified as strong sports fans.[15] Men, for example, are much more likely than women to read the sports pages in the newspaper.[16] And one interesting eavesdropping study of bank officers having lunch in a dining room found that although these professionals all had the same sorts of jobs, men lunching together talked about business, food and sports, whereas the women also discussed business, but primarily talked about friends, children, husbands and boyfriends.[17]

The Olympics are one of the few major sporting events that attract almost as many female viewers as male. The television executives achieve this high female viewership by focusing on the personal dimension. The president of NBC sports has noted:

> Men will sit through the Olympics for almost anything, as long as they get to see some winners and losers.... Women tend to approach this differently. They want to know who the athletes are, how they got there, what sacrifices they've made. They want an attachment, a rooting interest.

The TV brass think that women get the emotional connection from watching what critics call "maudlin" profiles, whereas men find the emotion in the competition itself, the results and the winners and losers.[18]

The coverage of the Olympics increasingly showcases gymnastics and diving, while devoting much less attention to boxing and wrestling. Female gymnastics and diving emphasize flexibility and beauty as much as strength and athleticism. So too does female ice skating, which is as much about grace and artistry as about strength and speed. The top stars are thrown flowers from the crowds and get bouquets from competition organizers. The whole tone is feminine. And the viewing statistics reflect the female bias: over 70 percent of girls follow figure skating, while fewer than 20 percent of boys do.[19]

Young women also follow tennis more than men do, and although it does not figure in the competition per se, here again there is more emphasis on grace and beauty than in most female sports. Competitors wear skirts and often devote considerable time to their appearance. The Women's Tennis Association's official magazine promises "Celebrities, Glamour, Profiles, Fashion, Lifestyles."[20] Television ratings for professional women's tennis are more than four times greater than for women's golf or basketball.[21] The commissioner of the women's golf tour recently received criticism when he hired a fashion, makeup and hair consultant for the golfers and averred that what the tour needed was three tall blondes.[22]

The emphasis on appearance is not just an attempt to draw in male viewers. In Barbie Super Sports, a computer game designed to appeal to young girls, Barbie's sports participation begins with the selection of her outfits for in-line skating and snowboarding.[23]

Moreover, despite men's consistently higher rates of sports participation, since 1991 women have out-purchased them in sports apparel.[24]

Columnist Ellen Goodman joins other feminists in praising the new emphasis on female athletes, but laments the fact that it is accompanied by far greater emphasis on female beauty.[25] But female beauty remains of inordinate importance to men and, as a result, to women. That over one and one half *billion* viewers, predominantly female, watched the 2002 Miss World pageant is testimony to this.[26]

Women apparently want their athletic heroines to care about their appearance. Most women prefer to watch female athletes who seem attractive and feminine. One academic study of college students, for example, found that women prefer stylish sports that "emphasize beauty and elegance of body position and movement but also stress speed, agility and strength." Their favorite sports do not involve "physical contact between competitors," and competitions are judged by comparative rankings "rather than in one winner/one loser fashion." In contrast, men prefer to watch combative sports where there is "direct physical contact between performers." Their favorite sports emphasize strength, stamina, power, domination, agility and speed. One party wins at the expense of an opposing party.[27]

Intercollegiate women's sports, as well as the less popular male sports, get a subsidy of sorts from the popularity of the major male sports. At the University of Virginia, a Division I university where I teach, 97 percent of total ticket revenues come from sales for men's games, and 3 percent from sales for women's games.[28] Nowadays, sports channels that want to acquire the rights to popular male sports often have to agree to take on less popular male and female sports. ESPN has recently televised every game of the collegiate baseball championships, and as part of their agreement with the NCAA, they also televised every game of the women's softball championships. This was not a commercial decision.[29]

In their book *Why Men Don't Iron,* Anne and Bill Moir observe that "to the majority of women, men's pastimes and their passionate attachment to their sporting heroes seem ridiculous."[30] The following "Cathy" cartoon illustrates more or less the same thing. On Thanksgiving Day in 2002, Gallup reported on CNN that 58 percent of men and 36 percent of women would watch an hour or more of sports over the holiday. We don't know how many of those women planned to watch sports because they wanted to be with their husbands, who predictably would be in front of the tube.

Early in 2002, University of Virginia football coach Al Groh told seventy football widows that for many men, football is "their weekly soap opera."[31] For some men, though, the addiction to multiple "soaps" becomes truly worrisome. One recovered "addict" even wrote a book about the affliction, *Not Now, Honey, I'm Watching the Game*. Questioning other "sportsaholics," he found that 85 percent felt great about the time they devoted to watching sports, while 69 percent of their wives felt "angry, jealous and frustrated" by husbands who spent thirty to forty hours a week watching televised games.[32]

Participation

The patterns that researchers have found in sports viewing preferences carry over consistently into male and female preferences for playing sports. Surveys of college students and prospective students invariably find that more men than women are interested in participating in intercollegiate athletics. One survey of college students found that 61 percent of enrolled students with this interest were male; another poll of prospective students found that 57 percent of the interest came from males.[33]

Satisfying current Title IX requirements by insisting that intercollegiate athletes be rigorously balanced by gender is even more difficult than these surveys suggest. This is partly because the burgeoning number of female high school athletes is a misleading indicator of how many women will be serious participants on intercollegiate teams. Women who go out for a team generally insist on playing in games, while men are more willing to ride the bench; coaches of both male and female teams agree that women are more likely than men to quit if they don't get to play in games. Many of the women who were accustomed to playing in high school games will be benchwarmers in college, and then stop coming out.[34] The female softball coach at Cal State Northridge says that in all sports, "most [women] tend to quit the team" once they "realize that they will not be able to play in games."[35]

As a result, while Division III men's baseball teams cut dozens of players to get their average squad size down to 30.4 players, "women's NCAA softball teams struggle to get their average squad up to 18."[36] And though in 1995, Brown University had seventeen women's teams and sixteen men's teams, the number of male and female athletes was nowhere near proportional and not just because the football team was so large. Almost all the women's teams had room for additional athletes (93 slots in total) whereas the men's teams "had a superabundance of players competing for available positions."[37] To get the numbers of women up, Brown had to launch "additional undersubscribed teams."

Brown and other schools also had to begin cutting the benchwarmers on male teams. The Brown track coach discouraged male applicants inquiring about whether they could come out for the team as walk-ons, whereas he gave female applicants detailed information about how to find him and the track. Several university officials told a *New York Times* reporter that male students interested in minor sports could try out only if they could recruit two women who would try out for women's teams.[38] The Brown athletic director found turning away the male walk-ons to be the hardest part of the whole Title IX process. "Eager, willing athletes" who would not travel and who would cost the university little or nothing had to be told to "stay in [your] dorms so [you] won't screw up the numbers."[39]

As a *60 Minutes* show in 2003 pointed out, the result of this obsession with numbers can be teams and slots on teams being cut for males who have been committed to their sports since early childhood, while new teams are being set up for women who have never played the sport before arriving at college. Since crew squads are large, crew for women has been a real growth sport (from 96 to 140 teams between 1997 and 2002). Crew coaches comb their campuses looking for tall, broad-shouldered females for their teams. Full scholarships are sometimes offered to women with no experience in the sport.[40]

The NCAA's Gender Equity Task Force has also encouraged schools to add new women's sports such as synchronized swimming, archery, bowling, equestrian teams and ice hockey, although there is not much evidence of interest in these sports among women in high school. For example, only eleven high schools in the nation offer archery teams.[41]

There are a number of reasons why someone might play a sport in high school or college, and not all of them involve a passion for competitive athletics. For example, participation might help win or maintain a scholarship, please parents, or give one prestige among one's peers. The best way to judge the strength of interest in playing competitive athletics may be to see how many women and men participate at the recreational level. Here the sex differences are extremely large.

One large study questioned high school seniors about their participation in a wide range of activities: sports, music, art, dance, religion, spending time with parents or friends, volunteering and religious activities, among others. Far and away the largest sex difference was in "non-school sports," with male participation exceeding female participation by a factor of three.[42] In college, anyone who is interested can play intramural sports, but again there are three to four times as many men as women who do so.

After college, adult women participate more in fitness activities than they once did, but they do not play competitive sports more often.[43] Fifty-two percent of gym members are now women, but the gender gap in the type of gym activities pursued is telling. While women participate most in dance and exercise classes, men constitute the majority of basketball and racquetball players; at one Manhattan club, 80 percent of gymnasts and figure skaters are women, while 90 percent of basketball, hockey and soccer players are men.[44]

Biology and Competitive Sports

Why are males more interested in sports? A look at early childhood, when socialization has just begun, can provide clues about the degree to which interest in sports is determined by culture. As with aggression and dominance-seeking behavior, sex differences in athletic interests begin early. Studies from the 1920s to the 1990s show that in the preschool years, girls are more interested in dance and boys in balls and rough-and-tumble play. These differences begin to appear before the age of two. By grade school the boys' games are more competitive, longer in duration, with more rules and interdependence between players and with clear winners and losers.[45] In contrast, girls avoid games where winning means that someone must lose; they like turn-taking games like hopscotch, where competition is less direct.[46]

One study of fourth and sixth graders showed that during free play, boys are competing with other boys 50 percent of the time whereas girls compete against each other only 1 percent of the time.[47] Boys often compete as part of a group, and their groups are larger than girls' groups. There are many arguments among the boys, but the disputes are not taken personally and are resolved by rules. Boys "seem to enjoy the adversarial cut-and-thrust" with friends and prefer to have the best players, not necessarily their friends, on their team. Girls, in contrast, want their friends to be on their team and don't want to compete against them. Girls usually prefer to play in smaller groups and will "abandon a game if it causes arguments."[48]

In her book *The Two Sexes,* Eleanor Maccoby concludes that:

> Boys, more than girls, are excited by threats, challenges, and competition.... The arousal that boys experience when involved in situations of challenge and competition with other boys appears to be something they like and seek. In traditional psychological language, certain challenging responses from peers appear to be more "reinforcing" for boys than for girls.[49]

These differing play preferences make team sports more attractive to boys. On the playground, ten- and eleven-year-old boys play football and basketball three times more often than girls. Studies have found that this ratio has remained unchanged between 1963 and 1994.[50]

For boys, the first sign of competitive physical activity is usually rough-and-tumble play. Across different cultures, boys more than girls prefer rough play, and among primates the proclivity toward rough play is much stronger in males than females.[51] Boys are physically aroused more easily than girls, reacting more quickly and more strongly to triggers.[52] Parents of preschool boys often describe them as "having a great deal of unnecessary energy."[53] The boys often work the energy off by play fighting, usually with friends; they will move from playing a game to having a wrestling match and then back to the game. Boys like contact play and accord it social significance: they, more than girls, know which of their friends is strongest and think it is important to win at games.[54]

Before age ten, girls are often as strong or stronger than boys, but they do not usually compete to see whom they can dominate. Instead, as noted in the last chapter, they generally let themselves be pushed around by the boys in the jockeying for popular toys.[55]

Some authors think that men therefore have learned as boys to push women around. Myriam Miedzian is among those who blame fathers for creating men who are too combative and competitive and ultimately too violent. Miedzian says that fathers who want to be sure their sons grow up to be strong and tough

> overstimulate them from an early age. They toss them about more, act loud and tough rather than soft and gentle as they do with their girls. . . . [I]n order to be able to take this kind of treatment, the organism becomes less sensitive.

By thus encouraging the values of "the masculine mystique" parents, and especially fathers, end up "encourag[ing] violent behavior in their sons."[56]

There are at least three problems with Miedzian's analysis. First, from the time of birth, boys display characteristics that Miedzian attributes to overstimulation. Second, she thinks that fathers avoid rough-and-tumble play with their girls, but in fact, children of both sexes go to dad for fun and exciting play. Moreover, research suggests that boys get more roughhousing because they seem to like it more, not because fathers are more "soft and gentle" with their girls. When the girls seem to like rough play, fathers give it to them.[57]

Finally, Miedzian, like many others, fails to distinguish between rough-and-tumble play and actual aggression.[58] Researchers find that rough-and-tumble play is important for a boy's healthy development. Those who engage in it learn to manage skills of "competition and aggression"; they learn not to go too far. Rough-and-tumble (R & T) play

> often leads to children's engagement in cooperative games with rules. The similarity of the motor patterns in both forms of play suggests that R & T provides practice for games with rules. For example, chasing behavior (a component of R & T) and tag (a rule-governed game) both involve running, dodging and reciprocal role taking.[59]

The researcher just quoted says that children disliked by their peers respond aggressively when those peers try to initiate rough-and-tumble-play. Children who have not been exposed to this kind of play are often less socially competent and less popular with peers. Thus, it is important that boys, especially those with aggressive tendencies, be introduced to rough-and-tumble play in a nonthreatening environment.

The males most likely to end up hypermasculine and violent when they become teenagers are those who are raised without a father, not those who are raised by a masculine father. The supposed villain, the overstimulating father, is in fact something of a hero. Fathers' rough play teaches not aggression but self-control. Paternal involvement in R & T "is associated with children's skills at regulating their emotional states."[60] Fathers take preschool boys, described by one mother as "a force barely under control,"[61] and teach them not to bite and kick in rough play. Fathers teach kids when "enough is enough" and when it is time to "shut it down." A committee brought together by the Board on Children and Families of the National Research Council has concluded that "fathers, in effect, give children practice in regulating their own emotions and recognizing others' emotional cues."[62]

Boys from an early age like ball games, roughhousing, competitive play and games with clear winners and losers. Other evidence suggests that males' greater interest in sports is hormonal rather than developmental. Experiments with other primates and "natural" experiments with girls exposed to high levels of male hormones produce compelling evidence that hormones are important determinants of that inclination.

Experiments with rhesus monkeys, for instance, show pretty conclusively that the embryonic environment is crucial. Prenatal exposure to androgens increases the frequency of female rough-and-tumble play; and for males, even neonatal castration does not reduce the frequency of such play.[63]

Similar results are found in human populations. Girls exposed to anomalous overdoses of androgens show more interest in rough-and-tumble play. They also are more interested in sports, including rough ones like football, and less interested in more typically female activities such as cheerleading. These results occur whether one looks at girls whose excess hormonal exposure comes from congenital adrenal hyperplasia (CAH) or from their mothers' receiving masculine hormone injections to sustain at-risk pregnancies. In one study, for example, "between 7 and 8 of every 10 girls affected by CAH engaged in athletic competition more frequently than the average unaffected girl."[64] Also relevant is a study showing that women sex-typed as masculine or androgynous are more likely than other women to participate in a sport for competitive reasons.[65] As previously argued, there are reasons to believe that women with masculine or androgynous personalities are more likely than most to have been exposed to high levels of embryonic androgens.

Theresa Crenshaw, an M.D. and hormonal expert, thinks that "women are the peacemakers" largely because of their hormonal makeup. "Mellowing them are their relatively high levels of serotonin compared to the male, oxytocin in abundant supply, and estrogen, a gentle, ordinarily soothing antidepressant hormone."[66] Richard Udry of the University of North Carolina has shown that exposure to above-average levels of testosterone can make women less peaceable and more assertive—a little more like men than most of their sisters.[67] In general, women are far more gentle and peaceable than the average man in part because biology makes them so. Hormonal differences help explain why women tend to be drawn to cooperation more than to competition and why they generally prefer the less aggressive and less combative sports.

As suggested in the last chapter, baseline androgens encourage males to engage in certain typically male behaviors, but so too does the testosterone boost that men get from successfully dominating or competing. Women enjoy winning, but unlike men, their testosterone levels do not rise when they win. When two women play tennis, both will experience a slight increase in testosterone levels, but their testosterone goes up most regularly if they feel they have played well, whether or not they have won.

When two men with similar testosterone levels play tennis, the winner will finish the match with a much higher level than the loser. Since a boost "creates a feeling of euphoria and exhilaration," men who compete and win have an incentive not enjoyed by women to compete and win again.[68]

Evolutionists believe these hormonal differences are explained by natural selection. Achievement in physical competition confers status on males by demonstrating an ability to protect the community and to provide safe harbor for women and children.

Talent at sports is a way of climbing the male pecking order and establishing dominance. Studies of boys show that toughness in early grade school predicts male dominance in early high school. Talent in sports is also associated with male dominance in high school.[69] Great athletes, such as Michael Jordan, are often known to possess an incredibly high need to dominate.[70] Boys constantly seek ways to improve their rank in male hierarchies. Thus, one study of children shows that "Even for activities that were not competitive by nature, the boys [much more than girls] often broke into teams to facilitate competition."[71]

Mating studies clearly show that women, more than men, value athleticism, strength and aggressiveness in a partner. A 1994 study even found that the mate attraction device *most* often noticed by females was "using risk in athletics."[72] The connection between male athletic ability, status and success with women may help explain why men have a greater passion for sports than women. To be sure, men who are looking to mate value a woman who is healthy and well conditioned. But as we've already shown, competitiveness and dominance-seeking in a mate are far less attractive to men. Additionally, other women consider competitiveness and dominance-seeking by a woman to be unattractive, but men are not similarly put off by such behavior in other men.[73] Thus, the high school football captain is still more likely to pursue the homecoming queen than the best female athlete.[74]

Back to Title IX

A week before beginning to write this chapter, I saw a replay of Christine Sinclair scoring the winning goal in sudden-death overtime as the University of Portland became the 2002 NCAA women's soccer champions. It's hard to believe that the joy expressed on her face at that moment could have been exceeded by a man's in similar circumstances. Women these days get a chance to experience the thrill of victory and the agony of defeat far more often than they used to. This is good news. In addition, the physical benefits of sports can reduce a woman's lifetime risk of developing heart disease, cancer and osteoporosis.[75] Sports have also been shown to increase a female's self-esteem; and high school athletes, male and female, are less likely than nonathletes to smoke or use illegal drugs.[76]

Sports encourage both competition and teamwork. A disproportionate number of female business executives were athletes in school. As explained earlier, above-average testosterone levels and relatively masculine or androgynous personalities may help explain both the athleticism and the business success. But participation in sports is almost certainly helpful to women who would advance in the corporate world. Team sports in particular can take women beyond the small groups they tend to gravitate toward and get them competing, cooperating, and striving to reach larger goals.[77]

Jessica Gavora, a leading critic of current Title IX regulations, has joined Title IX supporters in giving thanks that she grew up in a society with opportunities for her to play high school sports. But Gavora is critical of Title IX in part because she thinks that societal forces rather than the law and regulations are largely responsible for the opportunities she enjoyed. (She provides evidence showing that girls' gains in athletics began before passage of Title IX and "the greatest gains of girls and women occurred before implementing regulations existed to enforce [the law].")[78] Moreover, in *Tilting the Playing Field,* Gavora takes seriously the evidence showing that females in general seem less interested than males in competitive sports. If success in sports gains males more admiration from their peers and from potential mates, it is not surprising that they care more about such success than females do.

Although one might expect parents to encourage sports more for their boys than for their girls, research in this country has found little evidence that they do. Parents have a strong influence on the activities of younger children, and some think that parents these days, especially fathers, "are just as able to live vicariously through their daughters' athletic exploits as those of their sons."[79] As Barbara Whitehead further explains, fathers can "channel their traditional masculine impulses and ambitions into the school and sports careers of their female offspring."[80] Support for gender neutrality among parents is evident in one recent academic study that finds "no significant overall gender difference in sports participation [of children] at younger ages"; but as children grow older, and as parents have less control over their activities, girls participate less than boys.[81] One strong advocate of women's sports ruefully acknowledges this dropout problem as girls enter their teens, and explains, "They tend to think of themselves more as cheerleaders. They think about dating and not wanting their hair messed up. They get distracted."[82]

I don't think parents or society encourages young teenage girls to drop their sports so they can become cheerleaders and start mooning over boys. It hardly seems accidental that at puberty, when estrogen levels soar, there is a "marked rise" in the female preference for cooperation over competition and an "increasing gender gap" between boys and girls in their participation in competitive sports.[83]

For the many young women who do stay with sports, a feeling of connection with teammates and coaches is a crucial element in their persistence. Christine Brooks, a track coach for women at Penn State, and other coaches of female athletes agree that women often rely on their coach for personal advice, and, unlike for men, "the social and more emotional aspect comes before the skills." Anson Dorrance, longtime coach of many NCAA women's soccer championship teams at the University of North Carolina, agrees. Dorrance underscores the importance of a coach understanding the female "connective tissue." "A word or two of private praise or a short congratulatory note for a job well done often significantly boosts performance." But the praise must be private. Both Brooks and Dorrance point out that there is always a danger that weaker female athletes will react negatively toward the abler ones through what Brooks calls "gossip and 'catty' remarks." Both agree that setting particular athletes apart can cause major problems for a team. Dorrance thinks men can be disgusted with each other and still function fine on the playing field, but women need the sense of group support; they need to be getting along. Women also have a harder time competing against each other.[84]

Tony Kornheiser, sports columnist for the *Washington Post,* was struck by how the women's Olympic basketball team practiced foul shots during warm-ups:

> They set up in a circle around the foul line, and rotate so each player takes one free throw at a time. And the entire team cheers each made shot. You never see men do that. Men don't get that involved with their teammates unless they're in a conversation about agents.[85]

A Fairfax, Virginia, basketball league called Mothers of Basketball provides an even more striking example of women desiring connection and cooperation and resisting overt competition. More than sixty women, a mix of over-thirty homemakers and professionals, play on six teams. A reporter observes:

> Susan Crawford slaps an ill-timed jump shot almost clear out of the gym. Now it is time to talk some trash. You can feel it coming. But whoa. Crawford puts her hand on the opponent's shoulder and ... *apologizes?!*

In this league, if the woman Crawford was guarding had scored, Crawford would have joined everyone on both teams in cheers.

Unlike most basketball leagues, this one has no standings and no playoffs. Indeed, there could not be any, because no one ever keeps score. It's league policy. The founder explains: "I love the game . . . [but] I'm not very good, and I didn't want to go out there and screw up and have someone yell at me. So I found 59 other people like myself."

Bringing up this odd league is sure to anger female athletes who consider it a side show that diverts attention from their own love of competitive sport. One of the articles that discussed the Mothers of Basketball catalogued all women's basketball opportunities in the Washington, D.C., area, including six standard score-keeping leagues. Almost all of the leagues listed had end-of-the-year playoffs.

But the Mothers of Basketball is clearly worthy of attention: its members include women who have played varsity basketball in high school and college but now have chosen to play in this competition-free league. One ex-collegiate player explains that if you kept score, women with less experience would not want to enter a two-point game in the final minutes. "They'd be afraid of hurting the team. Besides, the idea of this league is to encourage everyone."

Perhaps there would be more female leagues that don't keep score if the participants didn't have to face the scorn of their score-keeping sisters—scorn that is added to the jeers of their husbands and sons back home. The league founder admits that the men in their lives wonder, "Why would you play if you are not keeping score?" But she won't budge. If they kept score, "we'd get all crazy and think we're losing, and it would get unpleasant."[86] As on the playground thirty years before, the girls want to keep things pleasant while the boys want to finish the game and declare winners and losers.

The Mothers of Basketball want to play a form of the game that seems comfortably feminine. The desire to mix a demanding sport with femininity is represented on the T-shirts with the league's logo: a high-heeled sneaker perched atop a basketball. This intention also appears in what one old hand sees as the four governing principles of the league. As a reporter watched, she explained these to a newcomer: "You always try to get the ball away from whoever has it on the other team. You shoot if you can. You say, 'excuse me' if you bump into someone, and you try not to break a nail."[87]

As a thought experiment, suppose you wanted to devise a somewhat more competitive sport that might appeal to most young women. From the analysis earlier in the chapter, it's not hard to put together the recipe for such a sport. Women like stylish sports that "emphasize beauty and elegance" but also require speed, agility and strength. The sport should not have clear winners and losers; it should instead be judged by comparative rankings. Such a system would allow more than half of the competitors to do well, perhaps by exceeding their previous scores even when "losing" by a typically male standard. The sport would not involve physical contact between competitors.

As it happens, there is such a sport that attracts hordes of young women and that might enable many colleges to meet the Title IX proportionality standard: it is competitive dance. Before age two, girls are already more attracted to dance than are boys, and Brown University has found that 91 percent of students interested in dance activities are women.[88] Competitive cheerleading is a related sport with a little less dance and a little more gymnastics.

On Thanksgiving Day in 2002, ESPN featured hours of competitive dance and competitive cheerleading, with high schools and colleges from all over the country taking part. The speed, flexibility and synchronization of the dance teams were remarkable. The cheerleaders put a little less emphasis on grace and flexibility, but their strength and airborne acrobatics were spectacular. The NCAA didn't have to pull strings to get these female athletes on television; they created their own fan base.

Cheerleading these days is, as the *Washington Post* puts it, "a high powered blend of dance and gymnastics,"[89] requiring strength and conditioning as well as grace, flexibility, agility, coordination and rhythm. Cheerleaders and competitive dancers often use the weight room and visit the trainer for injured knees and wrists.[90] Schools pay for cheerleading coaches, and some even offer cheerleaders financial aid. Cheerleading attracts some of the best female athletes in the school. They often practice ten months a year, and they would like their activities to be recognized as a sport. Some wear T-shirts with logos proclaiming,

> I *am* a girl
> I *am* an athlete
> CHEERLEADING
> is MY sport [91]

But the Office of Civil Rights in the Department of Education rules that cheerleading and competitive dance are not sports, and that participants do not count for Title IX compliance purposes. The principal problem seems to be that cheerleaders and dance teams usually perform to raise spirit at contests played by other, usually male, athletes.[92] As one ex-cheerleader told me, cheerleading has a selfless quality—it's getting people to yell for other people.

Apparently it doesn't matter if these people compete as well as cheer for others. The Office of Civil Rights deems that at least half their appearances must be in a competitive setting, or their activity is not a sport. In response, the University of Maryland recently divided its cheerleading team into a "spirit squad" and a competitive squad. The latter group will perform only at competitions and will be eligible for scholarship money, a move "designed to keep Maryland in compliance with Title IX while returning some scholarships to the school's eight underfunded men's programs."

Senior team member Erin Valenti opted to stay with the spirit squad, which must fundraise to cover its costs. "They're splitting us only so they can convince whoever the head of Title IX is that cheerleading can be considered a sport," she said. "To make it a sport, you're taking out the whole reason to do cheering to begin with." That is, the cheering part.[93]

The Women's Sports Foundation's Web page contains a position statement supporting the current policies that deny sports status to cheerleaders who compete less than they cheer for others.[94] But the Web page also has a "Women's Sports on TV" section that includes listings for yoga and aerobics shows.[95] If yoga and aerobics are sports, why aren't cheerleading and dance?

Here again we see the contrast between different kinds of women. Two female sociologists think it possible that "the more competitive the sport, the more likely that women have to be androgynous or masculine to feel comfortable participating."[96] As argued earlier, masculine, high-testosterone girls are more likely to enjoy playing football. Cheerleading and competitive dance, in contrast, have qualities that far more women look for in a sport. They demonstrate beauty, grace, agility and coordination as well as strength. They mean being part of a group and not having to stand out. They make it possible for everyone to be a winner if everyone executes the routine cleanly. The competition is occasional rather than regular; there is no physical contact between competitors; the competitors are ranked rather than being declared "winner" or "loser."

In college many women want to compete sometimes, but they don't want to miss the chance to build connections, community and school spirit by cheering and dancing for other sports, both men's and women's. University of Texas psychologist David Buss, among others, has shown that women across cultures "view group-oriented and group-facilitating acts" to be more desirable than men do.[97] But the Department of Education bureaucracy insists that an activity with too much community service—if it doesn't provide enough competitive opportunities to outweigh all the support performances—is not a sport.

Of cheerleaders, Jessica Gavora says it is "a measure of the scorn Title IX activists have for what they regard as traditionally female pursuits—and the perverse reverence they have for traditionally male activities—that they refuse to recognize these talented and dedicated young women as athletes."[98] In contrast, they approve of the NCAA's "emerging sports"—which are not really emerging. As noted above, a woman can get a full scholarship for crew although she has never been in a skull in her life. In 2002, there were a grand total of 88 high school crew teams in the whole country. Ice hockey, deemed an "emerging sport" by the NCAA, is attracting little interest among girls. In 1994, there were only 200 individual high school girls participating in the whole country. In the meantime, competitive dance aside, at the high school level there are 64,000 girls competing on cheerleading squads without any assistance from Title IX.[99]

The whole issue of proportional representation of the sexes on athletic teams arises only because women would rarely be able to compete on sexually integrated teams. Title IX outlaws discrimination on the basis of sex, but of course collegiate sports begin with de facto discrimination in that men are not allowed to try out for women's teams. Donna Lopiano, executive director of the Women's Sports Foundation, asks that we appreciate female athletes in the same way that we value lightweight boxers even though they cannot beat the heavyweights.[100] But a male lightweight champion will be superior in some ways, faster and quicker than his heavyweight counterpart, for example. The lightweight female boxer or basketball or soccer player, though lighter, cannot be faster or quicker than her male counterpart.

In my discussion I have not made much of men's greater ability in almost all sports; with public policy questions in mind, I have thought it more important to lay stress on relative levels of interest in participation. But it doesn't surprise me that most women as well as most men would rather watch a men's than a women's basketball game. As Stacey Pressman, a columnist for ESPN's Page 2, explains: "I'm bored out of my skull at women's basketball games.... I prefer a few women's events, like tennis, but I refuse to be politically correct about basketball. I'm sorry, but 40 minutes of underhanded layups is not entertaining."[101] By the same token, most men as well as most women would probably prefer to watch female dancers or figure skaters.

It seems there is a connection between the sports that women say they like best and those they are best at. Some researchers think women are actually better than men at activities involving "fluent sequential action." One experiment demonstrated that even with no prior experience, women are far better than men at picking up sequential dance steps.[102] And in dance, cheerleading, figure skating and gymnastics, women's grace and flexibility can compensate for men's greater speed and power.

How different such events are from collegiate football, which among many feminists provokes special disdain because it is such a violent sport. In football, when the two lines engage, each seeks complete domination. The defensive lineman tries to run over or past his opposite number and land a "good hit"—a very hard tackle—on the ball carrier. The offensive lineman aims to "pancake" the defender, lifting him off his feet and thumping him on his back, then pinning him to the ground with his own body. In the view of Miedzian and others, "brutal" sports such as football promote a "culture of violence."[103]

The studies on the correlation between football and off-the-field violence are mixed. Several have found that college athletes, and especially football players, are many times more likely than other students to commit violent crimes.[104] On the other hand, the best study of NFL football players shows they have assault rates less than half as great as for comparable groups in the general society. These differing results are perhaps explained by the fact that the landmark NFL study—published in the statistical journal *Chance*—takes account of socioeconomic background. Another characteristic that is related to violence but was not considered in any of the studies is the fact that football players are disproportionately mesomorphs—a muscular, big-boned body type. Mesomorphs are more likely to be assertive, easily angered and deviant than are people with other body types.[105] If socioeconomic class and mesomorphic body type were considered in the college comparisons, what seems to be excessive off-the-field violence by college football players might seem less extreme or even entirely normal.[106]

In comparing crime rates of athletes with those of nonathletes, a researcher must try to determine whether athletes are picked on or coddled by those enforcing the law. One recent study finds that athletes accused of sexual assault are far more likely to be arrested than are members of the general population accused of the same crime; on the other hand, once arrested, athletes are significantly less likely to be convicted of sexual assault than are members of the general population.[107] A low conviction rate for athletes is predictable. Since a much higher proportion of accusations against athletes are prosecuted, many of the prosecutions against athletes will be based on weaker-than-average evidence. On balance, there is no evidence that athletes are coddled.

Given the population it attracts, football probably does more to mitigate off-the-field violence than to encourage it. A British study mentioned in the last chapter found that the strongest predictor of crime was unsupervised peer groups. We also saw that many boys in unsupervised peer groups try to achieve status through violence. Football teams, in contrast, involve at least as much supervision, cooperation and coordination as in any other sport, and the violence is channeled and constrained by rules.

In 1998, the *Washington Post* published a series of articles on the football team at Anacostia High School, located in one of the toughest parts of the District of Columbia. Over the years, the football coach has been to funerals of half a dozen of his players or ex-players who have died violently. But football is not to blame. As the author points out, "Football is sometimes the only constant, the single component of their fragile lives with an actual game plan where you can lose and lose and lose and still come back to win, at least on the field, if only for a season."

The coach says a lot of the kids don't know who their fathers are, much less where they are. The coach provides a partial substitute for these missing fathers by visiting homes and telling mothers "I can't take him [for the team] if I can't correct him." On trips he talks dress code:

> You're representing D.C. I'm not having no raggedy mess out here from none of y'all. We're like a class operation, not a bunch of jerks from Southeast Washington . . . hat on backward, jersey on backward, all that silly mess.

The coach cuts nobody. "If a kid decides he'd rather play football than be out on the streets in trouble, he deserves a uniform."[108]

Football surely is not making things worse for these boys. It is far more likely to be preventing violence than creating it. Research shows that adolescent boys playing school sports are less likely than others to be involved in crime.[109]

The same could easily be true of college players. Editorialist William Raspberry suggests that street basketball in some neighborhoods can be as tough as football; there are no referees yet very few fights. Fighting makes a player unpopular because it breaks up the game—and all the boys want to keep playing the game. Similarly, in college athletics, if a player is violent off the field, he gets kicked off the team. He lets his teammates down, and *he can't play.* In this way the male love of sport fights crime.[110] Sports can civilize young men by mixing great fun with a sense of connection and responsibility to others, as well as rules that can channel their otherwise inchoate, competitive, dominance-seeking natures.

Another of the macho sports, wrestling, has been decimated by Title IX. Wrestling is growing at the high school level, where it attracts nearly 250,000 high school boys (and 3,400 girls). This makes it the sixth most popular male sport at the high school level. Intercollegiate wrestling has been around for close to a hundred years, and it ranks fourth in revenue production among all NCAA championships.[111] But under Title IX, between 1992 and 1999 alone, forty-three collegiate wrestling teams were discontinued.[112]

Unlike football players, wrestlers garner little glory on most campuses. And unlike football players, wrestlers come in all sizes. But given their height and weight, their toughness is unsurpassed. Wrestling is arguably the most physically and psychologically exhausting of sports. Wrestlers spend much of their time with their faces being ground into a mat. Everyone gets facial bruises, scratches and cuts, and there is the usual assortment of other athletic injuries as well. Recruiters for the SEALS and the Marines frequently bump into each other at wrestling tournaments because these professional warriors share with wrestlers "an intriguing predisposition to love" activities that make them feel "mentally and physically miserable." They also share an attraction to controlled and regulated violence. The wrestling mat has been called "a place to train gladiators."[113]

Wrestling has produced more than the usual number of testimonials about how a sport can turn lives around. In 2002, the *Washington Post* published a long feature on a 112-pound regional high school champion named Will Powars, who had a host of learning disabilities in addition to being short. Powars' mother said that wrestling had been her son's "saving grace" when school was not going well. "It really boosted his self-esteem, and that seemed to make all the difference for him." Powars himself said he used to doze off in school and run around afterward until wrestling "taught me how to focus and how to work hard. I realized that if I could be good at wrestling, I could be good at school, too."[114]

Speaker of the House Dennis Hastert was another lost boy until wrestling brought him some discipline and motivation. The late Senator Paul Wellstone thought wrestling did even more for him. A 1998 news story reported that when Wellstone was young he "didn't like much of anything, including himself." Wellstone described himself as "'a tough kid, in some trouble and headed for more.... Wrestling really saved me. It gave me self-confidence and self-respect.'"

Hastert fears that by dropping wrestling in colleges, administrators also indirectly diminish the number of qualified coaches needed to keep the high school programs going in the future.[115] In any case, the loss of the college programs is bound to reduce high school participation rates because athletes will no longer have college teams to shoot for.

Taking sex differences seriously means recognizing that dropping a sport like wrestling leaves many short but tough boys without a sport or other activity where they can bond with other boys and show their mettle in a rule-bound environment. Some of these boys seem certain to end up in the "unsupervised peer groups" that lead to violent crime.

Sports, like a father's rough-and-tumble play, probably help control male violence. Yet even if they don't, the current Title IX regime remains unjust. In their behavior and their voiced opinions, males show that they care more about competitive sports than females do. I have presented evidence showing some deep causes for these differences. The contrasting effects of estrogen and testosterone on interest in competitive activity at puberty, the more typically masculine behavior of girls exposed to extra testosterone *in utero*, the male toddler's attraction to playing with balls as opposed to the female toddler's attraction to dance—all lend credence to the conclusion that the greater love that boys and men show for sports is not merely socially constructed.

Moreover, interest aside, boys *need* sports more than girls do because boys have more difficulty than girls in making friends.

Eleanor Maccoby, perhaps the world's leading expert on sex differences in children, notes, "Boys' friendships tend to be less intimate than those of girls," and they are "based primarily on interest in, and participation in, the same activities." Among the activities boys love most are competitive games.[116]

The evolutionary psychologist Anne Campbell sees that a male's world is always "implicitly competitive and this pervasive sense of competition colours their sense of identity and relationships with others." They won't share depression, anxiety or fear with other men because these emotions show vulnerability. They reveal such feelings to women because they are not competing with women. Even then, "Deep inside, men are always on their own against the world."[117]

It can be lonely to be on your own against the world. Male connectedness depends on activity and often competitive activity. The less athletic males may compete via computer or video games, but far more males play traditional, long-established sports. Until some recent back problems, I had played tennis and squash all my life. I know that for me and for most of those I competed with, it doesn't get much better than having the opportunity to test ourselves against great competitors who are also fine sportsmen. I bonded with those sportsmen over many years, but now I never see them. Women in similar circumstances would still get together and talk; for me and my chums, when the activity ended, so did the connection. As important as our friendship was, talking would not bring it back.

The therapist and educator Michael Gurion makes my point more generally when he says,

> Male friendship is fragile in ways female friendship is not because male friendship is often not talk-dependent. It is proximity-and-activity-dependent.... As a result, it is harder to sustain than female friendship. When the war, task, work, or life-period of friendship is over, the friendship is generally over....
>
> Because females have the emotional advantage of being able to talk so much more thoroughly than males, they can get more out of fewer bonds. Males don't get as much emotional stimulation from two or three relationships as females do; they need lots of relationships, surrounding lots of activities, among lots of elders and peers, to get the same quantity and quality of emotional stimulation.[118]

I don't think it's an accident that, though my wife and I both attended single-sex colleges, her reunions almost never invite the husbands, whereas my college reunions always include the wives. Our wives don't want us because their conversations are inhibited when we are present; we want them around because they loosen our tongue-tied exchanges. The activities that brought us males together are gone, so when we gather we are at a loss as to how to proceed. Even with the best of old friends, we often circle around each other, wondering how much of our lives to expose. Our wives keep the conversations going and help us avoid the awkward silences.

Conclusion

Consider football again and the special animus that feminists feel towards it. The sport's violence is only part of the reason for this. At large NCAA Division 1-A universities, as many as 100,000 fans can flock to the Saturday football games. Football consumes 26 percent of the athletic budgets at these schools, but it also brings in 43 percent of the revenues.[119]

As many as a hundred young men are on a typical large university's football team, although dozens of them may never play. At public forums, Title IX advocates may speak contemptuously of these "hapless practice dummies." They are puzzled by what they see as the stupidity of grown men willing to be on a team when they never actually get to play.[120] And they are annoyed that the practice dummies appear to share in the "status, prestige, and preferential treatment" that football players get in comparison with almost any female athlete.[121]

Why are men, in all sports, more willing than women to ride the bench? *Males,* after all, have the big egos. But men will ride the bench because it allows them to connect with other men, a connection that's difficult for them to make apart from activities such as sport. The benchwarmer who plays in practice and cheers on game day is, throughout, a member of a team on a mission.

In the *60 Minutes* show on Title IX, the University of Maryland's athletic director, Debbie Yow, was asked how walk-on wrestlers react when told they can't come out for the team because of the Title IX numbers problem. Yow said, "They cry. A number of them do because it's so devastating to them to not be able to participate."

Similarly, Troy Aikman, the superstar pro quarterback, hung on in the NFL longer than his doctors advised. He suffered ten concussions during his career and four in his last twenty games. It wasn't the glory that kept him going against his better judgment. At the tear-filled news conference when he finally retired, he lamented, "I'm going to miss the camaraderie with my teammates. I'm going to miss the locker room after a big game."[122]

The benchwarmer is part player and part fan. He can practice against the star and share in the locker room joy after the big game. Men will put up with the benchwarming just to be a part of the team. Norma Cantu, a proponent and previous administrator of Title IX regulations, explains that women "are smarter than men. They decide that with no scholarship and no playing time they are better off doing other things." In other words, women offered the same type of opportunity as male counterparts—the seat on the bench—will often choose to pursue other interests.[123] They don't have the same need for sport as men.

Society needs activities that keep males like Denny Hastert and Paul Wellstone in school. The close attention that Title IX advocates pay to ratios of male and female college athletes seems even more misguided when one considers the fact that in high schools and colleges, girls outnumber boys in almost every extracurricular activity—student government, honor societies, school newspapers, debating clubs and choir, among others. Sports are one of the rare exceptions.[124] Moreover, girls are outperforming boys in virtually every academic category. An important 2000 Department of Education study of forty-four indicators of academic equity found that "Females are just as likely as males to use computers at home and at school"; that "Females and males take similar mathematics and science courses in high school"; and that "Females have consistently outperformed males in reading and writing.... The writing skills of female eighth-graders were comparable with those of 11th-grade males."[125]

The National Urban League reported in 2000 that only 37 percent of blacks in college are male. Men currently represent only 44 percent of all college students, and the federal government predicts that by 2010 the percentage will be down to 41 percent.[126] Women are also more likely than men to finish college—currently earning 25 percent more bachelor degrees than men do.[127] Yet Title IX bureaucrats tell the University of Wisconsin at Madison that although women now represent 50 percent of their intercollegiate athletes, this is not good enough. There are more female than male students, so women should have more than half the slots.[128]

Isn't the more serious problem that so few men are making it to college in the first place? Athletic opportunities commensurate with men's higher interest in sports will help address the larger issue of their lagging achievements in other areas.

Title IX began with noble intentions: giving interested women access to athletic participation. It became a pernicious form of social engineering only when it became part of a numbers game and an ideological agenda insisting that the way women are socialized (rather than the way they *are*) keeps them from loving sports as much as men do. Only when we begin to take sex differences seriously enough to see that men are intrinsically more attracted to sports—and need sports competition more than women do—will we be able to design public policies that are just, functional and sensible.

PART 4

WOMEN WANT THEIR WAY, TOO

8 NURTURING THE YOUNG

A friend of mine, she cries at night,
And she calls me on the phone—
Sees babies everywhere she goes,
And she wants one of her own.
She's waited long enough, she says,
And still he can't decide.
Pretty soon she'll have to choose,
And it tears her up inside.
She's scared—scared to run out of time.

To the beat of an insistent drum ticking off the seconds of a biological clock, country singer Bonnie Raitt's "Nick of Time" tells a story about something she says was on her mind and in her heart.[1] She was inspired to write it by friends in their middle to late thirties whose boyfriends refused to commit to marriage and children. Her friends cried themselves to sleep.

Raitt had been singing for a long time without becoming a star, but this particular song, with its haunting tune and poignant lyrics, was an enormous hit. In 1989, Raitt's rendition of "Nick of Time" won her two Grammys.

Ultimately, when the right man finally comes along, the life of the woman in Raitt's song is transformed from one of tears and broken promises to one fulfilled by "love in the nick of time." But many women do not find the right love in time.

Siobhan Darrow, a CNN war correspondent with a strong taste for adventure, writes in her autobiography, *Flirting with Danger,* of her late thirties "dream of motherhood" and obsession with her biological clock.[2] And the noted psychiatrist Kay Jamison, in *An Unquiet Mind*, calls her failure to have children of her own "the most intolerable regret" of her life.[3]

Sometimes the regrets are mixed with anger as well as sorrow. While most of the rage inspired by the sexual revolution is aimed at men, the "no baby blues" rage is often aimed at leaders of the feminist movement. In *Motherhood Deferred,* Anne Taylor Fleming lets loose at godmothers of feminism "Gloria! Germaine! Kate!" as she, "an agnostic midlife feminist," sends up "silent prayers to the fertility gods on high."[4] Similarly, an Australian feminist newswoman nearing her forties finds her life pointless, despite a great job and "trendy" inner-city pad. She is childless and angry: "Angry that I was so foolish to take the word of my feminist mothers as gospel. Angry that I was daft enough to believe female fulfillment came with a leather briefcase."[5]

Having children may not be central to a woman's happiness, but most mothers think it is. Ninety-three percent of all mothers think their children are a source of happiness all or most of the time.[6] Eighty-six percent of mothers of children under age eighteen say their relationship to their children is crucial to their personal happiness (10 on a 10-point scale).

These findings may be hard to reconcile with other research. Multiple studies of married people find that children depress marriage satisfaction levels in the middle years of marriage,[7] and some studies find that happiness is lower and that mental health problems are more common for women with children than for women without children. This result appears despite the general association of marriage with higher levels of physical and mental health.[8] There are studies, however, which find that having children in the home is associated with better health for women.[9]

That children might make a woman less satisfied with her marriage doesn't mean they do not add to her happiness. It's possible that children make women happy while simultaneously increasing stress in marriage.

Sylvia Hewlett's best-selling *Creating a Life: Professional Women and the Quest for Children,* makes it abundantly clear that large numbers of middle-aged career women regret being childless. When beginning her research, Hewlett had intended to write a turn-of-the-century book celebrating the lives of women of achievement. She had planned to write about mentors and their strategies for breaking through the glass ceiling. But after interviewing the first ten women, she was struck by the fact that they were all childless. After delicate probing, she learned that none of the ten had chosen their fate.

Hewlett then commissioned a national survey of high-achieving women (those making more than $60,000 in midcareer). She found that when these women graduated from college, only 14 percent of them knew that they did not want to have children. But in fact, 33 percent were childless, and of those involved in corporate

America, the figure was 42 percent. In her follow-up interviews Hewlett was "continually surprised—and humbled—by how raw and near to the surface the emotions" were. One woman told her it was "frightening, this yearning for a child—it's hard to fathom the desperate urgency." Another revealed the "gnawing hunger in the very cells of [her] body."[10]

Hewlett found that "hype trumped reality on the fertility front." Fully 89 percent of the younger high-achieving women thought they could get pregnant in their forties. Among the older high achievers, more than a quarter of those between 41 and 55 said they would still like to get pregnant, but only 1 percent of all those in that age group had had a first child after age 39.

It was different for the high-achieving men. First of all, well under half as many were childless at middle age. Second, their desire for kids was, as one female respondent said, "nonurgent" and "abstract." Her husband wanted kids, but his eyes were not drawn to other people's children, "while mine [were] drawn like magnets."[11]

Even among those high-achieving women who had children, 32 percent of those over forty had only one, and for many this too was "a source of deep regret." One spoke of an "aching loss" and wondered how "an imagined child [could] provoke such deep grief."[12] In 1996, at the age of 49, prominent high achiever Hilary Clinton remarked that she too might like to have another child.[13]

Unfortunately, the cure can be just as bad as the ailment. Aging women undergoing infertility treatments are "whiplashed by a treatment regime" that jerks them from "hope to despair."[14] Of those undergoing infertility treatment, 50 percent of women (but 15 percent of men) say this is the most upsetting experience of their lives.[15] A Harvard Medical School study found that "women undergoing infertility treatments had levels of depression comparable to patients with AIDS and cancer."[16] And childless women who miscarry have depression rates five times higher than those of comparable women who are not pregnant.[17]

Baby Times Are Good Times?

My wife and I have three sons, and as I've said, she teaches at an all-male college. About a decade ago she decided that she was being overexposed to testosterone, so she joined a women's aerobics class, which she has attended faithfully three times a week ever since.

One of the things she comments on is how nice and solicitous these fiftyish women are. Her experience is not uncommon. Studies regularly find that women are more empathetic, tender-minded and nurturing than are men.[18] Moreover, daughters are more likely than sons to take care of a sick parent, and women are more likely than men to take care of the family pet.[19]

It does not seem to be only compulsion that leads to these patterns. National surveys by UCLA's Higher Education Research Institute regularly find that about 68 percent of female freshmen but only 50 percent of male freshmen say that "helping others in difficulty" is a very important or essential life objective.[20] The nurturing tendencies of women can even have a beneficial impact on their health. One study finds that single women—whether in their seventies or in their twenties—can have significant reductions in blood pressure if they care for a dog or a cat.[21]

In my wife's aerobics experience, nurturing tendencies intensify when one of the women brings in an infant grandchild. The women cluster around the lucky grandmother, and most of them would like a chance to hold the baby. Everyone knows, however, that the infant will be unhappy if there is too much commotion or if there are too many unfamiliar women holding it. Each would be sorry and, perhaps, embarrassed to make the baby cry, so the women try to restrain themselves. But the ones who do get to hold the infant feel very fortunate indeed.

The behavior of these women is reminiscent of other female primates. As Sarah Hrdy writes, "Primatologists have long been aware of the magnetic appeal of babies. Young females from one troop will kidnap an infant from another." There are even recorded cases of a female monkey adopting a baby from another species and spontaneously lactating to suckle it. What seem to count most in eliciting such qualities are "generalized signals advertising the baby's vulnerability and newness."[22]

Actually raising an infant day after day is not always pleasurable. Mothers are often bone-tired, and marriages are sometimes strained as mothers hope for more help than they actually receive from fathers, or as fathers feel neglected.[23] One study finds that infancy competes with puberty as mothers' least favorite period of childrearing. However, infants soon become toddlers, and mothers enjoy caring for toddlers more than any other stage of childrearing.[24]

Even in their child's infancy there are signs that women, on balance, find being a mother enjoyable. One such indication is provided by the results of careful studies of first births—the most difficult for most mothers.[25] One study asked women if they agreed that "raising children and keeping house is more interesting than the kind of work most men do for a living."[26] The same women were asked this question both at the end of their second trimester and again three weeks after delivery. Although the second trimester is considered the happiest for most pregnant women, *after* giving birth and in the midst of the sleepless nights, 10 percent *more* women—62 percent as opposed to 52 percent before birth—now agreed with this statement. Satisfaction increases as the infant becomes just a little older. Another study that compared preferences for staying home versus returning to work found that more women chose the home alternative three months after becoming a mother than did so shortly after birth.[27]

Certainly women can be unpleasantly surprised by how they react to having to take care of a young child. The award-winning novelist Alice McDermott seems convinced, however, that in general women are pleasantly surprised by their reaction. She recalls a graduate school seminar where a middle-aged female student objected to writer Marilyn French's depiction of motherhood as an "unending mound of dirty dishes" and an endless stream of urine in the eye. The woman said that her time at home with her children was the most glorious of her life.

McDermott remembers that "we twenty-somethings in the class responded with pitying smiles. Clearly childbirth had addled the poor woman's mind." Yet a decade later,

> those of us who had so rationally disabused our older friend of any romantic notions about reproduction were sending birth announcements and gushing letters to one another across the country. The letters read like book jacket blurbs for some Vatican marriage manual. "Becoming a mother is the best thing I've ever done." "It's like floating in warm milk." "I could fill a stadium with babies."

McDermott wonders why the bliss they feel never appears in her or others' novels. After considering alternative explanations, she voices the suspicion that

> What we [writers] feel for our children is perhaps too satisfying, too marvelous to be carried fully into fiction. Fiction requires the attendant threat, the dramatic reversal. . . . [W]ithout them any depiction of our joy might appear overstated. We hesitate to include in our fiction what so often strikes us in life as something too good to be true.[28]

Mothers and Children in Differing Cultures

A female friend of ours, divorced with two children, remarried a decade later and had a baby boy named Ted. Both she and her new husband were at the time extremely busy professionals; her daughter by the first marriage was entering puberty. A number of years later, the daughter told them that there had been so little parental supervision in those years that she could have done "lots of things" if she had wanted to. Her mother asked her why she had not done them. She answered, "I knew that if you had caught me, you wouldn't have let me take care of Ted."

As we have already seen, in all cultures that have been studied, girls like dolls and play parenting more than boys do.[29] Four-year-old boys asked to care for a baby watch passively, while four-year-old girls tend to it actively.[30] Among both monkeys and humans, young females persist in seeking contact with infants even when the mother tries to keep them away.[31] Compared with males, female preadolescent rhesus monkeys raised in complete social isolation and therefore immune to the pressures of socialization are less aggressive and more nurturing toward infants presented to them for the first time.[32]

Among mammals, human males spend much more time with children than males of most other species do.[33] Nevertheless, the time that human mothers spend with their children dwarfs the time spent by human fathers. Sarah Hrdy notes that a baby born to a foraging mother living in a strenuous environment, such as that of the nomadic !Kung San tribe of the Kalahari Desert, will be carried by its mother some four thousand miles during its first years. The mother will provide its "cradle, protection, mobility, breakfast, midmorning juice, lunch, and dinner."[34] In societies all over the world—in Africa, Latin America, Japan and the United States—children age three to ten have been found to spend anywhere from two and a half to twelve times more time with their mothers than with their fathers. The sex differences are even greater in studies that focus on infants and toddlers.[35] Despite the general gender equality found in tribes such as the !Kung San, fathers in that community provide less than 7 percent of the care for children under two.[36] In the United States, cohabiting couples, compared with married couples, have a less traditional division of household labor with one notable exception: the care of infants.[37]

Sweden is a country that has made determined efforts to bring about a more androgynous pattern of child care. In the 1970s, Sweden changed some maternal leave policies to parental leave. Subsequently, one month of paid leave was made available to a family *only* if the father took it. At one stage there was a "massive advertising campaign" encouraging fathers to take care of their children.[38] Yet despite the incentive, fathers still did not make child care a priority. In one study of Swedish parenting patterns, many fathers who had planned to take leave later changed their minds. Others took leave at the same time as their wives. Even in families where fathers took leave and expressed a desire to be the primary caretaker of their new infant, the traditional parenting differences emerged nonetheless. For example, the "mothers displayed affectionate behavior, vocalized, smiled, tended, held, disciplined and soothed the infant more than the fathers did."[39]

Proponents of the Swedish measures were trying to create a much more androgynous society, but the results they sought have not materialized. Swedish mothers are more than twice as likely to take any leave as Swedish fathers, and their leaves last, on average, six times as long. One supporter of the Swedish gender equality goals calls the results "a disappointment if not a downright failure."[40]

The Israeli kibbutzim provide an even more compelling example of the staying power of traditional gender roles in child care. Begun in the early twentieth century, the kibbutzim aimed quite explicitly to break down historic, stereotypical sex roles. Children were placed in houses apart from their parents. Communal kitchens and laundries were created to further emancipate women from domestic obligations and allow them to work outside the home as men did.[41]

But the idea that children should be raised in common proved to be a major stumbling block. Over time, more and more kibbutzim revisited the question of where children should live and decided they should stay with their families. Today the family is "the basic unit of kibbutz social structure."[42]

The movement back toward family-centered child care was led by young mothers whose adamant lobbying convinced their husbands to vote in favor of the change.[43] The mothers' desire to devote more time to maternal activities violated the principles of the kibbutz and contravened the wishes of the men in their community. But the women's will prevailed. Although both parents continue to work outside the home while nurseries care for their young children, at the end of the day, when mothers get back home, they "are still far more frequently involved in child-care duties and in spontaneous interaction with the child" than fathers are.[44]

Biological Sources of Nurturing Differences

The failure of the Swedish and Israeli efforts to transform nurturing roles is powerful evidence that socialization alone cannot explain traditional child care roles. The similarities already mentioned between female humans and other female primates also suggest that nature must be considered important in explaining sex-differentiated patterns of childrearing.

Indeed, the sex differences in nurturing appear at an astonishingly early age—before any socialization could have occurred. One experiment exposed day-old infants to a battery of sounds including wild animal calls, computer-generated language and the unhappy cries of other infants. All the babies cried the most when they heard the sounds of other crying infants, but the female babies cried longer.[45] Another experiment exposed children age twelve to twenty months to the distress of other people. Girls responded with more empathy, and they were less likely to seem affectively indifferent.[46]

There are also pronounced increases in engagement with babies when women are in the midst of menarche or after they have given birth. One important study found that twelve- and thirteen-year-old girls who had gone through menarche were more interested in pictures of infants than girls of the same age who had not.[47]

Some scholars who emphasize socialization as the source of gender differences in nurturing behavior point out that in both the menarche and post-childbirth periods, social pressures to act "feminine" are at their height.[48] But perhaps the social expectations exist precisely because hormones cause females to become more nurturing at these times.[49]

Experiments on mice also indicate that biology is responsible for some of the sex differences in nurturing behavior of new mothers and fathers. Specific genes identified with maternal behavior have been identified. Moreover, injection of estrogen and progesterone can make virgin females much more interested in infants.[50] Similar experiments with males have "not been very successful" in eliciting nurturing behavior, a result attributed to male androgens blocking the effects of the nurturing hormones.[51]

The most important nurturing hormone is the peptide oxytocin. In both males and females, oxytocin promotes bonding and a calm, relaxed emotional state. In men it is released in large quantities during orgasm. In women, oxytocin is released in large quantities during pregnancy and breastfeeding.[52] In virgin female monkeys, injection of this hormone produces maternal behavior and a friendly demeanor.[53] In humans, women have more neural receptors for oxytocin than men do, and the number of receptors further increases during pregnancy.[54]

Oxytocin and prolactin, another hormone that surges during pregnancy and breastfeeding, change women's personalities in ways that make them better mothers. These hormones seem to make routine more tolerable. Compared with other women their age, pregnant and breastfeeding women have been found to be more tolerant of monotony. They are also more prone to please and obey—a trait some researchers think is nature's way of making them more ready "to 'take orders' from their babies."[55] Even the act of stroking her baby releases oxytocin in the mother, causing her to feel a "beatific calm" and somewhat sedated.[56]

Sarah Hrdy, author of a landmark 700-page book on mothers and infants, calls oxytocin "the kindest of natural opiates." Many women feel euphoric or exhilarated while nursing. A few even have orgasms.[57]

When nursing releases oxytocin in the mother, it is believed that some of the oxytocin reaches the child through the breast milk. By inducing a mutually pleasurable experience for mother and child, oxytocin increases the feeling of mutual attachment. Blood samples show that the more that oxytocin peaks during breastfeeding and the longer the time spent breastfeeding, the more mothers report feeling emotionally accessible and attached to their children. Breastfeeding mothers—more than bottle-feeders or "thwarted breastfeeders," who planned to breastfeed but were unable to—feel worse and are quicker to respond when their babies cry.[58]

Just as longer periods of breastfeeding promote attachment, so too does day-by-day contact. Under extreme circumstances of resource scarcity, mothers have been known to commit infanticide.[59] But this usually happens before mother and infant have established regular contact. Attachment grows stronger and stronger with increased contact. This process takes place with adoptive babies as well as those naturally born to the mother.[60] But nursing induces a profound connection. In Hrdy's words,

> Once nursing begins, bondage is a perfectly good description for the ensuing chain of events. The mother is endocrinologically, sensually, as well as neurologically transformed in ways likely to serve the infant's needs and contribute to her own posterity.... As the baby sucks, the mother experiences an exquisite relief from the pressure of milk that has built up in her glands. The baby sucking on the receiving end of this let-down reflex brings with it pleasurable sensations, bordering on and blending into the erotic....

Hrdy then discusses her own experience:

> My children's deliciousness rendered *me* more willing to be consumed by *them,* to give up bodily resources, and in my own contemporary example, most importantly, time—time, time, time ... and so to subordinate my own aspirations to their desires so we could all (more or less) contentedly take our places at posterity's table.[61]

Of course, fathers also bond to their babies. Many fathers react to their infant's crying with increased cortisol levels and increased arousal just as mothers do.[62] Moreover, as we've already seen, testosterone drops when fathers have a child, and this facilitates nurturing.[63] In fact, there is evidence of "an inverse relationship between free testosterone and nurturance—both within and between the sexes."[64] (The evidence comes in part from a study of girls with Turner's syndrome, who have an extra female chromosome and no exposure to male hormones. These girls have "an exaggerated interest in dolls, babies and mothering.")[65] Thus the bonding and nurturing instincts are not as strong in men as in women.[66] A father does not get a "neurochemical high" from cuddling a baby in the way a mother does.[67]

A mother can recognize her own infant's cry a few hours after birth; a father is much less likely to have this ability.[68] Men and women also have different physiological reactions to certain infant cries. In one experiment, the hormone levels of new parents were measured as they were exposed to recordings of day-old infants crying. One cry was that of a waking infant wanting to be fed, the other, that of a baby being circumcised. At the first sign of real distress—the circumcision—both mothers and fathers reacted with alacrity. But as Hrdy explains,

> If the cry was merely "I want" rather than "Help! Help!" the mother was the quicker to respond. It's possible that the mother's greater responsiveness and the physiological reactions that accompany it are learned. More probably her lower threshold for responding to infant signals is innate.[69]

A very different type of study found that childless women exposed to a video of a crying baby experienced acceleration of heart rate while childless men experienced a deceleration.[70] Mothers are lighter sleepers; fathers are less likely to hear the cry at night and more likely to be annoyed than concerned by it if they do.[71]

When mothers are with infants, there is a lot going on. In effect, a subtle conversation is taking place:

> During a feeding, dozens of events occur. The baby sucks, winces, squirms, relaxes, lets go of the nipple, burps, falls asleep, hiccups, smiles, roots, cries, opens his eyes, tenses his face or softens his expression. His mother rocks, sits still, hums, is silent, adjusts her position, tenses, relaxes, gazes, smiles, talks, pats, strokes, lifts the baby, puts him down. *Each event is a remark.*[72]

It is hard to determine whether the interactions of fathers with their infant children are similarly complex because it is difficult to find men who spend enough time with their babies to be studied in a natural setting. One researcher, however, attempted to do so by placing a microphone on infants age two weeks to three months. On average the ten fathers verbally communicated to their infants for 38 seconds per day. Moreover, "Fathers' verbalization decreased over time and mothers' increased."[73]

Researchers love to study role-reversed families, but they have a hard time finding them. One study of nontraditional families found on follow-up, just two years later, that only one-quarter of them were maintaining their nontraditional ways.[74] It is especially hard to find role reversals that involve fathers taking care of infants. Where one does find them, researchers discover that men simply do not recognize or appreciate the way that babies can "converse." Fathers are not as sensitive as mothers to the babies' abilities and methods of communication, and they become bored far more easily than mothers do.[75]

A researcher studying one male academic who attempted to adapt gender-neutral roles within his marriage found that he came up with "tricks" for getting through extended contact with his son. These tricks consisted of "toys and events which kept the baby distracted, and which thus decreased the father's level of attention."[76] The father told about trying "to get things done" during the time he was responsible for his child. He couldn't stand the crying and fussing, when there seemed to be no reason for it. Sometimes he would "go pound his fist in the wall." When he and his wife, also an academic, were both home at night, he would do housework rather than infant care. "I can whip dinner together in ten minutes," he explained, "but I'm not very original when it comes to seeing why my son or daughter is crying, what the problem is. Where she [his wife] could figure it out a lot better, or has the patience to do it."

When asked about interacting with the baby, the father emphasized that he was trying to teach him things—how to hold his bottle, how to roll over. This is a common pattern with fathers; they like to interact with children by teaching or playing. This repertoire works better when the child is above eighteen months in age, so it isn't surprising that research reveals that fathers prefer spending time with older children.[77] The academic quoted above "tremendously" enjoyed his two-year-old daughter. He noted that she could dress herself, take care of herself, go to the bathroom by herself. And she was more verbal, which meant she had "reached a stage where she and I can interact more."[78]

This well-educated father is not alone in his feeling about infant care. A study using national data finds that fathers with young children help more around the house with tasks such as dishwashing and household cleaning than fathers with older children, but they are not significantly more likely to help with child care.[79]

Mothers, more than fathers, simply find it pleasurable to care for infants. But with the greater attachment comes greater vulnerability. As noted above, the baby's cry disturbs them more. Moreover, mothers can find it excruciating to be away from their children for extended periods.[80] Mothers also seem to be more affected than fathers if their child is aberrant or performs poorly; thus mothers with delinquent children are more likely to be unhappy and in poor health.[81]

One study looked at families where each parent performed at least 35 percent of the child care. Fathers as well as mothers reported that mothers were more involved emotionally in their children's lives, and that mothers felt an intense connection with their child that fathers did not feel. Mothers worried more about their absent children and found separation from their children harder to endure.

> The women had more difficulty concentrating on other tasks when they themselves were not caretaking. "Fathers simply put a hold on their parenting functions when away from their children in a way women rarely do." Physical separation tended to leave the mothers feeling "empty and confused" as though "a part of her is missing."[82]

Additionally, divorce brings more depression for women with children than for women without them. This is not true for men.[83] After divorce, only one in six fathers maintains regular contact with his children.[84] Indeed, even fathers who have been good family men often lose contact with their children. Women who do not have custody are far more likely than men to maintain close contact.[85] We hear much talk today about the new sensitive father who provides hands-on child care, but in fact there has never been a time in our history when such a large number of fathers have been absent from their children's lives.[86]

Men tend to see their wife and children as a package deal. Even in a stable marriage, they do more child care and play with children more if they have a good relationship with their wife. On the other hand, the mother's attachment to her child "is not affected by the quality of the couple's relationship."[87]

Evolutionary Explanations

Evolutionists think that the patterns described above make perfect sense. The enumerated hormonal differences that foster female attachment and commitment are the result of a process of natural selection determining that women would have more success getting their genes through to subsequent generations if they cared more about children, and especially young children, than fathers did.

The core of the theory is the same as that which explains differences in sexuality. Both mating effort and parental effort advance reproduction. Men have plenty of sperm; the challenge for them is to find receptive women. Women have far fewer eggs; the greater challenge for them is to ensure that their eggs produce children and that these children thrive.

Evolutionists think that in the environment of evolutionary adaptation (EEA), men did little direct parenting. Aside from the fact that it would take time away from efforts to gain further mating opportunities, there is also the problem of uncertain paternity. Nurturing a child that may carry another man's genes would interfere with efforts to pass on one's own genes. Mothers, on the other hand, know which children are theirs. They also see firsthand that their babies are born with undeveloped brains and motor skills—thus needing lots of care.

During the EEA, human infants would not have been able to thrive—even live—without almost constant contact with their mothers. Because the fat and protein levels of human milk are low, babies need more of it every few hours; that is one reason why mothers carry their babies for months if not years while gathering food.[88] Human infants are born vulnerable and dependent upon at least one close relative, which could be a father, grandmother, niece or sibling. But Hrdy notes that in the majority of hunter-gatherer societies (thought to be the closest of existing societies to the EEA), "care of infants by fathers is unusual."[89]

> What makes a mother maternal is that she is (invariably) at the scene, hormonally primed, sensitive to infant signals, and related to the baby. These factors lower her threshold for giving of herself to satisfy the infant's needs. Once her milk comes in, the mother's urge to nurture grows stronger still.[90]

As I have already argued, women are attracted to men who can protect and provide for them and their children. This desire naturally encourages women to be attracted to dominant men. But dominant men are not usually kind, considerate and nurturing. And women also have a taste for men with these traits. Some women try to tame cads and then marry them (the romance-novel strategy). Others seek "nice guy" dads who will stick around and attend to the needs of a mother and her children.

Given their capacities and predispositions, men advertise their strength and looks and/or their commitment. The dad who emphasizes the quality rather than the quantity of progeny may do just fine.[91] But the good guys in this scenario are protectors and providers—not regular and enthusiastic caregivers for infants. One study of 186 societies finds that mothers are the principal or almost exclusive caretakers of infants (age two and under) in 90 percent of the societies. In 4 percent of the societies, the fathers have a "regular close relationship" with infants; in 20 percent they have rare or no "proximity"; in the vast majority of societies—76 percent—fathers have either frequent or occasional proximity. In most societies, fathers do hold their infants from time to time, but the societies in which men never hold their infants outnumber those in which men hold them regularly. And holding an infant is not the same as caring for it. One scholar sums up the situation as follows: "Human males around the world do very little caregiving during infancy."[92]

If women don't bond with their babies, their offspring won't survive. But why do women seem so attached to *all* babies? For one thing, caring about another woman's baby makes it more likely that she will care about yours. Moreover, Hrdy and others think "baby-lust improves the chances a new mother will care for her own baby."[93] Studies show that from early childhood to old age, females are more interested in infants than males. This is especially pronounced among children and adolescents, where there seems to be a "perceptual bias" that may lead young females "to seek out interactions with infants and allow them to gain important parenting skills."[94] Among other primates, early play-parenting is associated with later survival of one's offspring.[95]

Through history, women more often resided with their male partner's kin than with their own. *Allomothers,* female caretakers aside from the mother, could be crucial to the survival of young children. (Indeed, unlike most species, humans use the help of others in giving birth.)[96] But if no blood relatives were around, it became especially important for women to develop a capacity to form reciprocal and intimate relationships.[97]

The "tend-and-befriend" strategy discussed earlier is well suited to encouraging others to care for mothers and their children. There is recent evidence that success in befriending others can save a woman's life. One study followed the progress of patients dismissed from hospitals after recovery from congestive heart failure. For women, the absence of emotional support in their community increased death rates more than eightfold. For men, it made no difference at all.[98]

Women are more apt to have the qualities needed to establish intimate and mutually supportive relationships than men are. Experiments show, for instance, that across cultures women are better than men at recognizing emotions in faces. This talent seems to be more pronounced in women with higher levels of estrogen. Women are also better at detecting mood from body posture and gesture.[99]

Women find special pleasure in small groups of women—a preference that gives them practice at establishing intimate friendships. Today, women's groups may be book or investment clubs or aerobics classes. In an earlier era, they were quilting circles. Even in the relative isolation of 1950s suburbia, the Tupperware party helped fill the void.[100] All this "connection" can protect offspring. As we mentioned earlier, in neighborhoods where women borrow food from each other, lunch together and help each other with problems, crime rates are lower.[101]

Feminism

Recently, a number of prominent "first-wave" feminists have written about children and motherhood in rapturous terms. One reviewer called Anne Roiphe's book *Fruitful* "an elegiac essay on baby-hunger, mother-love, child-worship, parental passion."[102] For Roiphe, who complains that feminism has turned "a collective back on biology," motherhood is the most important thing in her life.[103]

Starting with her book *The Second Stage*, Betty Friedan has given increasing attention to women's "needs to give and get love and nurture, tender loving care."[104] When she uses phrases such as "profound human impulses" and "compelling life urges," Friedan hints that, like Roiphe, she thinks biology explains these sentiments.[105]

Germaine Greer manifests a more dramatic transformation. Her early feminist tract *The Female Eunuch* (1971) depicted childbearing as "constricting, suffocating, an enemy of a liberated woman's larger hopes." Now, thirty years later, she says she is "desperate for a baby.... She mourns her unborn babies ... and [has] pregnancy dreams, waiting with vast joy and confidence for something that will never happen."[106]

Second-wave feminist Naomi Wolf describes how pregnancy and childbirth have transformed her. "The ways in which the hormones of pregnancy affected me called into question my entire belief system about 'the social construction of gender.'" Wolf admits to feeling clingier, weepier, "stupidly domestic," and confesses that "the kind of sap that fills women's magazines" became comprehensible to her.[107] She felt a "childlike surge of need for repetitive, utterly simple affirmations that I was—that we, the baby and I, were—not going to be abandoned."

Even as this transformation through motherhood was occurring, Wolf thought to herself, "how pathetic"—she was "becoming one of those women with whom I had always refused to identify." Many of the other mothers Wolf talked to began sentences with "I never thought I'd be one of those mothers who, after having a baby ...," and then they would tell stories like those Wolf herself related. Wolf became convinced that the changes she and her friends felt were the result of increases in levels of estrogen and oxytocin.[108]

These powerful testimonials by leading feminists seem to have had little impact on the feminist movement as a whole.[109] For although these feminists have revised their positions on motherhood, they have not abandoned the core of the feminist agenda. They still want very much to make it easier for women to have careers, to encourage men to adopt a greatly expanded role in caring for their children, and to compel the government to subsidize day care much more heavily.[110]

The political agenda of feminism does not appear to be fully compatible with individual feminists' views about babies and the intrinsic power of motherhood. The influential feminist theorist Susan Okin says we should aim for a society where "childbearing would be so conceptually separate from child rearing and other family responsibilities that it would be a cause for surprise, and no little concern, if men and women were not equally responsible for domestic life or if children were to spend much more time with one parent than the other."[111] Political and academic feminists believe that as long as the historic division of labor in the family prevails, women will not obtain an equal share of valued resources and positions of power, and this belief leads them to downplay the force of the mother-child bond.

Most politically active feminists value resources and power and the competitiveness that men employ to achieve status; they do not have comparable respect for typically feminine values and pursuits. Legendary movement figures such as Simone de Beauvoir, Kate Millett and Gloria Steinem were all childless. When they discuss mothering they use words like "sacrifice" and "burden" and "onerous."[112] Though Beauvoir can, at times, wax lyrical about the joys of mothering,[113] feminists often take away from her writings what she probably intended they should: The housewife is "subordinate, secondary, parasitic." And nursing affords many women

> no pleasure; on the contrary, she is apprehensive of ruining her bosom; she resents feeling her nipples cracked, the glands painful; suckling the baby hurts; the infant seems to her to be sucking out her strength, her life, her happiness. It inflicts a harsh slavery upon her and it is no longer a part of her: it seems a tyrant; she feels hostile to this little stranger, this individual who menaces her flesh, her freedom, her whole ego.[114]

When discussing why she never had a baby, Beauvoir said she "had no desire to be a slave of such a creature."[115]

Motherhood and breastfeeding undoubtedly seem a burden to a minority of women. The women who find child care "boring" and "tedious"[116] tend to react negatively to those who discuss evidence of mother-infant attachment. Hrdy notes that there have been demonstrations against attachment theorists and a host of books attacking them. Diane Eyer's *Motherguilt,* for example, charges that much "mother bullying" is "midwifed" by popular psychologist "baby gurus." Another attachment critic blames the "psychobabble about attachment and bonding" of the baby gurus for a "backlash against working mothers."[117]

One popular gender text says that differences in nurturing behavior between men and women are few if one defines *nurturance* broadly as "caring for and promoting the welfare of others." Such a definition would mean that "mending a leaking roof" would count as a nurturing act.[118] Cross-cultural studies of manhood have indeed found that men have a distinctive nurturing style, and that "manhood ideologies always include a criterion of selfless generosity, even to the point of sacrifice."[119]

But the author of this gender text is not willing to leave things with "his" and "her" forms of nurturing. She insists that even the overwhelming research findings on women's greater pleasure in nurturing of babies "reveals a cloudy picture," and, in any case, "there seems little doubt that gender differences in nurturant behavior, where they are found, can be traced to social context, stereotyping and social pressure."[120]

Such a view insists that men avoid baby care because of the way they have been socialized, not because of their nature, and because patriarchal power enables them to avoid the boring and burdensome side of life.[121] However, several studies have determined that socialization cannot explain why females are more attracted to babies. University of Chicago researchers Dario Maestripieri and Suzanne Pelka summarize as follows:

> Many previous studies failed to identify any direct influence of socialization on sex differences in interest in infants. In one of these studies, Blakemore (1990) studied interactions of 4- to 7-year-old boys and girls with their infant siblings at home. Although older girls interacted with infants more than boys did, there was no evidence that direct maternal socialization was a determinant of this difference. In a related study, Blakemore (1991) reported that adults evaluated more positively children who interacted with babies than those who did not. However, the sex of the child did not affect the parent's evaluations.... Finally, Goldberg et al. (1982) failed to find any sociocognitive explanations to account for their reported association between menarche and increased interest in infants among girls.[122]

As for child care seeming boring to most females—the evidence offered above (and below) suggests otherwise. Despite generously funded day care, Swedish mothers readily take parental leave; when they go back to paying jobs, they prefer part-time work so they have more time to spend with their children. Similarly, U.S. mothers with children under eighteen are more likely to say they prefer part-time work than full-time work or no work.[123]

Perhaps feminists who describe the care of young children as boring are really saying that *too much* child care is burdensome. Women do far more child care than men, and when men do care for children, they are more apt to play than do less agreeable chores. One might then be inclined to predict that men would say they like parenting more than women, but in fact, "fathers report significantly lower parental satisfaction than mothers."[124]

Feminists insist there is a socially constructed "'motherhood mystique' which ensures that a woman will feel guilty at first for giving up any aspect of the traditional mothering role."[125] Joan Williams, a mother and prominent feminist legal theorist, acknowledges that to many women the mystique does not always feel coercive: "Society has nourished in them the belief that it is their birthright to be able to take time off from the grind and enjoy their children while they are small."[126]

Simone de Beauvoir wrote about the dangers of this sort of belief:

> What is extremely demoralizing for the woman who aims at self-sufficiency is the existence of other women of like social status, having at the start the same situation and the same opportunities, who live as parasites.... A comfortably married or supported friend is a temptation in the way of one who is intending to make her own success.[127]

Beauvoir's heirs combat the temptation with pleas to their sisters, reminding them about the importance of getting a career started before having children, not only because divorce is so common but also because doing so will help ensure that they will be more "independent" and less likely to let "their children define them."[128] They write books with titles like *How to Avoid the Mommy Trap* that recommend hard negotiating with spouses before starting a family.[129] They get angry at women who make "selfish decision[s] from the collective perspective of feminism" by resigning top jobs in business to care for children,[130] or who write books in which they explain that they let their barely started careers get off track for no better reason than "a hunger" for motherhood "gnawing at my belly."[131]

In 1975, Beauvoir declared that arguments and anger would not be enough to bring society where feminists wanted it to go; coercion would also be necessary.

> No woman should be authorized to stay at home to raise her children. Women should not have that choice, precisely because if there is such a choice, too many women will make that one. It is a way of forcing women in a certain direction.[132]

This sort of feminism, which favors saving women from themselves, is still present today. For example, politically active feminists usually support day care subsidies rather than increases in the tax deduction for dependants—a measure that would benefit nonworking as well as working mothers. They don't support tax relief because it would "encourage one person to stay home and that person usually would be the woman."[133]

A coercive proposal to get working men instead of their wives to stay home with the children was recently proposed in the *North Carolina Law Review.* The author, after noting how few Swedish men voluntarily take paternal leave, proposed a law for the United States that would make such leave mandatory for men for six weeks after the birth of a child.[134] Another proposal would require that fathers and mothers alternate post-birth leaves for several months at a time.[135]

In 1989, Felice Schwartz, a longtime friend of working women, came up with a proposal that would enable women to have children, stay attached to their jobs and still devote substantial time to their families. She proposed that female executives in business be given the option to choose a career track or a career-and-family track. Those choosing the latter would move up more slowly, probably aiming for middle management in the medium term, but they would have more time with their families when they wanted it.[136]

Schwartz's article in the *Harvard Business Review* provoked an uproar, with prominent feminists in the lead. Weighing in with a jointly authored letter were the National Organization for Women, the National Women's Political Caucus and several other groups who made it clear that the problem was not just that Schwartz had proposed that the career-and-family track be available only to women. They worried that even if Schwartz's proposal were applied to men as well, in practice it would become a "mommy track" cutting off "women's employment opportunities." The letter writers thought that Schwartz's article should instead have questioned the traditional distribution of child care between women and men. Moreover, it should not have assumed that young women would be able to predict whether they would be career- or family-oriented. Many women would undoubtedly choose family initially, but would regret their decision "when work becomes a passion that overtakes other goals."[137]

Several years later, Katha Pollitt acknowledged that "mommy tracks," like that proposed by Schwartz, might genuinely help women in the short run. But they should nonetheless be opposed, she believed, because such policies would tend to keep gender roles in the family from changing, and that kind of change should be the long-term goal.[138]

Not only do these feminists want to limit women's choices, but NOW also wants to withhold information that might lead women to make the "wrong" choices. I noted earlier that many highly educated women greatly overestimate their chances of getting pregnant after age forty. In the summer of 2002, the American Society for Reproductive Medicine wanted to place public service ads in shopping malls and movie theaters that could have helped correct this misinformation. The ads were designed to enable women to make reproductive choices based on the facts. In particular, they wanted to tell women how they could prevent infertility.

The opposition of groups such as NOW aborted the whole program. The ad that particularly angered NOW contained the message: "Advancing Age Decreases Your Ability to Have Children." NOW accused the doctors of using "scare tactics." They further argued that "the ads sent a negative message to women who might want to delay or skip childbearing in favor of career pursuits."[139]

Pregnancy, Childbirth and Work

Most feminists refuse to give ground on their goals of equal workplace time, effort and outcomes for women and men. Two incontestable biological differences pose major problems for achieving those goals: women are necessarily the sex that gets pregnant, and women are the sex that breastfeeds.

The mainstream feminist movement has not acknowledged these differences in its push for expanded family leave. On the contrary, NOW and most other feminist organizations have fought hard—and for the most part successfully—to ensure that *maternity* leave be defeated in the legislatures and the courts. Feminists instead promote *family* leave because it is available to either sex and thus provides "equal treatment." Giving only mothers a pregnancy-related leave is seen by most feminists as "special treatment" and a step backwards.[140]

If women are to advance in careers as rapidly as men, pregnancy must be viewed as no big deal. The feminist position goes something like this: "Sure, women have to have the babies. But men can take care of them as well as women. Sure, some women will stay home for a while to care for their babies. But in a fair world, because there is no fundamental difference between men and women, just as many men will choose to care for babies. And high-quality, subsidized day care will ensure that both sexes can get back to their careers soon enough."

Thus, having priorities straight means not letting pregnancy and childbirth interfere with careers. In this way of thinking, Pat Summitt of the University of Tennessee, the most successful women's basketball coach of all time, stands as a model for one female journalist who applauds the fact that Summitt "worked into her ninth month, and gave birth to her son, Tyler, after she went into labor on a recruiting trip."[141]

Liz Gallese looks for similar role models in her study of female Harvard Business School graduates. The overall story Gallese tells in *Women Like Us* is depressing to my female students and, it seems, to Gallese herself. Many of the single women she discusses are held back in their careers by their focus on finding a decent man who loves them and whom they can love; and, as mentioned before, the women who are happily married tend to pull back in their careers so as not to outshine their husbands.[142]

Gallese finds but one heroine—"Holly." A high-powered careerist, even Holly acknowledges that she would not have relocated to advance her career if her husband had not had a consulting business that he could do anywhere. And Holly further acknowledges that one of the reasons for her focus on her career is her *husband* Chuck's insistence on it. Gallese calls Chuck "Hemingwayesque"—a tall, strong fellow who is away from home twenty-four days a month and who once came back from weeks on the road and "declared that he was going on a ten day fishing trip with a group of friends." Holly decided against divorce because she had three young children, and her first instinct was to "preserve the family." Plus she still adored Chuck.[143]

Gallese is inspired by Holly because she has it all—husband, three kids under five and "most of all she has swung the door wide open for her future. The divisional vice-presidency [at one of the biggest corporations in the country] she had hoped for was at least a possibility."[144]

Gallese realizes that Chuck is in many ways more unusual than Holly. She wonders why he desires an ambitious woman like Holly. He tells Gallese he thinks she is an "incredible mother." He also admires her ability to thrive in a "rough and tumble man's business." Chuck, with "eyes narrowing into those hard little slits," tells Gallese that he likes "winning football teams" and "successful women."[145] He gives one particular example of Holly's virtues. "You're talking about a woman who dropped a baby [their third] on a Saturday afternoon and showed up at the company two weeks later for her mail. She didn't miss a step in a man's job in a man's company."[146]

Gallese seems as pleased as Chuck about Holly's priorities, but some of my female students say that Holly does *not* have it all. "She doesn't get to spend any real time with her children." And they are not wild about Chuck—in particular, his cheerleading for her quick return to work with a two-week-old baby and two other children under five at home.

I think my skeptical female students are right in this case. If one takes the effects of pregnancy and childbirth seriously, one finds many reasons to be cautious about fully engaging in high-powered careers during pregnancy and after childbirth. Indeed, since high-powered careers and stress go together, and stress felt by would-be mothers can hinder conception, the careers can prevent pregnancy itself.

Such was the conclusion of 43-year-old Connie Chung when, in 1990, she announced that she was quitting her high-stress job as a CBS anchorwoman "so that she could take a very aggressive approach to having a baby."[147] Programs that reduce stress have been found to increase fertility. Reducing anxiety reduces levels of cortisol—a stress-indicating hormone that can prevent a woman from releasing eggs. In evolutionary terms, it makes sense that periods of high stress would not be ideal times to have babies.

Doctors can deal with stress-induced infertility by reducing a patient's anxiety or by injecting fertility drugs. But as the head of the

Division of Reproductive Endocrinology and Infertility at the University of Pittsburgh's School of Medicine has noted, fertility drugs lead to ovulation and the possibility of pregnancy, but the mother is "still stressed. That probably isn't good for the fetal brain."[148]

So when women are stressed during pregnancy it is not just their own health that may be at issue. The idea that stress can damage the fetus remains somewhat controversial.[149] Some studies find that women in physically challenging occupations have higher rates of miscarriages and stillbirths. Other research indicates that chronic stress can lead to premature births.[150] But one study of pregnant medical school residents found no evidence of poor birth results unless the students worked more than one hundred hours a week. (They worked, on average, seventy hours a week.)[151]

Of course, even this study's finding that apparently normal babies of normal weight come out at the normal time doesn't mean there cannot have been more subtle kinds of damage. There certainly is evidence that the mother's stress hormones pass through to the baby. For example, acute stress in a pregnant woman has been shown to alter the fetus's heart-rate patterns. This supports the theory that the mother's state of mind "can shape the neurobehavioral development of the fetus." One study even found that the fetus grew agitated when a pregnant woman reported "she had *considered* having a cigarette."[152]

Expectant mothers will have less stress if they use relaxation techniques and if their husbands help more and are reassuring and comforting at home.[153] But the mothers also will have reduced stress if they work less. One study found that women working past thirty weeks into their pregnancy had significantly higher blood pressure readings during job time on work days than on other days. The 7 percent of women who developed clinically relevant high blood pressure during their pregnancies showed blood pressure readings 7.4 points higher during working hours than at other times.[154]

High blood pressure can lead to pre-eclampsia, which can lead to seizures resulting from toxemia, a condition that can be fatal to mother and baby. Another study comparing mothers who worked past the midpoint of pregnancy with mothers who did not work found that 4 percent of the working mothers and 1 percent of the nonworking mothers had pre-eclampsia.[155] In the study of pregnant medical school residents mentioned above, the incidence of pre-eclampsia was more than twice as high in the residents (8.8 percent) as in the doctors' wives (3.5 percent).[156]

Working leads to more exposure to germs, which can lead to respiratory infections such as the flu. For pregnant women, flu can increase the risk to the fetus of developing devastating conditions. Children whose mothers have a respiratory infection during the middle three months of pregnancy, for example, have double the risk of developing schizophrenia, a condition affecting about 1 percent of the population.[157]

Women in the midst of a normal pregnancy are subject to a number of maladies. One obstetrics text calls nausea and vomiting, backache and heartburn "common conditions." Fatigue is even more commonplace, affecting about three-quarters of all pregnant women.[158] Postpartum fatigue is equally normal. Backache, perineal pain and hemorrhoids are also common in substantial numbers of women who have given birth.[159]

Some studies look not just at postpartum maladies but also at postpartum functional status. Two different studies have found that at six months postpartum more than 75 percent of mothers have not achieved full functional status. One study specifically asked about daily activities that were limited because the mother was "tired or felt poorly"; 40 to 50 percent of mothers responded that six months after giving birth, they were "accomplishing less than usual," "not performing as carefully as usual," "limiting work or other activities"[160] and "requiring extra effort to perform work and activities." Another study concluded that more than 75 percent of the women who *were* back at work did not feel they were functioning at full capacity.[161]

The reduced ability to function is not just because of fatigue or pain. Pregnant and breastfeeding women feel "slightly sedated," are less anxious and have less muscle tension than other women their age. These effects are correlated with levels of the "natural opiate," oxytocin.[162] The combination of fatigue and the effects of oxytocin increases can leave women feeling they are "spaced out all the time."[163]

There are other studies that discuss postpartum working. One acknowledges that "it may be controversial to suggest that working women are subject to disability beyond 6 weeks after childbirth," but nonetheless reports that the employed women studied had "diminished levels of well-being ... at approximately 7 months after childbirth."[164] Another finds that "Women who had taken more than 24 weeks maternity leave had better mental health outcomes at 9 and 12 months postpartum. Mental outlook was also brighter for women who spent fewer hours at their job."[165]

We've already heard Naomi Wolf say that during her pregnancy she felt psychologically vulnerable and hence more dependent on her husband. She also felt more vulnerable physically:

> I took my husband's arm to cross a busy street—a street that single-girl icons I grew up admiring would have waltzed or skipped or gone striding across, hair flying—did nature mandate this temporary dependency? Is my lifetime of conviction about women's ability to go it merrily alone a complete evolutionary howler in the face of pregnancy? But the fact was I was vulnerable, he wasn't and I welcomed his help. At seven months, the ligaments in my hips had loosened to accommodate the baby, my center of gravity had pitched forward, and even walking was precarious and slow.[166]

Three weeks after giving birth, Wolf still felt vulnerable and "stunned with fatigue."[167] She developed new admiration for traditional societies where pregnant women are protected from stress[168] and postpartum women are "nurtured by the women of their community for some weeks . . .while they bond with their baby and recover from the rigors of childbirth."[169] Wolf wants society to acknowledge that pregnant women and new mothers should be nurtured, congratulated and "crown[ed] . . . with laurels upon having completed the arduous task."[170]

Such care and kudos are unlikely to come from most of her feminist sisters, because their whole work/family worldview is dependent on denying the fact that childbirth produces the fatigue and other maladies listed above. For political feminists, pregnancy and childbirth should not be regarded as especially taxing, physically or emotionally, for the mother. Otherwise the feminist insistence that fathers be eligible for the same parental leave would make little sense.

The comical nature of this charade was well demonstrated in the heat of the 1996 campaign. Democrat Blanche Lambert Lincoln decided not to run for reelection to the House of Representatives when she found that she was carrying twins. Haley Barbour, chairman of the Republican National Committee, was at the same time making the general point that Bill Clinton was not a popular President—even in his home state of Arkansas, where people knew him best. Thus at one press conference Barbour mentioned that every single Democratic official in Arkansas was retiring, like Lincoln, or abstaining from the race rather than running on the ballot with an unpopular Bill Clinton. The following exchange ensued:

Question: You're going to blame Clinton for Blanche Lambert Lincoln's twins?
Barbour: I think Blanche Lambert Lincoln's twins were an excuse. John Engler's [governor of Michigan] triplets didn't slow him down.
Question: May I point out a certain biological distinction here?
Barbour: Don't be sexist.[171]

In a subsequent letter to Barbour, Lincoln noted that she now had "a 50 inch waist and ankles to match." Anticipating her life after giving birth, she said that running for reelection while "boarding an airplane twice a week with two infants, a briefcase and a diaper bag wasn't my idea of quality parenting."[172] (Though Lincoln insisted that many male members of Congress also retire to spend time with their families, Washington insiders say that almost no man ever leaves a dream job for family reasons.)[173]

Haley Barbour's "don't be sexist" quip may seem a low blow. But that is precisely what NOW spokeswomen would have said if anyone other than Lincoln herself had questioned the advisability of a woman campaigning for Congress while expecting and delivering twins.

Breastfeeding

Breastfeeding may also have more of an impact on women and their children than many feminists are willing to concede. Breastfeeding can have some negative effects on infants and their mothers. Mothers who eat peanuts before breastfeeding, for example, can inadvertently make their babies allergic to peanuts. Breast milk lacks vitamin D, so nursing mothers should give their infants daily doses of this bone-building supplement.[174]

Almost everything else that can be said about the health effects of nursing is positive. For mothers, breastfeeding reduces postpartum bleeding, facilitates the return to pre-pregnant weight, reduces hip fractures in the postmenopausal period, and reduces the risks of ovarian and breast cancer. The breast cancer reduction effects are truly stunning. Using data from 47 epidemiological studies in 30 countries, a 2001 report in *The Lancet* found that each year of breastfeeding reduced breast cancer rates by 4.3 percent.[175]

The catalogue of breastfeeding's benefits to the infant is longer still, and most studies show that long-term breastfeeding is better than medium-term breastfeeding. In acknowledgement of this evidence, the American Academy of Pediatrics recommends that breastfeeding continue for at least one year and "thereafter for as long as mutually desired."[176] A U.S. surgeon general has added that "the lucky baby nurses until two."[177]

Infant formula cannot duplicate the benefits of human milk, in part because scientists have not yet begun to understand all that the two hundred constituents of mother's milk do. Science writer Natalie Angiers says of breast milk:

> Nothing does just one thing. Milk sugars offer calories, and milk sugars allow other nutrients to be fully metabolized. The sugars of human milk and of infant formula are quantitatively similar but qualitatively different. Lactoferrin permits the scarce iron in milk to be "bioavailable" to the baby, and it also prevents pathogenic bacteria from getting their maws on the metal, which they need to survive. There is no lactoferrin in infant formula.[178]

Her discussion of mother's milk continues detailing the nerve growth factors that it contains and the hormones that are ten times more prevalent in a mother's milk than in her blood stream, but of which "we don't have a clue" about the effect on the infant.[179]

Naomi Wolf further explains that

> Mothers and babies who are nursing are like one continually interacting, merged organism. They share the same REM sleep cycles. Since breast milk itself is a living organism, formula manufacturers cannot replicate it. Breast milk varies in density and nutrient levels according to the needs of each baby, becoming, for instance, one consistency for single babies, and another to better suit twins.[180]

Even today, when the benefits of mothers' milk are far better understood than they were in prior generations, between 35 and 40 percent of U.S. infants never taste mother's milk, and of those infants who are breastfed, less than 12 percent are still nursing at the time of their first birthday. [181]

Of course, things can turn out fine with formula. But the evidence that mother's milk is better for infants is overwhelming. The 1997 American Academy of Pediatrics statement that recommends breastfeeding for at least a year says there is strong evidence that breast milk protects against at least eight different maladies and some evidence that it protects against eight others. In the first category are respiratory, middle ear and urinary infections and bacterial meningitis. In the second category are lymphoma, insulin-dependent diabetes mellitus and ulcerative colitis. Evidence gathered since 1997 indicates that breast milk is in fact almost certainly protective against at least three of the eight illnesses against which it was thought to be only possibly protective in the 1997 statement: allergies, sudden infant death syndrome and impaired cognitive development (IQ). There is also new evidence that nursing protects against the later development of high blood pressure (in the child).[182]

Some mothers try to breastfeed and can't; other mothers don't try. Some doctors say that we should not be judgmental about those who make this decision. Other doctors emphasize their duty to tell mothers and society what optimum health requires even if, as with nutrition or smoking, many people will ignore the recommendations. Women weigh in with great passion on each side of this issue.[183]

Breastfeeding rates have been rising since 1990 but still remain under 30 percent. Even those who do breastfeed often supplement breast milk with formula.[184] The 1997 American Academy of Pediatrics statement gives a long list of "obstacles to the initiation and continuation of breastfeeding," including physician apathy and misinformation, insufficient prenatal breastfeeding education, disruptive hospital policies, commercial promotion of infant formula, lack of broad societal support, media portrayal of bottle-feeding as normative, and maternal employment (especially in the absence of workplace facilities and support for breastfeeding).[185] A 2000 study also notes mothers' perceptions of fathers' preferences for bottle-feeding and mothers' concerns about the adequacy of their milk, along with mothers' jobs outside the home.[186]

Maternal employment produces the most sparks. A number of studies suggest that tension exists between full-time work and breastfeeding. One study finds that only 18 percent of mothers working full-time breastfeed for six months, whereas 45 percent of nonworking mothers do so. Another study finds that 64 percent of mothers working under twenty hours a week nurse, whereas 36 percent of those working more than twenty hours a week do. A third study finds that longer maternal leaves and shorter hours at work mean longer-term breastfeeding. A fourth study concludes that there is a strong association between the timing of the transition from breastfeeding and the transition to employment.[187]

Historically, feminists with an eye on workplace equality have omitted or minimized discussions of breastfeeding as part of the effort to reconceptualize women "primarily as paid workers rather than mothers."[188] In this spirit, a representative from the Institute for Women's Policy Research finds the 1997 pediatricians' recommendations "a step backward" in efforts to make it possible for mothers "to enjoy their babies and their jobs."[189] But other liberal legislators and feminist organizations concentrate on laws ensuring workplace accommodations for nursing mothers and encouraging businesses to provide lactation locations for pumping or nursing.[190] NOW also backs such legislation in an unusual show of support for a female-specific protective policy.

Cultural conservatives react to the tension between full-time work and breastfeeding by urging new mothers, where possible, to work less or not at all. They also question whether expressed milk delivered by another through a bottle will really give a baby the same benefits as intimate contact through nursing at the mother's breast.[191]

In one famous experiment, an infant monkey was forced to choose between a wire-mesh "mother" with food and a softer, cloth-covered "mother" without food. The monkey would cling to the cloth-covered "mother" for sixteen to eighteen hours a day. But even the cloth-covered mother monkey replica could not provide the comfort that an actual mother would have given. Observing the "grief, the listlessness, the obvious and heart-rending despair" of infant monkeys deprived of mothers, the researcher declared, "Thank God, we only have to do it once to prove the point."[192]

How profound is the maternal presence? A sobbing baby will become calm in her mother's arms before the mother has even finished raising her shirt for nursing.[193] It could just be anticipation of food, but perhaps it's also the mother's smell, her voice, her heartbeat. Experiments show that a baby can hear her mother's heartbeat and voice in the womb, and will recognize and be calmed by both after birth.

Mother Love

There is ample evidence that women and mothers are more attached to young children than men and fathers are, and we are now beginning to accumulate a list of reasons why this affection is reciprocated by infants. When a rhesus monkey's mother holds her infant to her chest, the infant's natural opiates increase. Both the mother's touch and her heartbeat seem to bring this pleasure. After birth, the human mother's heartbeat is also familiar, reassuring and pleasurable for her child. Science writer Deborah Blum explains that mothers seem to know this instinctively:

> It's a fact that mothers preferentially carry infants on the left hip. It's true for right-handed mothers, who rationally explain that it makes sense to free their more useful hand for other chores. But it's also true for left-handed mothers, who rationally explain that it makes sense to use their stronger, dominant arm in holding the child safely.... It likely grows out of our evolution. Consider that ape females, too, prefer to cuddle their babies to the left. Perhaps in some distant past mothers learned that their infants settled and relaxed if they were held close to the heart.[194]

This left-side bias is not nearly as prevalent in fathers, even those who spend a lot of time caring for their young children. Mostly right-handed, the fathers tend to carry the baby in their stronger right arm "across the body from the heart."[195]

Some sleep scientists believe that the mothers' breathing and heartbeat would help prevent sudden infant death syndrome (SIDS) if Western mothers slept with their children. This view is controversial with some U.S. doctors who emphasize the instances of adults inadvertently suffocating babies who share their bed.[196] Nonetheless, the international comparisons are striking. The U.S. has far and away the highest rate of SIDS in the world (2 per 1,000)—ten times higher than Japan and one hundred times higher than Hong Kong, both countries where mothers routinely sleep with their children. In most of the world, parents sleep with their young children, and the lowest incidences of SIDS are in societies with widespread co-sleeping.

With co-sleeping, the sleep stages of infant and mother become entwined. In their coauthored book, *A General Theory of Love,* three medical doctors explain:

> Sleep is an intricate brain rhythm, and the neurally immature infant must first borrow the patterns from parents.
>
> Infants are born knowing this—the typical baby, whether placed on his mother's left or right, spends the entire night turned toward her, with ears, nose and occasionally eyes drinking in the sensory stimulation that sets his nocturnal cadences. The same principle allows a ticktocking clock to regularize the restless sleep of puppies newly taken from their mother, and enables the breathing teddy bear to stabilize the respirations of preemies.

The steady heartbeat and "regular tidal sweeps of breath" can thus "keep a sleeping baby alive."[197]

Though a mother's heartbeat holds a special place in her infant's early life, there is no evidence that infants have a general preference for female over male heartbeats. Not so for voices. Infants seem to prefer the high, soft and rhythmic voices of women, and even among women, the mother's voice is special. "By monitoring infants' physiologic reactions to novelty," researchers can prove that newborns recognize their mothers' (but not their fathers') voices at birth. "Within days, an infant recognizes and prefers not only his mother's voice but also her native language, even when spoken by a stranger."[198] When it hears its mother, "the heart of the infant slows, calms, and steadies, beating more gently as it hears that particular music of a mother's voice."[199]

A baby knows that it likes mother's heartbeat, voice and smell, but mom also has special talents that will protect it when it is in distress. Mother is better than father at distinguishing *her* baby's cry from other babies' cries, and she is better at distinguishing a cry of pain from one of hunger or of anger.[200]

Mothers are also better than fathers at reading body language and other nonverbal signals. Indeed, women in general are better than men at recognizing emotions in others' faces. They are especially skilled at reading babies' faces. One experiment showed that women are quicker and more accurate at identifying infant emotions such as joy, interest, sadness, fear, surprise and distress. Prior experience as a mother or a babysitter did not explain these sex differences.[201]

Evolutionists think superior female and maternal abilities in recognizing signs of infant distress were naturally selected for because they increased the survival of preverbal babies. Women have a number of other special skills that can be explained by means of an evolutionary argument. Their skin is more sensitive to touch than men's, especially on the arms, legs and trunk, where a baby in distress might make itself known. Mothers also use their delicate touch to see if their baby is cold, hot, rigid, shaky or soggy—all of which can be signs of distress.[202]

Women can detect fainter odors than men and identify more accurately what they smell. This skill can alert mothers to dangerous smoke or rotting meat. Women hear high sounds better than men, and they prefer lower volumes more than men, so they will be more likely to notice their child's slightest murmur, sigh or difficulty breathing. Women perceive and remember colors better than men, so they can spot both ripe fruit and signs of a baby's rash. In "deep history" mothers needed to feed and doctor "teary infants in the moonless grass." Perhaps as a result their night vision is better than men's. Men on the hunt, in contrast, needed superior day vision, which they in fact still have.[203]

To be sure, babies care about their fathers. Just like mothers, fathers hold, rock, talk to and smile at their children. Some scholars believe that with experience, fathers become as competent with infants as mothers are.[204] In the rare circumstances where fathers become solo caretakers, "infants form primary attachments to them."[205]

A mother, however, is likely to have superior senses for recognizing signs of infant distress, and the baby will have a special fondness for her milk, heartbeat and voice. A baby will usually prefer her and, over the full range of circumstances, mother will on average do baby more good than father. Sarah Hrdy is a feminist who asks that fathers "not sell short their own abilities to reassure—or harm." But she acknowledges that a baby will usually attach to its mother, and that the mother will have "a lower threshold for responding to infant needs."

Fathers often love to play with toddlers and older children, and children beyond infancy love to play with a rambunctious and stimulating dad. But babies don't respond as well to dad's playmaking as older children do; and fathers soon get bored. Studies find that fathers are less likely than mothers to acknowledge the utterances of an infant. Moreover,

> Mothers are more likely than fathers to follow their infant's looking behavior when presenting a new toy, and to build on the infant's behavior when encouraging a new behavior with a toy.... Fathers are also less successful than mothers in getting their infants to engage in specific actions with a toy.[206]

Thus, in play as in other realms, mothers seem to be more "tuned in" to their babies.

9

DAY CARE

If mothers are more attuned to their infants than fathers (or strangers) and enjoy caring for them more, a logical assumption would be that babies and mothers benefit from maternal child care. But the ongoing battle over day care indicates that this proposition is extremely controversial today.

A study mentioned earlier indicated that good news about day care gets far more press coverage than bad news about it. The anthropologist author of this study attributes the phenomenon to the likelihood that journalists have their own children in day care and find the good-news stories reassuring. This possible incentive to bias extends far beyond journalism. Often the academic psychologists publishing studies on day care have used day care for their children.[1]

Likewise, staffers of all stripes on Capitol Hill use day care regularly, and "most don't know too many stay at home mothers."[2]

Whether or not there is bias toward good news, any bad news about the effects of day care produces outrage among working mothers. "Oh great, *more* guilt for working mothers.... Most of us can't take our kids to work with us, so why make us feel worse for a situation that everybody already has some tension with?" So said one mother when a study about high turnover in day care staff followed hard on the heels of another study linking day care to aggressive behavior. Another parent said that hearing a radio report of one of these studies was "like a knife to the heart."[3]

Studies examining how trailblazing behavior of a whole generation of mothers has affected their children are bound to be controversial. In the following pages I will try to unravel the facts about day care and evaluate the extent to which public policy surrounding this issue has taken sex differences seriously.[4]

Disease

It is clear that young children in day care centers get sick much more often than other kids. Some of the diseases for which day care seems to put children at greater risk—for example, spinal meningitis and sudden infant death syndrome (SIDS)—are fatal. There are nearly three times as many cases of SIDS in organized child care settings as would be predicted from time of exposure in such settings; one-third of those who die of SIDS in day care do so in their first week there. The authors of one study note that their results are "especially striking, because the demographic characteristics of [the group studied] (white, born to older, more educated parents, and without a history of smoke exposure) would typically place these infants in the lowest risk category for SIDS."[5]

Because small children put their hands in their mouths every one to three minutes and because toys get passed around, high infection rates at day care centers are not surprising.[6] Day care providers pressure mothers to use antibiotics, and mothers, stressed by the prospect of more lost work days, pressure doctors to prescribe them. Overuse of antibiotics incubates deadly new germ strains. Studies show, for instance, that penicillin-resistant streptococcus pneumococci is strongly correlated with hours spent in day care. Though wider knowledge about the dangers of antibiotics overuse has led to decreased usage in communities at large, children in day care centers have not reduced their use of antibiotics. Drug-resistant germs spawned there often reach the wider community.[7]

Children in day care are also at greater risk of being reinfected with new strains of a virus, an occurrence that can lead to dangerous complications. Reinfection with new strains appears to be an important mechanism to make these children "a reservoir for horizontal transmission to adults and other children."[8]

Among the more serious infections are those of the middle ear, a malady which can lead to hearing loss and subsequent social difficulties. The placement of surgical tubes to drain children's ears, which costs three to four billion dollars a year, is almost seven times more common in day care children. Children of relatively high-income parents are more likely to come down with ear infections than are children of the poor—a result that may be explained in part by upper-middle-income parents' more frequent use of commercial day care.[9]

There is a silver lining in this dark cloud for working mothers and fathers who use center day care. All those germs and all that sickness may strengthen the immune systems of their kids. In this regard, the earlier they are in day care, the better. Later asthma rates are only 40 percent as high for children who have been in day care before they are six months old. Hay fever rates also are lower. Moreover, though children in day care centers have twice as many colds before age two as do those cared for at home, they have only one-third as many from ages six to eleven. Both groups appear to be equally protected thereafter.[10]

These recent studies pointing to the protective effects of early exposure to germs are provocative and important. But one reporter who canvassed researchers concluded that "no scientists are quite ready to recommend a retreat from high standards of hygiene."[11] In light of all the risks set forth above, it seems unlikely that we will ultimately decide that germ-filled day care does more physical good than harm for young children.

Attachment, Emotions, Behavior and Cognition

The real controversy over day care does not come from studies about the incidence of disease but rather from the research on attachment, behavior and cognition. This research is difficult to conduct; there are so many potentially important variables in child development that it is hard to pinpoint any one cause of a particular effect. Moreover, parents would not stand for research that randomly assigned their loved ones to various forms of care—the procedure that would produce the most convincing research results. Thus, the studies we are left with may yield misleading conclusions. It's possible, for example, that although professional child care centers in general may seem to put children at greater risk, only certain low-quality centers do so. Or, though the professional centers may seem to hamper development, differences between children at these centers and other children may instead result from characteristics of mothers who use day care or the amount of time the mothers work.

The National Institute of Child Health and Human Development (NICHD) was aware of these difficulties in 1991 when it brought together a wide range of behavioral scientists to conduct a long-term national survey of over 1,300 newborns in ten communities across the nation. Parents decided what kind of care their child would receive at every age. But trained observers, interviewers and testers were everywhere. Using videotape and other techniques, they measured the quality of mother-child interaction and the extent to which the home environment and "maternal vocabulary" (a proxy for maternal intelligence) "contributed to the optimal development of children." Data on family income and parental education was collected, as was detailed data on the quality of nonmaternal care. Researchers observed not just whether the child was in center-based care but also how caregivers responded when the child cried; whether they seemed involved, warm and responsive; whether they would ask the child questions; and whether they spoke to him or her positively or negatively.[12]

To date, results of this ongoing study have found risks to children in center-based care and to some extent in all forms of nonmaternal care. For children under three, nonmaternal care at home—often by fathers or grandmothers—was found to be generally superior to care at professional centers.[13] However, in the first three years of life, there existed an association between any kind of nonmaternal care and mothers who were "somewhat less positive" toward their children and vice versa. In particular, the researchers found that "more hours of [nonmaternal] care in the first 6 months of life were associated with lower maternal sensitivity";[14] likewise, more nonmaternal care in the first fifteen months was associated with less positive mothering at that age. Subsequently, at ages two and three, children exposed to more nonmaternal care engaged less positively with their mothers. The findings on maternal sensitivity are especially important because high scores on this measure strongly predict social competence and fewer problem behaviors.[15]

Next came some strong indications that "early and extensive nonmaternal care" is linked with a worrying increase in the odds of producing "needy, bragging, disobedient and aggressive children."[16] One important finding compared those children who were exposed to more than thirty hours per week of nonmaternal care beginning in their first year and those exposed to less than ten hours of nonmaternal care beginning in the first year. In the heavily exposed group, 17 percent displayed problem behaviors by age four and a half, whereas only 6 percent of the modestly exposed group did so. A later study, relying on reports of parents, child care workers and kindergarten teachers, found that early and extensive nonmaternal care was a risk factor for problem behavior in kindergarten as well.

The effect of early and extensive nonmaternal care on aggression—including fighting, cruelty and explosive behavior—was especially striking. The differences in aggression were significant even after researchers controlled for such factors as the quality of maternal and nonmaternal care, family income, parents' marital status and mothers' educational levels. The odds of troubled behavior increased even further for those children who had been in day care for over forty-five hours per week. It is not yet known whether early commencement of nonmaternal care or cumulative exposure to such care in the preschool years is the more problematic; studies disagree on this point.[17]

In addition to raising questions about the advisability of putting young children in child care centers, recent studies present doubts about the desirability of maternal employment itself. A 2002 study reports negative impacts of full-time maternal employment during the first nine months of a child's life. After holding other relevant variables constant, researchers found that new mothers with relatively extensive work experience outside the home—more than thirty hours per week—produced children who at age three had poorer cognitive and verbal development than children of stay-at-home mothers.[18] Researchers hypothesize that mothers who spend more time away from their infants are less equipped to help them deal with frustration or encourage their learning. Also, women with time-intensive jobs may come home stressed and depleted, with less patience and energy to engage their children skillfully and warmly.[19] Other research, however, shows verbal and memory gains in children exposed to center-based care, especially high-quality care, before the age of four and a half.[20] Maternal employment or professional day care at the toddler and preschool ages may improve subsequent cognitive development even though maternal care best stimulates cognitive development in infancy.

Evolution and Biology: A Reprise

The risks of nonmaternal care set forth above are apparent even after researchers control for the mother's assessment of a child's temperament at six months and after they control for maternal sensitivity.[21] We also know that both mothers and independent observers rate mothers as "more behaviorally and emotionally withdrawn" on days when the mothers report greater workloads and interpersonal stress at work. These observations suggest that the combination of a job and day care can reduce preexisting maternal sensitivity by increasing stress.[22] Moreover, as we will see below, women of all types will become more attached to their infants as they spend more time with them.

Though some uncertainty is inevitable on crucial day care issues, evolution-based arguments and some biological evidence support the NICHD findings about the importance of maternal care to healthy child development. Mothers love their babies more than others do, and babies fully reciprocate. And though babies love their fathers, their mothers are better at establishing an emotional dialogue, picking up subtle cues and establishing nonverbal communication.[23] Studies show that even "parental presence is not enough"; parents must be attentive to their babies because infant development varies in proportion to a parent's expressiveness and looking behavior.[24]

Studies measuring the levels of stress hormones provide additional evidence that day care is stressful for children. Children who spend long hours in day care have higher levels of cortisol than other children, and cortisol is at a higher level when a child is in day care than when he or she is at home. Though cortisol levels are typically highest in the morning, the cortisol level of children in day care rises as the day progresses. For boys, but not girls, this rise in cortisol is associated with more anxious and withdrawn behavior.[25]

In *Mother Nature,* Sarah Hrdy studies how the young are nurtured in different human cultures and in various animal species. As an evolutionary anthropologist who identifies with feminism, Hrdy cannot be accused of holding views intended to limit the life choices of contemporary women. Early in her book, Hrdy says that families in postindustrial societies "require more than one wage earner." This "economic reality" means that "most mothers, even if they want to, do not have the option of staying home to care for their babies. . . . Dual career mothers *still* need to balance their subsistence needs against the time, energy, and resources needed to rear their children." Negative outcomes are not deaths but "insecurities among infants, stress in their mothers."[26]

Hrdy thinks that educated, professional mothers like her simply face "irreconcilable dilemmas." As an illustration, Hrdy introduces Anke Ehrhardt, an eminent scientist, and sympathetically describes her "haunting words."

> Ehrhardt [is] a . . . woman every bit as impressive for her warmth and grace as for the accomplishments that made her the world's expert on children's development of gender identity. Over breakfast at a scientific conference in Prague this extraordinarily nurturing woman confided why she consciously decided never to have children. She said it was because she "knew too much" about what they need.[27]

Unlike Ehrhardt, Hrdy decided to combine career and motherhood. She describes herself as a mother who, like many women, "is aware of her infant's needs but who also aspires to a life beyond bondage to them." She is, however, unable to join some professional women in casually reconciling this conflict by dismissing mother/infant attachment theory as just "another facet of patriarchal oppression." Nor can she persuade herself that she can make up for ten-hour days, five days a week by "quality time" after dinner or on the weekends. Hrdy's knowledge of infants tells her that if a child looks up and fails "to detect 'the meeting eyes of love,' " he or she feels "anxiety, distress, terror, and, finally, desolation."[28]

Writing in 1999, Hrdy says she is unsure how "the rapid spread and highly experimental nature of paid communal daycare for very young infants" will work out. To her mind, the crux of the problem is the scarcity of committed allomothers, caretakers beyond the mother. Hrdy seems sure, however, of one thing:

> *Caretakers need not be the mother, or even one person, but they have to be the same caretakers.* . . . Human infants have a nearly insatiable desire to be held and to bask in the sense that they are loved. . . . If a baby does not perceive that he or she is growing up among committed kin, even a measure of care considered adequate for development within normal limits may not be enough to produce an adult who realizes his or her full human potential of empathy for others.[29]

"Quality Day Care"

There is no question that low-quality, center-based day care exacerbates the emotional, behavioral and cognitive problems associated with day care. But suppose a child has "quality day care." This is the lynchpin of the feminist agenda on day care—the saving grace of this social policy meant to allow mothers to feel they are doing well by their young children while still advancing in their careers as successfully as their husbands. The catch is that the problems enumerated above were significant even in studies that controlled for the quality of day care. Recent research supports the notion that even the most expensive and professionally staffed day care center is not of high quality compared with maternal care supplemented by the help of kin.

A cursory analysis of some current attempts to bring quality to day care indicates the intransigence of the problem. Center-care directors say that staff turnover is very tough on their charges. As one put it, "it's very hard for the younger ones, the infants and toddlers, to warm up to strangers. They're more fussy, crying." One large study of "better than average" child care centers found that between 1996 and 2000, 75 percent of the teaching staff and 40 percent of the directors had left their jobs.

One center-care director in Arlington, Virginia, lost four of her seven employees in one year, and within a short time all of their replacements also quit. (This record is not atypical: about half of all child care workers quit their jobs every year.)[30] She concluded, "If you can keep a teacher for a year, that's great." To do better, to really reduce turnover, she thought she would have to raise salaries to $12 an hour. That was currently impossible because it would raise the cost of child care to parents from $130 a week to $200 a week—more than her clients could afford.

If parents can't afford it, maybe Uncle Sam can help. To be sure, the federal government already helps a great deal by providing block grants to the states for subsidized child care and untaxed employer-provided child care benefits. The federal government also provides a tax credit for dual-earner families using commercial care—a credit that benefits families whose income is in the top third of the income bracket seventeen times more than those families in the bottom third. All in all, these subsidies amount to fifteen billion dollars a year.[31] But according to day care providers they are still not large enough to produce quality day care that parents can afford.

Subsidies for increases in pay for child care workers would merely scratch the surface. For true "quality" care, government would have to chip in enough extra to make sure that day care centers had "adequate" staff by the standards of the National Association for the Education of Young Children: at least one caretaker for every 4 babies and at least one caretaker for every 6 two-year-olds.[32]

Naomi Wolf has called as well for "on-site daycare so that we can see our children while we are at work and on-site nurseries so that mothers can nurse in the private sector for as long as they

ENCOUNTER BOOKS
900 Broadway
Suite 400
New York, New York 10003-1239

reasonably choose."[33] This upgrade could be very hard to bring about. In many small to medium-sized firms or buildings there will not be many mothers with infants in need of a nursery. The nursery staffing ratios may be one to one in some places or even one staff member and no baby when the only infant enrolled grows up.

After these improvements, what sort of quality will we be left with? First, turnover will be reduced, but it will be far from eliminated. Child care workers leave jobs for lots of reasons besides low pay. They may change professions, go back to school, get married and move away, have a baby and decide to take some time off. Or maybe they just decide they'd rather work for a different child care center—one that just opened up closer to home or that a friend has started.

Even if we could somehow keep all workers in the same center for their working lives, we wouldn't provide much continuity of care for the individual child. When the infants become toddlers, they will have new caretakers, and will probably move from the infant room and its staff to the toddler room and its staff. The very fact that the recommended staffing ratio changes from one staff member for every 4 children to one staff member for every 6 children will itself be enough to ensure that there will be new caretakers for many continuing children. With center-based child care it is simply impossible to regularly meet Hrdy's bottom-line standard for quality day care: the "*caretakers . . . have to be the same caretakers.*"[34]

Recall the last chapter's discussion of the subtle "conversation" that goes on between a mother and her baby—the speaking, smiling, pointing, exchanging of objects. How much of this elaborate "turn-taking" will happen between a child care worker and *every one* of her *four* infant charges? There will be too much diaper changing and feeding that must be done to allow much time for peaceful, unhurried cuddling, much less any subtler kind of interaction. And even if there *were* sufficient time, there is little reason to believe that day care workers will be as motivated to engage in repeated "conversations" with infants in the way that mothers are.

Mothers have a more-than-rational love for their children and enjoy types of care-giving that no one else will. After all, even among professorial mothers, more say they like to change their baby's diapers than say they dislike it. Similarly, Hrdy tells us that "many mothers find the smell of their breast fed infants' excrement entirely congenial. Few other individuals of either sex, however, can honestly say that they share this taste." Hrdy then gives a candid job description for a modern allomother:

> Wanted: someone to turn his/her life over to the whims and needs of a smaller, weaker, often unreasonable individual for a period of months or years. Low pay. Little prestige. No security or long term mutual obligation; faint prospect that any relationship formed will be maintained over time. Caution: if the infant comes to love you best, the mother may grow jealous and terminate the relationship early.[35]

Most professional women with resources hire nannies to care for their infants because they realize that nannies are less likely to be distracted by other infants than center-care workers are, and thus nannies will be more likely to give their infants prolonged, serious attention. But paid alloparents who are not kin are unlikely to provide the quality of care that, say, an unpaid grandmother might.

For one thing, the allomothers or nannies are apparently well aware of the dangers of becoming sucked in by a baby's charms only to be abandoned by the parents when their situation changes. A recent study of Latina nannies in Los Angeles, for example, indicated that they had learned not to get too deeply involved with the children in their care because the family might move or fire them. Cases certainly exist where mothers have quit their jobs and fired nannies precisely because the nannies were *too good* as substitute mothers. The kiss of death was when the children started calling their nannies "mommy."[36]

Camilla Benbow, a world-renowned expert on sex differences in gifted students, grew up on the college campus where her father taught, and through babysitting she came to know, love and then lose contact with several infants and toddlers. When she had her own first child, she said, "Now I have a baby that no one can take away from me."[37]

Barry Brazelton, the author of the 1969 classic *Infants and Mothers,* believed that mothers who knew they had to go back to work in the first months after birth distanced themselves from their babies in the same way that the Latina nannies do. They were afraid to bond fully because the pain of later separation would then be too great.[38]

Finally, for the mother the breastfeeding experience in an on-site nursery will be less pleasant than at home. The "beatific calm" and "warm sensations" that Hrdy experienced and believes occur in most breastfeeding mothers are unlikely to be possible when the office beckons in twenty minutes.[39] The mother may feel stressed and pressured to get back. High levels of cortisol, which subside as oxytocin increases during nursing, may be just what the office requires if a worker is to close a deal or finish a report. (One mother swears that her IQ dropped until she had weaned her baby: "A pleasant fog descends upon the brain.")[40] As a mother rushes away and her baby cries out for her, she is not likely to return to work as focused on the tasks ahead as when she left.[41] In general, the nursing experience is likely to be markedly less enjoyable.

Guilt

Surveys indicate that more than half of working mothers feel guilty about leaving their children in day care.[42] Some blame society for this guilt. "Where is it written, outside the culture that indoctrinates us, that mothers are so essential to their children?" asks one professional woman.[43] Similarly, an officer of the National Association for the Education of Young Children tells a reporter, "We've socialized women into feeling guilty. Child care is essentially viewed as . . . a *mother's* responsibility. This is what I wonder. Do you think working dads have the same level of guilt?"[44] Some working mothers don't blame society for their guilt, but instead agree with Hrdy's view that the guilt is a byproduct of an irreconcilable dilemma. For them, "the antiseptic talk of 'work-life balance' " does nothing to still the "ceaseless internal debates . . . the persistent, private kernel of doubt and remorse."[45]

What's clear is that many working women are stunned by their unexpected feelings. A big city newspaper reporter said,

> My friends who had gone back to work told me it would be hard. By hard I thought they meant I would feel reluctant, reticent, like going back to school in the fall after summer vacation. . . . I did not expect grief. . . . I did not expect guilt.[46]

Another woman, the vice president of a bank, put it this way:

> On some mornings it's just awful leaving for work. My older son says, "Mommy, I don't want you to go to work today." He gives me a big hug, then another, then another. It's *torture*. And my younger one, he gets these big tears and watches me through the window as I go to the car. Sometimes at night, my [elder] son asks me to lie down with him on his bed, and he says, "I'll hold your shirt so you don't go away."

> I'm always soul-searching.... You're trying to provide for a good life and that's sort of ironic. Because what is more important—the monetary aspects or being there for them?[47]

Having a really important job—one with the potential to do great good for society as a whole—is no protection against these feelings. Of all the moving stories I have encountered in researching this book, none are more poignant than those related by two prominent politicians who are also mothers and who reflected on their dual roles.

Madeleine Kunin, a survivor of the Holocaust who rose to become governor of Vermont, tells a fascinating political story in her autobiography. But her inner turmoil over pursuing a career while being the mother of four children was what most profoundly affected one reviewer.

> She tells us that she never broke free of the pull of domesticity and the accompanying guilt. Driving to an important political meeting she found her young son's beloved baby blanket in the back of the car. Should she go back home to return it? She did. During a campaign she came home to find that her family had already blown out her child's birthday candles. She had them do it over again so she could participate.
>
> "At least once a day," Kunin remembers, "I would feel a stab in my chest, thinking I should be at one place when I was at another." There was no cure for the anxiety; all she could do, she says, was "not to let it overwhelm me, not to let it pull me down, but to carry it as gracefully as I could."[48]

Golda Meir, former prime minister of Israel, tells a similar story:

> Such a struggle breaks out in you. Your heart goes to pieces. It's all running around, trying to be in two places at once, getting upset. All this can't help but be reflected in the structure of the family. I know that my children, when they were little, suffered a lot on my account. I left them alone so often. I was never with them when I should have been and would have liked to be. Oh, I remember how happy they were, my children, every time I didn't go to work because of a headache. They jumped and laughed and said, "Mamma's staying home! Mamma has a headache." If you only knew how many times I say to myself, "To hell with everything, to hell with everybody, I've done my share, now let the others do theirs, enough, enough, enough."[49]

Many prominent women give up on careers rather than put up with the tension, guilt and grief. Brenda Barnes resigned as president and chief executive of Pepsi-Cola North America when one of her three kids, all in elementary school, said she could keep working if she would "promise to be at home for all our birthdays." Every time she would "miss a child's birthday, a school concert or a parent-teacher discussion" she would "feel the tug."[50] Wendy Chamberlain gave up the plum assignment of ambassador to Pakistan at the height of the war against terrorism when bombings in Islamabad caused all dependants to be ordered home: Chamberlain refused to be apart from her thirteen- and fifteen-year-old daughters.[51]

Fathers don't feel this daily guilt and grief as a result of the time they spend away from their children. But then they usually don't believe they are as well equipped for child care as mothers are. A 1996 national survey found that 87 percent of men and 78 percent of women believed that women are biologically better suited to care for children.[52]

One study of sex differences in psychological stress among married couples concludes that for wives, but not husbands, it is especially stressful to be married and employed with minor children.[53] A second study of mothers finds that those who work have more stress than those who don't.[54] A third study, also of mothers, finds that those who work are far more conflicted about working than homemakers are about staying at home. And working moms' "pervasive internal struggle" is as common among those with teenagers as among those with preschoolers; even mothers with "supportive husbands" are "often" highly conflicted.[55] A fourth study shows that working moms with minors at home have higher levels of cortisol than do other women with the same jobs. This result was independent of marital status or social support.[56]

This stress is no doubt increased by the tendency of children to let mom know they'd like her around more. One sign that "quality day care" won't resolve women's difficulties in juggling work and family is that the children who want mom around are often well beyond day care age. Barnes' kids were all in elementary school, and Chamberlain's were teenagers.

Studies show that from 1965 to the late 1980s, the time that the average American child spent with a parent dropped by 43 percent.[57] A Carnegie report notes that adolescents "in survey after survey ... lament their lack of parental attention."[58] Other studies make it clear that mom does more good than dad when she stays home.

Although one might guess that having either parent at home more would lead to higher student achievement, studies that control for parental income and education as well as for quality of school reveal that lower maternal work hours increase student achievement, but lower paternal work hours *decrease* it.[59] It may not be surprising, then, that in another study, high maternal job satisfaction is associated with *lower* psychological well-being in girls, while paternal job satisfaction, in contrast, is associated with higher psychological well-being.[60]

Army Colonel Lois Beard, once considered the odds-on favorite to be the first mother ever to be promoted to the rank of general, resigned suddenly in 1999. She said she "loved being a commander, but I found myself saying I would be a better commander if I wasn't a parent and a better parent if I wasn't a commander." She thought her teenage daughters were withdrawing from her. Her sixteen-year-old told a reporter that while she missed both parents, she saved her ire for her mother. She admitted freezing her mom out, saying to herself, "You weren't there when I needed you, so why should I talk to you now?"[61]

Is this reaction of children simply a sign that they have tacitly accepted historic gender role stereotypes, despite having been exposed to all those school textbooks full of mothers with briefcases and none with aprons? Maybe. But maybe the kids think that mom has a more understanding and welcoming ear when they need to talk. And maybe men who hang around the home a lot are not at their best. Children give unemployed and partially employed fathers particularly low grades on making them feel "important and loved."[62] Statistical studies also find that unemployed mothers provide twice as much "undivided child care" per week as employed mothers; unemployed fathers, on the other hand, provide children with no more undivided child care than employed fathers do.[63]

Some might consider socialization responsible for weak father-child attachment. Three studies by three different sets of authors, however, find that weak father-son bonds are more likely the result of a wife's employment and subsequent nonmaternal care for her children: "Father-son attachments consistently emerge as at risk for insecurity when non-maternal care is initiated on a full- or near-full-time basis in the first year [after birth]."[64]

In any case, research to date does not provide support for the view that good relations with dad in early childhood can substitute for good relations with mom. Several studies ask young adults whether they feel high or low satisfaction with their early childhood relationships with their mothers, on the one hand, and their fathers, on the other, or whether they fall somewhere in between. The studies then compare these satisfaction levels with current levels of loneliness, depression, anxiety, self-esteem, relations with peers and other indicators of well-being. Perceived satisfaction with the mother in childhood correlates with better health, but in most of the studies, fond memories of dad do not correlate with good health.[65]

Maternal guilt, then, may reflect children's need to have their mothers present much of the time as they grow up. Evolutionists don't doubt that mother's guilt is an adaptive device with a biological basis.

> Surely ancestral women ... needed to coordinate emotionally with their young. Those who suffered when they saw a sick or unhappy infant devoted more time and energy to keeping this child alive. Emotionally attuned mothers raised children who were well adjusted. These children disproportionately lived—gradually selecting for women's superior ability to express sadness, pity, empathy, compassion, and other nurturing emotions.[66]

Mother's guilt, however, has its up side. Science writer Deborah Blum sympathetically discusses a piece of evidence from developmental psychologist Jay Belsky's studies of day care:

> The mothers who assert that their children are generally better off in day care—who are relaxed, casual, and relieved about leaving them there—are much more likely to have children who lack a secure attachment. In a sense, these mothers haven't pulled tight the emotional threads; they don't grieve at the door because they can let go easily. And their children are, perhaps, more emotionally adrift.[67]

Desire

In encouraging mothers to bond with their babies, Mother Nature uses the carrot of pleasure as well as the stick of guilt. Golda Meir's pain was partly guilt and a sense of duty to her children, but also partly a genuine desire to be there when she could not be. Madeleine Kunin had the candles relit and blown out again for her own benefit, not for that of her kids. Susan Estrich, even as she chides Brenda Barnes for letting down the feminist team with her resignation, emphasizes mothers' own need to spend time with their children.

> Even if our children would turn out fine without us, even if their peers matter more than we do, most of us, for our sake if not for theirs, do not want to miss the experience of watching them grow. Going days without seeing one's children, as many men actually do on the climb to the top, and in holding on once they get there, is viewed by most mothers as an unacceptable alternative.[68]

Despite the emphasis on androgynous roles in Sweden, women there are far less likely than men to report pleasure at returning to work at the end of their parental leaves.[69] In this country, far more women than men say that "their career was too big a sacrifice; it just wasn't worth it."[70] Many female professionals refuse to make the sacrifice. One attorney who resigned to be a stay-at-home mom said that the main benefit was "knowing all the minutiae" of her son's life.[71] Author Iris Krasnow puts these minutiae in perspective:

> I go over my day—wiping banana off the TV screen, scraping mud off sneakers with a Swiss army knife, reading *Pocahontas* to four boys who are looking at their mother with reverence. And I am reminded that This Is As Good As It Gets.[72]

A bright, likable and well-adjusted research assistant told me that she had been a day care baby from early in infancy. She didn't think it had harmed her at all; yet she planned to stay home with her kids in the early years. She said that her mother remembered very little of her early childhood. She wasn't there for the first words or the first walk. The research assistant wanted to be there for her children. (One national survey of 1,100 mothers finds that this desire to be present for the first words and the first walk is virtually universal.)[73]

In reflecting on the research assistant's comments, I remember thinking that although I have loved being a father and have tried hard to be a good dad to our three sons, I couldn't remember a thing about who began to walk or talk when. I didn't know if I was there or not and didn't think I had missed much if I wasn't. But what stories they liked at bedtime and what they were like to coach in youth basketball—that I was OK on.

Again, professional women regularly express amazement at the intensity of their maternal feelings. One says her return to work made it only as far as the Red Line subway platform.[74] Another wonders how she will explain to her boss, her colleagues—or even to herself—why staying home and reading *Hop on Pop* now seems so compelling.[75] Some professionals acknowledge these feelings only with foreboding. A journalist with a degree from Yale described the "huge and terrifying abyss" that opened up beneath her feet when she realized, "I *want* to mother this baby."[76]

It is not only guilt, but also a desire for hands-on parenting that incites many women to forego promising career opportunities or quit their jobs. Maria Shriver resigned as co-anchor of *Sunday Today* so she could spend more time with her baby daughter.[77] Massachusetts governor Jane Swift had a husband willing to be a stay-at-home dad, but nonetheless Swift commandeered a state helicopter to fly home to be with her young daughter because she couldn't "bear to have her very far away from me."[78] When Karen Hughes resigned as top adviser to President George W. Bush, a contributing factor was the realization that she was not getting a chance to see her teenage boy's *friends* grow up![79] And one of the most important reasons Cokie Roberts gave when leaving ABC's Sunday news show was a desire to spend more time with her grandchildren.[80]

Conclusion

In the late 1990s about 59 percent of mothers with kids under one year of age were in the work force—up from 31 percent in 1976. This dramatic increase does not, however, mean that working mothers have been beating down the doors of day care centers. Currently, only about 36 percent of women with children under twelve months old work full-time, and a substantial minority of these work at home.[81] Moreover, half the time, nonmaternal caretakers of infants are relatives. Of all children under one, only about 7 percent have working mothers who have placed them in day care centers. Even among all children under five with working mothers, only about 29 percent are in center-based care.[82]

Working women say they hold jobs because their families need the money. One survey showed that almost four times as many women say they work for financial reasons as say they do so to escape boredom or for self-fulfillment. In 1996, a different poll asked working women to imagine that they had enough money to live as comfortably as they would like. The pollsters wondered if, in that situation, they would prefer to work full-time, work part-time, do volunteer work, or work at home caring for their family:

> Thirty-one percent of the women replied that they would like to be at home with their children; another 33 percent replied that part-time work would be ideal; 20 percent expressed a preference for volunteer work; only 15 percent replied that they wanted to work full time.[83]

A third national survey summed up its findings as follows:

> For most mothers, being a working mother is not liberating, it's taxing and stressful. The feeling of most mothers seems to be, "A mother *should* be at home, I want to be at home, and I would be a better mother if I were at home."
>
> The stress of combining working with mothering, said 53 percent of working mothers, negatively affected their ability to be good mothers to their children even when they were at home. As one mother wrote, "You know that the minute you walk in the door it's time to tune in. But all you want to do is tune out."[84]

Regardless of their own preferences, working mothers believe that society is best served when mothers care for their own babies. One survey puts mother-care at the top with alternative types in the following order: care by another relative, mother and father "working in a tag team," church-run care, family friend, home day care provider, nanny, and center-based care.[85] Another survey of working women finds that they respect stay-at-home moms more than mothers who work full-time, and when women are asked whether the increased number of working mothers with young children is good or bad for society, women of all educational levels are more likely to think it is bad, but college-educated women—by a margin of more than three and a half to one—are particularly likely to think so.[86]

Americans are remarkably traditional. As one academic feminist acknowledges, the "vast majority of women and men continue to endorse the importance of husband as provider and wife as nurturer."[87] A 1996 Gallup survey found that about half of Americans and slightly more women than men agree with a statement suggesting the desirability of a strict and traditional division of labor: the "optimal family structure is one where the father works as a 'breadwinner' while the mother takes care of the children and the home." Another 21 percent said there should be such a clear division of labor but that it didn't matter whether mother or father stayed home.[88] Moreover, both men and women believe in stereotypes that,

I have argued, are actually not stereotypes at all—that men are less interested, patient and competent with infants than women are.[89]

Even though most women think it isn't good for young children when their mothers have demanding, time-intensive jobs, and even though the vast majority of mothers with young children do not themselves want full-time jobs, such mothers often work long hours because of "financial pressures."[90] Many commentators agree with an expert on child development who has said that people these days simply have no choice: "In the 50s a man could raise a family on his income while his wife stayed at home, but few can do that any more."[91] A vice president of the National Women's Law Center adds: "Both parents need to support the family and that produces this crunch for child care that we in this country need to respond to."[92] Or as the editor in chief of *Working Mother* magazine asserts, mothers must work "to ensure their children are safe and fed and clothed."[93]

All these statements come from a society where mothers with only a high school education are the least likely to return to work in the first year of their child's life, while those with graduate degrees are the most likely to do so.[94] Women with higher education are the socioeconomic group most likely to say that working moms are bad for kids, but also the group most likely to put their children in the type of care that seems worst for infants: center-based care.[95] Since women with high education levels are very likely to be married to men making above-average incomes, it is hard to credit the view that economics explain this remarkable and apparently contradictory situation.

The argument that "economic realities" make the two-career family essential these days is heard everywhere. But in fact, the median married male worker in 1959 made $27,579 in dollars adjusted to reflect their purchasing power in 2001; the same median worker in 2001 made $36,261.[96]

In the fifties a man could and did "raise a family on his income alone," but in the present era, much wealthier husbands and wives are assured that such an arrangement won't allow their families to meet their "subsistence needs." I don't doubt that many upper-middle-class women genuinely believe that their financial situation compels them to work and that they do so for the sake of their children—for private schools, music lessons and the like. These women, however, may not be aware that several studies find "income is not as important as commonly believed" in heading off children's problems.[97]

Moreover, the NICHD studies suggest that women should not discount the negative behavioral effects of extensive nonmaternal care of young children. Indeed, some studies indicate that the magnitude of the effect of nonmaternal care on child behavior is "virtually the same" as the magnitude of the effect of being raised in poverty and "substantially larger than" the magnitude of the effect of a lack of "sensitive-responsive parenting."[98]

By fostering and encouraging the common opinion that economic conditions compel the typical married woman to work, advocates of androgynous roles and day care can drum up support for further subsidization of center-based care, which both experts and the public think inferior to most other forms of care. But at least one good longitudinal study shows that after having their babies, mothers become increasingly sure that child care should be done by parents, whereas fathers become increasingly sure that nonparental care would be fine.[99] In light of such evidence it would be interesting to learn which spouse insists that the wife must work on account of "economic realities."[100]*

There is little evidence to support increased subsidization of day care. Two-career families who put their children in subsidized day care apparently produce a near tripling of the odds that these children will be disobedient and aggressive—hardly a trend the government should support financially.[101]

New subsidies for child care will not influence those who desperately need the money or those who would go crazy if they spent all day with their kids Those women will work regardless. Neither will subsidies affect those who are determined to stay home with their kids. They might influence those in the middle—those desiring to stay home with their kids but tempted by the ways an added income could help their families. Since day care is likely to have a negative impact on children's behavioral, emotional and even physical health, there seems to be little argument for subsidizing it further.[102]

Some might contend that subsidization would lead some parents to choose higher-quality care. But one careful study finds that subsidies lead parents to buy more hours of child care, not better child care.[103] In any case, very young kids do best with their parents.

---

*On a related subject, one female columnist has noted all the studies supposedly showing that *women* are choosing to delay childbirth, when in her experience it is often their *husbands* who want to delay childbirth because they are more interested in keeping their wives' market income flowing. [Mundy, 2000]

To subsidize and thus encourage inferior kinds of care in the hope they will become a little better is a bit like subsidizing low-tar cigarettes because they are not quite as bad as other kinds of cigarettes.

It would seem to make more sense to subsidize something that is good—to give a tax break to parents of very young children if one parent stays home with the child instead of working. According to polls, the public prefers such an approach over expanding day care subsidies by more than a two-to-one margin.[104] At the very least, we might increase the dependants' personal tax exemption, a policy which would provide mothers with money that could be used to pay for commercial day care if they should so wish, but could also be used to make staying home and caring for one's children more affordable.

It might be thought that mothers would be delighted to learn that something they like to do and do better than anyone else is vital to the well-being of their children and thus to society more broadly. But satisfaction will be delayed until the facts are better known and until the androgynous project can be seen as misogynist rather than as the road to female salvation.

CONCLUSION

Marriage underlies most of the foregoing discussion of cultural and policy issues. Fatherless families exist in the first place either because parents do not marry or because they divorce. The sexual revolution makes women unhappy because it interferes with men's ability to transform their sexual passions into a more enduring love that inspires them to commit to a long-term future. Title IX administration is troubling, in part, because by removing a positive outlet for men's aggression and urge for dominance, it eliminates one means of making them suitable for marriage. Finally, day care has proved a sorry substitute for the marital alternative, mothers, as the principal caretakers for children.

While most women want marriage and family to be at the center of their lives, some women want career to be coequal or even primary. I admire and respect such women and have taught many in my classes on sex differences, culture and policy. A number have become correspondents and friends; I follow their lives with real interest. I am eager for their happiness.

Jan, a radical gender feminist through and through, sparred with me in class, sometimes angrily. I hired her as a research assistant, and she did very well. She could fully set forth an argument she disagreed with as well as any student I have ever had. Now working toward a Ph.D. in sociology at one of the country's best universities, Jan will not like this book. Though a serious scholar, her career in academia will be largely concerned with trying to transform gender roles toward androgyny. Career will always come first for Jan.

Christie went on to a top law school and became Christine. She refused to go through doors when men opened them for her because she didn't need the help and thought she should have as much opportunity to perform that courtesy as any man. Christie really wanted to learn. Someone with my views would have a difficult time persuading her, but with Christie a reasoned view always had a chance.

Lisa was a bundle of energy, hilarity and ambition for a career as a journalist. She loved to argue and shared my view that the best of all worlds includes lovable people who disagree about fundamentals but don't let these disagreements alter their affection for each other.

All three of these women clearly have above-average interest in careers by any standard, male or female. Yet none of the three seems masculine. Despite her tough-minded views, Jan is shy; and both Christine and Lisa are sociable in the way that appealing young women often are. All three would serve as illustrations of Socrates' belief that interesting human beings often display a mix of masculine and feminine traits.

If these young women had grown up when I did, they would have scanned the "female help wanted" ads for a narrow range of jobs that almost always paid less than those in the "male help wanted" ads, and it is unlikely that all of them would have gone on to pursue advanced degrees or well-suited professional careers. Jan, Christine, Lisa and many others are in debt to the women who were instrumental in expanding the possibilities for those who followed. The whole country benefits when such talents are unleashed.

But for Christine and Lisa the road may not be easy. Each wants to marry, and they are attracted to ambitious men. But we have seen that men with ambition may prefer women who are less ambitious. And if these women's careers should outshine those of their husbands, they are less likely to be happy in their marriages and divorce will be more likely. Children will further complicate their career paths. The women who want full-blown careers as well as a complete family life have a difficult path to navigate. Still, many do so successfully. And it's wonderful that they have opportunities to pursue a life plan of their choosing.

Though the *New York Times* may think it "belittling" to identify women as housewives or homemakers, the women in my classes seem wary of what they regard as the feminist propaganda pervading the schools and the media. When I taught my course on sex differences in the spring of 2003, I asked the students to imagine that they had a sixteen-year-old daughter. I then asked which of the articles read for that week's reading assignment, which I called "The Contemporary Debate," they would most want her to read. The articles included works by Gloria Steinem and Katha Pollitt from a feminist perspective, and by Danielle Crittenden and Carolyn Graglia who emphasized the importance of marriage and children. In most years I have some conservative, traditional female students, but that spring I had none; all the female students regarded themselves either as feminists or as moderates on gender issues. So I was amazed when most said they would want their daughters to read conservatives Crittenden or Graglia.

In explaining their choices, my students said it wasn't that they thought these authors more persuasive than their adversaries, but rather that their views were important and nowhere to be found in the primary and secondary schools they had attended, where only the feminist perspective on careers and family was represented. One student said her daughter should "hear both sides." Another said she should be exposed to arguments expressing the "value in mothering." Still another young woman, who would be off to Duke medical school in the fall, thought Graglia helped combat the media publicity and social pressure against stay-at-home moms.

In the midst of this same semester I was back in touch with a very bright student, Meg, who had been the most outspoken feminist in the same course a few years earlier. She wrote asking for a letter of recommendation for further study and let drop the following comment: "Needless to say, my strong opinions on gender equality have evolved somewhat in the past few years, particularly since becoming engaged."

I asked for more detail in my response, and Meg wrote back as follows:

> As for my evolving views, I must admit that I've been forced to reconsider something you said in class; you stated your view that if an alien came to our planet and asked you to show him what happiness looked like, you'd show him a recently engaged woman. I believe I argued the point at the time, but based on my own recent experiences and those of my female friends, most of them in their mid- to late twenties now—I think there may be more truth to that than I was willing to acknowledge at the time. My opinion now is that many women are far more concerned with marriage and family than they admit, perhaps because in this cultural moment it's not popular to do so.

As our correspondence continued, she elaborated:

> Often, I think, women fool themselves into thinking they don't have traditional desires for marriage and family. An example comes to mind. One of my good friends was telling me how she never really had planned on getting married or even wanted to get married. It all seemed silly and traditional to her. However, when her boyfriend, who she had been living with for five years, finally surprised her by proposing, she said, "yes, yes, yes" and then wept uncontrollably for two days. She told me this story without any acknowledgement of the irony. And I'm thinking, does a woman who never really wanted to get married weep uncontrollably for two days when her boyfriend proposes?
>
> My point is that contemporary culture has somehow made women feel ashamed of having conventional aspirations like marriage and children. I'm twenty-five, for example, and even though I have every intention of continuing my career, you wouldn't believe the looks of disbelief I get when I tell friends that I would also like to start our family within the next three years. This seems shocking to many of my friends, even though we know numerous couples in their mid- to late thirties who desperately want children but are now facing fertility problems.

Meg said, in conclusion, that she thought we need to teach girls and women to be more honest with themselves about their own desires.

I wrote Meg and asked if she did not think that people have a tendency to say that things—like marriage—are not all that important to them if they think that there is a decent chance they won't happen. Psychologically, it's tough to get through days if things you desperately want aren't happening; it seems logical to downplay their importance. So perhaps it can be tough for women to be honest with themselves about their own desires.

She replied in the affirmative:

> I'd say your point about downplaying goals that seem out of reach is quite valid. The problem is that it's self-perpetuating; for societal reasons marriage and family become difficult to obtain, thus women deny that they want these things, thus they become even more difficult to obtain because they've been deprioritized.

What Most Women Want

Most women want most of all a loving husband and children. They have always been more attracted to people than to things. They love strong, long-term relationships; casual, uncommitted sex soon loses its attractions, if indeed it ever had any. The marital ideal—one man and one woman bound in body and soul, sharing, comforting, communicating through good times and bad—is very appealing even, or perhaps particularly, in a cynical age. This vision includes romantic and committed sex along with children, to whom most women have been drawn since childhood and who seem even more precious once pregnancy and breastfeeding bathe women in hormonal pleasure.

One 1997 national survey of women by the Pew Research Center found that 93 percent of mothers regard their children as a source of happiness all or most of the time; 90 percent say the same about their marriage. Meanwhile, only 60 percent of working women find their careers a source of happiness all or most of the time. On a 10-point scale, 86 percent of mothers rate their children a 10 for their importance to personal happiness; just 30 percent of employed women rate their job as a 10. Even *unmarried, childless* women are more likely to say that personal relationships, with mothers (31 percent) or friends (24 percent), are more important to their happiness than careers (11 percent) or hobbies (10 percent).[1]

Given the priorities that most women give to family on the one hand and job on the other, it seems unlikely that the job gains of the last forty years have compensated for the deterioration that has occurred on the home front. A 1995 poll found that more than twice as many women thought the feminist movement had made it harder to combine jobs and families as thought the movement had made it easier.[2] Similarly, a 1998 poll found that about five times as many men *and* women thought changing gender roles had made it harder for marriages to be successful as thought it had made it easier. Of those surveyed, about six times as many thought changing roles had made it harder to raise children as thought it had made it easier.[3] And whatever the cause, women are far less likely to get the marriages and children they say they want than in the past. More than twice as many women nearing forty are unmarried today (28 percent) compared with 1960 (13 percent).[4] As recently as 1980, only 9 percent of women in their early forties had not had a child; now the number is 16 percent: a truly staggering rise, especially when juxtaposed with the statistics on women's happiness and priorities.[5]

Although the national media might make us think that Mr. Moms are popping up all over, they are not. For one thing, women are rarely attracted to such men. Sociologist Catherine Hakim surveys the evidence and concludes, "Even the most qualified and high-earning women reject role reversal in favor of a partner who is at least equal, preferably superior, in earnings, status or power."[6] Hakim, whose recent book looks at a substantially different body of research than I have, nonetheless agrees with me that women, even more than men, prefer gendered roles in which the husband spends more time earning money.[7] She finds that the women's movement has not narrowed the gender gap in this regard.[8] Evolutionary psychologist David Buss and his colleagues agree. They look at mate preferences over the last half-century and see no sign that women value domestic skills in a marriage partner more than they used to.[9]

Hakim finds that 20 percent of married women, many of whom have no children, are work-centered. Another 20 percent of married women want no part of work outside the home, whether full-time or part-time. The majority of women, however—approximately 60 percent—can be best classified as adaptive. They are frequently ambivalent, torn between the conflicting pulls of family and employment. They seek a more balanced life than work-centered women do.[10] Often their work patterns depend on whether they marry and on their husband's earning capacity. Many respond to job opportunities based on family circumstances. Because they have multiple goals and priorities, these women seem less focused or single-minded than either career or home-centered women. When they are working, they are more likely than men to think of their work as jobs rather than long-term, inflexible careers.[11] They frequently work part-time or only after the children are in school. Hakim finds that the "vast majority" of career-oriented women change their perspective and priorities after they have children.[12]

On balance, part-time female workers are more satisfied with both jobs and children than are full-time female workers, possibly because such women usually see themselves as secondary earners and are thus more able than husbands to renounce high-paying jobs for work they enjoy in a friendly environment.[13] Taken as a whole, working women are as satisfied—if not more satisfied—with their jobs as men are. But even though women work less than men on average, their most frequently cited complaint is long hours.[14]

Evidence provided in an article published in a 2003 issue of the *Journal of Marriage and the Family* shows that between 1973 and 1994, working women increasingly came to see home, not work, as their haven; for men there has been no change.[15] A second article in the same issue found that marital quality went down when wives worked extended hours or in demanding jobs.[16]

What Most Men Need

It is harder to bring into focus the males who have taken my sex difference courses than it is the females. Sex differences themselves can actually help explain this. First, when the course ends, the men are less likely than the women to stay in touch. Second, as evidenced by enrollment figures, the course material interests them less. I teach courses on political economy, and the classes are two-thirds male. My courses on sex differences are three-quarters female. For the women, class discussions about men, sex, relationships, babies, career and family just continue on an academic level what they and their girlfriends talk about all the time; the women seem like they're on the edges of their seats—as if each feels that "this is my life we're talking about." In contrast, many of the men seem bored.

The men who are not bored are usually interested for one or more of three reasons: they take a scientific interest in the subject; they think the evidence confirms their culturally conservative views; or they take their religion very seriously. Those who are seriously religious are often not sexually active, and they are more mature and far more likely to think about marrying at graduation or within a year or two after.

Tom, a brilliant law student now clerking at the Supreme Court, was scientifically curious, culturally conservative and religious. Tall and handsome, toward the end of law school he settled on a nurturing fiancée, and it is hard to imagine anything other than happily ever after for these two.

Brit was as conservative but not as religious. When we discussed *The Rules* in class, he blurted out, "I think my girlfriend used *The Rules* with me." He and his girlfriend had dated for years and were, as he put it, "engaged to be engaged." After college, she followed him to New York, but within four months they had broken up and she was back in the South. He said, "In some ways I feel like I should have known better than cohabiting, but I was not willing to make a commitment like marriage without a 'test-drive.' Maybe therein lies the whole problem."

There is another group of men who lament that they are all the girls' "friends" but never their "boyfriends." Sometimes they are "nerds," too shy and perhaps too nice for their own good. In time, when the girls become more sensible and these young men mature a little, they will surely marry and be good family men.

Finally, there are those who are very much enjoying having casual sex with undergraduate women. One of these, a tall, good-looking and charismatic guy, Pat, told me he could easily sleep with a different woman every weekend night all year long. His sister would be coming to the university in the fall, and he planned to make "damn sure" that she knew what was going on so she could avoid becoming prey for sexually rapacious males.

Over the last year or two, I have asked students to comment on my draft chapters, and one man, Luke, said the following in response to an anecdote in the sexual revolution chapter:

> "Sleeping with a woman who has already submitted is like playing a computer game you have already won." WOW. It is true though. It is interesting that a number of my friends will usually only call someone they had a one night stand with late at night, after they have already tried and failed to find new people to have sex with that night. The "sluts" become safeties. If you can't find anyone else new to have sex with, then there is a back-up plan. Just like if u don't have a new video game to play, you just go back to the one you have won already because you have nothing else to do.

Though women readers may feel that Pat and Brit will never be marriage material, I can also report on a third "player," Jack, every bit as committed to casual sex when I knew him. He was a little older when at UVA, and two years after leaving, he wrote of a wife and a son, saying they were "blissfully happy." He added, "I remember a story you told in class about your father who was 'tamed' by marriage and childbirth. I feel a little bit that way myself! And to be honest, I rather like it."

Like Jack, most men in time end up pleased with marriage. But it is easy to see why the idea might take some getting used to. Compared with women, they are more used to time alone and time in large groups. Women have far more experience with best-friend relationships built on communication. Boys and men are attracted to competitive challenges more than to opportunities for intimacy.

They do not generally understand female-style emotional support. They are used to helping a pal by downplaying his troubles or giving advice, not by sympathetically hearing him out. In one study, 98 percent of wives reported that they wanted their husbands to talk more about their thoughts and feelings.[17] For men, problems call for advice or action, not talk. When told he should show his wife more affection, one man went home and washed her car.[18]

Some feminist texts complain about men's pitiful performance in the "emotion work" of a marriage. In marriages, wives work to keep conversations going and are more thoughtful than their husbands about sentimental things. Janice Steil notes that all this takes "time, energy, effort and skill," and it proves to be still "another aspect of family work . . . that women disproportionately perform."[19]

One of the most common marital disputes occurs between a wife who desires more intimacy and a husband who "withdraws and feels pressured."[20] In olden days, new brides went to their mothers with their disappointments about marital intimacy; mothers might tell them, "That's just the way men are" and suggest having lunch with old girlfriends. A footnote in Janice Steil's book discusses a study finding that couples have better marriages when wives make up for intimacy deficits with their husbands through their female friendships. Steil rejects this way of resolving the problem because it "fails to address the issue of the costs of unfulfilled expectations. Most women probably do not enter into marriage with the expectation that the work of intimacy will be nonreciprocal."[21] Among the costs of the unfulfilled and unrealistically androgynous expectations are the large number of wives (with clean cars?) who file for divorce because, as Sanford Braver's book on the subject shows, they do not feel "loved and appreciated."[22]

No matter how good their relationships, men are far more likely than women to report that they need free time to relax and pursue hobbies away from their mate. Yet they sense that marriage means less time for hobbies and more time spent with children and kin, activities that women tend to enjoy more than men do. Making a marriage work requires flexibility and a willingness to change some habits. But men are more stubborn and less flexible than women.[23]

For all these reasons, men are less attracted to and less well equipped for marriage than women. Men, nonetheless, need marriage. Communities of unmarried young men are prone to engage in violence and predatory sex. Compared with the married, young unmarried men tend to be lazy and unfocused. Or worse, they may drop out of society altogether, or undermine it. Unmarried men are five times more likely than unmarried women to be homeless, and they disproportionately fill our prisons.

Marriage compels men to grow up. This is why the newly engaged young man looks more serious as well as more happy. As poll results suggest, men know that marriage means new responsibilities and worries. They will now have to become good providers and set good examples for their children. Their love for and commitment to their wives can be increased by their common commitment to their children. Their families will make the loner males more sociable and community-oriented. They have a new reason to care about their community's schools and the Parent Teacher Association. Crime rates and community drug problems have new saliency for them.[24]

Married men usually take well to the provider role. Even among those with top educational credentials, men are more likely than women to choose a job because it offers better financial prospects. Polls show that men are more likely than women to depend upon work for a sense of purpose and identity.[25] These polls also show that men are more than twice as likely as women to say they would continue to work full-time even if they could live as comfortably as they would like without doing so.[26]

Despite its constraints, work caters to a part of men's nature. It allows them to roam beyond the family fire. It provides a competitive outlet. A salary gives a tangible indicator of progress. Men who marry and who plan a family have more motivation to work hard, and with rising personal responsibilities, their work effort and salaries rise concurrently.[27] Moreover, "the mental health of women is unrelated to their earnings, while among men there is a strong, positive association between earnings and mental health."[28]

Men are more aggressive than women, and they more regularly seek to dominate. Dominance, assertiveness and the drive that sustains ambition are thought to belong to the same behavioral family.[29] In the workplace, men are more likely than women to grab the floor in meetings and to claim credit, whether deserved or not, for the ideas that carry the day. Women seem to care more about protecting the feelings of subordinates; men worry more about hurting the feelings of their bosses. Women generally seek more ties with their coworkers; men, however, with their eyes and ambitions directed upward, are more likely to ask their boss's boss to lunch.[30]

This male drive, however, does not extend to the domestic sphere. Even in those few modern American families where the parents try to share child care equally, the husbands often push for more paid care so there are fewer total hours they must divide with their spouses. In most cases of marital conflict regarding child care, "mothers wanted more than their husbands thought was necessary: more protectiveness, more attention, more interaction."[31] The fathers in families where time with children is shared equally acknowledge that their wives are more emotionally involved with the children, often to the extent that they find it harder to concentrate on other tasks when away from them.[32] In contrast, husbands in two-career families are more stressed than wives if child care breaks down and they must stay home from work to tend to children.[33]

A study of 33-year-olds in the United Kingdom found that children and child care were "crucial factors shaping marital and life satisfaction for women" but not for men.

> Involvement with their children . . . had no effect on [men's] satisfaction with their marriage and with life in general. If anything, the opposite was sometimes observed: men who were closely involved in the care and social development of their children were most unhappy with their marriage, and with life generally.[34]

Ironically, research suggests that a good way to induce fathers to become more attached to their children is for their wives to work less outside the home.[35]

Marital Dynamics and Vulnerabilities

The theme of female vulnerability recurs throughout this book. Because women tend to bond with those they sleep with, men's more cavalier attitude about sex can leave women bitter and emotionally devastated. Pregnancy, delivery and nursing can drain women's energy, often leaving them in need of being nurtured themselves. Women's outsized love of their children produces a bond that makes them more dependent on their husbands to provide the resources enabling them to spend as much time with their children as they wish.

Women's stronger attachments to friends and family also make them more vulnerable to loss. An experiment at the National Institute of Mental Health asked men and women to recall deaths, divorces and other sad events in their lives while PET scans viewed their brains. The limbic system glowed in both sexes, but the area was eight times as big in the women. In her book *Sex on the Brain*, Deborah Blum reports on the views of Ellen Frank, a researcher at the University of Pittsburgh:

> Women are genetically preprogrammed to be more affiliative. Interpersonal attachment is a bigger deal for women than men, and that's true in all cultures and times. It has an adaptive significance for the survival of the species. If women didn't attach, babies wouldn't survive.... If we have one half of the human race that's more preprogrammed for attachment, then that's the half that's going to be more vulnerable.[36]

That so much of women's happiness is dependent on a good marriage and happy children makes women especially vulnerable. One study of full-time dual-career couples found that problems at work increased psychological distress equally for men and women, but that problems in the marriage led to much more distress for women than for men.[37] Women's vulnerability affects their physical as well as their mental health. When wives perceive that their family and marriage are not going well, their blood pressure goes up. When husbands perceive trouble, their blood pressure does not increase, but the husband's perception of trouble will send his wife's blood pressure up.[38] Similarly, after having an argument with her spouse, a woman's immune function decreases much more than a man's, and changes persist for at least twenty-four hours.[39]

Men's distress in marriage has other sources entirely. Husbands' mental and physical health deteriorate when they think their wives are failing in the domestic arena or when they feel they themselves are not fully meeting their providing and protecting duties. Husbands are happy in their marriage if their wife is attractive—and more attractive than they are—and if she performs well domestic tasks such as cooking and shopping.[40] Fathers in dual-earner families watch the children more often than do fathers providing the family's only income, but they also fight more with their wives and find their marriages less satisfactory.[41] (Working wives in turn are unhappy, reporting less satisfaction with "the love and affection they receive from their husbands" than do nonworking wives.)[42] Moreover, though wives' success in their careers means more family income, a deeper physiological effect seems to occur: one large study finds that when a wife's income goes up, her husband's odds of dying earlier go up as well.[43]

Other research shows that wives' careers, and especially their working long hours,

> often [have] negative effects on men's psychological well-being, as measured by levels of depression, self-esteem, and satisfaction with job, marriage and life in general. While one would expect that the "breadwinner" role would be less important to marital satisfaction among men with nontraditional sex-role attitudes, this does not seem to be the case.[44]

The world-renowned Framingham heart study has found that unsupportive bosses can harm the health of wives,[45] but also that the wives' unsupportive bosses have an even more dramatic effect on the health of their husbands! After researchers control for the usual variables, husbands of white-collar wives who have unsupportive bosses are over three times more likely to die of heart disease. Why? The authors of the Framingham study note that men will want to be protective when their wives are hassled by their bosses, but they will be "relatively powerless to assist or change the situation."[46] Their wives will probably want to talk problems out even when there are no solutions and the men can take no action. The subsequent male anger and frustration apparently kill them at remarkably high rates.

Women's Work

The biggest issues in contemporary marriages surround women's work, in and out of the home. Women like to care for children much more than men do, and they also like housework more than men do. When vocational counselors use the Strong Interest Inventory to help guide clients to appropriate occupations, "Some of the largest sex differences are found on such tasks as cooking, sewing and 'home economics.'"[47] There is reason to think that such differences have a biological basis. Preteen and teenage girls exposed to unusually high levels of testosterone *in utero* are more interested than other girls in a career other than homemaking. Correspondingly, women who have Turner's syndrome and thus produce no testosterone typically have unusually high interests in housekeeping.[48]

Before marriage, women do about one-third more housework than men. Though newly married men will respond to their wives' pressure to do more housework, they don't prioritize it as their wives do. Jennifer Roback Morse makes the same point this way:

> When I want my husband to do "his half" of household chores, what I really want is for him to do half of everything on my list of important things. But he has his own list. He values some things that I do not; he does not value all the things that I do.[49]

Even when husbands do domestic work, they rarely do it as well as wives want it done. They may give the child a bath, but as Caitlin Flanagan points out, they won't "straighten the bath mat and wring out the washcloths." They may take the toddler to nursery school, but

> They won't spend ten minutes chatting with the teacher and collecting the art projects. They will, in other words, do what men have always done: reduce a job to its simplest essentials and utterly ignore the fillips and niceties that women tend to regard as equally essential.

Flanagan remarks that a lot of women "feel cheated and angry and even—bless their hearts—surprised about this." In the old days, women could take pride in men's inability to perform women's work competently, but now when she gets home after a late deposition and finds Legos all over the floor and pizza boxes in the kitchen, the contemporary woman gets "madder than a wet hen."[50]

The subject of Flanagan's essay is not domestic work but sexless marriages, a modern phenomenon that has led to several books and much discussion. As Flanagan sees it, the women staring at the Legos and pizza boxes are left with two options:

> Endlessly haranguing their husbands to be more womanly, or silently fuming and (however wittingly) launching a sex strike of an intensity and a duration that would have impressed Aristophanes. The men who cave to the pressure to become more feminine—putting little notes in the lunch boxes, sweeping up after snack time, the whole bit—may delight their wives but they probably don't improve their sex lives much, owing to the thorny old problem of *la différence.*

We are right back to the same problem faced by the less angry, androgynous couples discussed in Chapter 3. No sex. The wives described there got plenty of help around the house, but in many cases this spousal help didn't make much difference: they had little or no desire to sleep with unmanly men.

What to do? One option would be to get rid of the "late depositions." Flanagan comments that earlier generations of married women knew that "one way to keep the springs of the marriage bed in good working order" was to plan days that allowed time and energy to be "physically and emotionally able to make love on a regular basis." Most women would prefer such days—days made up of part-time work outside the home or full-time homemaking. Today, cultural pressures to work and even the preferences of many men prevent women from bringing such days into being. Eagly and others have noted that while men may not desire a woman who will dominate or surpass them, they may think they would like a mate with a good income.[51]

The problem for women is that men are not letting up on other requirements. As Buss, Eagly, and the young men in the Doonesbury cartoon observe, they still want their women to be babes. At the same time, they don't want to be bothered with much house-

work.[52] Too often the contemporary man's agenda is to try to convince his partner that she shouldn't sweat the Legos and pizza boxes; she should just hire someone to clean the place a little and look after the kids.

The result is angry, exhausted mothers desperate for a house that looks and feels like a home and for more time with their children.[53] One way out would be for women to start telling their boyfriends, husbands and the rest of the world that they are not the same as men are. Being constantly on the go in a competitive world may work for men but not for many women who want to get pregnant or who want to nurse. They need to relax. And carrying and delivering a baby can be exhausting. Nursing takes time. In order to be fulfilled emotionally and psychologically, mothers need to spend enough time with the kids. And, as corroborated by study after study, the kids need more time with their mothers. Loving *is* doing something. As the heroine Kate Reddy says in Allison Pearson's *I Don't Know How She Does It,* families need "a lubricant." Who can better provide the lubricating love and nurturing than the mother?[54]

This philosophy will usually require men to provide the business plan. Men like challenges. Women might ask them to step up and be real providers, leaving the women more time and capacity to better fulfill the domestic role.

Such a scenario sounds regressive in an era like our own that pays plenty of lip service to a revolutionary approach to sex roles, but it's pretty much what most men and women believe works best even today. Especially after marriage, most men and women in the United States and western Europe continue to support a division of labor in which men are ultimately responsible for breadwinning and women for the domestic realm.[55] This division continues to produce happy and stable couples, and it enables men to be manly, protective and competent. Both husbands and wives are likely to be happier in a family where he makes $70,000 a year and she $30,000 rather than in one where they each make $50,000, and not just because she will be more relaxed and have more time at home. In the first scenario, a husband will be more successful in the male status hierarchy, which will please both him and his wife. She will care less about income-based success and more about the significance of her work; she is more likely to compete with her peers through looks, home, and healthy, happy kids.[56]

Before men marry, they may think they would prefer a wife with high earnings, but they seem to change their minds when their wives' careers lead to family chaos. Husbands are no happier about wives taking depositions at 6:00 P.M. than are the wives who worry about dinner, the state of the house and their children as they race home afterward. It is not that they can't stand to see their wives succeed. Husbands want happy wives. They don't want a frantic spouse and turmoil at home. Inherently men believe they must be doing something wrong if their wives are overwhelmed as they scramble to cope with both work and family. Their wives' hectoring bosses may send husbands the message that they are failing as protectors; their wives' exhaustion may indicate to them that they are failing as providers. In both cases, stress sends the husband's health downhill.

Research is mixed on the question of whether marital division of housework and child care is a significant source of tension. There is considerable evidence showing that most mothers, even those who work full-time, think the imbalance in the division of household labor is fair. Because married couples tend to define equality in their relationship in terms of mutual respect, commitment and reciprocity over time, rather than in terms of precisely divided tasks, most mothers continue to view the inequality in household and child care tasks as equitable.[57] Nonetheless, our parental-leave study and several other national surveys have found that wives are much more likely than husbands to think they should have more spousal help with household labor. In some surveys, one-half to two-thirds of women offer complaints on this score.[58]

Since women like both child care and housework more than men do, they are likely to do more of it in any foreseeable world. But even if they dislike it less than their husbands do, many wives don't enjoy housework. Even those who somewhat enjoy it may prefer other activities. When husbands do domestic work and contribute by cleaning up after themselves, they are showing that they love their wives, are attuned to what they care about and appreciate the importance of their work.

Surprisingly, marriages in which both partners think the distribution of work is fair are more likely than most to end in divorce. The ones least likely to end in divorce are those in which both partners think the distribution of labor is somewhat unfair to the wife.[59] I believe that this situation occurs because women's work in the home is devalued by much of society. A man who believes that his wife does more than her share notices and appreciates what she does. And wives indicate their marriages are happiest not when their spouse performs housework equally, but when their mate shows affection and appreciation.[60]

The affection and love of their mates mean so much to women because they signal that it is safe to nest. Women may want to nest, but with the disappearance of societal safeguards such as alimony and of the stigma facing men who run off with younger women, they need evidence that it is safe to do so. Far more than their husbands, married women will be happy only if their marriage is good. A wife's success in marriage, however, is dependent on the right response from her husband.[61] It's no wonder she will try so hard to be a peacemaker and find ways to make her marriage work.

Feminists who continue to think of gender as socially constructed deny with passion the idea of deep-seated female vulnerability. They usually believe that men's power in the home comes from their power in the marketplace. Writing in *Ms.*, one family therapist sets forth her golden rule of marriage: "Whoever has the gold makes the rules."[62] Having the gold does not, apparently, mean controlling the checkbook. In most families, women do that already. The therapist probably means that women must bring home the gold before they can control its expenditure and make the rules.

Something is wrong with the theory. Employed wives who continue to do the bulk of the domestic work are already bringing home a large share of the family income; it seems unlikely that they will make the rules even if they bring home the larger share. At home these high-achieving wives, especially the younger ones, "attempt to be especially attractive and sexual for their husbands, and they report indulging husbands' whims and salving egos."[63]

Even if higher income were the recipe for greater marital power, wives are especially unhappy in wife-dominated marriages. The dominated husband often just tunes out and focuses on other things. Since the marriage is so important to the wife's happiness, she becomes miserable. Evidently marriage cannot be seen as a struggle for power or economic influence in which the winner gains happiness.

In one way, men and women in a traditional marriage both get exactly what they want. As noted earlier, when asked how they would like to be described, men use words like *dominant, assertive, independent*. Women asked the same question say *loving, generous, sensitive*.

If marriage means bringing together one person with a taste for assertion and another with a taste for generosity, we should not be surprised to find that the former is, in some sense, the head of the family. This doesn't mean he rules like an absolute dictator. Indeed, it's still quite common to hear of small, feminine women who have their strong, masculine husbands "wrapped around their little fingers." Happy women usually rule indirectly. They can rule because their husbands love and want to please them. They can also rule because, as psychological studies have demonstrated, women can read men better than men can read women.[64] What matters, then, is only that men be the ostensible heads of households. In such cases, both parties emerge happy.

One way to get men to dominate less and be open to their wives' influence is to create what Brad Wilcox calls "soft patriarchs." Such figures can be found in conservative Protestant churches, which urge husbands to be "servant leaders" who attend to their wives' needs for communication and affection as well as to the family's needs for economic wherewithal and moral leadership.[65] While the emotional work of marriage may not be inherently pleasurable or come naturally to men, it can become central to their lives if it is seen as a duty or as intrinsic to a mission. (Men hate to iron, but even a Marine, who typically loves risk-taking and excitement, can take to ironing his dress uniform with attentive skill.)[66]

The Protestant churches that Wilcox describes appeal to men by giving them a sense of importance and reminding them of their sacred obligation to use their familial power to serve their families. They appeal to the male sense of honor by encouraging the husband to imagine himself in a central, heroic role. Just as Christ sacrificed himself for the sake of others, husbands must be ready to sacrifice themselves for their wives and children. By making the male role in marriage vital, these churches make it more attractive to men; and by condemning extramarital sex, they make alternatives to marriage less attractive and less available.

A more secular approach might challenge men by pointing to the importance of biological fathers to the healthy development of children. Civilization needs family-oriented men. If we took sex differences seriously, we would not be looking for new ways to weaken the historic role of men in the family. By challenging the titular familial leadership of the male and undermining the centrality of his role as provider for his family, modernity has reduced the number of men to whom marriage seems desirable. But the titular familial leadership of the male survives. The Census Bureau used to ask, "Who is the head of the household?" Perhaps they expected to get less patriarchal answers when they changed the question to a nearly incomprehensible "Who is the 'family householder?'"[67] In 1994, nevertheless, 91 percent of American couples said it was the husband.

Wives doubtful about whether to grant titular household leadership to husbands should realize they may not have to give up much more than the title. Some studies have shown that husbands overestimate their decision-making power, while wives underestimate theirs. Yet an early study "found that the most satisfied husbands were those who believed they had the greater decision-making power even where there was no independent evidence of it."[68]

A woman who seeks power outside the family through a dominant and aggressive personality will have to be as agile as Spiderman if she is to be happily married as well. My female students often warm to Anne Moir and David Jessel's description of another type of female power, which is "something subtler, the force that creates relationships, binds families and builds societies."[69] This is a kind of power we desperately need. It is past time for both sexes to appreciate its importance.

ACKNOWLEDGMENTS

Students in my sex differences courses have been my testing boards and my advisors. Thanks to them for their help.

Over the ten years that I have worked on this project, a number of the students have helped with the research itself. I am lucky to teach at the University of Virginia, where talented and hard-working undergraduates are so plentiful. Apologies to those students whose aid I have no doubt forgotten. I remember fondly and with appreciation the assistance of Michael Anderson, Heather Bates, Bryan Boyle, Kim Brooks, Toby Bryce, Lindsay Bunting, Tracey Burnett, John Burrows, Andrea Byler, Jason Chin, Jay Cost, Catherine Crump, Sarah Dinan, Julie Eckert, Claire Edwards, Marie Fishpaw, Michael Fitzgerald, Leah Friedman, Lisa Gschwandtner, Emma Hand, Asia Hastings, Ben Hatch, Anne Marie Herron, Emily Hodge, Katherine Kirks, Jens Knudsen, Angela Lee, Jennifer Lerner, Mindy Martin, Ann Mason, Mancy Master, Justin Nance, Tyce Palmaffy, Heather Perry, Haiyan Qu, Christine Ribeiro, Andrew Rogers, Meghan Sullivan, Whitney Wilson.

Ex-students Kimberly Brooks, Catherine Crump and Ben Hatch were talented researchers as well as careful readers and commentators on the manuscript. Jay Lasus read the entire manuscript, offered thoughtful comments and frequently forwarded articles that ended up informing the argument of the book.

Once I began writing, Erica Hemphill and over an even longer period Emily Swafford proved they could do anything—notes, research, bibliography, rewriting a paragraph—and always with great skill, efficiency, stick-to-it-ness and good cheer.

Thanks to Charmaine Yoest, my graduate student, colleague and friend for helping to shape and carry out our parental leave research and for assorted aid and good judgment throughout the years.

Thanks to expert readers Jay Belsky, Steve Camorata, Janice Carter, Debbie Gordon, David Lubinski, Steve Nock, Lauren Noyes, Gabrielle Schoppa and J. Richard Udry. Patricia Haussman and Brad Wilcox were perceptive readers and also unendingly helpful in pointing me to important sources.

Financial support from the Brady Foundation gave me time to write the book and the Alfred P. Sloan Foundation's support of my parental leave research, discussed in the first chapter here, is also gratefully acknowledged. The University of Virginia provided crucial financial support over the years: a semester with pay as a Sesquicentennial Associate at the Center for Advanced Studies, summer support from the Bankard Fund, research support from the Department of Politics' Egger Fund, and permission fees for the cartoons within from the Dean of the College of Arts and Sciences and the Vice President for Research and Graduate Studies.

Beyond financial support,Virginia's Library Express On Grounds for Alderman Library never tired of tracking down what must have seemed an unending number of requested sources. My department chair, Robert Fatton, has been a jewel in big ways and small.

Thanks to Frank Fukuyama, Larry Sabato and James Q. Wilson for encouragement and advice about publishing and to my agent, Don Gastwirth, for successfully seeing me through the always tension-filled business of finding the book a good home.

Special thanks to Peter Collier of Encounter Books, a superb editor who took my "finished" manuscript, gave it a well-deserved licking and left me with a much better book. Carol Staswick, my copy editor at Encounter, has improved the text as well as cleaned it up. Amy Packard and Judy Hardin have given the book a fair chance to reach an interested public.

Julia Salasky has been my rock on many, many occasions—researching, rereading and reshaping the argument over succeeding drafts. She is a brilliant editor who knows a good argument when she sees one and has no reticence in telling an author when she does not see one. I am most grateful to her.

Son John's technical skills and son Christopher's acumen in shaping the argument about parental leave and editing some chapters were crucial at important stages.

My wife Diana has read every word of every draft of all my books. She does some research, crafts paragraphs and improves wording throughout. As always, she is my indispensable editor and, more importantly, my muse.

I have not produced a book worthy of such talent, and I am solely responsible for errors of fact and interpretation.

NOTES

Introduction

1. Diamond, 1982, p. 182.
2. Diamond, 1982, p. 183.
3. Winkler, 2000.
4. Diamond, 1982, p. 183; Harris, 1998, pp. 222–23.
5. Lorber, 1994; Richardson et al., 1997, p. 38.
6. Colapinto, 1997 and 2000.
7. Colapinto, 1997 and 2000; Winkler, 2000; Murphy, 1997.
8. Imperato-McGinley et al., 1979.
9. Legato confirmed by phone the accuracy of news story quotation.
10. Pool, 1994, p. 175.
11. U.S. Department of Education, National Center for Educational Statistics, 2002.
12. Belkin, 2003; Shields, 2003.
13. Tyre and McGinn. 2003; Employment Policy Foundation, 2003.
14. Moore, 1997.

Part 1: Nature Matters

Chapter 1: Androgynous Parenting at the Frontier

1. Lippa, 1998a, pp. 179–80; Lubinski and Humphreys, 1990, pp. 342–43.
2. Cunningham and Antill, 1984.
3. Harris and Firestone, 1998, p. 250.
4. Betz and Fitzgerald, 1987.
5. Berman and Pedersen, 1987, p. 224; Goldschneider and Waite, 1991, pp. 128–29.
6. Zhang and Farley, 1995, pp. 195–205.

7. For a more technical discussion see Rhoads, 2004.
8. Yoest, 2003.

Chapter 2: Masculinity/Femininity

1. Percy; Arnold cited in Campbell, 1999, p. 71.
2. O'Leary, 1997, pp. 155, 160.
3. O'Leary, 1997, ch. 10; Fausto-Sterling, 2000, pp. 3–4; Walsh, 1997, p. 7.
4. Drash, 2000.
5. Peplau, 1985, p. 261.
6. C-Span, 2000.
7. Millet, 1970, p. 26; Polatnick, 1982, pp. 22–23; Biskupic, 1995.
8. Fausto-Sterling, 2000, p. 3.
9. Muldoon and Reilly, 1998; Campbell, 1999; Sommers, 2000, p. 86; O'Leary, 1997, p. 112.
10. Djikstra, 1997, p. 442.
11. George et al., 1996, p. 31.
12. Okin, 1989, p. 171.
13. Lorber, 1986; Janet Gornick quoted in Hymowitz, 2002.
14. Biskupic, 1995.
15. Nussbaum, M., 1997, pp. 91–97; Joan Williams as quoted in Hymowitz, 2002.
16. Miller, David, 1990.
17. Campbell, 1999, p. 73.
18. Eagly, 1995, p. 155.
19. Lueptow, 2001.
20. Lueptow et al., 2001, pp. 7, 10.
21. Lueptow et al., 2001, p. 23.
22. Campbell, 2002, pp. 122–23.
23. Travis, 1991, p. 117; Tavris, 1992, p. 53; Rosser, 1992; Epstein, 1996.
24. Pool, 1994, p. 7; Lott, 1997; Walsh, 1997, p. 22; Tavris, 1992, p. 289; Udry et al., 1995, p. 365; de Waal, 1999, p. 94.
25. Fausto-Sterling, 1992, p. 212; Campbell, 1999, p. 59; Kimura, 1999, p. 52.
26. Pool, 1994, p. 18.
27. Naomi Weisstein as quoted in Walsh, 1997, p. 7.
28. Walsh, 1997, p. 8.
29. Sommers, 2000, p. 89.
30. Sommers, 2000, p. 90.
31. Sommers, 2000, p. 10.
32. Benbow, 1996, phone interview, 11 January; Djikstra, 1997.
33. McGuinness, 1996, phone interview, 11 January; Kimura, 1999, p. 8.

34. Udry, 1999, interview, June.
35. Lips, 2001, p. 170.
36. Walsh, 1997, pp. 1–2.
37. Pool, 1994, pp. 6–10.
38. Pool, 1994, p. 7.
39. Williams and Best, 1990a, p. 307.
40. Halpern as quoted in Moir, 1999, p. 117; Pool, 1994, p. 6; Sommers, 1999, p. 10.
41. Pool, 1994, p. 6; Kimura, 1990, pp. 42, 7–8.
42. Maccoby, 2000.
43. Gorney, 1985; Cowan, 1997, p. 16; Stein, 1993, p. 190; Caccioppoli, 1997; Rosenfeld 1995; Bannon, 2000.
44. Blum, 1998, lecture at University of Virginia, June.
45. Hales, 1992, p. 121; Pool, 1994, pp. 36–37.
46. Valian, 1998, preface.
47. Valian, 1998, pp. 26–27, 332; Maccoby, 1998; Walsh, 1997, p. 34.
48. Life Is Short, 2002.
49. Sommers, 2000, pp. 73–74.
50. Shirley and Campbell, 2000, p. 9; Ridley, 1999, pp. 217–18; Maccoby, 1998, pp. 84–88; Lewis, 1969; McGuinness, 1977, Lippa, 1998b.
51. Ridley, 1999, p. 217.
52. Delk et al., 1986.
53. Harris, 1998, p. 221; Maccoby, 1998, ch. 6; Walsh, 2001, p. 34.
54. Blum, 1997, pp. 66–67; Moir and Jessel, 1989, p. 86.
55. Gottman, 1994a, p. 275.
56. Feingold, 1994.
57. Wiederman and Allgeier, 1992, p. 178.
58. Gallup Organization, 1996; Eaton, 1986; Widiger, 2000.
59. Harris, 1998, p. 224.
60. Tiger, 1987; Rossi, 1985; Layng, 1993.
61. Hansen and Campbell, 1985, p. 81; Willingham, 1997, pp. 147–49.
62. Cornwall et al., 2000.
63. Mealey, 2000, pp. 71–72; Burnham and Phelan, 2000, pp. 41–42; Maccoby, 1998, p. 91.
64. Gaulin and McBurney, 2001, p. 88; Badcock, 2000, pp. 11–16.
65. Geary, 1998, p. 288; Ridley, 1993, p. 251.
66. Gaulin and McBurney, 2001, p. 88; Badcock, 2000, pp. 11–16.
67. Eisenman, 1998.
68. Kimura, 1999, pp. 132–35.
69. Moir and Jessel, 1989, p. 40.
70. Hotz, 2000.

71. Moir, 1999, p. 125; Fisher, 1999, pp. 11, 60–61, 116–17.
72. Moir, 1999, p. 125; Udry et al., 1995.
73. Hoyenga, 1993, p. 179; Udry, 2000, p. 152.
74. Dabbs, 2000, pp. 88–89; Pool, 1994, p. 179; Mazur and Lamb, 1980.
75. Udry, 2000.
76. Udry, 1994, p. 562.
77. Ridley, 1993, p. 255; Berch and McCauley, 1990, p. 164.
78. Dabbs, 2000, p. 57.
79. Moir, 1999, p. 123.
80. Campbell, 2002, p. 216.
81. Dittmann et al., 1990a.
82. Berenbaum, 1990; Kimura, 1999, pp. 108–9; Rowe, 1994, pp. 177–78; Berenbaum and Hines, 1990; Pool, 1994, ch. 4; Collaer et al., 2002.
83. Berenbaum, 1990.
84. Miller, 1998, pp. 36–37; Hales, 1999, p. 77; Collaer et al., 2002, p. 87; Grimshaw et al., 1995; Dabbs, 2000, p. 13.
85. Udry et al., 1995; Udry, 1994; Udry, 2000.
86. Udry, 2000, pp. 450–51.
87. Cashdan, 1995; Gaulin, 1993; D'Amico, 1983, pp. 41–42.
88. Baucom et al., 1985, p. 1224; Bardwick, 1971, pp. 102–6.; Moir, 1999, p. 123.
89. Alexander and Sherwin, 1993; Sherwin, 1988; Hales, 1999, p.79; Gallagher, 1988, pp. 77, 82.
90. Purigoy and Koopmans, 1979; W. Gallagher, 1998; Bancroft et al., 1983, p. 515.
91. Moir, 1999, pp. 124–26; Collaer et al., 2002, p. 95; Kimura, 1999, ch. 5.
92. Hales, 1999, p. 80; Baucom et al., 1985, p. 1218.
93. McGuinness, 1985, pp. 138–40; Lubinski et al., 1993, pp. 17–20; Lubinski and Humphreys, 1997, pp. 177–78; Subotnik, 1988; Hausman, 1999; Govier and Feldman, 1999; Benbow et al., 2000; Webb, Lubinski and Benbow, 2002.
94. Curry et al., 1994; Ehrhardt et al., 1981, p. 296; Charlesworth and Dzur, 1987.
95. Gilmore, 1990; Nock and Brinig, 2001.
96. Dabbs, 2000, pp, 36, 59, 156; Kimura, 1999, ch. 5, p. 110; Lubinski and Humphreys, 1990, p. 343; Lippa, 1998a; Toto, 2002.
97. Dabbs, 2000, p. 211.
98. Williams and Best, 1990b, pp. 187, 196; Feldman et al., 1981.
99. Hochschild, 1989.
100. Steinem, 1995.
101. Nasar, 2001, pp. 228–29.

102. Cringely, 2000.
103. Berselli, 1998.
104. Gohm et al., 1998; Humphreys et al., 1993.
105. Span, 1999.
106. Ahrens, 2000.
107. Moir, 1999, pp. 253–55; Lubinski et al., 1993, p. 702.
108. Collaer et al., 2002, pp. 77, 87; Berenbaum, 1990; Signorella and Jamison, 1986.
109. Miller, p. 50—as cited in Ellis and Ebertz, 1998; Inoff-Germain et al., 1988, pp. 129–39.
110. Williams and Best, 1990b, p. 156; Hakim, 2000, pp. 84–85.
111. Hunt, 2000; Bellafante, 1998; Quinn, 1992.
112. Jones and Brayfield, 1997, p. 1239.
113. Jones and Brayfield, 1997.
114. Moir, 1999, pp. 271–73.
115. Graglia, 1998, p. 1; Hakim, 2000.
116. Buunk et al., 2000.
117. Steil, 1997.
118. Graglia, 1998, p. 364; McDermott, 1993.
119. Graglia, 1998, p. 52.
120. Davis-Floyd, 1994, p. 201.
121. Davis-Floyd, 1994; Hakim, 2000, p. 94.
122. Genevieve and Margolis, 1987, p. 1000.
123. Graglia, 1998.
124. Valian, 1998, p. 179.
125. Angier, 1999b, p. 363.
126. Hakim, 2000, p. 111.
127. Marcus, 1997, pp. 88–90.
128. Navarro, 2001; Berlage, 1986, pp. 55–59; Alexander, 2002; Cyr, 1999.
129. Purefoy and Koopmans, 1979.
130. Dabbs, 2000, pp. 12–13.
131. Navarro, 2001, p. D1
132. Graglia, 1998, p. 96.
133. Russell as quoted in Krasnow, 1999; Crittenden, 1999, p. 175.
134. Estrich, 2000, O'Leary, 1997, p. 122.
135. Graglia, 1998, pp. 108, 96.
136. Williams and Best, 1990b, p. 195; Tannen, 1990, p. 177.
137. Morin, 2002.
138. Shalit, 1997; Buss, 1994a, p. 147; Akerlof et al., 1996.
139. Samuelson, 1999, p. 59.
140. Murray, 2000; Morin, 2000.
141. Seligman, 1999—as quoted in Scrapbook, 1999, p. 2.
142. Sommers, 1994, ch. 3; Rothman, 1995, pp. 133–36.

143. Paul C. Vitz as quoted in Graglia, 1998, p. 416; Noddings, 1998, p. 18; Powers, 1997, p. 29.
144. Ravitch, 2003, p. 86.
145. Ravitch, 2003, p. 94.
146. Quinn, 1992.
147. Tavris, 1998.
148. Hoyenga, 1993, p. 13; Gottesman et al., 1997, p. 1266.
149. Symons, 1981.
150. Pool, 1994, p. 12; Ehrhardt, 1985, p. 92.
151. Sommers, 2000.

Part 2: Men Don't Get Headaches

Chapter 3: Sex

1. Konner, 1999.
2. Mealey, 2000, p. 272; Buss and Barnes, 1986, p. 568; Buss, 1994a.
3. Buss, 1994a, chs. 2 & 3; Sprecher et al., 1994; Kenrick and Keefe, 1992.
4. Pinker, 1998.
5. Miller, G., 2000, p. 86.
6. Smuts, 1992, p. 255.
7. Lips, 2001, pp. 207–24; Golombok and Fivush, 1994; Schmitt et al., 2001.
8. Schmitt et al., 2001.
9. Blum, 1997, p. 228.
10. Archer, 1996, p. 42; Crenshaw, 1996, p. 38.
11. Schmitt, 2003; Baumeister, 2000, p. 362.
12. Moir and Jessel, 1989, p. 130.
13. Weeks, 1999.
14. Geary, 1998, p. 145.
15. Clark and Hatfield, 1989; Moir and Jessel, 1989, p. 109; Mealey, 2000, p. 266.
16. Buss statement in Sileo, 1995.
17. Reality Check: The Gender Revolution, 1998.
18. Schwartz and Rutter, 1998, pp. 52–53; Linda Alperstein quoted in Strauss, 1998; Strauss, 1998, p. 39.
19. Veroff et al., 1998, p. 166; Riessman, p. 46; Schwartz and Rutter, 1998, pp. 128–29; National Council on Aging, 1998; Baumeister, 2000, p. 361.
20. Thompson and Walker, 1989, p. 847; Crenshaw, 1996, p. 90.
21. Carroll et al., 1985, pp. 137–38; Maccoby, 1998, pp. 215–16.
22. Carroll et al., 1985, pp. 137–38; Schwartz and Rutter, 1998, p. 54; Mealey, 2000, p. 299; Blum, 1997, p. 242; Murstein, 1974, pp. 431–32; V. S. Naipaul on "sexual release" in Weeks, 2001.

23. Murstein, 1974, p. 424; Rasche, 1991, pp. 46–48.
24. Alexander et al., 1997; Alexander and Sherwin, 1993; Udry, 1988; Crenshaw, 1996, p. 140; Geary, 1998, p. 146.
25. Udry, 1988; Paikoff and Brooks-Gunn, 1990, p. 216; Sherwin, 1988.
26. Money as quoted in Townsend, 1998, pp. 203–4, 238–39; Gallagher, 1998; Blum, 1997, pp. 30, 234; Fisher, 1999, p. 196; Crenshaw, 1996, pp. 171–72; Moir, 1999, p. 222; of related interest is Udry et al., 1986, p. 224.
27. Crenshaw, 1996, p. 143; Moir and Jessel, 1989, p. 137; Block as quoted in Campbell, 2002, p. 108.
28. Moir, 1999, p. 235.
29. Jenkins, 2001; Townsend, 1998, p. 239; Schwartz and Rutter, 1998, pp. 46–47.
30. Moir and Jessel, 1989, pp. 134–35.
31. Fisher, 1999, p. 267; Waite and Joyner, 2001, p. 258; Kolodny as quoted in *Washington Post,* 29 March 1994; Moir and Jessel, 1989, pp. 134–35; related Buss, 1994a, p. 81; Mealey, 2000, p. 267.
32. Cited in Gaulin and McBurney, 2001, p. 205.
33. Hoyenga et al., 1993, p. 384; Fisher, 1999, p. 247; Gaulin and McBurney, 2001, p. 205.
34. Geary, 1998, p. 146; Buss, 1994a, p. 82; Hicks and Leitenberg, 2001; Gallagher and Waite, 2000, p. 93.
35. Schwartz and Rutter, 1998, p. 51; Fisher, 1999, pp. 198–99.
36. Ellis and Symons, 1997, p. 544; quote in Buss, 1994a, p. 82.
37. Bowman, 2001, p. 13; Farrell, 1993, p. 290.
38. Parke and Sawin, 1976.
39. Blum, 1997, p. 230.
40. McCarthy, 1999; Marlowe, 2000; Jeter, 1998.
41. Fisher, 1992, p. 95; Fisher, 1999, pp. 201–8.
42. Fisher, 1992, p. 95.
43. Tavris, 1992, pp. 211–12.
44. Tavris, 1992, pp. 229–31.
45. Blum, 1997, p. 227; Golombok and Fivush, 1994, p. 228; Young, 1999, p. 31.
46. Blum, 1997, p. 242.
47. Blum, 1997, p. 227.
48. Buss et al., 2001; Gaulin and McBurney, 2001, p. 216.
49. Buss, 1994a, p. 54; Divakruni, 2000, p. 24.
50. Fisher, 1999, p. 234; Gaulin and McBurney, 2001, p. 220; Townsend, 1998, p. 230.
51. Feingold, 1990; research of Daniel Hamermash and Jeff Biddle reported in Gerencher, 2001.

52. Townsend, 1998, p. 64.
53. Townsend, 1998, p. 63.
54. Williams, Margorie, 1998.
55. Estrich, 1997.
56. The Reliable Source, 1998.
57. Steinem, 1992, p. 220.
58. Crittenden, 1999, p. 153; Bushnell, 1995, p. 11; Unger and Crawford, 1996, pp. 317–18.
59. Buss, 1994a, p. 54; Birds Do It, Bees Do It, 1997, p. 60.
60. Etcoff, 1999, p. 137; Buss, 1994a, p. 54; Berry, 2000, pp. 273–342.
61. Buss, 1994a, pp. 38–40.
62. Heightism: Short Guys Finish Last, 1995.
63. Heightism: Short Guys Finish Last, 1995.
64. Botting, 1996.
65. Mealey, 2000, p. 268; Etcoff, 1999, pp. 177–78.
66. Etcoff, 1999, pp. 152–59.
67. Gaulin and McBurney, 2001, pp. 220–23; Etcoff, 1999, chs. 5 & 6, esp. p. 159; Mealey, 2000, pp. 225–26; Perrett et al., 1998; Booth, Carver et al., 2000, pp. 1028–29; Finkelhor et al., 1997; Penton-Voak and Perrett, 2000.
68. Etcoff, 1999, pp. 151–58.
69. Etcoff, 1999, pp. 149–58; Brown, 1994; U.S. News & World Report, 2000.
70. Estrogen and the Younger Look, 1999.
71. Campbell, 2002, p. 191; Kenrick, 1996; Kenrick, 1992; Kenrick, 1990; Pawlowski, 1999.
72. Estrogen and the Younger Look, 1999.
73. Mealey, 2000, p. 274.
74. Fallon and Rozin, 1985; Mealey, 2000, p. 220.
75. Etcoff, 1999, p. 192.
76. Etcoff, 1999, pp. 190–95; Geary, 1998, pp. 150–51; Mealey, 2000, p. 217; Burnham and Phelan, 2000, pp. 162–63; Tassinary and Hansen, 1998; Kalick et al., 1998; Sociobiology: A Beauty Contest, 1998; Streeter and McBurney, 2003, pp. 88–98.
77. Etcoff, 1999, p. 192.
78. Gaulin and McBurney, 2001, pp. 209–11; Etcoff, 1999, pp. 161–62; Hume and Montgomerie, 2001; Birds Do It, Bees Do It, 1997, p. 60; Betzig, 1997, p. 5; Rhodes et al., 2001; Blum, 1997, p. 100.
79. Birds Do It, Bees Do It, 1997, pp. 60–61.
80. Hughes et al., 2002.
81. Campbell, 2002, pp. 172–73.
82. Mealey, 2000, p. 221.
83. Buss, 1994a, p. 71.

84. Stossel, 2002.
85. Stepp, 2002.
86. Kenrick, 1995, p. 57; Morin, 2000.
87. Kanazawa and Still, 2000, p. 18.
88. Mealey, 2000, p. 271.
89. R. S. Miller as quoted in Mealey, 2000, p. 271.
90. Rockwell, 1986.
91. Abdollahi and Mann, 2001.
92. Etcoff, 1999, p. 68.
93. Muggeridge, 1995.
94. Abrahamse, 1995, p. 72.
95. Crittenden, 1999, p. 147.
96. South, 2001; Riessman; Blumstein and Schwartz, 1983; Buckle et al., 1996, p. 374; Smock and Manning, 1997; Etcoff, 1999, p. 79; Geary, 1998, pp. 127–28; Finnas, 2000; Brosnan, 2000; Jalovaara, 2003.
97. Betzig, 1989; Gardner, 2003.
98. Buss, 1994a, p. 24; Gaulin and McBurney, 2001, p. 212; Geary, 1998, p. 128.
99. Townsend, 1998, pp. 74–76; Etcoff, 1999, p. 79; Howard et al., 1987.
100. Buss, 1994a, pp. 24–25; Geary, 1998, pp. 127–28.
101. Sweeney, 2002.
102. Kenrick and Li commentary on Eagly and Wood, 2000.
103. Buss, 1994a, p. 46.
104. Buss, 1994a, pp. 45–47; Townsend and O'Neill, 1990, pp. 78–79, 93, 243; Wiederman and Allgeier, 1992; Townsend et al., 1995, pp. 199–200.
105. Buss, 1994a, p. 46.
106. Tooley, 2002, p. 167.
107. Eagly and Wood, 1999, p. 420.
108. Townsend, 1998, pp. 64–68, 88, 91.
109. Mealey, 2000, p. 235.
110. Buss, 1994a, p. 46; Feingold, 1992; Geary, 1998, pp. 127–28; Hakim, 2000, pp. 196–98, 207–17.
111. Henry Kissinger in Buss, 1994a, p. 26; Blum, 1997, p. 266.
112. Grossman, 1998, p. 11.
113. Roberts, 1993, p. D1.
114. Roberts, 2000.
115. Marlowe, 2000; discussion of Martha in Gallese, 1985.
116. Kayden, 1990, p. 107.
117. Whitehead and Popenoe, 2000, p. 9.
118. Levine, 1992, p. 292; Cashdan, 1996, p. 142.
119. Graglia. 1988, p. 15.

120. Steil, 1997, pp. 50–55.
121. Steil, 1997, p. 54; Thompson and Walker, 1989; Krebs, 2001.
122. Steil, 1997, p. 53; Geary, 1998, p. 128; Nock, 2001.
123. Buss, 1994a, p. 26.
124. Townsend, 1998, p. 65; related see Gaulin and McBurney, 2001, p. 352.
125. Kenrick, 1995, p. 57.
126. Thompson and Walker, 1989, p. 853.
127. Low as quoted in Blum, 1997, p. 266; Fisher, 1999, pp. 38–39.
128. Cashdan, 1996, p. 141; Kayden, 1990, p. 121.
129. Sommers, 1994, pp. 262–66.
130. Hatkoff and Lazwell; Tooley, 2002, p. 167; Townsend, 1998, pp. 64–65.
131. Rossi, 1995, p. 186.
132. Stossel, 2002.
133. Trollope, 1991.
134. Fielding, 1996, p. 274.
135. Fielding, 1999, p. 245.
136. Ahrens, 1997a.
137. Mealey, 2000, pp. 267, 272.
138. Hax, 1997a.
139. Levine, 1992, pp. 266–67, 348.
140. Williamson, 1992; Batten, 1992, p. 96; Ellis and Symons, 1997, pp. 210–11; Sommers, 1994, pp. 267–68.
141. Laura Taylor, *Anticipation,* ch. 11; Crenshaw, 1996, p. 61, on *Bridges of Madison County.*
142. Cowan and Dunn, 1994, and Fischer and Byrne, 1978, as cited in Baumeister, 2000.
143. Baumeister, 2000.
144. Crenshaw, 1996, pp. 185–87; Lynch, 2000.
145. Baumeister, 2000, p. 367.
146. Crenshaw, 1996, p. 186.
147. Tasker, 1995; Merkin, 1996.
148. West, pp. 116–17, 137; Paglia, 1997.
149. Fisher, 1999, p. 200.
150. Apt and Hurlbert, 1994, p. 498.
151. Davis, 2004.
152. Fisher, 1999, p. 199; Laumann et al., 1994.
153. Friend, 1994, p. 50.
154. Dabbs, 2000, p. 11.
155. Heyman, 1995, p. 155.
156. Taylor—interview from 1988 shown on *CNN People,* 1 September 2002.

157. Apt and Hurlbert, 1994, p. 497.
158. Miller et al., 2000; Buss, 1994a, p. 26; Gilmore, 1990, p. 200; McCombs, 2003.
159. Gray-Little and Burks, 1983; Weisfeld et al., 1992; Felmlee, 1994.
160. Gottman, 1994b.
161. Gallese, 1985, p. 238.
162. Gardner, 2003.
163. Jalovaara, 2003; Popenoe, 1993.
164. Schwartz, Pepper, 1994.
165. Ruth, p. 63.
166. Prose, 1998; Margaret Carlson's Competition, 1998, p. 2.
167. Chris Matthews, *Hardball,* 16 October 1998.
168. Prose, 1998.
169. Dowd, 1998.
170. Graglia, 1998, pp. 258–59.
171. Sneed, 1992, p. D1; Quinn, 1992; Roberts, 2000.
172. Quinn, 1992; Kass, 1997, pp. 49–50.
173. Farnham and Lundberg, 1947, p. 161; Carlson, 1999, pp. 4–7; Todd, 2000, pp. 237–39; Sunstein, 1975, pp. 249, 253; Nixon, 1971, pp. 122–23.
174. Graglia, 1998, pp. 14–16; N. Emery, 1999, pp. 9–11; Tooley, 2002, pp. 70–77.
175. Townsend, 1998, p. 65.
176. Pearson, 2002.
177. Fielding, 1999.
178. Kurtz, 2001.
179. Crenshaw, 1996, pp. 113, 116.
180. West, p. 130.
181. Rossi, 1995, pp. 186–87.
182. Marlowe, 2000.
183. Crenshaw, 1996, p. 35.
184. Riessman, 1990.
185. Nevid, 1984, p. 409.
186. Townsend, 1998, p. 67.
187. Sidak, 2000, pp. 26–27; McLellan, 2000.

Chapter 4: Fatherless Families

1. Popenoe, 2001, p. 24.
2. Gallagher and Waite, 2000, p. 125; Fagan and Rector, 2000; Parcel and Dufur, 2001; Rountree and Warner, 1999; Cookston, 1999; Osgood and Chambers, 2000; Flanagan, Shaw et al., 1999; Hoyenga and Hoyenga, 1993, p. 223; Heiss, 1996; Chen and

Kaplan, 2001; Roscigno, 2000; Morse, 2001; De Goede, 2000; "Number of Troubled Children Increases," 2000; Pampei and Williamson, 2001; Batten, 1992, pp. 196–98.

3. Glenn, Nock et al., 2002, p. 37.
4. Glenn, Nock et al., 2002, pp. 39–40.
5. Glenn, Nock et al., 2002.
6. Weitoft, Hjern et al., 2002; Whitehead, 2003.
7. Weitoft, Hjern et al., 2002; Whitehead, 2003..
8. Wilcox, forthcoming.
9. Glenn, Nock et al., 2002, p. 42.
10. Sommers, 2000, p. 130; Heiss, 1996; Kawachi, Kennedy et al., 1999; Ousey, 2000.
11. Briggs-Gowan, 2001; R. Emery, 1999, p. 41.
12. Hilton and Devall, 1998, p. 47.
13. Glenn, Nock et al., 2002, pp. 39–40.
14. Gallagher and Waite, 2000, p. 131; Mansfield, 1999; Burr, Hartman et al., 1999.
15. Cherlin, 1999, p. 423.
16. Caspi, DeFries et al., 2000, p. 435.
17. Cherlin, 1999, p. 426.
18. Amato and Sobelewski, 2001.
19. McLanahan and Sandefur, 1994, p. 5.
20. R. Emery, 1999, p. 37.
21. R. Emery, 1999, p. 35.
22. R. Emery, 1999, p. 40; Gallagher and Waite, 2000, pp. 132, 36; Buchanan, Brinke et al., 2000.
23. Mealey, 2000, p. 296; Blackmore, 2000; Buehler and Pasley, 2000; Watts and Nagy, 2000; Perry-Jenkins and Gillman, 2000.
24. Gallagher and Waite, 2000, pp. 127–28.
25. Briggs-Gowan, 2001.
26. Broude, 1999, p. 14; Hetherington, Bridges et al., 1998, p. 176; Parke and Brott, 1999, pp. 180–81; Wilcox, forthcoming.
27. Campbell, 2002, p. 59; Mintz, 1998, p. 23.
28. Anderson, Holmes et al., 1999, p. 438.
29. Belsky, Steinberg et al., 1991, p. 661; Harris, 1998, p. 302.
30. Harris, 1998, p. 302; Amato, 1998, pp. 256–57.
31. McMunn, 2001; McLanahan and Sandefur, 1994, pp. 89–91; Big Breasts and a Bogus Broadcast, 1996; Harris, Furstenberg et al., 1998; Rodgers and Rose, 2002.
32. Popenoe, 1996, pp. 150–51.
33. Wilcox, 2004; Jayakody and Kalil, 2002.
34. Wilcox, forthcoming.
35. Brody, 1998; Gallagher and Waite, 2000, p. 135; Finkelhor, Moore et al., 1997; Padu and Peltzer, 2000; McCabe, 1997; Scholer,

Edward F. Mitchel et al., 1997.

36. Cited in Boodman, 1999b.
37. Popenoe, 2001, p. 18.
38. Ellis et al., 1999.
39. Betzig, 1997, pp. 3–4; Rossi, 1997, pp. 6–7; Mealey, 2000, p. 258.
40. Ellis and Garber, 2000; Betzig, 1997, pp. 3–4; Rossi, 1997, pp. 6–7; Mealey, 2000, p. 258.
41. Belkin, 2000.
42. Belkin, 2000; Betzig, 1997, pp. 3–4; Rossi, 1997, pp. 6–7; Smith, 1997, p. 339; Booth, Carver et al., 2000, p. 1027; Goleman, 1991.
43. Ellis and Garber, 2000, p. 498.
44. Ellis, Bates et al., 2003.
45. Mealey, 2000, p. 257; Gaulin and McBurney, 2001, p. 227; Mundy, 2000.
46. Mealey, 2000, p. 258; Gaulin and McBurney, 2001, pp. 227–28; Belkin, 2000; Cashdan, 1996, p. 139; Campbell, 2002, p. 187.
47. Gaulin and McBurney, 2001, pp. 227–28; Mealey, 2000, pp. 257–58.
48. Belsky, Steinberg et al., 1991, p. 661; Smith, 1997.
49. Anderson, 1994, pp. 11–12.
50. Campbell, 2002, p. 207.
51. Cashdan, 1996, p. 137.
52. Anderson, 1994; Campbell, 2002, p. 226.
53. Anderson, 1994.
54. Anderson, 1994, p. 9.
55. Anderson, 1994, pp. 31, 18; Crawford, 2001.
56. Dyson, 2001, pp. 23, 130, 84–86, 96; Rosen, 2001; Johnson, 2001.
57. Anderson, 1994, pp. 37–76.
58. Wilson, 2002, pp. 168–69; Popenoe, 1996, p. 31, 53–56; Nock, 1998, pp. 34–35.
59. Moyers, 1986, pp. 7–8; Court Upholds Limits on Man's Ability to Have Kids, 2001.
60. Gaulin, 2001, p. 434; Guo and Stearns, 2002.
61. Gaulin, 2001, p. 434.
62. Harden, 2001; McLaughlin and Lighter, 1997; Hofferth, Smith et al., 2000; Raspberry, 2000b; Broder, 2002; Toner, 2002.
63. Harden, 2001; Morin and Dean, 2002; McLaughlin and Lighter, 1997; Hofferth, Smith et al., 2000; Raspberry, 2000b; Broder, 2002; Toner, 2002.
64. Vedantam, 2002a.
65. Batten, 1992, pp. 184–85; Cready, Fossett et al., 1997; Daddy's Home, But Which Home? 2001; Finnas, 2000; Townsend, 1998, p. 135.

66. Anderson, 1994, p. 17.
67. Cashdan, 1996, pp. 139–40.
68. South, 1993, pp. 366–68; Campbell, 2002.
69. Jencks and Edin, 1995, p. 187; Rodríguez, 2000.
70. Courtwright, 1996, pp. 242–43.
71. Mealey, 2000, p. 267.
72. Dyson, 2001, p. 185.
73. Sawhill, 2002, p. 78; Rumbelow, 2002.
74. Sawhill, 2002, pp. 78–79; Stewart, 2003.
75. Buss, 1994a, pp. 114–17, 67–69.
76. Mealey, 2000, p. 296.
77. Gaulin and McBurney, 2001, p. 228.
78. Dyson, 2001, p. 199; Milloy, 1999.
79. Prior and Hayes, 2001.
80. Matthews and Gump, 2002.
81. Associated Press, 1997.
82. Wilmouth and Koso, 2002.
83. Rector and Johnson, 2002; Hewlett, 2002, pp. 189–91; Gallagher and Waite, 2000, chs. 4–8; Pienta, Hayward et al., 2000; Murray, 2000; Sephton, Sapolsky et al., 2000; Demo and Acock, 1996; McDonough, Walters et al., 2002.
84. Parker, Ortega et al., 1995.
85. Gallagher and Waite, 2000, pp. 52–54, 68–70; for contrary study see Vedantam, 2003.
86. Waite and Luo, 2002.
87. Zengerle, 1997; Collison, 1991; Oberman, 1994.
88. Crenshaw, 1996, pp. 121–22.
89. Udry, 1988, p. 711.
90. Udry, Talbert et al., 1986, pp. 224; Carroll, Volk et al., 1985.
91. Udry and Billy, 1985; Udry and Billy, 1987; Udry, 1988; Udry, Billy et al., 1985; Baumeister, 2000.
92. Barras, 2000, pp. 91, 70, 93, 90, 1; Raspberry, 2000a; Glenn and Marquardt, 2001, pp. 53–56.
93. Nock, 1995.
94. Thompson and Walker, 1989, p. 852; Kristol, 1991, p. 492.

Chapter 5: The Sexual Revolution

1. Akerlof, 1996.
2. Rabkin, 1997; Darling, 1999; Oberman, 1994; Baumeister, 2000.
3. Hymowitz, 1995; Fox-Genovese, 1996.
4. Darling, 1999; Crittenden, 1999, pp. 28–29; Dalton, 2000.
5. Hymowitz, 1995; Bloom, 1987, p. 99; Shalit, 1997; Roiphe, 1993; Tanenbaum, 1999; Ehrenreich et al., 1987, pp. 194–96.
6. Thompson quoted in Tanenbaum, 1999, p. 105; Shalit, 1997, p. 44; Shalit, 1999, pp. 64–65; Buss, 1994a.

7. Hymowitz, 1995; Levine, 1995.
8. Shalit, 1997; Crittenden, 1999.
9. Tanenbaum, 1999.
10. Lips, 2001, pp. 24–25; Hyde, 1996; Hax, 1997b; Charlottesville City School Board, 1997.
11. Tavris, 1992, pp. 244–45; Phillips, 1999, pp. 129–32.
12. Greer, 1999, p. 10.
13. Sally Cline quoted.in Shalit, 1999, p. 192; Nussbaum, 1997, p. 97; Greer, 1999.
14. Browne, 1997, p. 27.
15. Michigan Supreme Court decision (501 N.W.2d 155 (Mich. 1993))—as quoted in Browne, 1997, p. 30.
16. Lips, 2001, pp. 224–25; Weaver, 1999a; Herwig, 2001.
17. Townsend and Klein, 1995; Wright, 1994, p. 40; Buss, 1994a, pp. 68–69.
18. Buss, 1994a, p. 69.
19. Salasky, 2001; see also Shalit, 1999, pp. 108–9.
20. Glenn, 2001, p. 24. Much of what follows draws heavily on this source.
21. Glenn, 2001, p. 13.
22. Glenn, 2001, p. 14.
23. Glenn, 2001, p. 15; Shalit, 1999, p. 236; Salasky, 2002.
24. Glenn, 2001; Shalit, 1999, p. 92.
25. Glenn, 2001, p. 20.
26. Glenn, 2001, p. 19.
27. Glenn, 2001, p. 15; Fillion, 1996.
28. Townsend, 1998, pp. 47, 48, 51; Salasky, 2002.
29. Glenn, 2001, p. 267; Townsend, 1998; Hayes, 2000, p. 78.
30. The 1994 report of the Sexuality Information and Education Council (SIECUS) discussed in Shalit, 1997, p. 44; Kean, 2000.
31. The 1994 report of SIECUS discussed in Shalit, 1997, p. 44; National Campaign to Prevent Teen Pregnancy, 2000.
32. The 1994 report of SIECUS discussed in Shalit, 1997, p. 44; National Campaign to Prevent Teen Pregnancy, 2000; see also Hales, 1999, p. 142.
33. Glenn, 2001, pp. 16–19.
34. Townsend and Kline, 1995.
35. Townsend, 1998, p. 47.
36. Townsend, 1998, p. 46; Nordlinger, 1999; Noguchi, 2001.
37. Townsend, 1998, p. 50.
38. Townsend, 1998, p. 51.
39. See also Shalit, 1999, p. 91.
40. Townsend and Klein, 1995, p. 187.
41. Townsend and Klein, 1995, pp. 190–93.
42. Townsend, 1998, pp. 54–55.

43. Townsend, 1998, pp. 45–46.
44. Hax, 2002; Townsend, 1998, p. 55.
45. Townsend, 1998, pp. 46–47.
46. Townsend, 1998, pp. 55–56.
47. Townsend, 1998, p. 58.
48. Townsend, 1998, p. 58; Harris, 1997; Hyde in Buss, 1996, pp. 114–16.
49. Arana-Ward, 1997; Roiphe, 1997.
50. Fillion, 1996.
51. Weaver, 1999b, p. 4; Frey, 1999.
52. Frank and Young in Frank, 2000, p. 96.
53. Frank and Young in Frank, 2000, pp. 95–98.
54. Murphy, 2000, p. 512.
55. Whitehead, 1998.
56. Kaiser Family Foundation, 2000.
57. Finer, Darroch et al., 1999.
58. Kaiser Family Foundation, 2000.
59. Division of Sexually Transmitted Disease Prevention, 1999.
60. Kaiser Family Foundation, 2000; Brown, 2000a; Manlove, 2002.
61. Simeone, 2001; Charlottesville City School Board, 1997.
62. Baumgardner, 2000, particularly pp. 28–30.
63. Hales, 1999, p. 32; Science Notebook (Mating and the Immune System), 2000; Blum, 1997, p. 247.
64. Hales, 1999, pp. 31–32; Booth, Carver et al., 2000, p. 1028; Blum, 1997, pp. 235–39; Science Notebook: The Pill's Olfactory Effect, 2001.
65. Blum, 1997, p. 235; Hales, 1999, pp. 31–32; Booth, Carver et al., 2000, p. 1028; Blum, 1997, pp. 235–39; Science Notebook: The Pill's Olfactory Effect, 2001.
66. Hales, 1999, p. 32; Booth, Carver et al., 2000, p. 1028.
67. Mealey, 2000, pp. 282–83.
68. Blum, 1997, pp. 235–39.
69. Fillion, 1996; Blum, 1997, pp. 233–34.
70. Graglia, 1998, p. 173.
71. Graglia, 1998, p. 176.
72. Graglia, 1998, p. 173.
73. Fein, 1995, rule #15.
74. Cited in Gallagher, 2000, pp. 86–87; Harris, 1997.
75. Waite, 1999/2000, p. 32.
76. Waite, 2001, p. 258; Krasnow and Yoest, 1998, p. 47.
77. Cowan, 1985, p. 465; Mattox, 1996.
78. Reuters, 2002.
79. Gallagher, 2000.
80. Waite, 2000, pp. 6, 13.

81. Schlessinger, 1994, p. 95.
82. Smock, 2000, p. 15; Shalit, 1999, pp. 249–50.
83. Stanley and Markham quoted in Gallagher, 2000, p. 85.
84. Popenoe, 1999; Shalit, 1999, p. 202; Peterson, 2002.
85. Peterson, 2002.
86. Geary, 1998, pp. 163–64; Betzig, 1997, pp. 7–8, 400; Gaulin, 2001, p. 201; Buss, 1994a, pp. 63–64.
87. Entertainment Network, 14 May 2002.
88. Powell, 1998; Powell, 2001.
89. Munson, 1999; See, 1999; Harrington, 2001; Yardley, 1999.
90. *Charlottesville Daily Progress*, 13 October 1999; Merida, 1998.
91. Maccoby, 1998, p. 210.
92. Podhoretz, 1991, p. 32; Gallagher, 2001; see also discussion of Paglia in Bellafante, 1998, p. 58.
93. Blum, 1997, pp. 226, 239, 277.
94. Sileo, 1995.
95. Stepp, 1999b.
96. Harris, 1999; Gilder, 1989.
97. Kristol, 1995, p. 56; see also Dilulio, 1996, p. 17; Podhoretz, 1991, p. 33; Wilson, 1993.
98. Harris, 1999.
99. Virginia Slims Poll on women's attitudes toward men conducted by Harris in 1970 and Roper in subsequent years; Townsend, 1990.
100. Anderson, 1997, p. 34.
101. Virginia Slims Poll on women's attitudes toward men conducted by Harris in 1970 and Roper in subsequent years.
102. Bechtel, 2000, p. 15; Symons, 1981.
103. Oberman, 1994.
104. See Dr. Drew and others in Nordlinger, 1999, p. 19; Bates, 2001.
105. Harris, 1997; Shalit, 1999, p. 30.
106. Waite, 2000, p. 15.
107. Dalton, 2000.
108. EN 333: Shakespeare's Histories and Comedies.
109. Whitehead, 1999, pp. 120–21; Powers, 1997; Caldwell, 1982, pp. 36–37.
110. Barker, 1991; Anders, 1996.
111. Hewlett, 2002.
112. Graman, 2001.
113. Treistman, 1999.
114. Reid, 1998.
115. Whitehead, 1998.
116. Waite, 2000, p. 35.
117. Waite, 2000, p. 15.

118. Wilson, 1993.
119. Merida and Vobejda, 1998.
120. Krasnow and Yoest, 1998.
121. Inoff-Germain, 1988, p. 136; Tannen, 1990, pp. 176–78.
122. Townsend, 1998, p. 56.
123. Townsend, 1998, p. 56; Hakim, 2000, p. 268; Rossi, 1987; Moir and Jessel, 1989; Tannen, 1990, pp. 268–70.
124. Whitehead and Popenoe, 2002.
125. Pew Research Center Survey, 1996; Krasnow, 2000.
126. Glenn, 2001, p. 31; Wolfe, 1998; Harvey, 2002.
127. Gallagher, 2000, pp. 106–9.
128. See Chapter 3; Campbell, 2002, p. 191; Miller, 2000, pp. 213, 244; Kenrick, 1990; Kenrick, 1996; Kenrick, 1992; Pawlowski, 1999; Mealey, 2000, p. 274; Crittenden, 1999, ch. 5, pp. 37–38; Whitehead, 1999.
129. Glenn and Marquardt, 2001.
130. Glenn and Marquardt, 2001, p. 12.
131. Gueorguieva, 2001; Brown, 2000b.
132. Vedantam, 2002b.
133. Tough, 2002.
134. Fretts, 1995.
135. Hansen, 2002; Nelson, 2003.
136. Miller, 2000, p. 244.
137. Nelson, 2003; Crittenden, 1999, pp. 156–57.
138. Hewlett, 2002, p. 87.
139. Crittenden, 1999, ch. 5; Waite, 2000; Townsend, 1990, pp. 255–56; Gaughan, 2002, p. 69.
140. Hewlett, 2002, pp. 169–70.
141. Fein, 1995, rule #7.
142. Laner, 2000.
143. Moore, 1997.
144. Fein, 1995, rule #17.
145. Goodman, 1996.
146. Fein, 1995, rule #2.
147. Fein, 1995, rule #6; Martin, 1984; Martin, 1985.
148. Fein, 1995, rule #13.
149. Fein, 1995, rule #14.
150. Fein, 1995, rule #15.
151. Glenn, 2001, p. 40; Tanenbaum, 1999, pp. 104–5.
152. Podles, 1997; Buss, 1994a, p. 116.
153. Fein, 1995, rule #22; Townsend, 1998, pp. 25, 56; Schaub, 1998.
154. Shalit, 1999, p. 198; Parke and Brott, 1999.
155. Buss, 1994a, pp. 114–16; Bailey, 1989, pp. 94–95; Campbell, 2002, pp. 197, 199.

156. Shalit, 1999, pp. 185–93.
157. Shalit, 1999, pp. 208–9; Mundy, 2000.
158. Mundy, 2000.
159. Buss, 1994a, pp. 114–16.
160. Pipher, 1994, p. 207; Roffman, 1999; Stepp, 1999a, 1999b.
161. Mundy, 2000, p. 21.
162. McGuinness, 1979, pp. 83, 85.
163. Mencimer, 1998.
164. Crittenden, 1999, pp. 35, 43; Liesen, 1994, p. 8; Shalit, 1999, pp. 91, 227.
165. Rabkin, 1997, p. 55.
166. Pipher, 1994, p. 182.
167. Shalit quoted in McLure, 1999.
168. Britt, 1998.
169. Shalit, 1999, p. 22; compare with Bailey, 1989, pp. 94–95.
170. McLaughlin, 2002, p. 87; Raspberry, 2001; Glenn, 2001, pp. 62, 64, 68.
171. Hymowitz, 1995.

Part 3: Men Want Their Way

Chapter 6: Aggression, Dominance and Competition

1. Quart, 1998.
2. Baumrind, 1972, p. 88; Gottman, 1994a, pp. 279–81.
3. Ahrens, 1997a; McPherson, 1997; Matus, 1999; Colburn, 1991.
4. Moir, 1999, p. 266; Campbell, 2002, p. 65.
5. Gross, 1998.
6. Mealey, 2000, p. 307; D'Amico, 1983, p. 63; Eagly and Steffen, 1986; Browne, 1995, pp. 1017–19; Blumstein and Schwartz, 1983, Appendix A.
7. Pool, 1994, p. 220; Rensberger, 1994.
8. Mealey, 2000, p. 245; Rowe, 1994, pp. 183–85.
9. Barkow, 1992; Ginsburg and Miller, 1982.
10. Ginsburg and Miller, 1982; Maccoby, 1998, p. 53.
11. Zorpette, 1999; Moir, 1999, p. 161.
12. Beard, May 1998.
13. Browne, 1995, pp. 1029–30; Chen, Baker et al., 2000, p. 1580.
14. Gaulin and McBurney, 2001, p. 254; Browne, 1995, p. 1029; Badcock, 2000, p. 14.
15. In the Nation, 2001; Kaufman, 1999b; Baker, Lamb et al., May 2001; Colburn, 1998.
16. Campbell, 2002, pp. 74–78.
17. Caldwell, 1996, p. 16.
18. Guttmann, 1998.

19. Johnson, 1996; Morin, 1997.
20. In Florida, Warmth Rises from the Ashes, 1998; Dabbs and Dabbs, 2000, ch. 8.
21. On TV, 8 March 2002.
22. Golombok and Fivush, 1994, pp. 140–41.
23. Mealey, 2000, p. 307.
24. Golombok and Fivush, 1994, p. 141; Mealey, 2000, p. 307; Pinker, 1997, p. 510.
25. Weisfeld, Muczenski et al., 1987, p. 129.
26. Gilmore, 1990, pp. 169, 223.
27. Gilmore, 1990, p. 110.
28. Harrington, 1985.
29. Campbell, 2002, p. 191; Morin, 2001.
30. Campbell, 2002, pp. 191, 221; Nisbett and Cohen, 1999a; Gaulin and McBurney, 2001, p. 359.
31. Dishion, 1999, p. 757.
32. Pinker, 1997, pp. 510–11; Browne, 1995, p. 1020.
33. Smuts, 1996; p. 254.
34. Low, 2000, p. 241; Smuts, 1996, p. 240; Yardley, 2002.
35. West, 1997, p. 92; Fagan and Johnson, 2002; Smuts, 1996, p. 240.
36. Batten, 1992, p. 89; Buss, 1994a, p. 130; Dabbs and Dabbs, 2000, p. 112.
37. Campbell, 2002.
38. Buss, 1994a, p. 157; Campbell, 2002, p. 254.
39. Campbell, 2002.
40. Campbell, 2002, pp. 254–57.
41. Campbell, 2002, pp. 254–57; Sheets, 2002, p. 100.
42. Campbell, 2002, p. 244.
43. Betzig, 1997, p. 9; Rogers, 2000.
44. Burch and George Gallup, 2000, pp. 429–35; Platek, 2002, p. 84.
45. McLain, Setters et al., 2000.
46. Campbell, 2002, pp. 194–96.
47. Campbell, 2002, p. 92.
48. Campbell, 2002, p. 92; Maccoby, 1998, pp. 40–41; Fisher, 1999, p. 43; Stepp, 2002.
49. Campbell, 2002, p. 228.
50. Van Creveld, 2000.
51. Taylor, Klein et al., 2000, pp. 417–18; Golombok and Fivush, 1994, p. 175.
52. Rasche, 1991, p. 46; Mishra, 1997; Dabbs and Dabbs, 2000, p. 79.
53. Mealey, 2000, p. 284.
54. Campbell, 2002, p. 167.

55. Inoff-Germain, 1988; Campbell, 2002, p. 128.
56. Campbell, 2002, pp. 84–85; Moir, 1999, p. 161; Crenshaw, 1996, p. 184; Rushton, 2002, p. 41.
57. Christiansen and Knussman, 1987; Daitzman and Zuckerman, 1980; Uzych, 1992; Crenshaw, 1996, pp. 30, 158.
58. Crenshaw, 1996, p. 30.
59. Golombok and Fivush, 1994, p. 137.
60. Dabbs and Dabbs, 2000, p. 160.
61. Dabbs and Dabbs, 2000, pp. 78–82; Crenshaw, 1996, p. 158; Christiansen and Knussman, 1987, p. 178.
62. Booth and Dabbs, 1993; Crenshaw, 1996, p. 148.
63. Browne, 1995, p. 1018; Sommers, 2000, p. 90; Moir, 1999, p. 264.
64. Stein, 2002.
65. Pool, 1994, pp. 180–81; Reinisch, 1981; Nyborg, 1994, p. 58.
66. Albert, Walsh et al., 1993, esp. pp. 406–8.
67. Constantino, Grosz et al., 1993; Dittmann, Kappes et al., 1990a; Dittmann, Kappes et al., 1990b.
68. Sapolsky, 1997, pp. 154–57.
69. Dabbs and Dabbs, 2000, pp. 80–81; Burnham, 2001.
70. Dabbs and Dabbs, 2000, pp. 88–89; Pool, 1994, p. 179; Mazur and Lamb, 1980; Blum, 1997, pp. 180–81.
71. Dabbs and Dabbs, 2000, p. 88; Moir, 1999, p. 169.
72. Lips, 2001, pp. 124, 122.
73. Quoted in Sommers, 2000, pp. 128, 131.
74. Pipher, 1994, p. 68.
75. Lips, 2001, pp. 124, 122.
76. Fischer and Mosquera, 2001, pp. 13, 14, 19.
77. Dowling, 2000, chs. 6 & 7.
78. Van Creveld, 2000.
79. Weiss, 1995, p. 7; Geary, 1998, p. 214.
80. Mealey, 2000, p. 371.
81. Barkow, 1992, p. 538.
82. Maccoby, 1998, p. 43.
83. Sommers, 2000, p. 42; Townsend, 1998, p. 240.
84. Campbell, 2002, pp. 216, 231; Browne, 1995, p. 1027.
85. Campbell, 2002, p. 231.
86. Archer, 1996, p. 914; Browne, 1998, p. 10.
87. U.S. Department of Justice, 1997, p. 54.
88. Pratto, 204, p. 206; Gaulin and McBurney, 2001, p. 359.
89. Laub, Nagin et al., 1998; 2000, p. 23.
90. Popenoe, 1996, p. 75; Boothroyd, 2002, p. 69.
91. Popenoe, 1996, p. 75.
92. Courtwright, 1996, p. 163; Schaub, 1997.

93. Booth, Carver et al., 2000, pp. 1027, 1029; Parke and Brott, 1999, p. 20; Gallagher and Waite, 2000, pp. 53–55; Daly and Wilson, 1999, p. 14.
94. Booth, Carver et al., 2000, pp. 1027, 1029.
95. Hetherington, Bridges et al., 1998, p. 176; Kaufman and Uhlenberg, 1998; Broude, 1999; Lewis, Fari Amini et al., 2000, pp. 203–4, 218.
96. Boys with Absentee Fathers Twice as Likely to Be Jailed, 1998; Gallagher and Waite, 2000, p. 134; McLanahan and Sandefur, 1994, p. 76; Sommers, 2000, p. 130.
97. Darby, 1998.
98. Cubbin, Pickle et al., 2000; Kawachi, Kennedy et al., 1999.
99. Gallagher and Waite, 2000, p. 135; Anderson, Holmes et al., 1999, p. 446.
100. Veysey and Messner, 1999; Dishion, 1999; Heiss, 1996; Raspberry, 1999.
101. Cookston, 1999; Florsheim, Tolan et al., 1998; Ross and Mirowsky, 2001.
102. Rountree and Warner, 1999.
103. Cook, Church et al., 1996.
104. Mathews and Strauss, 2000.
105. Osgood and Chambers, 2000.
106. De Goede, 2000.
107. Nisbett and Cohen, 1999b, pp. 16–19; Mealey, 2000, p. 372; Fischer and Mosquera, 2001, p. 17; Kennedy, 1999.
108. Weisfeld, Muczenski et al., 1987.
109. Golombok and Fivush, 1994, p. 142; Mazur and Booth, 1998, p. 387.
110. Mazur and Booth, 1998, p. 362; Grant in Mazur and Booth, 1998, p. 376.
111. Goldberg, 1993, p. 69; Dabbs and Dabbs, 2000, p. 155; Nyborg, 1994, p. 58.
112. Dabbs and Dabbs, 2000, p. 164.
113. Dabbs and Dabbs, 2000, p. 160.
114. Dabbs and Dabbs, 2000, pp. 63, 137.
115. Meredith, 2000.
116. Rasche, 1991, p. 48.
117. Miller cited in LaCroix and Haynes, 1987, p. 114.
118. Hewlett, 2002, p. 134; Gallese, 1985.
119. Mealey, 2000, p. 376; Fisher, 1999, p. 52.
120. Fisher, 1999, p. 30.
121. Rosaldo, 1980, pp. 393–95; Fisher, 1992, pp. 283, 286; Goldberg, 1993, p. 14; Rosen, 2002, p. 6.
122. Mann, 2001.

123. Emery, 2000a.
124. Kaufman, 2000; Arnhart, 1998, p. 137.
125. Only Widows and Orphans, 1999.
126. Gallese, 1991; Gallese, 1985.
127. Gallese, 1985.
128. Moir and Jessel, 1989, p. 130.
129. Campbell, 2002, pp. 72, 110, 116.
130. Hewlett, 2002, pp. 41, 55, 57, 59, 60, 165, 175, 197; Browne, 1995, p. 1088; Gaulin, 1993; D'Amico, 1983, pp. 41–42.
131. Hewlett, 2002, p. 178; Kayden, 1990, pp. 121–22.
132. Campbell, 2002, pp. 117–18; Cashdan, 1995; Cashdan in Mazur and Booth, 1998, p. 366.
133. Campbell, 2002, pp. 119–20.
134. Dabbs and Dabbs, 2000, pp. 5, 13–14, 129–30, 138–39; Fisher, 1992, p. 287; Fisher, 1999, p. 29; Ehrhardt, Ince et al., 1981, p. 296; Inhoff-Germain et al. in Cashdan, 1995, p. 354; Mealey, 2000, p. 309; Duke, 2001; Charlesworth and Dzur, 1987.
135. Crenshaw, 1996, pp. 150–53; Mazur and Lamb, 1980; Moir, 1999, pp. 170–71.
136. Bateup, 2002; Mazur and Booth, 1998, p. 362; Fisher, 1999, p. 42; Fisher, 1992, p. 287; Blum, 1997, p. 181; Moir, 1999, pp. 170, 171.
137. Golombok and Fivush, 1994, pp. 164–65.
138. Buss in Browne, 1995, p. 1024; Knight and Kagan, 1977.
139. Lips, 2001, p. 127.
140. Fisher, 1999, p. 29.
141. Fisher, 1992, p. 287.
142. Fisher, 1999, pp. 36–37; Maccoby, 1998, p. 38.
143. Campbell, 2002, pp. 114–15; Lips, 2001, pp. 127, 323.
144. Stolba, 1999.
145. Campbell, 2002, p. 105.
146. Maccoby, 1998, pp. 62–64; Harris, 1998, p. 237; Lips, 2001, p. 323.
147. Campbell, 2002, p. 105; Maccoby, 1998, p. 64.
148. Harris, 1998, p. 236.
149. Maccoby, 1998, pp. 62–63.
150. Maccoby, 1998. p. 150.
151. Maccoby, 1998, p. 37.
152. Maccoby, 1998, p. 51.
153. Freedman and DeBoer, 1979, pp. 594–95.
154. Harris, 1998, pp. 237–38; Maccoby, 1998, p. 72.
155. Lueptow, 2001; Campbell, 2002, pp. 122–23; Voss, 2002.
156. Ahlgren and Johnson, 1979; Golombok and Fivush, 1994, p. 243; Maccoby, 1998, p. 39.

157. Browne, 2002, p. 15; Golombok and Fivush, 1994, p. 243; Blum, 1997; Maccoby, 1998, p. 39; Hoyenga and Hoyenga, 1993, p. 319; Knight and Kagan, 1977.
158. Guinier, Tannen in Hartocollis, 2001.
159. Hartocollis, 2001.
160. Hoyenga and Hoyenga, 1993, p. 319; Browne, 1995, p. 1020.
161. Hoyenga and Hoyenga, 1993, p. 319; Campbell, 2002, p. 118.
162. Blair, 1999.
163. *American Enterprise*, September 2000, p. 9.
164. Browne, 1995, p. 1021.
165. Browne, 1995, pp. 132–33.
166. Moir, 1999, p. 173; Polefrone and Manuck, 1987, p. 26.
167. Maccoby, 1998, p. 104.
168. Baucom, Besch et al., 1985, Maccoby, 1998, pp. 104, 115.
169. Browne, 1995, pp. 1021–22; Campbell, 2002, p. 108; Moir, 1999, p. 174.
170. Browne, 2002, p. 19.
171. Campbell, 2002, pp. 190, 120–21; Browne p. 17; Lips, 2001, p. 127; Fisher, 1992, p. 222; Cashdan, 1998.
172. Campbell, 2002, p. 118.
173. Browne, 1995, p. 1027; Pool, 1994, pp. 54–55.
174. Crenshaw, 1996, p. 104.
175. Geary, 1998, p. 247; Campbell, 2002, pp. 116–17; Browne, 1995, p. 1027.
176. Geary, 1998, pp. 250–51.

Chapter 7: Sports, Aggression and Title IX

1. Riley, 1997.
2. Republican National Committee, 2000.
3. Whiteside, 2001.
4. U.S. Department of Education, Secretary's Commission for Opportunity in Athletics, 2003.
5. Reynolds, 2003.
6. Irving, 2003; National Women's Law Center, 2002, p. 7.
7. Kennedy, 2003.
8. Gavora, 2002, pp. 52–55.
9. U.S. Department of Education, Secretary's Commission for Opportunity in Athletics, 2003.
10. Sullivan, Emmet G., http://www.dcd.uscourts.gov/Opinions/2003/Sullivan/02-72.pdf.
11. U.S. Department of Education, Secretary's Commission for Opportunity in Athletics, 2003, p. 40.
12. Solomon, 2003.
13. Quoted in Brady, 2003.

14. U.S. Department of Education, Secretary's Commission, 2003.
15. Farhi, 2001.
16. Willingham and Cole, 1997, pp. 147–48.
17. Tannen, 2001 p. 236.
18. Farhi, 1996; Tuggle and Owen, 1999, p. 172.
19. Genzale, 2002, pp. 20, 144.
20. Nichols, 2002; Givhan, 2001; Rivers, 2002.
21. Genzale, 2002.
22. Lipstick on the Links, 2002.
23. Barbie Super Sports on Amazon.com.
24. The Future of Women's Sports and Fitness, 2001.
25. Goodman, 1999; Chisolm, 1999; Bruce, 1998.
26. Goodman, 2002.
27. Sargent, Zillmann et al., 1998, pp. 52–53; Genzale, 2002, p. 20.
28. Data from University of Virginia Athletic Department, 2000.
29. E-mail, 21 June 2001, and later conversation with ESPN official.
30. Moir, 1999, p. 166.
31. Galinsky, 2002.
32. Maurer, 1997.
33. Gavora, 2002, p. 27; Roach, 1995; Hollander, 2002.
34. Gavora, 2002, p. 68.
35. Furchtgott-Roth and Stolba, 2001, p. 146.
36. Gavora, 2002, p. 64.
37. Roach, 1995; Gavora, 2002, p. 79.
38. Pennington, 2002; Gavora, 2002, pp. 68–69.
39. Roach, 1995.
40. Gavora, 2002, pp. 65–67; Barr, 2002.
41. Gavora, 2002, p. 65.
42. Willingham and Cole, 1997, p. 151.
43. Sporting Goods Manufacturers Association, 1998.
44. Tierney, 2003.
45. Power, 2000, p. 252.
46. Campbell, 2002, p. 106.
47. Browne, 2002, p. 16.
48. Campbell, 2002, p. 106; Browne, 2002, p. 15.
49. Maccoby, 1998, p. 115.
50. Geary, 1998, pp. 227–28.
51. Maccoby, 1998, pp. 37–38; Pool, 1994, p. 212.
52. Maccoby, 1998, p. 103.
53. Maccoby, 1998, p. 102; Sommers, 2000, pp. 96–97; Eaton and Enns, 1986.
54. Campbell, 2002, p. 106.
55. Maccoby, 1998, pp. 63–64.
56. Miedzian, 1991, p. 84.

57. Maccoby, 1998, p. 16; Browne, 2002, p. 97.
58. Sommers, 2000.
59. Pellegrini and Perlmutter, 1988, pp. 15–17; Christine Drea quoted in Blum, Beuhring et al., 2000, p. 50; Humphreys and Smith, 1987; Power, 2000, p. 178.
60. Geary, 1998, p. 115.
61. Maccoby, 1998, p. 102.
62. Quoted in Popenoe, 1996, p. 144; Maccoby, 1998, pp. 93, 111.
63. Geary, 1998, p. 222; Taylor, Klein et al., 2000, p. 414(n); Pool, 1994, p. 212.
64. Geary, 1998, p. 228; Campbell, 2002, pp. 126–27; Maccoby, 1998, p. 112.
65. Myers and Lips, 1978.
66. Crenshaw, 1996, p. 184.
67. Udry, Morris et al., 1995; Udry, 2000.
68. Moir, 1999, pp. 170–71; Blum, 1997, p. 181; Burnham, 2001; Yalom, Green et al., 1973; Dabbs and Dabbs, 2000, p. 89; Crenshaw, 1996, p. 150.
69. Freedman and DeBoer, 1979, p. 594.
70. Leahy, 2002; Weisfeld, Bloch et al., 1983.
71. Tannen, 2001, p. 157; Blue Marlin Fishing, 1997.
72. Cited in Mealey, 2000, p. 269; Howard, Blumstein et al., 1987; Buss, 1994b, p. 248.
73. Tannen, 2001, p. 158.
74. Miller, 2000, pp. 254–56.
75. http://www.feminist.org/research/sports6.html.
76. http://www.girlsnsports.com/benefits.html.
77. Pate et al., 2000; Berlage, 1986, pp. 55–59; Bursik and Young, 2000, p. 251; National Women's Law Center, 2002; Frisch, 1987; Welch, 1998; Cyr, 1999, pp. 29–30.
78. Gavora, 2002, pp. 2, 32.
79. Gavora, 2002, p. 5; Girl Wrestler Fights for Spot, 1998.
80. Whitehead, 2003, p. 86.
81. Hofferth and Sandberg, 2001.
82. Span, 1997, p. 23.
83. Crenshaw, 1996, p. 104; Golombok and Fivush, 1994, p. 247; Campbell, 2002, pp. 116–17; Browne, 1995, p. 1027; Hofferth and Sandberg, 2001, p. 304.
84. Brooks, 1979; Scheck, 1996; Roaf, 1979, pp. 9–10; Brennan, 1993.
85. Kornheiser, 1996.
86. Tousignant, 1996; Hudgens, 1997, p. 8.
87. Tousignant, 1996; Hudgens, 1997, p. 6.

88. Gavora, 2002, p. 77.
89. Argetsinger, 1999.
90. Cantu and Mueller, 1999.
91. Argetsinger, 1999, pp. A1, A12; Chaney, 2000.
92. Women's Sports Foundation, 2002, p. 4.
93. Badger, 2003.
94. Women's Sports Foundation, 2002.
95. http://www.womenssportsfoundation.org.
96. Myers and Lips, 1978, p. 578.
97. Buss in Browne, 1995, p. 1024.
98. Gavora, 2002, p. 144.
99. Gavora, 2002, pp. 144, 65.
100. Goodman, 2003.
101. Tierney, 2003.
102. McGuinness, 1985, p. 87.
103. Gavora, 2002, p. 129; Miedzian, 1991, pp. 184–85.
104. Crenshaw, 1996, p. 151; Ellin, 1995; From Box Scores to the Police Blotter, 1995.
105. Bardwick, 1971, p. 106; Gove, 1985, p. 138.
106. Blumstein and Benedict, 1999, pp. 12–15; Shapiro and Heath, 2000.
107. From Box Scores to the Police Blotter, 1995.
108. Fountain, 1998a, 1998b.
109. Gurian, 1999, pp. 54–55.
110. Raspberry, 1997; Maccoby, 1998, p. 39; Low, 2000, p. 196.
111. National Wrestling Coaches Association, 2002.
112. Gavora, 2002, p. 53.
113. Robinson, 1999.
114. El-Bashir, 2002.
115. Gugliotta, 1998.
116. Maccoby, 1998, pp. 54–56.
117. Campbell, 2002, pp. 108–9.
118. Gurian, 1999, pp. 53, 48–49.
119. Gavora, 2002, p. 62.
120. Gavora, 2002, p. 56; Greenberger, 2002.
121. Women's Sports Foundation, 2002.
122. Aikman Settles on Retirement, 2001.
123. Brady, 2003.
124. Fletcher, 2002.
125. Bae, 2000.
126. Fletcher, 2002.
127. Knapp, 2001.
128. Gavora, 2002, pp. 17, 51, 143–45.

Part 4: Women Want Their Way, Too

Chapter 8: Nurturing the Young

1. Morse, 1989, p. B13; Raitt, 1989.
2. Darrow, 2000, pp. 140–41.
3. Jamison, 1995.
4. Fleming, 1994, pp. 149–50.
5. Haussegger, 2002.
6. Pew Research Center Survey, 1997.
7. Burr, 1970; Luckey and Bain, 1979; Rollins and Feldman, 1970; Boulton, 1983, pp. 18–19; Whyte, 1990, pp. 140–41; Hakim, 2000, p. 181; Hales, 1999, p. 192.
8. Boulton, 1983, pp. 3–7; Goodbody, 1987, p. 428; Hakim, 2000, p. 181.
9. Khlat, Sermet and Le Pape, 2000.
10. Goldin, 1997, pp. 43–49; Hales, 1993, p. 193; Beyette, 1999; Lewis and Yoest, 1996; Pew Research Center Survey, 1997; Waxman, 1998, p. B1.
11. Hewlett, 2002, pp. 47–48; also see Miller, 1980.
12. Hewlett, 2002, pp. 1–3, 10, 40–42, 48, 86–87, 89, 94, 98, 119–20.
13. Thomson, 1997; Trafford, 1996; Pew, 1997.
14. Hewlett, 2002, p. 49; Hales, 1999, p. 194.
15. Hales, 1999, p. 199.
16. Charen, 1998, p. 22.
17. Miscarriage Raises Women's Risk of Major Depression, 1997.
18. Feingold, 1994, pp. 429–56; Vox, 1985, pp. 489–502; Lippa, 1998b, pp. 996–1009.
19. Gehrke, 1997, pp. 417–18; Wolfe, 1991, p. 164.
20. Astin, et al., 1997; Sommers, 2001.
21. Lewis, 1997.
22. Hrdy, 1999, p. 156.
23. Genevie, 1987, p. xxv; Jones, 1985, p. 105.
24. Genevie, 1987, pp. 125–51.
25. Genevie, 1987, pp. 125–35; Hewlett, 2002, p. 24; Valian, 1998, p. 272; Graglia, 1998, pp. 24, 89; Lewis and Yoest, 1996, pp. 18, 80–81, 98; Kahlenberg, 2002; Rasche, 1991, p. 47.
26. Entwisle, 1981, p. 290.
27. Hock, 1984, pp. 425–31; Cowan, 1993, pp. 169–70; Corter and Felming, 1995—as cited in Browne, 2002, p. 181.
28. McDermott, 1993, pp. 1, 7, 9–13; Tooley, 2002, p. 77; Graglia, 1998, p. 364.
29. Geary, 1998, pp. 234–35, 43; Whiting, 1973, pp. 171–88; Maccoby, 1998; Pool, 1994, p. 213; Fisher, 1999, pp. 76, 120–21.

30. Parke, 1999, pp. 109–10; Blakemore, 1990.
31. Rossi, 1987; Maccoby, 1998, pp. 98, 331.
32. Popenoe, 1996, p. 169.
33. Geary, 1998, p. 116.
34. Hrdy, 1999, pp. 100, 301, 540; Rossi, 1987.
35. Geary, 1998, pp. 99–101; Whiting, 1973; Rossi, 1987.
36. Geary, 1998, p. 101; Campbell, 2002, p. 57.
37. Nock, 1999.
38. Doyle, 1998, p. 110.
39. Campbell, 2002, p. 57; Geary, 1998, p. 101; Wilson, 2002, p. 188; Hoem, 1995, pp. 293–95; Knudson, 2002.
40. Doyle, 1998, p. 111; Selmi, 2000.
41. Browne, 2002, p. 106.
42. Browne, 2002, p. 107; Tiger, 1987; Smith, 2000.
43. Fuchs, 1988, p. 70; Tiger, 1987, p. 349.
44. Campbell, 2002, p. 57.
45. Fisher, 1999, p. 123; Blum, 1997, p. 66.
46. Geary, 1988, p. 219.
47. Goldberg, 1982; Geary, 1998, p. 234; Robertson, 2003, pp. 38–39.
48. Frodi, 1978; Berman, 1980.
49. Geary, 1998, p. 223.
50. Fisher, 1999, p. 124; Maccoby, 1998, p. 114; Geary, 1998, p. 103; Crenshaw, 1996, p. 101.
51. Maccoby, 1998, p. 114.
52. Moir, 1999, p. 224; Hrdy, 1999, pp. 137–39; Campbell, 2002, pp. 55, 99.
53. Angier, 1999b, p. 312.
54. Hrdy, 1999, p. 138; Moir, 1999, p. 271.
55. Uvnas-Moberg, 1990, p. 271.
56. Hrdy, 1999, pp. 137–39, 536; Angier, 1999b, pp. 314–15; Hales, 1999, p. 210; Booth, Carver et al., 2000.
57. Hrdy, 1999, pp. 137, 537–38; Angier, 1999b, pp. 514–15; Crenshaw, 1996, p. 98.
58. Entwisle, 1981, p. 157.
59. Hrdy, 1999, p. 538.
60. Hrdy, 1999, p. 538.
61. Hrdy, 1999, pp. 537, 40.
62. Geary, 1998, p. 104.
63. Parke, 1999, p. 20.
64. Hausman, 1999, p. 53; Dittmann, 1990a; Storey, 2000; Moir, 1999, p. 270.
65. Mitchell and Helsons, 1990.
66. Jones, 1985, p. 99.
67. Moir, 1999, pp. 272–73.

68. Moir, 1999, p. 272; Wiesenfeld, 1981.
69. Hrdy, 1999, p. 212; Moir, 1999, pp. 172–73; Wiesenfeld, 1981.
70. Furedy, 1989; Wiesenfeld, 1981.
71. Moir, 1999, p. 273; LaRossa, 1981, p. 192.
72. Stein quoted in Moir and Moir, 1989, p. 146.
73. Jones, 1985; Rebelsky and Hanks, 1971.
74. Parke, 1999, p. 124; but see Aldous, 1998, p. 818.
75. Rossi, 1987.
76. LaRossa, 1981, pp. 49–67; Thompson and Walker, 1989, p. 861.
77. Rossi, 1987; Power, 2000, p. 333.
78. La Rossa, 1981, pp. 189–97.
79. Goldscheider, 1991, p. 130.
80. Lewis et al., 2000, p. 203; Becker, 1992, pp. 146–48; Lewis and Yoest, 1996, p. 98.
81. Ambert, 1999; Tooley, 2002, p. 86.
82. Ehrensaft, 1990.
83. Riessmann, 1990, pp. 123–24.
84. Campbell, 2002, p. 59.
85. Browne, 2002, p. 22.
86. Popenoe, 2001.
87. Campbell, 2002, p. 59; Becker, 1992; Geary, 1998, pp. 106–7; Parke, 1999, p. 117.
88. Trevathan, 1987, pp. 223–34.
89. Hrdy, 1999, p. 498.
90. Hrdy, 1999, p. 500.
91. Mealey, 2000, pp. 236, 93; Geary, 1998, pp. 97, 117; Campbell, 2002, pp. 177–79.
92. Popenoe, 1996, p. 182.
93. Hrdy, 1999.
94. Maestripieri, 2002, pp. 327–44.
95. Geary, 1998, p. 223.
96. Hales, 1999, p. 210.
97. Geary, 1998, p. 321.
98. Harvard Heart Letter, 1997.
99. Fisher, 1999, pp. 92–94.
100. Fisher, 1999, pp. 84, 91–93; Spake, 1999, p. 82.
101. Rountree and Warner, 1999.
102. Raskin, 1996, p. B1; Crittendon, 1999, p. 82.
103. Span, 1996, p. D11.
104. Friedan, 1981—in Tooley, 2002, p. 10.
105. Quoted in Tooley, 2002, p. 48; Crittenden, 1999, p. 160.
106. Quoted in Tooley, 2002, pp. 86, 51.
107. Wolf, 2002, pp. 115–16.
108. Wolf, 2002, ch. 8; Geary, 1998, p. 322; Thompson and White,

1989, p. 863; Hakim, 2000, p. 235.
109. Sommers, 1996; Catton, 1996; Tooley, 2002, p. 10.
110. Graglia, 1998, pp. 130–31; Friedan, 1989; Fox-Genovese, 1998.
111. Okin, 1992, p. 171; Nussbaum, 1992.
112. Graglia, 1998, pp. 17, 87, 107, 363–64; Selmi, 2000; O'Leary, 1997; Levine, 1992, pp. 125–26; Mintz, 1998—in Booth and Crouter, 1998, p. 26; Kristol, 1996; Shreve, 1987.
113. Tooley, 2002.
114. Beauvoir, 1978, p. 508.
115. N. Emery, 1999, p. 11.
116. Graglia, 1998, pp. 363–64.
117. Eyer quoted in Hrdy, 1999, pp. 491–92.
118. Lips, 2001, p. 130
119. Gilmore, 1990, p. 229.
120. Lips, 2001, pp. 130, 362–67; Moir, 1999, p. 268.
121. Poltnick, 1982, p. 23; see Friedman comments in Vedantam, 2001; Fisch, 2002.
122. Maestripieri, 2002, p. 341.
123. Pew Research Center Survey, 1996.
124. Rogers and White, 1998, pp. 300–1.
125. Lips, 2001, p. 366.
126. Williams, 1992, pp. 106, 109.
127. Beauvoir, 1978—as quoted in Tooley, 2002, pp. 76–77.
128. Quoted in Crittenden, 1999, p. 155.
129. Shields, 2002; Kahlenberg, 2001.
130. Estrich quoted in Furchtgott-Roth, 2000; Okin, 1992—quoted in O'Leary, 1997, p. 122.
131. Walsh, 1994.
132. Tooley, 2002, p. 76.
133. Martha Burke—quoted in Crittenden, 1999, p. 178; Childcare Initiative Triggers "Mommy Wars," 1998; Bergmann, 2000.
134. Selmi, 2000, p. 773.
135. Bergmann, 1997, pp. 278–79.
136. Schwartz, 1989.
137. Friedan, 1989, p. 196; Young, 1999, p. 45; Gallese, 1989; Thiers, 1986.
138. Pollitt, 1994; Williams, 1989, pp. 107–8; Hewlett, 2002, pp. 282–82.
139. Weiss, 2002.
140. Wisensale, 2001, pp. 135–41; Elving, 1995, pp. 22–33.
141. Jenkins, 2002.
142. See Chapter 3 above, p. 26; Gallese, 1985, p. 250.
143. Gallese, 1985, pp. 226–27.
144. Gallese, 1985, p. 225.

145. Gallese, 1985, p. 225.
146. Gallese, 1985, p. 223; Krasnow and Yoest, 1998.
147. Sharbutt, 1990.
148. Ianzito, 2002; Gindoff, 2002.
149. Stein, 2003b.
150. Sandman et al., 1999, pp. 333–45; Luke et al., 1999, pp. 1172–79.
151. Reuters, 1990; Walker, 2001, p. 364; Samiei, 2002.
152. Wolf, 2002, p. 111.
153. Oh, Baby, 2002; Richardson, 1983, pp. 93–111.
154. Walker, 2001.
155. Walker, 2001.
156. Klebanoff, 1996; Dabbs, 1991, pp. 1480–85—as cited in Walker, 2001, pp. 361–65.
157. The Fetus Is Father of the Man, 1999.
158. Gabbe et al., 1991, pp. 222–29; Lee and Zaffke, 1999, pp. 183–91; Elek et al., 1997, pp. 49–54.
159. Brown and Lumley, 1998, pp. 156–61; Gjerdingen and Chaloner, 1994, pp. 465–72; Glazener et al., 1995, pp. 282–87; Brown, 1999; McGovern et al., 1997.
160. Kline et al., 1998; McGovern et al., 1997, pp. 507–21.
161. Kline et al., 1998.
162. Uvnas-Moberg, 1990, pp. 170–72.
163. Upton, 2000.
164. Mike et al., 1994, pp. 214–29.
165. Gjerdingen and Chaloner, 1994, p. 471.
166. Wolf, 2002, pp. 119–20; Adams, 2004.
167. Wolf, 2002, p. 208
168. Wolf, 2002, pp. 111–14.
169. Wolf quoted in Tooley, 2002, p. 227.
170. Wolf, 2002, p. 114; Greer in Tooley, 2002, p. 82.
171. Yang, 1996.
172. Lincoln, 1996.
173. Leibovich, 2002.
174. Breast Feeding, Eating Nuts Linked to Allergies, 2001; Squires, 2000.
175. American Academy of Pediatrics, 1997; Beral, 2002; Okie, 2002; Zheng, 2000.
176. American Academy of Pediatrics, 1997.
177. Blum, 1993.
178. Angier, 1999b, pp. 152–53; Bachrach et al., 2003.
179. Angier, 1999b, pp. 152–53; Carbajal et al., 2003.
180. Wolf, 2002, p. 269.
181. Angier, 1999b, p. 153; Wolf, 2002, p. 269; Li, 2003.

182. American Academy of Pediatrics, 1997; Kaufman, 1999a; Squires, 1999; Smoking, Breast-Feeding Connected to SIDS, 2001; Mortensen, 2002, pp. 2365–71; Singhai, 2001; Roberts, 2001; Kaufman, 2001; Wolf, 2002, p. 269; Angier, 1999b, p. 154; Bachrach et al., 2003.
183. Sargent, 2000, p. 143; Wolf, 2002, p. 270; Mozingo, 2000; Trafford, 1997; The Pros and Cons of Breast-Feeding, 1998, p. 4; Breast-Feeding Successes and Failures, 2000, p. 4.
184. American Academy of Pediatrics, 1997; Breast-Feeding Rates Rise, 2002.
185. American Academy of Pediatrics, 1997.
186. Cited in Wolf, 2002, p. 269.
187. Ryan, 1989, pp. 524–31; Gielen, 1991, pp. 298–305; Roe, 1999; Lindberg, 1996, pp. 144–48; Miller, 1996, p. 434.
188. Galtry, 2000, p. 304.
189. Zuckerman, 1998.
190. Kamen, 2001; Hopkinson, 2002; Galtry, 2000.
191. Graglia, 1998, pp. 367–68.
192. Graglia, 1998, p. 185; Parke, 1999, p. 18.
193. Wolf, 2002, p. 267.
194. Blum, 1997, pp. 65–67; Hales, 1999, pp. 39–40.
195. Blum, 1997, p. 65; Lewis, 2000, p. 196.
196. Stein, 2003a.
197. Lewis et al., 2000, p. 196.
198. Lewis et al., 2000, p. 114; Popenoe, 1996, p. 213.
199. Blum, 1997, p. 69.
200. Babchuck, 1985; Wiesenfeld, 1981; Parke, 1999, p. 25.
201. Babchuck, 1985; Wiesenfeld, 1981; Fisher, 1999, pp. 92–93.
202. Pool, 1994, p. 41; Fisher, 1999, p. 86.
203. Fisher, 1999, pp. 88–93; Pool, 1994, p. 41; Blum, 1997, pp. 67–69.
204. Lips, 2001, p. 130; Parke, 1999, p. 25; Mealey, 2000, pp. 342–43.
205. Hrdy, 1999, p. 214.
206. Power, 2000, pp. 543–45.

Chapter 9: Day Care

1. Robertson, 2003, ch. 2 and pp. 96–97.
2. Lopez, 1998.
3. Strauss, 2001.
4. Strauss, 2001; Vedantam, 2001; Lewis, Fari Amini et al., 2000.
5. Moon, 2000; Redmond, 1984.
6. Wald, 1988, pp. 540–46.
7. Belongia, 2001; Nyquist, 1999.
8. Bale, Petheram et al., 1996.

9. Alaimo, 2002; Berman, 1995; Thrane et al., 2001; Vernon-Feagans, 1996; Wald, 1988; Zeisel, 1995.
10. Okie, 2000.
11. Redfearn, 2002; Robertson, 2003, pp. 85–91.
12. Peth-Pierce, 2002, Russell, 1999.
13. Peth-Pierce, 2002, Russell, 1999.
14. Peth-Pierce, 2002; Robertson, 2003, p. 76.
15. Belsky, 2002; Belsky, Steinberg et al., 1991; Boodman, 1999a; Power, 2000.
16. Belsky, 2001; Robertson, 2003, pp. 48, 52.
17. Belsky, 2002; Vedantam, 2001; Sweney, 2001; Belsky, 2001; National Institute of Child Health and Human Development Early Child Care Research Network, 2003.
18. Devitt, 2002; Fisch, 2002; Han and Waldfogel, 2001.
19. Belsky, 1999; Fisch, 2002.
20. National Institute of Child Health and Human Development Early Child Care Research Network, 2003; but see contrasting view of Robertson, 2003, pp. 82–85.
21. Belsky, Steinberg et al., 1991.
22. Luecken, Suarez et al., 1997; Repetti and Wood, 1997.
23. Babchuck, 1985; Wiesenfeld, 1981; Fisher, 1999, pp. 92–93.
24. Power, 2000, p. 365, Lewis, Fari Amini et al., 2000, pp. 198–203, Rossi, 1981 p. 498.
25. Tout, 1998, pp. 1247–62; Belsky, 1991, pp. 647–70; Twenge, 2000, pp. 1007–21; Booth, Carver et al., 2000, p. 243; Watamura et al., 2003.
26. Hrdy, 1999, p. 109.
27. Hrdy, 1999, p. 492, p. 407.
28. Hrdy, 1999, p. 492, p. 535.
29. Hrdy, 1999, pp. 506–8, 493, 116; Greenspan, 1997, pp. 264–65.
30. Robertson, 2003, p. 70.
31. Robertson, 2003, pp. 7–13, 122–24.
32. Vobejda, 1997; Strauss, 2001, pp. A1, A6; Peth-Pierce, 2002; Shreve, 1987.
33. Wolf, 2002, p. 284.
34. Hrdy, 1999, p. 508; Robertson, 2003, pp. 38–39, 76.
35. Hrdy, 1999, p. 504.
36. Hondagneu-Sotelo, 1997; Morse, 2001, p. 140.
37. Benbow, personal correspondence.
38. Rosenfield, 1985; Robertson, 2003, pp. 141–42.
39. Hrdy, 1999, pp. 137–39, 536.
40. Crittenden, 1999.
41. Crittenden, 1999; Hrdy, 1999; Krasnow and Yoest, 1998, p. 48.
42. Robertson, 2003, p. 131.

43. Williams, 2001.
44. Frey, 2001b; Biskupic, 1995.
45. Williams, 2001.
46. Lewis and Yoest, 1996, p. 98; Robertson, 2000, p. 165.
47. Crittenden, 1999, pp. 114, 139; Lewis, Fari Amini et al., 2000, p. 203.
48. Garment, 1994.
49. Lewis and Yoest, 1996; p. 47, Robertson, 2000, p. 163.
50. Deogun, 1997; Fisher, 1999, p. 47.
51. Envoy to Pakistan Plans to Step Down, 2002.
52. Ford, 2002, p. 285.
53. Cleary, 1983.
54. Walker and Best, 1991, p. 81.
55. Genevie, 1987, pp. 382–83.
56. Luecken, Suarez et al., 1997.
57. Eberstadt, 2001.
58. Morris, 1997; Russek, Schwartz et al., 1998.
59. Parcel and Dufur, 2001.
60. Perry-Jenkins and Gillman, 2000.
61. Becker, 1999.
62. Grimsley and Salmon, 1999.
63. Shapiro, 1997.
64. Belsky, 2001.
65. Hojat, 1998.
66. Fisher, 1999, p. 123.
67. Blum, 1997, p. 84.
68. Estrich, 2000, p. 103.
69. Browne, 2002, p. 183.
70. Fisher, 1999, p. 47.
71. Thompson, 1998, p. 27.
72. Lewis and Yoest, 1996, p. 47.
73. Genevie, 1987, p. 385.
74. Thompson, 1998, p. 30; Tooley, 2002, p. 86.
75. Crittenden, 1999, p. 116.
76. Walsh, 1994.
77. Sharbutt, 1990.
78. Schaefer, 2000.
79. Balz and Allen, 2002.
80. Kurtz, 2002.
81. Post Labor Laboring, 2000.
82. Klerman and Leibowitz, 1990, pp. 284–88; Sonenstein et al., 2000; Who's Minding the Children? 1998; Okie, 2000; U.S. Department of Health and Human Services, 1997, p. 69; Sommers, 1994.
83. Thompson and Walker, 1989, p. 862.

84. Genevie, 1987, pp. 386, 389.
85. Yoest, 1998, p. 48.
86. Pew Research Center Survey, 1997.
87. Steil, 1997.
88. The Gallup Organization, 1996, p. 13, tables 18 & 19; Robertson, 2003, p. 131.
89. McKee, 1982, p. 130; The Gallup Organization, 1996, p. 1.
90. Purtilo, 1996, p. 197.
91. Kelly, Marguerite, 1998.
92. Post Labor Laboring, 2000.
93. Roberts, 2002.
94. Post Labor Laboring, 2000.
95. U.S. Department of Health and Human Services. 1997, p. 69; Capizzano, Adams et al., 2000; Outside the Court, Chaos Too, 1997.
96. U.S. Census Bureau, 1964 ; U.S. Census Bureau, 2002.
97. Hofferth and Sandberg, 2001, pp. 302–6; Eberstadt, 2001; Robertson, 2003, pp. 33–35.
98. Belsky, 2002, p. 169.
99. Cowan, Cowan et al., 1993, p. 170; Becker, 1992, p. 148; Hakim, 2000, pp. 120–22.
100. Gelernter, 1996, p. 28; Robertson, 2003, pp. 126, 150.
101. Belsky, 2003a.
102. Peth-Pierce, 2002; Prosser and McGroder, 1992, p. 47.
103. Pearlstein, 1998.
104. Robertson, 2003, pp. 129, 131.

Chapter 10: Conclusion

1. Pew Research Center Survey, 1997; Bowman, 1998, p. 24.
2. Gallup poll in *American Enterprise*, May/June 1995, p. 19.
3. Reality Check, 1998.
4. Gallagher and Waite, 2000.
5. Trafford, 2002, citing National Center for Health Statistics, 2002.
6. Hakim, 2000, pp. 111, 141, 153, 155; Steil, 1997.
7. Hakim, 2000, pp. 88, 94, 257, 262; Steil, 1997; Genevie and Margolies, 1987, pp. 358–61.
8. Hakim, 2000, esp. pp. 143, 154.
9. Buss, Larsen, 2001, p. 502.
10. Hakim, 2000, p. 276.
11. Hakim, 2000, pp. 152–66.
12. Hakim, 2000, pp. 164, 235.
13. Browne, 2002, p. 174; Barker, 1993; Hakim, 2000, pp. 71, 90–91; Families and Work Institute, 1995, p. 54.
14. Browne, 2002, p. 136.

15. Kiecolt, 2003.
16. Amato et al., 2003.
17. Moir and Jessel, 1989, pp. 135–36.
18. Moir and Jessel, 1989.
19. Steil, 1997, pp. 85–86; Ehrenreich, 1993.
20. Cancian, 1985; Steil, 1993, p. 214.
21. Steil, 1997, p. 88.
22. Braver, 1998.
23. Williams and Best, 1990b, pp. 187, 196; Feldman et al., 1981.
24. Bloom, 1987, p. 186.
25. Fox-Genovese, 1996, p. 122.
26. Families and Work Institute, 1995.
27. Hakim, 2000, pp. 138–41; Gordon and Strober, 1978.
28. Kessler and McCrae, 1982, p. 225.
29. Moir and Jessel, 1989, p. 83.
30. Tannen, 1994.
31. Deutsch, 1999, pp. 34–35.
32. Ehrensaft, 1990.
33. Barnett and Rivers, 1996.
34. Hakim, 2000, pp. 147–48.
35. Belsky, 2001.
36. Blum, 1997, p. 217.
37. Barnett et al., 1995, p. 847; Barnett and Baruch, 1987, p. 136.
38. Musante et al., 1990.
39. Okie, 1996.
40. Moir and Jessel, 1989; Thompson and Walker, 1998; Weisfeld, 1992.
41. Barnett and Baruch, 1987; Thompson and Walker, 1989; Stanley, Hunt and Hunt, 1986; Kessler and McRae, 1992; Juster and Stafford, 1991; Huston and Ashmore, 1986; Huston, 1996.
42. Wilcox, 2004, ch. 6.
43. McDonough et al., 1999.
44. Browne, 2002, pp. 172–73; Stolzenberg, 2001.
45. Haynes and Feinleib, 1980.
46. Eaker, Haynes and Feinleib, 1983; Rovner, 1983.
47. Browne, 2002, p. 170.
48. Ridley, 1993, p. 255; Berch and McCauley, 1990, p. 164; Moir and Moir, 1999, pp. 245–55; Collins, 1993.
49. Roback, 1993, p. 129.
50. Flanagan, 2003; also see Gardner, 2003.
51. Sweeney, 2002.
52. Browne, 2002, p. 170.
53. Reality Check, 1998.
54. Pearson, 2002.

55. Hakim, 2000, pp. 100, 268; Reality Check, 1998; Steil, 1997; Robertson, 2003, p. 131; Ford, 2002, p. 285.
56. Browne, 2002, p. 173.
57. Nock, 2000; Steil, ch. 4.
58. Walsh and Spurgeon, 1997; Hetherington, 2002.
59. Nock and Brinig, 2001; Nock, 2000.
60. Huston and Ashmore, 1986, p. 199; Moir and Jessel, 1989.
61. Cancian, 1985.
62. Carter and Peters, 1996.
63. Thompson and Walker, 1989.
64. Begley, 1995, p. 51; Fisher, 1999, pp. 92–94; Geary, 1998, pp. 250–51; Brown, 1997; Thompson and Walker, 1989, p. 848.
65. Wilcox, 2004b.
66. Moir and Moir, 1999, p. 251.
67. Presser, 1998; Carlson, 2003.
68. Weisfeld et al., 1992.
69. Moir and Jessel, 1989, p. 129.

BIBLIOGRAPHY

Abdollahi, P., and T. Mann. 2001. Eating Disorder Symptoms and Body Image Concerns in Iran: Comparisons between Iranian Women in Iran and in America. *International Journal of Eating Disorders* 30 (3): 259–68.

Abrahamse, Adele. 1995. Review of *Hot Flashes: Women Writers on the Change of Life,* by Ione. *Iris: A University of Virginia Journal about Women.*

Adams, Caralee. 2004. The Unexpected When Expecting. *Washington Post,* 17 February.

Ahlgren, Andrew, and David W. Johnson. 1979. Sex Differences in Cooperative and Competitive Attitudes from the 2nd through the 12th Grades. *Developmental Psychology* 15 (1): 45–49.

Ahrens, Frank. 1997a. Armchair Generals: As Their Armies March and Fall, Men Relax at the War Games Store. *Washington Post,* 18 June.

———. 1997b. Unextinguishable Desire. *Washington Post,* 26 October.

———. 2000. Tin Soldiers for Techno-Geeks. *Washington Post,* 11 October.

Aikman Settles on Retirement. 2001. *Charlottesville Daily Progress,* 10 April.

Akerlof, George, Janet L. Yellen and Michael L. Katz. 1996. An Analysis of Out-of-Wedlock Childbearing in the United States. *Quarterly Journal of Economics* 111 (2): 277–317.

Alaimo, Katherine, et al. 2002. Food Insufficiency, Family Income and Health in US Preschool and School-Aged Children. *American Journal of Public Health* 91 (5): 781–86.

Alan Guttmacher Institute. 1999. *Fact Sheet on Teen Sex and Pregnancy,* September. http://www.guttmacher.org/pubs/fb_teen_sex.html.

Albert, D. J., M. L. Walsh and R. H. Jonik. 1993. Aggression in Humans: What Is Its Biological Foundation? *Neuroscience and Biobehavioral Reviews* 17 (4): 405–25.

Aldous, Joan, Gail M. Mulligan and Thoroddur Bjarnason. 1998. Fathering over Time: What Makes the Difference. *Journal of Marriage and the Family* 60 (4): 809–20.

Alexander, Gerianne M., and Barbara B. Sherwin. 1993. Sex Steroids, Sexual Behavior, and Selection Attention for Erotic Stimuli in Women Using Oral Contraceptives. *Psychoneuroendocrinology* 18 (2): 91–102.

Alexander, Gerianne M., Ronald S. Swerdloff, Christina Wang, Tina Davidson, Veronica McDonald, Barbara Steiner and Melissa Hines. 1997. Androgen-Behavior Correlations in Hypogonadal Men and Eugonadal Men. *Hormones and Behavior* 31 (2): 110–19.

Alexander, Rachel. 2002. Women Racing to Prominence. *Washington Post,* 29 September.

Amato, Paul. 1998. More Than Money? Men's Contributions to Their Children's Lives. In *Men in Families,* ed. A. Booth and A. C. Crouter. Mahwah, NJ: Lawrence Erlbaum Associates.

Amato, Paul R., et al. 2003. Marital Quality between 1980 and 2000. *Journal of Marriage and the Family* 65 (1): 1–22.

Amato, Paul, and Juliana Sobolewski. 2001. The Effects of Divorce and Marital Discord on Adult Children's Psychological Well-Being. *American Sociological Review* 66 (6): 900–21.

Ambert, Anne Marie. 1999. The Effect of Male Delinquency on Mothers and Fathers: A Heuristic Study. *Sociological Inquiry* 69 (4): 621–40.

American Academy of Pediatrics. 1997. Breastfeeding and the Use of Human Milk. *Pediatrics* 100 (6): 1035–39.

Anders, Gigi. 1996. Banking on Love. *Washington Post,* 21 October.

Anderson, Bobbi Jo, Malcolm D. Holmes and Erik Ostresh. 1999. Male and Female Delinquents' Attachments and Effects of Attachments on Severity of Self-Reported Delinquency. *Criminal Justice and Behavior* 26 (4): 435–52.

Anderson, Elijah. 1994. Sex Codes among Inner-City Youth. In *Sexuality, Poverty and the Inner City,* ed. Jayne Garrison et al. Menlo Park, CA: Kaiser Family Foundation.

Anderson, Kristi. 1997. Gender and Public Opinion. In *Understanding Public Opinion,* ed. B. Norrander and C. Wilcox. Washington, D.C.: Congressional Quarterly Books.

Angier, Natalie. 1999a. Men, Women, Sex and Darwin. *New York Times Magazine,* 21 February.

———. 1999b. *Woman: An Intimate Geography.* Boston: Houghton Mifflin.

Apt, Carol, and David Farley Hurlbert. 1994. Female Sexual Desire, Response, and Behavior. *Behavior Modification* 18 (4): 488–504.

Arana-Ward, Marie. 1997. Review of *Last Night in Paradise,* by Katie Roiphe. *Washington Post,* 5 May.

Archer, John. 1996. Sex Differences in Social Behavior. *American Psychologist* 51 (9): 909–17.

Argetsinger, Amy. 1999. When the Cheerleaders Are the Main Event. *Washington Post,* 10 July.

Arnhart, Larry. 1998. *Darwinian Natural Right.* Albany, NY: State University of New York Press.

Associated Press. 1997. Married People More Likely to Cut Back on Drinking, Using Drugs. 2 February.

Astin, Alexander W., Sarah A. Parrott, William S. Korn and Linda J. Sax. 1997. *The American Freshman: Thirty Year Trends.* Los Angeles: University of California Press, Higher Education Research Institute.

Babchuk, Wayne A., Raymond B. Hames and Ross A. Thompson. 1985. Sex Differences in the Recognition of Infant Facial Expressions of Emotion: The Primary Caretaker Hypothesis. *Ethnology and Sociobiology* 6 (2): 89–101.

Bachrach, Virginia R. Galton, Eleanor Schwartz and Lela Rose Bachrach. 2003. Breastfeeding and the Risk of Hospitalization for Respiratory Disease in Infancy: A Meta-Analysis. *Archives of Pediatric and Adolescent Medicine* 157 (3): 237–43.

Badcock, Christopher. 2000. *Evolutionary Psychology.* Malden, MA: Blackwell Publishers.

Badger, Emily. 2003. In the Spirit of Title IX: U-Md. Makes Cheerleading a Sport. *Washington Post,* 27 September.

Bae, Yupin, Susan Choy, Claire Geddes, Jennifer Sable and Thomas Snyder. 2000. *Trends in Educational Equity for Girls and Women.* Washington, D.C.: U.S. Department of Education.

Bailey, Beth L. 1989. *From Front Porch to Back Seat.* Baltimore: Johns Hopkins University Press.

Baker, Susan P., Margaret W. Lamb, Jurek G. Grabowski, George Rebok and Guohua Li. 2001. Characteristics of General Aviation Crashes Involving Mature Male and Female Pilots. *Aviation, Space and Environmental Medicine* 72 (5): 447–52.

Bale, James F., Jr., Susan J. Petheram, Inara E. Souza and Jody R. Murphy. 1996. Cytomegalovirus Reinfection in Young Children. *Journal of Pediatrics* 128 (3): 347–52

Balz, Dan, and Mike Allen. 2002. Hughes to Leave White House. *Washington Post,* 24 April.

Bancroft, John, Diana Sanders, David Davidson and Pamela Warner. 1983. Mood, Sexuality, Hormones, and the Menstrual Cycle. *Psychosomatic Medicine* 45 (6): 509–16.

Bannon, Lisa. 2000. Why Boys and Girls Get Different Toys. *Wall Street Journal,* 14 February.

Bardwick, Judith. 1971. *Psychology of Women.* New York: Harper and Row.

Barker, Kathleen. 1993. Changing Assumptions and Contingent Solutions: The Costs and Benefits of Women Working Full- and Part-Time. *Sex Roles* 28 (1/2): 47–71.

Barker, Vicki. 1991. Women at Work. *Washington Post,* 27 January.

Barkow, Jerome H., Leda Cosmides and John Tooby. 1992. *The Adapted Mind: Evolutionary Psychology and the Generation of Culture.* Oxford: Oxford University Press.

Barnett, Rosalind C., and Grace K. Baruch. 1987. Social Roles, Gender, and Psychological Distress. In *Gender and Stress*, ed. R. Barnett, L. Biener and G. Baruch. New York: The Free Press.

Barnett, Rosalind C., Robert T. Brennan, Stephen W. Raudenbush, Joseph H. Pleck and Nancy L. Marshall. 1995. Changes in Job and Marital Experiences and Change in Psychological Distress: A Longitudinal Study of Dual-Earner Couples. *Journal of Personality and Social Psychology* 69 (5): 839–50.

Barnett, Rosalind, and Caryl Rivers. 1996. Look Who's Talking about Work and Family. *Ms. Magazine,* July/August, 34–36.

Barr, Josh. 2002. Title IX Still Has a Tough Deed at 30. *Washington Post,* 9 May.

Barras, Jonetta Rose. 2000. *Whatever Happened to Daddy's Little Girl? The Impact of Fatherlessness on Black Women.* New York: Ballantine Publishing Group.

Bates, Heather. 2001. Observations on the Dating Habits and Sexual Experiences of My Peers. Report for Steven E. Rhoads, Department of Politics, University of Virginia, Charlottesville.

Bateup, Helen S., Alan Booth, Elizabeth A. Shirtcliff and Douglas A. Granger. 2002. Testosterone, Cortisol and Women's Competition. *Journal of Evolution and Human Behavior* 23 (3): 181–92.

Batten, Mary. 1992. *Sexual Strategies: How Females Choose Their Mates.* New York: G. P. Putnam's Sons.

Baucom, Donald H., Paige K. Besch and Steven Callahan. 1985. Relation between Testosterone Concentration, Sex Role Identity, and Personality among Females. *Journal of Personality and Social Psychology* 48 (5): 1218–26.

Baumeister, Roy F. 2000. Gender Differences in Erotic Plasticity: The Female Sex Drive as Socially Flexible and Responsive. *Psychological Bulletin* 126 (3): 347–74.

Baumgardner, Jennifer, and Amy Richards. 2000. *Manifesta: Young Women, Feminism, and the Future.* New York: Farrar, Straus and Giroux.

Baumrind, Diana. 1972. From Each According to Her Ability. *University of Chicago School Review* 80 (2): 161–97.

Beard, Patricia. 1998. Dangerous Minds. *Elle,* May.

Beauvoir, Simone de. 1978. *The Second Sex.* New York: Knopf.

Bechtel, Stefan. 2000. Cover Story. *C-Ville Weekly,* 4 July.

Becker, Elizabeth. 1999. Motherhood Deters Women from Army's Highest Ranks. *New York Times,* 29 November.

Becker, Mary. 1992. Maternal Feelings: Myth, Taboo, and Child Custody. *Review of Law and Women's Studies* 1 (1): 133–224.

Begley, Sharon. 1995. Gray Matters. *Newsweek,* 27 March: 48–54.

Belkin, Lisa. 2000. The Making of an 8-Year-Old Woman. *New York Times Magazine,* 24 December.

———. 2003. A Dad Says Caring for an Infant Is Work, Too. *New York Times,* 8 June.

Bellafante, Ginia. 1998. Feminism: It's All about Me! *Time,* 29 June: 54–57.

Belongia, Edward A., et al. 2001. A Community Intervention Trial to Promote Judicious Antibiotic Use and Reduce Penicillin-Resistant Streptococcus Pneumoniae Carriage in Children. *Pediatrics* 108 (3): 575–83.

Belsky, Jay. 1999. Quantity of Nonmaternal Care and Boys' Problem Behavior/Adjustment at Ages 3 and 5: Exploring the Mediating Role of Parenting. *Psychiatry: Interpersonal and Biological Processes* 62 (1): 1–21.

———. 2001. Developmental Risks (Still) Associated with Early Child Care. *Journal of Child Psychology and Psychiatry* 42 (7): 845–60.

———. 2002. Quantity Counts: Amount of Child Care and Children's Socioemotional Development. *Journal of Developmental and Behavioral Pediatrics* 23 (3): 167–70.

———. 2003a. The Dangers of Day Care. *Wall Street Journal,* 16 July.

———. 2003b. Does Amount of Time Spent in Child Care Predict Socioemotional Adjustment during the Transition to Kindergarten? *Child Development* 74 (4): 976–1005.

Belsky, Jay, Mary Lang and Ted L. Huston. 1986. Sex Typing and Division of Labor as Determinants of Marital Change across the Transition to Parenthood. *Journal of Personality and Social Psychology* 50 (3): 517–22.

Belsky, Jay, Laurence Steinberg and Patricia Draper. 1991. Childhood Experience, Interpersonal Development, and Reproductive Strategy: An Evolutionary Theory of Socialization. *Child Development* 62 (4): 647–70.

Benbow, Camilla Persson, David Lubinski, Daniel L. Shea and Hossain Eftekhari-Sanjani. 2000. Sex Differences in Mathematical Reasoning Ability at Age 13: Their Status 20 Years Later. *Psychological Science* 11 (6): 474–80.

Beral, Valerie, et al. 2002. Breast Cancer and Breast Feeding. *Lancet* 360 (9328): 187–95.

Berch, Daniel B., and Elizabeth McCauley. 1990. Psychosocial Functioning of Individuals with Sex Chromosome Abnormalities. In *Psychoneuroendocrinology: Brain, Behavior, and Hormonal Interactions,* ed. C. S. Holmes. New York: Springer-Verlag.

Berenbaum, Sheri A. 1990. Congenital Adrenal Hyperplasia: Intellectual and Psychosexual Functioning. In *Psychoneuroendocrinology: Brain, Behavior, and Hormonal Interactions,* ed. C. S. Holmes. New York: Springer-Verlag.

Berenbaum Sheri A., and Melissa Hines. 1992. Early Androgens Are Related to Childhood Sex-Typed Toy Preferences. *Psychological Science* 3 (3): 203–6.

Bergmann, Barbara. 1997. Work Family Policies and Equality between Women and Men. In *Gender and Family Issues in the Workplace,* ed. F. D. Blau and Ronald G. Ehrenberg. New York: Russell Sage Foundation.

———. 2000. Subsidizing Child Care by Mothers at Home. *Feminist Economics* 6 (1): 77–88.

Berlage, Gai Ingham. 1986. If Your Daughter Wants a Business Career, Should You Encourage Her to Play Team Sports? *Proteus* 3 (3): 55–59.

Berman, Phyllis W. 1980. Are Women More Responsive Than Men to the Young? A Review of Developmental and Situation Variables. *Psychological Bulletin* 88 (3): 668–95.

Berman, Phyllis, and Frank A. Pedersen. 1987. *Men's Transitions to Parenthood: Longitudinal Studies of Early Family Experience.* Hillsdale, NJ: Lawrence Erlbaum Associates.

Berman, Stephen. 1995. Otitis Media in Children. *New England Journal of Medicine* 332 (23): 1560–64.

Berry, Diane S. 2000. Attractiveness, Attraction, and Sexual Selection: Evolutionary Perspectives on the Form and Function of Physical Attractiveness. *Advances in Experimental and Social Psychology* 32: 273–343.

Berselli, Beth. 1998. Girls Tired of Nuking Aliens Get Software to Call Their Own. *Washington Post,* 2 February.

Betz, N. E., and L. F. Fitzgerald. 1987. *The Career Psychology of Women.* Orlando, FL: Academic Press.

Betzig, Laura. 1989. Causes of Conjugal Dissolution: A Cross-Cultural Study. *Current Anthropology* 30 (5): 654–69.

———. 1997. *Human Nature: A Critical Reader.* New York: Oxford University Press.

Beyette, Beverly. 1999. Reality of Modern Motherhood Examined. *Charlottesville Daily Progress*, 19 September.

Big Breasts and a Bogus Broadcast. 1996. *Washington Post,* 19 May.

Birds Do It, Bees Do It. 1997. *Economist,* 30 August.

Birnbaum, Cara. 2002. The Secrets of Sexual Surrender: No Cosmo Girl Likes to Give up Control, but Being Able to Abandon Your Inhibitions Is Essential to Achieving Full-Blown Bedroom Bliss. Here's How. *Cosmopolitan,* February: 118–19.

Biskupic, Joan. 1995. Ruth Bader Ginsberg: Feminist Justice. *Washington Post,* 17 April.

Blackmore, Susan. 2000. The Power of Memes. *Scientific American,* October: 64–73.

Blair, Anita K. 1999. In Search of the Noble Warrior. *Women's Quarterly,* Summer.

Blakemore, Judith E. Owen. 1990. Children's Nurturant Interactions with Their Infant Siblings: An Exploration of Gender Differences and Maternal Socialization. *Sex Roles* 22 (1/2): 43–57.

Bloom, Allen. 1987. *The Closing of the American Mind.* New York: Simon and Schuster.

Blue Marlin Fishing: It's the Game That Counts. 1997. *Economist,* 5 April.

Blum, Deborah. 1997. *Sex on the Brain.* New York: Viking Press.

———. 1998. Lecture at University of Virginia, Charlottesville. 25 March.

Blum, Linda. 1993. Mothers, Babies, and Breastfeeding in Late Capitalist America. *Feminist Studies* 19 (2): 291–311.

Blum, Robert, Trisha Beuhring, Marcia Shew, Linda Bearinger, Renee Sieving and Michael Resnick. 2000. The Effects of Race/Ethnicity, Income, and Family Structure on Adolescent Risk Behaviors. *American Journal of Public Health* 90 (12): 1879–84.

Blumstein, Alfred, and Jeff Benedict. 1999. Criminal Violence of NFL Players Compared to the General Population. *Chance* 12 (3): 12–15

Blumstein, Philip, and Pepper Schwartz. 1983. *American Couples: Money, Work, Sex.* New York: William Morrow and Co.

Boodman, Sandra G. 1999a. At-Home Mothers Score Slightly Better with Tots. *Washington Post,* 9 November.

———. 1999b. Girls and Puberty: How Young Is Too Young? *Washington Post,* 26 October.

Booth, Alan, Karen Carver and Douglas A. Granger. 2000. Biosocial Perspectives on the Family. *Journal of Marriage and the Family* 62 (4): 1018–34.

Booth, Alan, and Ann C. Crouter. 1998. *Men in Families.* Mahwah, NJ: Lawrence Erlbaum Associates.

Booth, Alan, and James M. Dabbs. 1993. Testosterone and Men's Marriages. *Social Forces* 72 (2): 472–73.

Boothroyd, Lynda. 2002. The Effect of Parenthood on Physical Aggression. Paper presented at Annual Meeting of the Human Behavior and Evolution Society, Rutgers University. 19–23 June.

Botting, Kate, and Douglas Botting. 1996. Men Can Be Sex Objects Too! *Cosmopolitan,* August: 90–91.

Bowman, Karlyn. 1988. Poll Pourri: Listen to Mom. *Women's Quarterly,* Spring.

———. 2001. Poll Pourri: Love Sweet Love. *Women's Quarterly,* Winter.

Boys with Absentee Fathers Twice as Likely to Be Jailed. 1998. *Washington Post,* 21 August.

Brady, Erik, and Thomas O'Toole. 2002. Justice Answers Suit, Not Title IX's Merits. *USA Today,* 30 May.

Braver, Sanford. 1998. *Divorced Dads: Shattering the Myths.* New York: Jeremy P. Tarcher/Putnam.

Breast-Feeding, Eating Nuts Linked to Allergies (compiled from reports by the Associated Press). 2001. *Washington Post,* 4 April.

Breast-Feeding Rates Rise. 2002. *Washington Post,* 18 January.

Breast-Feeding Successes and Failures (Interactions). 2000. *Washington Post,* 20 June.

Brennan, Christine. 1993. Henrich's Weight Dilemma Meant Life on an Apple a Day. *Washington Post,* 25 December.

Briggs-Gowan, Margaret J., et al. 2001. Prevalence of Social-Emotional and Behavioral Problems in a Community Sample of 1- and 2-Year-Old Children. *Journal of the American Academy of Child and Adolescent Psychiatry* 40 (7): 811–19.

Britt, Donna. 1998. Sex, Courtship and the Hopes of Today. *Washington Post,* 8 May.

Broder, David S. 2002. Welfare Reform's Progress. *Washington Post,* 27 January.

Brody, Jane. 1998. Genetic Ties May Be Factor in Violence in Stepfamilies. *New York Times,* 10 February.

Brooks, Christine. 1979. Is There a Difference in Coaching Men and Women? *Coaching Women's Athletics* 5 (3).

Brosnan, Michael, Virgil Sheets and Samuel Schnitzer. 2000. Reproductive Exchange and the Decision to Divorce. Paper presented at Annual Meeting of the Human Behavior and Evolution Society, Amherst College. 7–11 June.

Broude, Gwen J. 1999. Boys Will Be Boys. *Public Interest* 136 (1): 3–17.

Brown, David. 1994. Attractive Facial Features Aren't Just Average Matter. *Washington Post,* 21 March.

———. 1997. Girls May Inherit Intuition Gene from Fathers. *Washington Post,* 12 June.

———. 2000a. Gonorrhea Decline Reverses; Cases Up 9%. *Washington Post,* 6 December.

———. 2000b. Number and Rate of U.S. Births Rise. *Washington Post,* 29 March.

Brown, Stephanie, and Judith Lumley. 1998. Maternal Health after Childbirth: Results of an Australian Population Based Survey. *British Journal of Obstetrics and Gynaecology* 105 (2): 156–61.

Brown, Warren. 1999. Study Warns against Driving Late in Pregnancy. *Washington Post,* 25 February.

Browne, Kingsley R. 1995. Sex and Temperament in Modern Society: A Darwinian View of the Glass Ceiling and the Gender Gap. *Arizona Law Review* 37 (3): 973–1106.

———. 1997. An Evolutionary Perspective on Sexual Harassment: Seeking Roots in Biology Rather Than Ideology. *Journal of Contemporary Legal Issues* (University of San Diego School of Law) 8: 5–78.

———. 1998. An Evolutionary Account of Women's Workplace Status. *Managerial and Decision Economics* 19 (7/8): 427–40.

———. 2002. *Biology at Work: Rethinking Sexual Equality.* New Brunswick, NJ: Rutgers University Press.

Bruce, Toni. 1998. Audience Frustration and Pleasure: Women Viewers Confront Televised Women's Basketball. *Journal of Sport and Social Issues* 22 (4): 373–97.

Buchanan, Ann, JoAnn Ten Brinke and Eirini Flouri. 2000. Parental Background, Social Disadvantage, Public "Care," and Psychological Problems in Adolescence and Adulthood. *Journal of the American Academy of Child and Adolescent Psychiatry* 39 (11): 1415–23.

Buckle, Leslie, Gordon G. Gallup Jr. and Zachary A. Rodd. 1996. Marriage as a Reproductive Contract: Patterns of Marriage, Divorce, and Remarriage. *Ethnology and Sociobiology* 17 (6): 363–77.

Buehler, Cheryl, and Kay Pasley. 2000. Family Boundary Ambiguity, Marital Status and Child Adjustment. *Journal of Early Adolescence* 20 (3): 281–308.

Burch, Rebecca, and George Gallup Jr.. 2000. Perceptions of Paternal Resemblance Predict Family Violence. *Evolution and Human Behavior* 21 (6): 429–35.

Burnham, Terry. 2001. Review of *Heroes, Rogues and Lovers: Testosterone and Behavior,* by James M. Dabss. *Evolution and Human Behavior* 22 (3): 213–15.

Burnham, Terry, and Jay Phelan. 2000. *Mean Genes.* Cambridge, MA: Perseus Publishing.

Burr, Jeffrey A., John T. Hartman and Donald W. Matteson. 1999. Black Suicide in U.S. Metropolitan Areas: An Examination of the Racial Inequality and Social Integration-Regulation Hypothesis. *Social Forces* 77 (3): 1049–81.

Bursik, Krisanne, and Jennifer Young. 2000. Identity Development and

Life Plan Maturity: A Comparison of Women Athletes and Nonathletes. *Sex Roles* 43 (3/4): 241–54.

Bushnell, Dana E., ed. 1995. *Nagging Questions*. Lanham, MD: Rowman and Littlefield.

Buss, David M. 1994a. *The Evolution of Desire*. New York: Basic Books.

———. 1994b. The Strategies of Human Mating. *American Scientist* 82 (3): 238–49.

———. 1999. *Evolutionary Psychology: The New Science of the Mind*. Boston: Allyn and Bacon.

Buss, David M., and Michael Barnes. 1986. Preferences in Human Mate Selection. *Journal of Personality and Social Psychology* 50 (3): 559–70.

Buss, David M., Randy Larsen, Lee A. Kirkpatrick and Todd K. Shackelford. 2001. A Half-Century of Mate Preferences: The Cultural Values. *Journal of Marriage and the Family* 63 (2): 491–503.

Buss, David M., and Neil M. Malamuth, eds. 1996. *Sex, Power, Conflict: Evolutionary and Feminist Perspectives*. Oxford: Oxford University Press.

Buunk, Bram P., Esther S. Kluwer, Mieke K. Schuurman and Frans W. Siero. 2000. The Division of Labor among Egalitarian and Traditional Women: Differences in Discontent, Social Comparison, and False Consensus. *Journal of Applied Social Psychology* 30 (4): 759–79.

Caccioppoli, Vera. 1997. Feminist Mother, Triplet Sons. *Washington Post*, 10 November.

Caldwell, Christopher. 1996. The Feminization of America. *Weekly Standard*, 23 December.

Caldwell, Mayta A., and Letitia Anne Peplau. 1982. Sex Differences in Same-Sex Friendship. *Sex Roles* 8 (7): 721–32.

Campbell, Anne. 1999. Gender, Evolution and Psychology: Nine Feminist Concerns Addressed. *Psychology, Evolution and Gender* 1 (1): 57–80.

———. 2002. *A Mind of Her Own*. New York: Oxford University Press.

Cancian, Francesca M. 1985. Gender Politics: Love and Power in the Private and Public Spheres. In *Gender and the Life Course*, ed. A. S. Rossi. New York: Aldine Publishing Co.

Cantu, Robert C., and Frederick O. Mueller. 1999. Fatalities and Catastrophic Injuries in High School and College Sports, 1982–1997: Lessons for Improving Safety. *The Physician and Sportsmedicine* 27 (8): 34–48.

Capizzano, Jeffery, Gina Adams and Freya Sonenstein. 2000. Child Care Arrangements for Children under Five: Variation across States. *New Federalism*, March.

Carbajal, Ricardo, Soocramanien Veerapen, Sophie Courderc, Myriam

Jugie and Yves Ville. 2003. Analgesic Effect of Breast Feeding in Term Neeonates: Randomized Controlled Trial. *British Medical Journal* 326 (7379): 13–17.

Carlson, Allan. 1999. When They Called Feminism a Mental Illness: A Lesson from the 1950's. *The Family in America,* July: 4–7.

———. 2003. The Curious Case of Gender Equality. *The Family in America,* November: 1–7.

Carroll, Janell Lucille, Kari Doray Volk and Janet Shibley Hyde. 1985. Differences between Males and Females in Motives for Engaging in Sexual Intercourse. *Archives of Sexual Behavior* 14 (2).

Carter, Betty, and Joan K. Peters. 1996. Remaking Marriage and Family. *Ms. Magazine,* November/December: 57–65.

Cashdan, Elizabeth. 1995. Hormones, Sex, and Status in Women. *Hormones and Behavior* (29): 354–66.

———. 1996. Women's Mating Strategies. *Evolutionary Anthropology* 5 (4): 134–43.

———. 1998. Are Men More Competitive Than Women? *British Journal of Social Psychology* 37: 213–29.

Caspi, Avshalom, John C. DeFries, Thomas G. O'Connor and Robert Plomin. 2000. Are Associations between Parental Divorce and Children's Adjustment Genetically Mediated? An Adoption Study. *Developmental Psychology* 36 (4): 429–37.

Catton, Pia. 1996. Fruitless Feminists. *Weekly Standard,* 9 December.

Chaney, Jen. 2000. Perspective: Of Poms and Cheerleaders. *Washington Post,* 22 September.

Charen, Mona. 1998. It May Not Be Destiny but Biology Determines Our Roles More Than We Like to Admit. *Women's Quarterly,* Spring: 22.

Charlesworth, William R., and Claire Dzur. 1987. Gender Comparisons of Preschoolers' Behavior and Resource Utilization in Group Problem Solving. *Child Development* 58: 191–200.

Charlottesville City School Board. 1997. The Family Life Education Curriculum, 10th Grade. Charlottesville, VA.

Chen, Li-Hui, Susan P. Baker, Elisa R. Braver and Gouhua Li. 2000. Carrying Passengers as a Risk Factor for Crashes Fatal to 16- and 17-Year-Old Drivers. *Journal of the American Medical Association* 283 (12).

Chen, Zeng-Yin, and Howard B. Kaplan. 2001. Intergenerational Transmission of Constructive Parenting. *Journal of Marriage and the Family* 63: 17–31.

Cherlin, Andrew J. 1999. Going to Extremes: Family Structure, Children's Well-Being, and Social Science. *Demography* 36 (4): 421–28.

Childcare Initiative Triggers "Mommy Wars." 1998. *Washington Post,* 26 January.

Chisholm, Ann. 1999. Defending the Nation: National Bodies, U.S. Borders, and the 1996 U.S. Olympic Women's Gymnastics Team. *Journal of Sport and Social Issues* 23 (2): 126–39.

Christiansen, Kerrin, and Rainer Knussman. 1987. Androgen Levels and Components of Aggressive Behavior in Men. *Hormones and Behavior* 21: 170–80.

Clark, Russell D., and Elaine Hatfield. 1989. Gender Differences in Receptivity to Sexual Offers. *Journal of Psychology and Human Sexuality* 2.

Cleary, Paul D. 1983. Sex Differences in Psychological Distress among Married People. *Journal of Health and Social Behavior* 24: 111–21.

Colapinto, John. 1997. The True Story of John/Joan. *Rolling Stone,* 11 December: 54–97.

———. 2000. The Women's Quarterly Symposium, Summer.

Colburn, Don. 1991. The Way of the Warrior: Are Men Born to Fight? *Washington Post,* 29 January.

Collaer, Marcia L., Mitchell E. Geffner, Francine R. Kaufman, Bruce Buckingham and Melissa Hines. 2002. Cognitive and Behavioral Characteristics of Turner Syndrome: Exploring a Role for Ovaria Hormones in Female Sexual Differentiation. *Hormones and Behavior* 41: 139–55.

Collins, Eliza G. C. 1993. Managers and Lovers. *Harvard Business Review,* September/October.

Collison, Michelle. 1991. A Sure Fire Winner Is to Tell Her You Love Her. *Chronicle of Higher Education* 38 (12).

Constantino, John N., Daniel Grosz, Paul Saenger, Donald W. Chandler, Reena Nandi and Felton J. Earls. 1993. Testosterone and Aggression in Children. *Journal of the American Academy of Child and Adolescent Psychiatry* 32 (6): 1217 (6).

Cook, Thomas D., Mary B. Church, Subira Ajanaku, William R. Shadish Jr., Jeong-Ran Kim and Robert Cohen. 1996. The Development of Occupational Aspirations and Expectations among Inner-City Boys. *Child Development* 67: 3368–85.

Cookston, Jeffrey T. 1999. Parental Supervision and Family Structure. *Journal of Divorce and Remarriage* 31 (1/2): 107–27.

Corter, C. M., and A. S. Fleming. 1995. Psychobiology of Maternal Behavior in Human Beings. In *Handbook of Parenting*, ed. M. H. Bornstein. Hillsdale, NJ: Lawrence Erlbaum Associates.

Court Upholds Limits on Man's Ability to Have Kids. 2001. *Washington Post,* 24 November.

Courtwright, David T. 1996. *Violent Land: Single Men and Social Disorder from the Frontier to the Inner City*. Cambridge: Harvard University Press.

Cowan, Carolyn Pape, Philip A. Cowan, Gertrude Heming, Ellen Garrett, William S. Coysh, Harriet Curtis-Boles and Abner J. Boles III. 1985. Transitions to Parenthood: His, Hers, and Theirs. *Journal of Family Issues* 6 (4): 451–81.

Cowan, Gloria, and Kerri F. Dunn. 1994. What Themes in Pornography Lead to Perceptions of the Degradation of Women. *Journal of Sex Research* 31 (1): 11–21.

Cowan, Philip A., Carolyn Pape Cowan and Patricia K. Keirg. 1993. Mothers, Fathers, Sons and Daughters: Gender Differences in Family Formation and Parenting Style. In *Family, Self and Society: Toward a New Agenda for Family Research,* ed. P. A. Cowan, D. Field, D. A. Hansen, A. Skolnik and E. G. Swanson. Hillsdale, NJ: Lawrence Erlbaum Associates.

Crawford, Mary. 2001. Talking Difference: On Gender and Language. In *Taking Sides: Clashing Views on Controversial Social Issues,* ed. K. Finsterbusch. Guilford, CT: McGraw-Hill/Dushkin.

Cready, Cynthia M., Mark A. Fossett and K. Jill Kiecolt. 1997. Mate Availability and African American Family Structure in the U.S. Nonmetropolitan South, 1960–1990. *Journal of Marriage and the Family* 59: 192–203.

Crenshaw, Theresa. 1996. *The Alchemy of Love and Lust.* New York: G. P. Putnam's Sons.

Cringely, Robert X. 2000. The New New Bill Gates: A Revisionist Look at the Richest Man on Earth. 23 November. http://www.pbs.org/cringely/pulpit/pulpit20001123.html.

Crittenden, Danielle. 1999. *What Our Mothers Didn't Tell Us: Why Happiness Eludes the Modern Woman.* New York: Simon and Schuster.

Cubbin, Catherine, Linda Williams Pickle, and Lois Fingerhut. 2000. Social Context and Geographic Patterns of Homicide among U.S. Black and White Males. *American Journal of Public Health* 90 (4): 579.

Cunningham, John D., and John K. Antill. 1984. Changes in Masculinity and Femininity across the Family Life Cycle: A Reexamination. *Developmental Psychology* 20 (6): 1135–41.

Curry, Carol, Karen Trew, Irene Turner and Jennifer Hunter. 1994. The Effect of Life Domains on Girls' Possible Selves. *Adolescence* 29: 113.

Cyr, Daine. 1999. Sharp Shooter: WNBA Star Cynthia Cooper Shows She's Got Game—Whether It's on the Court or in the Boardroom. *Working Woman,* September.

Dabbs, James M. 1991. Salivary Testosterone Measurements: Collecting, Storing, and Mailing Saliva Samples. *Physiology and Behavior* 49: 815–917.

Dabbs, James M., and Mary Godwin Dabbs. 2000. *Heroes, Rogues, and Lovers: Testosterone and Behavior.* New York: McGraw-Hill.

Dabbs, James M., Robert Frady et al. 1987. Saliva Testosterone and Criminal Violence in Young Adult Prison Inmates. *Psychosomatic Medicine* 49 (2): 174–82.

Daddy's Home; But Which Home? 2001. *Washington Post,* 10 June.

Daitzman, Reid, and Marvin Zuckerman. 1980. Disinhibitory Sensation Seeking, Personality and Gonadal Hormones. *Personality and Individual Differences* 1: 103–10.

Dalton, Patricia. 2000. Daughters of the Revolution: Too Many Young Women Have a Faulty Blueprint of What Liberation Means. *Washington Post,* 21 May.

Daly, Martin, and Margo Wilson. 1999. Machismo. *Scientific American* 10 (2).

D'Amico, Ronald. 1983. Status Maintenance or Status Competition? Wife's Relative Wages as a Determinant of Labor Supply and Marital Instability. *Social Forces*. 61 (4): 1186–205.

Darby, Patrick J. 1998. Analysis of 112 Juveniles Who Committed Homicide: Characteristics and a Closer Look at Family Abuse. *Journal of Family Violence* 13: 365–74.

Darling, Lynn. 1999. 1969: One Pill Makes You Larger. *Washington Post,* 26 December.

Darrow, Siobhan. 2000. *Flirting with Disaster.* London: Virgo Press.

Davis, Michele Weiner, 2004. *The Sex-Starved Marriage*. New York: Simon and Schuster.

Davis-Floyd, Robbie E. 1994. Mind over Body: The Pregnant Professional. *Pre- and Perinatal Psychology Journal* 8 (3): 201–26.

De Goede, Martjin. 2000. Family Problems and Youth Unemployment. *Adolescence* 35: 595–600.

Delk, J. L., R. B. Madden, M. Livingston and T. Ryan. 1986. Adult Perceptions of the Infant as a Function of Gender Labeling and Observer Gender. *Sex Roles* 15: 527–34.

Demo, David H., and Alan C. Acock. 1996. Family Structure, Family Process, and Adolescent Well-Being. *Journal of Research on Adolescence* 6: 457–88.

Deogun, Nikhil. 1997. Top PepsiCo Executive Picks Family over Job. *Wall Street Journal,* 24 September.

Deutsch, Francine M. 1999. *Halving It All: How Equally Shared Parenting Works*. Cambridge: Harvard University Press.

Devitt, James. 2002. Teacher's College, Social Work Professors Find Association between Mothers Working Full-Time and Young Children's Cognitive and Verbal Development. *Columbia News,* 17 July. http://www.columbia.edu/cu/news/02/07/working_mothers.html.

De Waal, Frans B. M. 1999. The End of Nature versus Nurture. *Scientific American,* December.

Diamond, Milton. 1982. Sexual Identity, Monozygotic Twins Reared in Discordant Sex Roles and a BBC Follow-Up. *Archives of Sexual Behavior* 11 (2).

Dishion, Thomas J., Joan McCord and Francois Poulin. 1999. When Interventions Harm. *American Psychologist* 54 (9): 755–54.

Dittmann, Ralf W., Michael H. Kappes, Marianna E. Kappes, Doris Borger, Hendrik Stegner, Rolf H. Willig and Hedwig Wallis. 1990a. Congenital Adrenal Hyperplasia I: Gender-Related Behavior and Attitudes in Female Patients and Sisters. *Psychoneuroendocrinology* 15 (5/6): 401–20.

Dittmann, Ralf W., Michael H. Kappes, Marianne E. Kappes, Doris Borger, Heino F. L. Meyer-Bahlburg, Hendrik Stegner, Rolf H. Willig and Hedwig Wallis. 1990b. Congenital Adrenal Hyperplasia II: Gender-Related Behavior and Attitudes in Female Salt-Wasting and Simple-Virilizing Patients. *Psychoneuroendocrinology* 15 (5/6): 421–34.

Divakruni, Chitra. 2000. Uncertain Objects of Desire. *Atlantic Monthly,* March: 22–27.

Division of STD Prevention. 1999. *Sexually Transmitted Disease Surveillance, 1998.* Department of Health and Human Services, Atlanta: Centers for Disease Control and Prevention (CDC), September.

Dowd, Maureen. 1998. In All His Featherbed Glory. *New York Times,* 6 July.

Dowling, Colette. 2000. *The Frailty Myth.* New York: Random House.

Doyle, James A., and Michelle A. Paludi. 1998. *Sex and Gender: The Human Experience.* Boston: McGraw-Hill.

Drash, Wayne. 2000. *All Girl All Tech Nationwide Program Offers Girls-Only Computer Training.* CNN.com. http://www.cnn.com/2000/TECH/computing/07/11/tech.camp/index.html (accessed 11 July 2000).

Duke, Lynne. 2001. The New Christie Mandate. *Washington Post,* 23 April.

Dyson, Michael Eric. 2001. *Holler If You Hear Me: Searching for Tupac Shakur.* New York: Basic Books.

Eagly, Alice H. 1995. The Science and Politics of Comparing Women and Men. *American Psychologist* 50 (3): 145–58.

Eagly, Alice H., and Valerie J. Steffen. 1986. Gender and Aggressive Behavior: A Meta-Analytic Review of the Social Psychological Literature. *Psychological Bulletin* 100 (3): 283–308.

Eagly, Alice H., and Wendy Wood. 1999. The Origins of Sex Differences in Human Behavior. *American Psychologist* 54 (6): 408–23.

———. 2000. A Call to Recognize the Breadth of Evolutionary Perspectives: Sociocultural Theories and Evolutionary Psychology. *Psychological Inquiry* 11 (1): 52–55.

Eaker, Elaine C., Suzanne G. Haynes and Manning Feinleib. 1983. Spouse Behavior and Coronary Heart Disease in Men: Prospective Results from the Framingham Heart Study. II. Modification of Risk in Type A Husbands According to the Social and Psychological Status of Their Wives. *American Journal of Epidemiology* 118 (1).

Eaton, Warren O., and Lesley Reid Enns. 1986. Sex Differences in Human Motor Activity Level. *Psychological Bulletin* 100 (1): 19–28.

Eberstadt, Mary. 2001. Home-Alone America. *Policy Review,* June: 5–23.

Ehrenreich, Barbara. 1993. The Politics of Talking in Couples: Conversus Interruptus and Other Disorders. In *Feminist Frameworks,* ed. A. M. Jaggar and P. S. Rothenberg. New York: McGraw-Hill.

Ehrenreich, Barbara, Elizabeth Hess and Gloria Jacobs. 1987. *Remaking Women: The Feminization of Sex.* Garden City, NY: Anchor Books.

Ehrensaft, Diane. 1990. *Parenting Together: Men and Women Sharing the Care of Their Children.* Illini Books ed. Urbana: University of Illinois Press.

Ehrhardt, Anke A. 1985. The Psychobiology of Gender. In *Gender and the Life Course,* ed. A. S. Rossi. New York: Aldine Publishing Co.

Ehrhardt, Anke A., Susan E. Ince and Heino F. L. Meyer-Bahlburg. 1981. Career Aspiration and Gender Role Development in Young Girls. *Archives of Sexual Behavior* 10 (3).

Eisenman, Russell. 1998. Sex Differences and Anti-Research Attitudes. *Women's Freedom Network Newsletter,* May/June.

El-Bashir, Tarik. 2002. Testing Your Limits. *Washington Post,* 1 March.

Elber, Lynn. 1998. Girl Power Seen Easily on Networks. *Charlottesville Daily Progress,* 8 June.

Elek, Susan M., Diane Brage Hudson and Margaret Ofe Fleck. 1997. Expectant Parents' Experience with Fatigue and Sleep during Pregnancy. *Birth* 24 (1): 49–54.

Ellin, Abby. 1995. Out of Bounds? Is Student-Athlete Crime Out of Control? *Link: The College Magazine,* October/November.

Ellis, Bruce J., et al. 1999. Quality of Early Family Relationships and Individual Differences in the Timing of Pubertal Maturation in Girls: A Longitudinal Test of an Evolutionary Model. *Journal of Personality and Social Psychology* 77: 387–401.

Ellis, B. J., J. E. Bates, K. A. Dodge, D. M. Fergusson, J. L. Horwood, G. S. Petit and L. Woodward. 2003. Does Father Absence Place Daughters at Special Risk for Early Sexual Activity and Teenage Pregnancy? *Child Development* 74 (3): 801–21.

Ellis, Bruce J., and Judy Garber. 2000. Psychosocial Antecedents of Variation in Girls' Pubertal Timing: Maternal Depression, Stepfather Presence, and Marital and Family Stress. *Child Development* 71 (2): 485–501.

Ellis, Bruce J., and Donald Symons. 1997. Sex Differences in Sexual Fantasy: An Evolutionary Psychological Approach. In *Human Nature: A Critical Reader,* ed. L. Betzig. New York: Oxford University Press.

Ellis, Lee, and Linda Ebertz. 1998. *Males, Females, and Behavior.* Westport, CT: Praeger.

Elving, Ronald D. 1995. *Conflict and Compromise: How Congress Makes the Law.* New York: Simon and Schuster.

Emery, Noemie. 1999. Feminist Doormats. *Women's Quarterly,* Spring.

———. 2000a. The Real Key to the Presidency. *Weekly Standard,* 18 September.

———. 2000b. Talking Feminist Blues. *Commentary,* December: 78, 80.

Emery, Robert E. 1999. *Marriage, Divorce, and Children's Adjustment.* London: Sage Publications.

Employment Policy Foundation. 2003. News Release. 26 March.

Entwisle, Doris R., and Susan G. Doering. 1981. *The First Birth: A Family Turning Point.* Baltimore, MD: Johns Hopkins University Press.

Envoy to Pakistan Plans to Step Down. 2002. *Washington Post,* 11 May.

Epstein, Cynthia Fuchs. 1996. Take the Focus off Gender Differences. *New York Times,* 17 September.

Estrich, Susan. 1997. *Making the Case for Yourself: A Diet Book for Smart Women.* New York: Riverhead Books.

———. 2000. *Sex and Power:* New York: Riverhead Books.

Estrogen and the Younger Look. 1999. *Washington Post,* 19 July.

Etcoff, Nancy. 1999. *Survival of the Prettiest.* New York: Random House.

Eyer, Diane. 1996. *Motherguilt: How Our Culture Blames Mothers for What's Wrong with Society.* New York: Times Books.

Fagan, Patrick F., and Kirk A. Johnson. 2002. Marriage: The Safest Place for Women and Children. *Heritage Foundation Backgrounder* 1535. http://www.heritage.org/Research/Family/BG1535.cfm.

Fagan, Patrick F., and Robert Rector. 2000. The Effects of Divorce on America. *Heritage Foundation Backgrounder* 1373. http://www.heritage.org/Research/Family/BG1373.cfm.

Fallon, April E., and Paul Rozin. 1985. Short Reports: Sex Differences in Perceptions of Desirable Body Shape. *Journal of Abnormal Psychology* 94 (1): 102–5.

Families and Work Institute. 1995. *Women: The New Providers.* Whirlpool Foundation Study.

Farhi, Paul. 1996. Tuning Out Testosterone: NBC Tailors Coverage to Attract Women. *Washington Post,* 23 July.

———. 2001. They Got Game but Few Fans. *Washington Post,* 7 June.

Farnham, Marynia F., and Ferdinand Lundberg. 1947. *Modern Woman: The Lost Sex*. New York: Harper Brothers Publishers.

Farrell, Warren. 1993. *The Myth of Male Power: Why Men Are the Disposable Sex*. New York: Simon and Schuster.

Fausto-Sterling, Anne. 2000. *Sexing the Body*. New York: Basic Books.

Fein, Ellen, and Sherrie Schneider. 1995. *The Rules: Time-Tested Secrets for Capturing the Heart of Mr. Right*. New York: Warner Books.

Feingold, Alan. 1990. Gender Differences in Effects of Physical Attractiveness on Romantic Attraction: A Comparison across Five Research Paradigms. *Journal of Personality and Social Psychology* 59 (5): 981–93.

———. 1992. Gender Differences in Mate Selection Preferences: A Test of the Parental Investment Model. *Psychological Bulletin* 112 (1): 125–39.

———. 1994. Gender Differences in Personality: A Meta-Analysis. *Psychological Bulletin* 116 (3): 429–56.

Felmlee, Diane. 1994. Who's on Top? Power in Romantic Relationships. *Sex Roles* 31 (5).

The Fetus Is Father of the Man. 1999. *Economist,* 25 September.

Fielding, Helen. 1996. *Bridget Jones's Diary*. London: Picador.

———. 1999. *Bridget Jones: The Edge of Reason*. New York: Penguin.

Fillion, Kate. 1996. *Lip Service: The Truth about Women's Darker Side in Love, Sex and Friendship*. New York: HarperCollins.

Finer, Lawrence B., Jacqueline E. Darroch and Sesheela Singh. 1999. Sexual Partnership Patterns as a Behavioral Risk Factor for Sexually Transmitted Diseases. *Family Planning Perspectives* 31 (5): 228–36.

Finkelhor, David, David Moore, Sherry L. Hamby and Murray A. Straus. 1997. Sexually Abused Children in a National Survey of Parents: Methodological Issues. *Child Abuse and Neglect* 21 (1): 1–9.

Finnas, F. 2000. Economic Determinants of Divorce in Finland. *Ekonomiska Samfundets Tidskrift* 53 (2): 121.

Fisch, Audrey. 2002. *Where's Poppa?* Salon.com (accessed 5 August 2002).

Fischer, Agneta H., and Patricia M. Rodriguez Mosquera. 2001. What Concerns Men? Women or Other Men? *Psychology, Evolution, and Gender* 3 (1): 5–25.

Fisher, Helen. 1992. *Anatomy of Love*. New York: Fawcett Columbine.

———. 1999. *The First Sex: The Natural Talents of Women and How They Are Changing the World*. New York: Random House.

Fisher, William A., and Donn Byrne. 1978. Sex Differences in Response to Erotica? Love versus Lust. *Journal of Personality and Social Psychology* 36 (2): 117–25.

Flanagan, Caitlin. 2003. The Wifely Duty. *Atlantic Monthly,* January/February.

Flanagan, Clare, Daniel S. Shaw and Emily B. Winslow. 1999. A Prospective Study of the Effects of Marital Status and Family Relations on Children's Adjustment among African American and European American Families. *Child Development* 70: 742–55.

Fleming, Anne Taylor. 1994. *Motherhood Deferred: A Woman's Journey.* New York: G. P. Putnam's Sons.

Fletcher, Michael A. 2002. Degrees of Separation: Gender Gap among College Graduates Has Educators Wondering Where the Men Are. *Washington Post,* 25 June.

Florsheim, Paul, Patrick Tolan and Deborah Gorman-Smith. 1998. Family Relationships, Parenting Practices, the Availability of Male Family Members, and the Behavior of Inner-City Boys in Single-Mother and Two-Parent Families. *Child Development* 69 (5): 1437–47.

Ford, Lynne E. 2002. *Women and Politics: The Pursuit of Equality.* Boston: Houghton-Mifflin.

Fountain, John. 1998a. For Players, a Difficult Journey. *Washtingon Post,* 5 January.

———. 1998b. The Kickoff: No Lockers, Few Players, Lots of Hope. *Washington Post,* 4 January.

Fox-Genovese, Elizabeth. 1996. *Feminism Is Not the Story of My Life.* New York: Doubleday.

———. 1998. Review of *Beyond Gender,* by Betty Friedan. *Women's Freedom Network Newsletter,* May.

Frank, Ellen. 2000. *Gender and Its Effects on Psychopathology.* Washington, D.C.: American Psychiatric Press.

Freedman, Daniel G., and Marilyn M. DeBoer. 1979. Biological and Cultural Differences in Early Child Development. *Annual Review of Anthropology* (8): 579–600.

Fretts, Ruth C., Julie Schmittdiel, Frances H. McLean, Robert H. Usher and Marlene B Goldman. 1995. Increased Maternal Age and the Risk of Fetal Death. *New England Obstetrical and Gynecological Survey and Journal of Medicine* 333 (15): 953–57.

Frey, Jennifer. 1999. Germaine Greer's Trouble with Men; The Feminist Author and Icon Has Definitely Let Them Get under Her Skin. *Washington Post,* 12 June.

———. 2001a. Then and NOW. *Washington Post,* 19 July.

———. 2001b. Working Moms and Day Care: It's Life with a Guilt Edge. *Washington Post,* 21 April.

Friedan, Betty. 1981. *The Second Stage.* New York: Summit Books.

———. 1989. Letter to the Editor Regarding "Management Women and the New Facts of Life" by Felice Schwartz in January/February 1989 issue of Harvard Business Review. *New York Times,* 21 May.

Friend, Tad. 1994. Yes: That's the Message from a New Generation of Women Thinkers, Who Are Embracing Sex (and Men!); Call Them "Do Me" Feminists; but Can They Save the Penis from the Grassy Field of American History? *Esquire,* February.

Frisch, Rose E. 1987. Body Fat, Menarche, Fitness and Fertility. *Human Reproduction* 2 (6): 521–33.

Frodi, Ann M., and Michael E. Lamb. 1978. Sex Differences in Responsiveness to Infants: A Developmental Study of Psychophysiological and Behavioral Responses. *Child Development* 49: 1182–88.

From ABC, Conflicting Reports at a News Division in Disarray. 2002. *Washington Post,* 6 May.

From Box Scores to the Police Blotter, 1995 Was a Rough Year for Athletes and the Law. 1995. *Los Angeles Times,* 27 December.

Fuchs, Victor R. 1988. *Women's Quest for Economic Equality.* Cambridge, MA: Harvard University Press.

Furchtgott-Roth, Diana. 2000. Susan Estrich's America. *Weekly Standard,* 13 November.

Furchtgott-Roth, Diana, and Christine Stolba. 2001. *The Feminist Dilemma: When Success Is Not Enough.* Washington, D.C.: AEI Press.

Furedy, John J., Alison S. Fleming, Diane Ruble, Hal Scher, Jacque Daly, David Day and Ruth Loewen. 1989. Sex Differences in Small-Magnitude Heart-Rate Responses to Sexual and Infant-Related Stimuli: A Psychophysiological Approach. *Physiology and Behavior* 46.

The Future of Women's Sport and Fitness. 2001. http://www.womenssportsfoundation.org/partners/girlzone/issues/business/article.html?record=882.

Gabbe, Steven G., Jennifer R. Niebyl and Joe Leigh Simpson, eds. 1991. *Obstetrics: Normal and Problem Pregnancies.* 2nd ed. New York: Churchill Livingstone.

Galinsky, John. 2002. John's Class Helps Women Tackle Football Facts. *Charlottesville Daily Progress,* 18 April.

Gallagher, Maggie. 2001. Pornography Still Segregated by Sex. *Charlottesville Daily Progress,* 26 May.

Gallagher, Maggie, and Linda Waite. 2000. *The Case for Marriage.* New York: Random House.

Gallagher, Winifred. 1998. Sex and Hormones. *Atlantic Monthly,* March.

Gallese, Liz Roman. 1985. *Women Like Us.* New York: William Morrow and Co.

———. 1989. The Mommy Trap. *Best of Business Quarterly,* Fall.

———. 1991. Blame Male Managers. *Across the Board,* April: 19–22.

The Gallup Organization. 1996. *Gender and Society: Status and Stereotypes.* Princeton, NJ: Gallup.

Galtry, Judith. 2000. Extending the "Bright Line": Feminism, Breast-feeding, and the Workplace in the United States. *Gender and Society* 14 (2): 295–317.

Gardner, Ralph, Jr. 2003. Alpha Women, Beta Men. *New York Metro.* http://www.newyorkmetro.com/nymetro/news/features/n_9495 (accessed 17 November 2003).

Garment, Suzanne. 1994. The Buck Stopped with Her. *Washington Post,* 20 March.

Gaughan, Monica. 2002. The Substitution Hypothesis: The Impact of Premarital Liaisons and Human Capital on Marital Timing. *Journal of Marriage and the Family* 64 (2): 407–19.

Gaulin, Steven J. C. 1993. How and Why Sex Differences Evolve, with Spatial Ability as a Paradigm Example. In *The Development of Sex Differences and Similarities in Behavior,* ed. M. Haug. Netherlands: Kluwer Academic Publishers.

———. 2001. Review of *Adaptation and Human Behavior: An Anthropological Perspective,* by N. Chagnon et al. *Evolution and Human Behavior* 22: 431–38.

Gaulin, Steven J. C., and Donald H. McBurney. 2001. *Psychology: An Evolutionary Approach.* Upper Saddle River, NJ: Prentice Hall.

Gavora, Jessica. 2002. *Tilting the Playing Field: Schools, Sports, Sex and Title IX.* San Francisco: Encounter Books.

Geary, David C. 1998. *Male, Female: The Evolution of Human Sex Differences.* Washington, D.C.: American Psychological Association.

Gehrke, Brad C. 1997. Results of the 1997 AVMA Survey of U.S. Pet-Owning Households Regarding Use of Veterinary Services and Expenditures. *Journal of the American Veterinary Medical Association* 211 (4): 417–18.

Gelernter, David. 1996. Why Mothers Should Stay Home. *Commentary* 101 (2): 25.

Genevie, Louis, and Eva Margolies. 1987. *The Motherhood Report: How Women Feel about Being Mothers.* New York: Macmillan Publishing Co.

Genzale, John, ed. 2002. *By the Numbers: The Authoritative Annual Research Guide and Fact Book, 2002.* Charlotte, NC: Street and Smith's Sports Business Journal.

George, Mark S., Terence A. Ketter, Priti I. Parekh, Peter Herscovitch and Robert M. Post. 1996. Gender Differences in Regional Cerebral Blood Flow during Transient Self-Induced Sadness or Happiness. *Biological Psychiatry* 40 (9): 859.

Gerencher, Kristen. 2001. Good-Looks Bias More Potent for Men. *CBS.MarketWatch.com.*

Gielen, A. C., R. R. Faden, P. O'Campo et al. 1991. Maternal Employment during the Early Postpartum Period: Effects on Initiation and Continuation of Breast-feeding. *Pediatrics* 87 (3): 298–305.

Gilder, George. 1989. *Men and Marriage.* Gretna: Pelican Publishing Co.

Gilmore, David D. 1990. *Manhood in the Making: Cultural Concepts of Masculinity.* New Haven: Yale University Press.

Gindoff, Paul, M.D. 2002. The Mind-Body Link to Fertility. *Washington Post,* 9 April.

Ginsburg, Harvey J., and Shirley M. Miller. 1982. Sex Differences in Children's Risk-Taking Behavior. *Child Development* 53: 426–28.

Girl Wrestler Fights for Spot. 1998. *Washington Post,* 5 June.

Givhan, Robin. 2001. Gold Medal Covers: Vogue, Elle Celebrate the Beauty of the Athlete. *Washington Post,* 12 January.

Gjerdingen, Dwenda K., and Kathryn Chaloner. 1994. The Relationship of Women's Postpartum Mental Health to Employment, Childbirth, and Social Support. *Journal of Family Practice* 38 (5): 465–72.

Glazener, Cathryn M. A., Mona Abdalla, Patricia Stroud, Simon Naji, Allan Templeton and Ian T. Russell. 1995. Postnatal Maternal Morbidity: Extent, Causes, Prevention and Treatment. *British Journal of Obstetrics and Gynaecology* 102: 282–87.

Glenn, Norval, and Elizabeth Marquardt. 2001. *Hooking Up, Hanging Out, and Hoping for Mr. Right: College Women on Dating and Mating Today.* New York: Institute for American Values, commissioned by Independent Women's Forum.

Glenn, Norval D., Steve Nock and Linda J. Waite. 2002. Why Marriage Matters: Twenty-one Conclusions from the Social Sciences. *American Experiment Quarterly* 5 (1): 34–44.

Gohm, C. L., Humphreys and Yao. 1998. Underachievement among Spatially Gifted Students. *American Education Research Journal* 35 (3): 515–31.

Goldberg, Steven. 1993. *Why Men Rule: A Theory of Male Dominance.* Chicago: Open Court.

Goldberg, Susan, Susan L. Blumberg and Alberto Krieger. 1982. Men - arche and Interest in Infants: Biological and Social Influences. *Child Development* 53: 1544–50.

Goldin, Claudia. 1997. Career and Family: College Women Look to the Past. In *Gender and Family Issues in the Workplace,* ed. F. D. Blau, and Ronald G. Ehrenberg. New York: Russell Sage Foundation.

Goldscheider, Frances K., and Linda J. Waite. 1991. *New Families No Families.* Berkeley: University of California Press.

Goleman, Daniel. 1991. Sex for Survival? *New York Times,* 30 July.

Golombok, Susan, and Robyn Fivush. 1994. *Gender Development.* Cambridge: Cambridge University Press.

Golombok, Susan, Fiona MacCallum and Emma Goodman. 2001. The Test-Tube Generation: Parent-Child Relationships and the Psychological Well-Being of In Vitro Fertilization Children at Adolescence. *Child Development* 72 (2): 599–608.

Goodman, Ellen. 1996. How to Capture Mr. Right: A Best Selling Book of Dubious Advice. *Boston Globe,* 31 October.

———. 1999. Women in Motion Exemplify What Movement Was About. *Charlottesville Daily Progress,* 16 July.

———. 2002. The Women's Issue of Interest: Beauty. *Charlottesville Daily Progress,* 6 December.

———. 2003. Go Annika Go. *Boston Globe,* 27 May.

Gordon, Francine E., and Myra H. Strober. 1978. Initial Observations on a Pioneer Cohort: 1974 Women MBAs. *Sloan Management Review* 19 (2): 15–23.

Gorney, Cynthia. 1985. Boys Just Want to Have Guns. *Washington Post,* 4 August.

Gottesman, Irving I., Stephanie L. Sherman, John C. DeFries, John C. Loehlin, Joanne M. Meyer, Mary Z. Pelias, John Rice and Irwin Waldmen. 1997. Recent Developments in Human Behavioral Genetics: Past Accomplishments and Future Directions. *American Journal of Human Genetics* 60 (6): 1265–75.

Gottman, John Mordechai. 1994a. *What Predicts Divorce?* Hillsdale, NJ: Lawrence Erlbaum Associates.

———. 1994b. *Why Marriages Succeed or Fail.* New York: Simon and Schuster.

Gove, Walter R. 1985. The Effect of Age and Gender on Deviant Behavior: A Biopsychosocial Perspective. In *Gender and the Life Course*, ed. A. S. Rossi. New York: Aldine Publishing Co.

Govier, Ernest, and Janice Feldman. 1999. Occupational Choice and Patterns of Cognitive Abilities. *British Journal of Psychology* 90: 99–108.

Graglia, F. Carolyn. 1998. *Domestic Tranquility.* Dallas: Spence Publishing Co.

Graman, Marilyn. 2001. Marriage-Minded Go to School. *Metro,* 9 April.

Gray-Little, Bernadette, and Nancy Burks. 1983. Power and Satisfaction in Marriage: A Review and Critique. *Psychological Bulletin* 93 (3): 513–38.

Greenberger, Marcia. 2002. Co-President of the National Women's Law Center. Paper presented at Journalism and Women's Society conference, Montana.

Greer, Germaine. 1999. *The Whole Woman.* New York: Alfred A. Knopf.

Grimshaw, Gina M., M. Phillip Bryden and Jo-Anne K. Finegan. 1995.

Relations between Prenatal Testosterone and Cerebral Lateralization in Children. *Neuropsychology* 9 (1).

Grimsley, Kirstin, and Jacqueline Salmon. 1999. For Working Parents, Mixed News at Home. *Washington Post,* 27 September.

Gross, Jane. 1998. Male Bonding but No Strippers. *New York Times,* 7 February.

Grossman, Jennifer. 1998. He's Tall When He Stands on His Money. *Women's Quarterly,* Autumn.

Gueorguieva, Ralitza V. 2001. Effect of Teenage Pregnancy on Educational Disabilities in Kindergarten. *American Journal of Epidemiology* 154: 212–20.

Gugliotta, Guy. 1998. On the Hill, Ex-Wrestlers Go to the Mat for the Sport. *Washington Post,* 30 April.

Guo, Guang, and Elizabeth Stearns. 2002. The Social Influences on the Realization of Genetic Potential for Intellectual Development. *Social Forces* 80: 881–910.

Gurian, Michael. 1999. *A Fine Young Man.* New York: Putnam.

Guttmann, Monika. 1998. Who's Healthier: Men or Women? *USA Weekend,* 2 January.

Hakim, Catherine. 2000. *Work-Lifestyle Choices in the Twenty-first Century.* New York: Oxford University Press.

Hales, Dianne. 1999. *Just Like a Woman.* New York: Bantam Books.

Halpern, D. F. 2000. *Sex Differences in Cognitive Abilities.* 3rd ed. Mahwah, NJ: Lawrence Erlbaum Associates.

Han, Wen-Jui, and Jane Waldfogel. 2001. The Effects of Early Maternal Employment on Later Cognitive and Behavioral Outcomes. *Journal of Marriage and the Family* 63 (2): 336–54.

Hansen, Jo-Ida C., and David P. Campbell. 1985. *User's Guide for the SVIB-SCII Strong-Campbell Interest Inventory.* Palo Alto: Stanford University Press.

Hansen, Michele, Jennifer J. Kucinczuk, Carol Bower and Sandra Webb. 2002. The Risk of Major Birth Defects after Intracytoplasmic Sperm Injection and In Vitro Fertilization. *New England Journal of Medicine* 346 (10): 725–30.

Harden, Blaine. 2001. Two-Parent Families Rise after Change in Welfare Laws. *New York Times,* 12 August.

Harrington, Richard. 2001. Upcoming in Book World; A Review of *Q: The Autobiography of Quincy Jones. Washington Post,* 20 December.

Harrington, Walter. 1985. The Boys of Selby. *Washington Post Magazine.* 23 June.

Harris, John F. 1999. The Lost Lessons of Watergate: Book Says Presidents Have Not Comprehended New Rigors of Scrutiny. *Washington Post,* 13 June.

Harris, Judith Rich. 1998. *The Nurture Assumption*. New York: Touchstone.

Harris, Kathleen Mullan, Frank F. Furstenberg Jr. and Jeremy K. Marmer. 1998. Paternal Involvement with Adolescents in Intact Families: The Influence of Fathers over the Life Course. *Demography* 35: 201–16.

Harris, Lynn. 1997. Casual Sex: Why Confident Women Are Saying No. *Glamour,* September: 314–17.

Harris, Richard J., and Juanita M. Firestone. 1998. Changes in Predictors of Gender Role Ideologies among Women: A Multivariate Analysis. *Sex Roles* 38 (3/4): 239–52.

Hartocollis, Anemona. 2001. Women Lawyers: Justice Is Blind; also a Lady. *New York Times,* 1 April.

Harvard Heart Letter. 1997: 2–3.

Harvey, Phillip D. 2002. Adulthood without Sex. *Washington Post,* 12 May.

Hatkoff, Terry S., and Thomas E. Laswell. 1979. Male-Female Similarities and Differences in Conceptualizing Love. In *Love and Attraction: An International Conference,* ed. M. Cook and G. Wilson. New York: Pergamon Press.

Hauslaib, Lara. 2003. Medical Uses of the Oral Contraceptive Pill: A Guide for Teens. Center for Young Women's Health. Children's Hospital, Boston.

Hausman, Patricia. 1999. On the Rarity of Mathematically and Mechanically Gifted Females: A Life History Analysis. Dissertation, The Fielding Institute.

Haussegger, Virginia. 2002. The Sins of Our Feminist Mothers. *The Age.* http://www.theage.com (accessed 23 July 2002).

Hax, Carolyn. 1997a. The Rules for Men. *Washington Post,* 12 December, 5.

———. 1997b. Tell Me About It: Advice for the Under-Thirty Crowd. *Washington Post,* 22 August.

———. 2002. Tell Me About It: Advice for the Under-Thirty Crowd. *Washington Post,* 9 June.

Hayes, Allison, Brian McManus and Elizabeth L. Paul. 2000. Hookups: Characteristics and Correlates of College Students' Spontaneous and Anonymous Sexual Experiences. *Journal of Sex Research* 37 (1): 76–88.

Haynes, Suzanne G., and Manning Feinleib. 1980. Women, Work and Coronary Heart Disease: Prospective Findings from the Framingham Heart Study. *American Journal of Public Health* 70 (2).

Heightism: Short Guys Finish Last. 1995. *Economist.* 23 December: 19–21.

Heiss, Jerold. 1996. Effects of African American Family Structure on School Attitudes and Performance. *Social Problems* 43: 246–64.

Herwig, Paige. 2001. The Not-So-Good-Old Days. *Washington Post,* 4 August.

Hetherington, E. Mavis, Margaret Bridges and Glendessa M. Insabella. 1998. What Matters? What Does Not? Five Perspectives on the Association between Marital Transitions and Children's Adjustment. *American Psychologist* 53 (2): 167–84.

Hetherington, E. Mavis and John Kelly. 2002. For Better or for Worse: Divorce Reconsidered. 1st ed. New York: W. W. Norton and Co.

Hewlett, Sylvia Ann. 2002. *Creating a Life: Professional Women and the Quest for Children.* New York: Talk Miramax.

Heyman, C. David. 1995. *Liz: An Intimate Biography of Elizabeth Taylor.* New York: Birch Lane Press.

Hicks and Leitenberg. 2001. Sexual Fantasies about One's Partner. *Journal of Sex Research:* 43–50.

Hilton, Jeanne M., and Esther L. Devall. 1998. Comparison of Parenting and Children's Behavior in Single-Mother, Single-Father, and Intact Families. *Journal of Divorce and Remarriage* 29 (3/4).

Hochschild, Arlie Russell. 1989. *The Second Shift.* New York: Avon Books.

Hock, Ellen, M. Therese Gnezda and Susan L. McBride. 1984. Mothers of Infants: Attitudes toward Employment and Motherhood Following Birth of the First Child. *Journal of Marriage and the Family* 46 (2): 425–31.

Hoem, Britta. 1995. The Way to the Gender-Segregated Swedish Labour Market. In *Gender and Family Change in Industrialized Countries,* ed. Karen Mason and Ann-M. Jensen. Oxford: Clarendon Press.

Hofferth, Sandra L., and John F. Sandberg. 2001. How American Children Spend Their Time. *Journal of Marriage and the Family* 63 (2): 295–308.

Hofferth, Sandra L., Julia Smith, Vonnie C. McLoyd and Jonathan Finkelstein. 2000. Achievement and Behavior among Children of Welfare Recipients, Welfare Leavers, and Low-Income Single Mothers. *Journal of Social Issues* 56 (4): 747–73.

Hojat, Mohammadreza. 1998. Satisfaction with Early Relationships with Parents and Psychosocial Attributes in Adulthood: Which Parent Contributes More? *Journal of Genetic Psychology* 159 (2): 203–20.

Hollander, Sophia. 2002. Sports Lure Men to Former Women's Campuses. *New York Times*, 20 November.

Hopkinson, Natalie. 2002. Breast-Feeding Debate Recast by Findings. *Washington Post,* 20 July.

Hotz, Robert Lee. 2000. Women Use More of Brain When Listening, Study Says. *Los Angeles Times,* 29 November.

Howard, Judith A., Philip Blumstein and Pepper Schwartz. 1987. Social or Evolutionary Theories? Some Observations on Preferences in Human Mate Selection. *Journal of Personality and Social Psychology* 53 (1): 194–200.

Hoyenga, Katharine Blick, and Kermit T. Hoyenga. 1993. *Gender-Related Differences: Origins and Outcomes.* Boston: Allyn and Bacon.

Hrdy, Sarah Blaffer. 1999. *Mother Nature: A History of Mothers, Infants, and Natural Selection.* New York: Pantheon Books.

Hudgens, Dallas. 1997. Leagues of Their Own: More Women Are Taking It to the Hoop Than Ever Before. *Washington Post,* 7 November.

Hughes, S. M., Marissa A. Harrison and Gordon G. Gallup Jr. 2002. The Sound of Symmetry: Voice as a Marker of Developmental Instability. *Evolution and Human Behavior* 23: 173–80.

Humphreys, Anne P., and Peter K. Smith. 1987. Rough and Tumble, Friendship, and Dominance in Schoolchildren: Evidence for Continuity and Change with Age. *Child Development* 58: 201–12.

Humphreys, Lloyd G., David Lubinski and Grace Yao. 1993. Utility of Predicting Group Membership and the Role of Spatial Visualization in Becoming an Engineer, Physical Scientist, or Artist. *Journal of Applied Psychology* 78 (2): 250–61.

Hunt, Albert. 2000. American Opinion: Women, Politics and the Marketplace; Major Progress, Inequities Cross Three Generations; Grandmother, Mother, Daughter Reveal a Tempered Optimism amid Universally Held Views. *Wall Street Journal,* 22 June.

Huston, Ted L. 1996. Path to Parenthood. *Discovery: Research and Scholarship at the University of Texas* 14.

Huston, Ted L., and Richard D. Ashmore. 1986. Women and Men in Personal Relationships. In *The Social Psychology of Male-Female Relations,* ed. R. D. Ashmore et al. Orlando, FL: Academic Press.

Hyde, Janet Shibley. 1996. *Half the Human Experience: The Psychology of Women.* Washington, D.C.: Heath and Co.

Hymowitz, Kay S. 1995. The "L" Word: Love as Taboo. *City Journal* 5 (2): 30–38.

———. 2002. The End of Herstory. *City Journal* 12 (3).

Ianzito, Christina. 2002. Relax to Conceive? *Washington Post,* 2 April.

Imperato-McGinley, Julianne, Ralph E. Peterson, Teofilo Gautier and Erasmo Sturla. 1979. Androgens and the Evolution of Male-Gender Identity among Male Pseudohermaphrodites with Reductase Deficiency. *New England Journal of Medicine* 300 (22).

In Florida, Warmth Rises from the Ashes. 1998. *Washington Post,* 12 July.

Inoff-Germain, Gale, Gina Snyder Arnold, Editha D. Nottelmann, Elizabeth J. Susman, Gordon B. Cutler and George P. Chrousos. 1988.

Relations between Hormone Levels and Observational Measures of Aggressive Behavior of Young Adolescents in Family Interactions. *Developmental Psychology* 24 (1): 129–39.

In the Nation. 2001. *Baltimore Sun,* 3 July.

Irving, John. 2003. Wrestling with Title IX. *New York Times,* 28 January.

Jalovaara, Marika. 2003. The Joint Effect of Marriage Partner's Socioeconomic Positions on the Risk of Divorce. *Demography* 40: 67–81.

Jamison, Kay Redfield. 1995. *An Unquiet Mind.* 1st ed. New York: A. A. Knopf.

Jayakody, Rukmalie, and Ariel Kalil. 2002. Social Fathering in Low-Income, African American Families with Preschool Children. *Journal of Marriage and the Family* 64: 504–16.

Jencks, Christopher, and Kathryn Edin. 1995. Do Poor Women Have a Right to Bear Children? *American Prospect,* December: 43–45.

Jenkins, Sally. 2001. When Fairy Tales Don't Crown Prince Charming. *Washington Post,* 9 June.

———. 2002. Judgment Call for the Mystics. *Washington Post,* 21 September.

Jeter, Joe. 1998. Moseley-Braun in Trouble. *Washington Post,* 1 October.

Johnson, Mal. 2001. What I Learned in School. In *Not Guilty: Twelve Black Men Speak Out on Law, Justice and Life,* ed. J. Asim. New York: HarperCollins.

Johnson, Ronald C. 1996. Attributes of Carnegie Medalists Performing Acts of Heroism and of the Recipients of These Acts. *Ethology and Sociobiology* 17 (5): 355.

Jones, L. Colette. 1985. Father-Infant Relationships in the First Year of Life. In *Dimensions of Fatherhood,* ed. Shirley M. H. Hansen and Frederick W. Bozett. London: Sage Publications.

Jones, Rachel K., and April Brayfield. 1997. Life's Greatest Joy? European Attitudes Toward the Centrality of Children. *Social Forces* 75 (4): 1239–70.

Juster, F. Thomas, and Frank P. Stafford. 1991. The Allocation of Time: Empirical Findings, Behavioral Models, and Problems of Measurement. *Journal of Economic Literature* 29: 471–522.

Kahlenberg, Rebecca R. 2001. The Tender Trap. *Washington Post,* 29 April.

———. 2002. When Stay-at-Home Moms Want a Second Job. *Washington Post,* 7 February.

Kaiser Family Foundation. 2000. Sexually Transmitted Diseases in the United States. *Fact Sheet 3003.* http://www.kff.org/womens-health/3003-index.cfm.

Kalick, Michael S., Leslie A. Zebrowitz, Judith H. Langlois and Robert

M. Johnson. 1998. Does Human Facial Attractiveness Honestly Advertise Health? *Psychological Science* 9 (1): 8.

Kamen, Al. 2001. In the Loop: Lactation Situation. *Washington Post,* 30 March.

Kanazawa, Satoshi, and Mary C. Still. 2000. Teaching May Be Hazardous to Your Marriage. *Evolution and Human Behavior* 21 (3): 18.

Kass, Leon. 1997. The End of Courtship. *Public Interest,* Winter.

Kaufman, Gayle, and Peter Uhlenberg. 1998. Effects of Life Course Transitions on the Quality of Relationships between Adult Children and Their Parents. *Journal of Marriage and the Family* 60: 924–38.

Kaufman, Marc. 1999a. Breastfeeding Said to Cut Children's Asthma Risk. *Washington Post,* 27 April.

———. 1999b. Fatherhood: No Longer a Lost Cause. *Washington Post,* 5 October.

———. 2000. Profiles Offer a Peek Inside the Presidential Psyche. *Washington Post,* 7 August.

———. 2001. Breast-Feeding May Cut Obesity. *Washington Post,* 16 May.

Kawachi, Ichiro, Bruce P. Kennedy and Richard C. Wilkinson. 1999. Crime: Social Disintegration and Relative Deprivation. *Social Science and Medicine* 48: 719–31.

Kayden, Zandra. 1990. *Surviving Power.* New York: The Free Press.

Kean, Tom, and Isabel Sawhill. 2000. More Teens Just Say "No." *Washington Post,* 5 September.

Kennedy, David M. 1999. Boston Proves Something Can Be Done. *Washington Post,* 23 May.

Kennedy, Edward. 2003. Statement of Senator Edward M. Kennedy on the Department of Education's Announcement of Next Steps on Title IX.

Kenrick, Douglas T. 1995. Evolutionary Theory versus the Confederacy of Dunces. *Psychological Inquiry* 6 (1).

Kenrick, Douglas T., and Richard C. Keefe. 1992. Age Preferences in Mates Reflect Sex Differences in Human Reproductive Strategies. *Behavioral and Brain Sciences* 15 (1): 75–133.

Kenrick, Douglas T., Richard C. Keefe, Cristina Gabrielidis and Jeffrey S. Cornelius. 1996. Adolescents' Age Preferences for Dating Partners: Support for an Evolutionary Model of Life-History Strategies. *Child Development* 67 (4): 1499–1511.

Kenrick, Douglas T., Edward K. Sadalia, Gary Groth and Melanie Trost. 1990. Evolution, Traits, and the Stages of Human Courtship: Qualifying the Parental Investment Model. *Journal of Personality* 58 (1): 97–116.

Kessler, Ronald C., and James A. McRae Jr. 1982. The Effect of Wives'

Employment on the Mental Health of Married Men and Women. *American Sociological Review* 47.

Khlat, Myriam, Catherine Sermet and Annick Le Pape. 2000. Women's Health in Relation with Their Family and Work Roles: France in the Early 1990s. *Social Science and Medicine.*

Kiecolt, K. Jill. 2003. Satisfaction with Work and Family Life: No Evidence of a Cultural Reversal. *Journal of Marriage and the Family* 65: 23–25.

Kimura, Doreen. 1990. Profile: Vive la Difference: Doreen Kimura Plumbs Male and Female Brains. *Scientific American,* October.

———. 1999. *Sex and Cognition.* Cambridge, MA: MIT Press.

Klebanoff, M. A., P. H. Shiono and G. G. Rhoads. 1990. Outcomes of Pregnancy in a National Sample of Resident Physicians. *New England Journal of Medicine* 323 (11): 1040–45.

Klerman, Jacob Alex, and Arleen Leibowitz. 1990. Child Care and Women's Return to Work after Childbirth. *American Economic Review* 80 (2): 284–88.

Kline, Carolyn R., Diane P. Martin and Richard A. Deyo. 1998. Health Consequences of Pregnancy and Childbirth as Perceived by Women and Clinicians. *Obstetrics and Gynecology* 92 (5): 842–48.

Knapp, Laura G., et al. 2001. *Postsecondary Institutions in the United States: Fall 2000 Degrees and Other Awards Conferred 1999–2000.* National Center for Education Statistics. December: 15.

Knight, George P., and Spencer Kagan. 1977. Development of Prosocial and Competitive Behaviors in Anglo-American and Mexican-American Children. *Child Development* 48: 1385–94.

Konner, Melvin. 1999. Darwin's Truth, Jefferson's Vision. *American Prospect,* July/August.

Kornheiser, Tony. 1996. In Women's Sports, Team Is a Winning Concept. *Washington Post,* 3 August.

Krasnow, Iris. 1999. It's Time to End the Mommy Wars. *Washington Post,* 7 May.

———. 2000. Being Single, Seeing Double. *Washington Post,* 11 September.

Krasnow, Iris, and Charmaine Yoest. 1998. Discovering Motherhood. *American Enterprise,* May/June: 45–50.

Krebs, Paula M. 2001. Why Family First Is Not a Win for Academic Feminists. *Chronicle of Higher Education,* 2 November.

Kristol, Elizabeth. 1996. Song of Myself: Review of *What Women Want,* by Patricia Ireland. *Commentary,* September: 83–84.

Kristol, Irving. 1995. *Neoconservatism: The Autobiography of an Idea.* New York: The Free Press.

Kristol, William. 1991. Women's Liberation: The Relevance of Tocqueville. In *Interpreting Tocqueville's Democracy in America*, ed. K.

Masugi. Lanham, MD: Rowman and Littlefield.

Kurtz, Howard. 2001. Media Shy Chelsea Clinton Ends Her Silence. *Washington Post,* 9 November.

———. 2002. At ABC, a Shaken News Dynasty. *Washington Post,* 6 March.

LaCroix, Andrea Z., and Suzanne G. Haynes. 1987. Gender Differences in the Health Effects of Workplace Roles. In *Gender and Stress,* ed. R. C. Barnett, L. Beiner and G. K. Baruch. New York: The Free Press.

Laner, Mary Reige, and Nicole A. Ventrone. 2000. Dating Scripts Revisited. *Journal of Family Issues* 21 (4): 488–500.

LaRossa, Ralph, and Maureen Mulligan LaRossa. 1981. *Transition to Parenthood: How Infants Change Families.* Beverly Hills: Sage Publications.

Laub, John, Daniel Nagin and Robert Sampson. 1998. Trajectories of Change in Criminal Offending: Good Marriages and the Desistance Process. *American Sociological Review* 63: 225–38.

Laumann, Edward O., et al. 1994. *The Social Organization of Sexuality: Sexual Practices in the United States.* Chicago: University of Chicago Press.

Layng, Anthony. 1993. Evolution Explains Traditional Gender Roles. In *Male/Female Roles*, ed. J. Petrikin. San Diego: Greenhaven Press.

Leahy, Michael. 2002. Going One-on-One against Father Time. *Washington Post*, 14 June.

Lee, Kathryn A., and Mary Ellen Zaffke. 1999. Longitudinal Changes in Fatigue and Energy during Pregnancy and the Postpartum Period. *Journal of Obstetric, Gynecologic, and Neonatal Nursing* 28 (2): 183–91.

Leibovich, Mark. 2002. The Double-Standard Excuse. *Washington Post,* 24 April.

Levine, Judith. 1992. *My Enemy, My Love.* New York: Doubleday.

———. 1995. The Sexual Revolution Is Not Immoral. In *Sexual Values: Opposing Viewpoints,* ed. Charles P. Cozic. San Diego, CA: Greenhaven Press.

Lewis, Deborah Shaw, and Charmaine Crouse Yoest. 1996. *Mother in the Middle.* Grand Rapids, MI: Zondervan Publishing House.

Lewis, Michael. 1969. Infant's Responses to Facial Stimuli during the First Year of Life. *Developmental Psychology* 1 (2): 75–86.

Lewis, Nicole. 1997. On the Pulse. *Washington Post,* 25 March.

Lewis, Thomas, M.D., Fari Amini, M.D., and Richard Lannon, M.D. 2000. *A General Theory of Love.* New York: Random House.

Li, Ruowei, et al. 2003. Prevalence of Breastfeeding in the United States: The 2001 National Immunization Survey. *Pediatrics* 111: 1198–201.

Liesen, Laurette T. 1994. Review, *Of Mice and Women: Aspects of Female Aggression,* by K. Bjorqvist and P. Niemela. *Politics and the Life Sciences* 13 (1): 150–51.

Life Is Short: Autobiography as Haiku. 2002. *Washington Post,* 18 August.

Lightning. 1998. *Washington Post,* 23 June.

Lincoln, Blanche Lambert. 1996. Letter to Haley Barbour, 6 June.

Lindberg, Laura Deuberstein. 1996. Women's Decisions about Breast-feeding and Maternal Employment. *Journal of Marriage and the Family* 58 (1): 239–51.

Lippa, Richard. 1998a. Gender-Related Individual Differences and National Merit Test Performance: Girls Who Are "Masculine" and Boys Who Are "Feminine" Tend to Do Better. In *Males, Females, and Behavior: Toward Biological Understanding*, ed. L. Ellis and L. Ebertz. Westport, CT, and London: Praeger.

———. 1998b. Gender-Related Individual Differences and the Structure of Vocational Interests: The Importance of the People-Things Dimension. *Journal of Personality and Social Psychology* 4: 996–1009.

Lips, Hilary M. 2001. *Sex and Gender.* Mountain View, CA: Mayfield Publishing Co.

Lipstick on the Links. 2002. *National Public Radio,* 1 August.

Lopez, Kathryn Jean. 1998. Day Care Capital. *Women's Quarterly,* Spring: 18–19.

Lorber, Judith. 1986. Dismantling Noah's Ark. *Sex Roles* 14 (11/12): 567–80.

———. 1994. *Paradoxes of Gender.* New Haven: Yale University Press.

Lott, Bernice. 1997. Cataloging Gender Differences: Science or Politics? In *Women, Men, and Gender: Ongoing Debates,* ed. M R. Walsh. New Haven: Yale University Press.

Low, Bobbi S. 2000. *Why Sex Matters: A Darwinian Look at Human Behavior.* Princeton, NJ: Princeton University Press.

Lubinski, David, C. P. Benbow and C. E. Sanders. 1993. Reconceptualizing Gender Differences in Achievement among the Gifted. In *International Handbook of Research and Development of Giftedness and Talent,* ed. K. A. Heller, F. J. Monks and A. H. Passow. London: Pergamon Press.

Lubinski, David, and Lloyd G. Humphreys. 1990. A Broadly Based Analysis of Mathematical Giftedness. *Intelligence* 14: 327–35.

———. 1997. Incorporating General Intelligence into Epidemiology and the Social Sciences. *Intelligence* 24 (1): 159–201.

Luecken, L. J., E. C. Suarez et al. 1997. Stress in Employed Women: Impact of Marital Status and Children at Home on Neurohormone Output and Home Strain. *Psychosomatic Medicine* 59 (4): 352–59.

Lueptow, Lloyd B., Lore Garovich-Szabo and Margaret B. Lueptow. 2001. Social Change and the Persistence of Sex Typing: 1974–1997. *Social Forces* 80 (1): 1–35.

Luke, Barbara, Michal Avni, Linda Min and Ruda Misiunas. 1999. Work and Pregnancy: The Role of Fatigue and the "Second Shift" on Antenatal Morbidity. *American Journal of Obstetrics and Gynecology* 181 (5): 1172–79.

Maccoby, Eleanor E. 1998. *The Two Sexes*. Cambridge, MA: Harvard University Press, Belknap Press.

———. 2000. Paper presented at University of Virginia's Center for Children, Families and the Law. 27 March.

Maestripieri, Dario, and Suzanne Pelka. 2002. Sex Differences in Interest in Infants across the Lifespan: A Biological Adaptation for Parenting? *Human Nature* 13 (3).

Males, Mike. 1992. Adult Liaison in the "Epidemic" of "Teenage" Birth, Pregnancy, and Venereal Disease. *Journal of Sex Research* 29 (4): 525–45.

Manlove, Jennifer, Elizabeth Terry-Humen, Angela Romano Papillo, Kerry Franzetta, Stephanie Williams and Suzanne Ryan. 2002. Preventing Teenage Pregnancy, Childbearing, and Sexually Transmitted Diseases: What the Research Shows. *Child Trends Research Brief*, May.

Mann, Judy. 2001. Women Should Reach for Governorships. *Washington Post*, 13 April.

Mansfield, Christopher J. 1999. Premature Mortality in the United States: The Roles of Geographical Areas, Socioeconomic Status, Household Type, and Availability of Medical Care. *American Journal of Public Health* 89: 893–98.

Marcus, Mary Brophy. 1997. "If You Let Me Play": A Basketball or a Hockey Puck May Shatter the Glass Ceiling. *U. S. News and World Report*, 27 October, 88–90.

Marcus, Ruth. 1985. Enid Waldholtz: Savvy Politician or Duped Wife. *Washington Post*, 26 November.

Margaret Carlson's Competition. 1998. *Weekly Standard*, 20 July.

Marlowe, Anne. 2000. Wages of Sin: A Review of *4 Blondes*, by Candace Bushnell. http://www.salon.com/books/feature/2000/09/22/bushnell.

Martin, Judith. 1984. *Miss Manners' Guide to Rearing Perfect Children*. New York: Penguin.

———. 1985. Playing Coy Makes the Heart Grow Fonder. *Washington Post*, 27 March.

Mathews, Jay, and Valerie Strauss. 2000. Head Start Works for Girls. *Washington Post*, 10 October.

Matthews, Karen A., and Brooks B. Gump. 2002. Chronic Work Stress and Marital Dissolution Increase Risk of Posttrial Mortality in Men from the Multiple Risk Factor Intervention Trial. *Archives of Internal Medicine* 162: 309–15.

Mattox, William R., Jr. 1996. Marital Bliss. *American Enterprise,* May/June: 45–46.

Matus, Victorino. 1999. Jane's Lovers: Boys and Their Toys. *Weekly Standard,* 17 May.

Maurer, David. 1997. Dealing with a Sportsaholic. *Charlottesville Daily Progress,* 28 September.

Mazur, Allan, and Alan Booth. 1998. Testosterone and Dominance in Men. *Behavioral and Brain Sciences* 21: 353–97.

Mazur, Allan, and Theodore Lamb. 1980. Testosterone, Status and Mood in Human Males. *Hormones and Behavior* 14: 236–46.

McCabe, Kristen M. 1997. Sex Differences in the Long Term Effects of Divorce on Children: Depression and Heterosexual Relationship Difficulties in the Young Adult Years. *Journal of Divorce and Remarriage* 27 (1/2): 123.

McCarthy, Sheryl. 1999. Neither Senator nor Former Senator Have Behaved Well in This Little Tiff. *Charlottesville Daily Progress,* 7 November.

McCombs, Phil. 2003. Comeback of the Alpha Male. *Washington Post,* 16 March.

McDermott, Alice. 1993. Books and Babies. *Washington Post,* 9 May.

McDonough, Peggy, Vivienne Walters and Lisa Strohschein. 2002. Chronic Stress and the Social Patterning of Women's Health in Canada. *Social Science and Medicine* 54: 767–82.

McDonough, Peggy, David R. Williams, James S. House and Greg J. Duncan. 1999. Gender and the Socioeconomic Gradient in Morality. *Journal of Health and Social Behavior* 40: 17–31.

McGovern, Patricia, Bryan Dowd, Dwenda Gjerdingen, Ira Moscovice, Laura Kochevar and William Lohman. 1997. Time off Work and the Postpartum Health of Employed Women. *Medical Care* 35 (5): 507–21.

McGuinness, Diane. 1979. How Schools Discriminate against Boys. *Human Nature,* February: 82–88.

———. 1985. *When Children Don't Learn.* New York: Basic Books.

McGuinness, Diane, and John Symonds. 1977. Sex Differences in Choice Behaviour: The Object-Person Dimension. *Perception* 6: 691–93.

McKee, Lorna. 1982. Fathers' Participation in Infant Care: A Critique. In *The Father Figure*, ed. L. McKee and M. O'Brien. New York: Tavistock.

McLain, D. Kelly, Deanna Setters, Michael P. Moulton and Ann E. Pratt. 2000. Ascription of Resemblance of Newborns by Parents and Nonrelatives. *Evolution and Human Behavior* 21 (1): 11–23.

McLanahan, Sara, and Gary Sandefur. 1994. *Growing Up with a Single Parent*. Cambridge: Harvard University Press.

McLaughlin, Diane K., and Daniel T. Lighter. 1997. Poverty and the Marital Behavior of Young Women. *Journal of Marriage and the Family* 59: 582–94.

McLaughlin, Emma, and Nicola Kraus. 2002. *The Nanny Diaries*. New York: St. Martin's Press.

McLellan, Diana. 2000. Reagan's Letters, Sealed with a Kiss. *Washington Post,* 6 September.

McLure, Ivy. 1999. Springtime for Virginity. *Women's Quarterly,* Summer: 22.

McMunn, Anne N., J. Nazruu, M. Marmot, R. Boreham and R. Goodman. 2001. Children's Emotional and Behavioural Well-Being and the Family Environment: Findings from the Health Survey for England. *Social Science and Medicine* 53 (4): 423–40.

McPherson, James M. 1997. What's the Matter with History? A Noted Civil War Historian Takes a Critical Look at His Profession. *Princeton Alumni Weekly,* 22 January.

Mealey, Linda. 2000. *Sex Differences: Developmental and Evolutionary Strategies*. San Diego: Academic Press.

Men, Women and Marriage. 1993. *Washington Post,* 5 December.

Men, Women and Sports. 1991. *Washington Post,* 1 December.

Mencimer, Stephanie. 1998. When You Must Make a Lasting Impression. *Washington Post,* 19 April.

Meredith, Tiffany. 2000. By Taming Horses, Prisoners Learn to Change Their Lives. *Washington Post,* 27 November.

Merida, Kevin. 1998. Like Other Rookies, Tracy McGrady Guards against the Sucker Play. *Washington Post,* 10 March.

Merida, Kevin, and Barbara Vobejda. 1998. Battles on the Home Front. *Washington Post,* 24 March.

Merkin, Daphne. 1996. Spanking: A Romance. *New Yorker,* Special Women's Issue, 26 February.

Miedzian, Myriam. 1991. *Boys Will Be Boys*. New York: Doubleday.

Mike, Deborah, Patricia McGovern, Laura Kochevar and Cecilia Roberts. 1994. Role Function and Mental Health in Postpartum Working Women. *American Association of Occupational Health Nurses* 42 (1): 214–29.

Miller, David. 1990. *Market, State, and Community: Theoretical Foundations of Market Socialism*. Oxford: Oxford University Press.

Miller, Edward M. 1998. Evidence from Opposite Sex Twins for the Effects of Prenatal Sex Hormones. In *Males, Females, and Behavior*, ed. L. Ellis and L. Ebertz. Westport, CT: Praeger.

Miller, Geoffrey F. 2000. *The Mating Mind*. New York: Doubleday.

Miller, Linda R., Rakhee N. Bilimoria and Nisha Pattni. 2000. Do Women Want "New Men"? *Psychology, Evolution and Gender* 2 (2): 3.

Miller, Nancy H., David J. Miller and Melissa Chism. 1996. Breast-feeding Practices among Resident Physicians. *Pediatrics* 98 (3): 434.

Miller, Warren B. 1980. First Child Decision Questionnaire Part II. (Answer to question D). In *National Institute of Child Health and Development. The Psychology of Reproduction. Appendix 4: Instruments Used for the Measurement of Psychological Traits.* Springfield, Virginia: National Technical Information Service.

Millet, Kate. 1970. *Sexual Politics.* New York: Doubleday.

Milloy, Courtland. 1999. Why Are These Girls Laughing? *Washington Post,* 5 May.

Mintz, Steven. 1998. From Patriarchy to Androgyny and Other Myths: Placing Men's Family Roles in Historical Perspective. In *Men in Families,* ed. A. Booth and A. C. Crouter. Mahwah, NJ: Lawrence Erlbaum Associates.

Miscarriage Raises Women's Risk of Major Depression. 1997. *Washington Post,* 5 February.

Mishra, Raja. 1997. Jessup's New Warden Lets Prisoners Know Who's Boss. *Washington Post,* 22 November.

Mitchell, Valory, and Ravenna Helsons. 1990. Women's Prime of Life. Is It the 50's? *Psychology of Women Quarterly* 1: 451–70.

Moir, Anne, and David Jessel. 1989. *Brain Sex: The Real Difference between Men and Women.* New York: Delta.

Moir, Anne, and Bill Moir. 1999. *Why Men Don't Iron.* New York: Citadel Press.

Montgomery, David. 1997. Paint It Green. *Washington Post,* 9 November.

Moon, Rachel T. 2000. Sudden Infant Death Syndrome in Child Care Settings. *Pediatrics* 106: 295–300.

Moore, David W. 1997. Today's Husband More Involved in Household Duties Than Post-WWII Generation (Results of Survey on Husbands' Involvement in Household Duties). *Gallup Poll Monthly* 378: 8–13.

Morin, Richard. 1997. Is There a Heroism Gender Gap? *Washington Post,* 26 January.

———. 2000. Why Married Men Shouldn't Teach. *Washington Post,* 6 August.

———. 2001. Boy Trouble. *Washington Post,* 24 June.

———. 2002. Catching a Divorce. *Washington Post,* 4 August.

Morin, Richard, and Claudia Dean. 2002. The Ideas Industry: Welfare Reform Reforms Teens, Study Says. *Washington Post,* 28 May.

Morris, Betsy. 1997. Is Your Family Wrecking Your Career? *Fortune,* 17 March.

Morse, Jennifer Roback. 2001. *Love and Economics. Why the Laissez-Faire Family Doesn't Work*. Dallas: Spence Publishing Co.

Morse, Steve. 1989. Bonnie Raitt Shows Renewed Spirit. *Boston Globe,* 19 March.

Mortensen, Erik Lykke, Kim Fleisher Michaelson, Stephanie A. Sanders and June Manchover Reinisch. 2002. The Association between Duration of Breastfeeding and Adult Intelligence. *Journal of the American Medical Association* 287 (18).

Moyers, Bill. 1986. The Vanishing Family: Crisis in Black America. *CBS News*.

Mozingo, Johnie, Mitzi W. Davis, Patricia G. Droppleman and Amy Meredith. 2000. Women's Experiences with Short-Term Breastfeeding. *Journal of Maternal and Child Nursing* 25 (3).

Muggeridge, Anne Roche. 1995. Give a Little Whistle! *Women's Quarterly,* Winter: 9–10.

Muldoon, O., and J. Reilly. 1998. Biology. In *Gender and Psychology,* ed. K. Trew and J. Kremer. London: Arnold.

Mundy, Liza. 2000. Sex and Sensibility. *Washington Post,* 16 July.

Munson, Steven C. 1999. Sex, Death, and Picasso (Metropolitan Museum of Art Exhibit of Pablo Picasso's Ceramic Works). *Commentary* 108 (1): 70.

Murphy, Caryle. 1997. Can an Infant's Sex Be Changed? *Washington Post,* 18 March.

Murphy, J. M., N. M. Laird, R. R. Monson, A. M. Sobol and A. H. Leighton. 2000. Incidence of Depression in the Stirling County Study: Historical and Comparative Perspectives. *Psychological Medicine* 30 (3): 505–14.

Murray, John E. 2000. Marital Protection and Marital Selection: Evidence from a Historical-Prospective Sample of American Men. *Demography* 37 (4): 511–21.

Murstein, Bernard I. 1974. *Love, Sex, and Marriage through the Ages.* New York: Springer Publishing Co.

Musante, Linda, Frank A. Treiber, William B. Strong and Maurice Levy. 1990. Individual and Cross-Spouse Correlations of Perceptions of Family Functioning, Blood Pressure and Dimensions of Anger. *Journal of Psychosomatic Research* 34 (4): 393–99.

Myers, Anita, and Hilary Lips. 1978. Participation in Competitive Amateur Sports as a Function of Psychological Androgyny. *Sex Roles* 4 (4).

Nasar, Sylvia. 2001. *A Beautiful Mind.* New York: Simon and Schuster.

National Campaign to Prevent Teen Pregnancy. 2002. *Not Just Another Thing to Do.* http://www.teenpregnancy.org (accessed 30 June 2000).

National Council on Aging. 1998. National Council on Aging Study. *Washington Post,* 13 October.

National Institute of Child Health and Human Development, Early Child Care Research Network. 2003. Does Amount of Time Spent in Child Care Predict Socioemotional Adjustment during the Transition to Kindergarten? *Child Development* 74 (4): 976–1005.

National Survey of Family Growth. 1997. Vital and Health Statistics.

National Women's Law Center. 2002. Equal Opportunity for Women in Athletics: A Promise Yet to Be Fulfilled. In *Report to the Commission on Opportunity in Athletics,* August.

National Wrestling Coaches Association. 2002. Amateur Wrestling Fact Sheet 2001–2002.

Navarro, Mireya. 2001. Women in Sports Cultivating New Playing Fields. *New York Times,* 13 February.

Nelson, Kathleen. 2003. Infertility Therapy Fraught with Health Risks. *Women's ENews* (cited 10 July 2003). Available via e-mail: womensnewstoday@womensenews.org.

Nevid, Jeffrey S. 1984. Sex Differences in Factors of Romantic Attraction. *Sex Roles* 11 (5/6).

Nichols, Rachel. 2002. All Eyes Are Watching. *Washington Post,* 3 July.

Nisbett, Richard, and Dov Cohen. 1999a. Men: The Scientific Truth about Their Work, Play, Health and Passions. *Scientific American* 10 (2).

———. 1999b. Men, Honor and Murder. *Scientific American* 10 (2).

Nixon, Edna. 1971. *Mary Wollstonecraft: Her Life and Times.* London: J. M. Dent and Sons, Ltd.

Nock, Steven L. 1995. Commitment and Dependency in Marriage. *Journal of Marriage and the Family* 57: 503–14.

———. 1998. *Marriage in Men's Lives.* Oxford: Oxford University Press.

———. 1999. The Problem with Marriage. *Society* 36 (5): 20–28.

———. 2000. Time and Gender in Marriage. *Virginia Law Review* 86 (8): 1971–87.

———. 2001. The Marriages of Equally Dependent Spouses. *Journal of Family Issues* 22 (6): 755–75.

Nock, Steven L., and Margaret F. Brinig. 2001. Weak Men and Disorderly Women: Divorce and the Division of Labor. In *The Law and Economics of Marriage and Divorce,* ed. A. W. Dnes and R. Rowthorn. Cambridge: Cambridge University Press.

Noddings, Nel. 1998. Perspectives from Feminist Philosophy. *Educational Researcher* 27 (5): 17–18.

Noguchi, Irene. 2001. Hooking Up in College. *Washington Post,* 28 August.

Nordlinger, Pia. 1999. Daughters of the Sexual Revolution. *Women's Quarterly,* Summer: 18–20.

Number of Troubled Children Increases. 2000. *Washington Post,* 6 June.

Nussbaum, Martha C. 1992. Justice for Women! *New York Review of Books* 39 (16).

———. 1997. Women in the Sixties. In *Reassessing the Sixties: Debating the Political and Cultural Legacy,* ed. S. Macedo. New York: W. W. Norton and Co.

Nyborg, Helmuth. 1994. *Hormones, Sex and Society.* Westport, CT: Praeger.

Nyquist, Ann-Christine. 1999. Antibiotic Use and Abuse in Clinical Practice. *Pediatric Annals* 28 (7): 453.

Oberman, Michelle. 1994. Turning Girls into Women: Re-evaluating Modern Statutory Rape Law. *Journal of Criminal Law and Criminology* 85: 15–79.

Oh Baby. 2002. *Living Well* (newsletter of Southern Health HMO), Summer.

Okie, Susan. 1996. Stress and Colds. *Washington Post,* 10 December.

———. 2000. Day Care, Older Siblings Protect against Asthma. *Washington Post,* 24 August.

———. 2002. Mothers Who Nurse Have Less Breast Cancer Risk. *Washington Post,* 19 July.

Okin, Susan Moller. 1992. *Justice, Gender, and the Family.* New York: Basic Books.

O'Leary, Dale. 1997. *The Gender Agenda: Redefining Equality.* Lafayette, LA: Vital Issues Press.

Only Widows and Orphans. 1999. *Economist,* 8 May.

Osgood, D. Wayne, and Jeff M. Chambers. 2000. Social Disorganization Outside the Metropolis: An Analysis of Rural Youth Violence. *Criminology* 38 (1): 81–115.

Ousey, Graham C. 2000. Deindustrialization, Female-Headed Families, and Black and White Juvenile Homicide Rates, 1970–1990. *Sociological Inquiry* 70 (4): 391–419.

Outside the Court, Chaos Too. 1997. *Economist,* 8 January.

Padu, S. N., and K. Peltzer. 2000. Risk Factors and Child Sex Abuse among Secondary School Students in the Northern Province (South Africa). *Child Abuse and Neglect* 24 (2): 259–68.

Paikoff, Roberta L., and J. Brooks-Gunn. 1990. Associations between Pubertal Hormones and Behavioral and Affective Expression. In *Psychoneuroendocrinology: Brain, Behavior, and Hormonal Interactions,* ed. C. Holmes. New York: Springer-Verlag.

Pampei, Fred C., and John B. Williamson. 2001. Age Patterns of Suicide and Homicide Mortality Rates in High-Income Nations. *Social Forces* 80: 251–92.

Parcel, Toby L., and Mikaela J. Dufur. 2001. Capital at Home and at School: Effects on Student Achievement. *Social Forces* 79 (3): 881.

Parke, Ross D., and Armin A. Brott. 1999. *Throwaway Dads: The Myths and Barriers That Keep Men from Being the Fathers They Want to Be*. Boston: Houghton Mifflin Co.

Parke, Ross D., and Douglas B. Sawin. 1976. The Father's Role in Infancy: A Re-Evaluation. *Family Coordinator* 25 (4): 365–71.

Parker, Keith D., Suzanne T. Ortega and Jody VanLaningham. 1995. Life Satisfaction, Self Esteem, and Personal Happiness among Mexican and African Americans. *Sociological Spectrum* 15: 131–45.

Pate et al. 2000. Sports Participation? *Archives of Pediatric and Adolescent Medicine* 154.

Pawlowski, B., and R. I. M. Dunbar. 1999. Impact of Market Value on Human Mate Choice Decisions. *Biological Sciences* 266: 281–85.

Pearlstein, Steven. 1998. Subsidies May Not Mean Parents "Trade Up on Day Care." *Washington Post,* 1 February.

Pearson, Allison. 2002. *I Don't Know How She Does It: The Life of Kate Reddy, Working Mother.* New York: Knopf.

Pellegrini, A. D., and Jane C. Perlmutter. 1988. Rough-and-Tumble Play on the Elementary School Playground. *Young Children* 43 (2): 14–47.

Pennington, Bill. 2002. Men's Teams Benched as Colleges Level the Field. *New York Times,* 9 May.

Penton-Voak, I. S., and D. I. Perrett. 2000. Female Preference for Male Faces Changes Cyclically: Further Evidence. *Evolution and Human Behavior* 21 (1): 39.

Peplau, Letitia Anne. 1985. Women and Men in Love: Gender Differences in Close Heterosexual Relationships. In *Women, Gender, and Social Psychology,* ed. V. E. O'Leary, R. K. Unger and B. S. Wallston. Hillsdale, NJ: Lawrence Erlbaum Associates.

Perrett, D. I., K. J. Lee, I. Penton-Voak, D. Rowland, S. Yoshikawa, D. M. Burt, S. P. Henzi, D. L. Castles and S. Akamatsu. 1998. Effects of Sexual Dimorphism on Facial Attractiveness. *Nature* 394 (6696).

Perry-Jenkins, Maureen, and Sally Gillman. 2000. Parental Job Experiences and Children's Well-Being: The Case of Two-Parent and Single-Mother Working Class Families. *Journal of Family and Economic Issues* 21 (2).

Peterson, Karen S. 2002. Cohabiting Can Make Marriage an Iffy Proposition. *USA Today,* 8 July.

Peth-Pierce, Robin. 2002. *The NICHD Study of Early Child Care.* http://www.nichd.nih.gov/ (accessed 11 October 2002).

Pew Research Center for the People and the Press Survey. 1997. *As American Women See It: Motherhood Today—A Tougher Job, Less Ably Done* (State of the Union Mother's Day Poll). http://people-press.org/dataarchive/#1997 (accessed 9 May 1997).

Phillips, Melanie. 1999. *The Sex-Changed Society.* London: Social Market Foundation.

Pienta, Amy Mehrahan, Mark D. Hayward and Kristi Rahrig Jenkins. 2000. Health Consequences of Marriage for Retirement Years. *Journal of Family Issues* 21 (5): 559–86.

Pinker, Steven. 1997. *How the Mind Works.* New York: W. W. Norton and Co.

———. 1998. Boys Will Be Boys. *New Yorker,* 9 February.

Pipher, Mary. 1994. *Reviving Ophelia: Saving the Selves of Adolescent Girls.* New York: Ballantine Books.

Platek, Steven, Rebecca L. Burch, Ivan S. Panyavin, Brett H. Wasserman and Gordon G. Gallup Jr.. 2002. Reactions to Children's Faces; Resemblance Affects Males More Than Females. *Evolution and Human Behavior* 23: 159–66.

Podhoretz, Norman. 1991. Rape in Feminist Eyes. *Commentary* 92 (4): 29–36.

Podles, Mary Elizabeth. 1997. Courtship and *The Rules. American Enterprise,* March: 24–25.

Polatnick, M. Riva. 1982. Why Men Don't Rear Children: A Power Analysis. In *Mothering: Essays in Feminist Theory,* ed. J. Trebilcot. Totowa, NJ: Rowman and Allanheld.

Polefrone, Joanna M., and Stephen B. Manuck. 1987. Gender Differences in Cardiovascular and Neuroendocrine Response to Stressors. In *Gender and Stress,* ed. R. C. Barnett, L. Beiner and G. K. Baruch. New York: The Free Press.

Pollitt, Katha. 1994. Feminism at the Crossroads. *Dissent* 41 (2): 192–96.

Pool, Robert. 1994. *Eve's Rib.* New York: Crown Publishers.

Popenoe, David. 1993. Parental Adrogyny. *Society,* September.

———. 1996. *Life without Father.* New York: The Free Press.

———. 2001. Single Father's Day. *Weekly Standard,* 2 July.

Popenoe, David, and Barbara Whitehead. 1999. Should We Live Together? Paper presented at The National Marriage Project. New Brunswick, NJ: Rutgers, The State University of New Jersey.

———. 2001. Who Wants to Marry a Soul Mate? In *The State of Our Unions 2001: The Social Health of Marriage in America.* The National Marriage Project. New Brunswick, NJ: Rutgers, The State University of New Jersey.

Post Labor Laboring. 2000. *Charlottesville Daily Progress,* 24 October.

Powell, Michael. 1998. The Plutocratic Party. *Washington Post,* 6 February.

———. 2001. Bloomberg: Coming into Focus. *Washington Post,* 31 December.

Power, Thomas G. 2000. *Play and Exploration in Children and Animals.* Mahwah, NJ: Lawrence Erlbaum Associates.
Powers, Elizabeth. 1997. A Farewell to Feminism. *Commentary,* January.
Presser, Harriet B. 1998. Decapitating the U.S. Census Bureau's "Head of Household": Feminist Mobilization in the 1970's. *Feminist Economics* 4: 145–58.
Prior, P. M., and B. C. Hayes. 2001. Marital Status and Bed Occupancy in Health and Social Care Facilities in the United Kingdom. *Public Health* 115: 401–6.
The Pros and Cons of Breast-Feeding. 1998. Letter to the Editor. *Washington Post,* 6 January.
Prose, Francine. 1998. Waiting to Inhale Bill. *New York Observer,* 9 February.
Prosser, William R., and Sharon M. McGroder. 1992. The Supply and Demand for Child Care: Measurement and Analytic Issues. In *Child Care in the 1990s: Trends and Consequences,* ed. A. Booth. Hillsdale, NJ: Lawrence Erlbaum Associates.
Purifoy, Frances E., and Lambert H. Koopmans. 1979. Andostenedione, Testosterone, and Free Testosterone Concentration in Women of Various Occupations. *Social Biology* 26 (3).
Purtilo, Ruth B. 1996. Narratives on Pain and Comfort. *Journal of Law, Medicine and Ethics* 24.
Quart, Alissa. 1998. Neo-Counterculture. *Washington Post,* 7 June.
Quinn, Sally. 1992. Who Killed Feminism? *Washington Post,* 19 January.
Rabkin, Jeremy. 1997. Feminism: Where the Spirit of the Sixties Lives On. In *Reassessing the Sixties,* ed. S. Macedo. New York: W. W. Norton and Co.
Raitt, Bonnie. 1989. *The Nick of Time.* CD. Capitol Records.
Rasche, Christine E. 1991. *Special Needs of the Female Offender: A Curriculum Guide for Correctional Officers.* Tallahassee, FL: Florida State Department of Education.
Raskin, Barbara. 1996. The Mommy Faces of Feminism. *Washington Post,* 8 October.
Raspberry, William. 1997. The Way They Play on the Mean Streets. *Washington Post,* 12 December.
———. 1999. Learning about Boys from Elephants. *Charlottesville Daily Progress,* 5 March.
———. 2000a. Little Girls and the Father Factor. *Washington Post,* 15 May.
———. 2000b. Should We Save Money or Help Poor? *Charlottesville Daily Progress,* 6 June.
———. 2001. What's Love Got To Do with It? *Charlottesville Daily Progress,* 27 July.

Ravitch, Diane. 2003. *The Language Police: How Pressure Groups Restrict What Students Learn.* New York: Alfred A. Knopf.

Reality Check: The Gender Revolution. 1998. *Washington Post,* 22 March.

Rebelsky, Freda, and Cheryl Hanks. 1971. Fathers' Verbal Interaction with Infants in the First Three Months of Life. *Child Development* 42 (1).

Rector, Robert, and Kirk A. Johnson. 2002. The Effects of Marriage and Maternal Education in Reducing Child Poverty: The Heritage Center for Data Analysis.

Redfearn, Suz. 2002. The Dirt on Bad Hygiene, Good Health. *Washington Post,* 12 November.

Redmond, Stephen R., and Michael E. Pichichero. 1984. Hemophilus Influenza Type B Disease: An Epidemiological Study with Special Reference to Day Care Centers. *Journal of the American Medical Association* 252: 2581–84.

Reid, T. R. 1998. Bridget Jones' Lonely Hearts Club Fans. *Washington Post,* 18 May.

Reinisch, June Machover. 1981. Prenatal Exposure to Synthetic Progestins Increases Potential for Aggression in Humans. *Science* 211: 1171–73.

The Reliable Source. 1998. *Washington Post,* 12 January.

Rensberger, Boyce. 1994. Anthropology: Violence Is Nothing New. *Washington Post,* 30 May.

Republican National Committee. 2000. Republican Platform 2000: Renewing America's Purpose Together: Higher Education: Increased Access for All.

Reuters. 1990. Stressful Jobs Seen as No Risk to Childbirth. *Washington Post,* 11 October.

Reuters. 2002. Married Women Enjoy Best Sex. 12 November.

Reynolds, Gerald. 2003. Further Guidance on Title IX. U.S. Department of Education, Office for Civil Rights.

Rhoads, Steven E., and Christopher H. Rhoads. 2004. Gender Roles and Infant Toddler Care: The Special Case of Tenure Track Faculty. Paper presented at Annual Meeting of the MidWest Political Science Association. 16 April. http://www.faculty.virginia.edu/familyandtenure/genderrolesandinfantcare.pdf.

Rhodes, Gillian, Leslie A. Zebrowitz, Alison Clark, S. Michael Kalick, Amy Hightower and Ryan McKay. 2001. Do Facial Averageness and Symmetry Signal Health? *Evolution and Human Behavior* 22: 31–46.

Richardson, Laurel, Verta Taylor and Nancy Whittier. 1997. *Feminist Frontiers IV.* New York: McGraw-Hill Co.

Richardson, Peggy. 1983. Women's Perceptions of Change in Relationships with Their Husbands during Pregnancy. *Maternal-Child Nursing Journal* 12 (1): 1–19.

Ridley, Matt. 1999. *Genome: The Autobiography of a Species in 23 Chapters*. New York: HarperCollins.

Riessman, Catherine K. 1990. *Divorce Talk: Women and Men Make Sense of Personal Relationships*. New Brunswick, NJ: Rutgers University Press.

Rivers, Caryl. 2002. Do Men Pant for Anna K. Because She Loses? *Women's ENews,* 4 September.

Roach, David. 1995. Will Title IX Be the End of Equal Opportunity in Sports? *Washington Post*, 5 October.

Roaf, P. 1979. Coaching Women. *Coaching Review* 2 (12).

Roback, Jennifer. 1993. Beyond Equality. *Georgetown Law Journal* 82: 121–33.

Roberts, Roxanne. 1993. Fabio, the Model of Romantic Perfection at Hecht's: Swoontime with the Italian Hunk. *Washington Post,* 23 October.

———. 2000. Splitsville. *Washington Post,* 5 January.

———. 2002. The Whole Mom Catalogue. *Washington Post,* 12 November.

Roberts, Susan B. 2001. Prevention of Hypertension in Adulthood by Breastfeeding? *Lancet* 357 (9254).

Robertson, Brian C. 2000. *There's No Place Like Work*. Dallas: Spence Publishing Co.

———. 2003. *Day Care Deception: What the Child Care Establishment Isn't Telling Us*. San Francisco: Encounter Books.

Robinson, Tom. 1999. SEALs Aim to Recruit Wrestlers. *Virginian-Pilot* (Norfolk), 11 April.

Rockwell, Susan. 1986. Our Woman in Damascus Learns about Love, Life and Dentistry. *Washington Post,* 16 March.

Rodgers, Kathleen Boyce, and Hilary A. Rose. 2002. Risk and Resiliency Factors among Adolescents Who Experience Marital Transitions. *Journal of Marriage and the Family* 64: 1024–37.

Rodríguez, Cindy. 2000. From Morocco with Love. *Boston Sunday Globe,* 11 June.

Roe, Brian, Leslie A. Whittington, Sara Beck Fein and Mario F. Teisl. 1999. Is There Competition between Breast-Feeding and Maternal Employment? *Demography* 36 (2): 151–71.

Roffman, Deborah M. 1999. Parents Can Influence Young Teens Not to Engage in "New" Fad: Oral Sex. *Charlottesville Daily Progress,* 25 July.

Rogers, Lois. 2000. One in Seven Fathers "Not the Real Parent." *London Sunday Times,* 22 January.

Rogers, Stacy J., and Lynn K. White. 1998. Satisfaction with Parenting: The Role of Marital Happiness, Family Structure, and Parents' Gender. *Journal of Marriage and the Family* 60: 293–308.

Roiphe, Katie. 1993. *Sex, Fear, and Feminism.* Boston: Little, Brown and Co.

———. 1997. When Two's a Crowd: The Downside of the Safe Sex Crusade. *Washington Post,* 23 March.

Rosaldo, M. Z. 1980. The Use and Abuse of Anthropology: Reflections on Feminism and Cross-Cultural Understanding. *Journal of Women in Culture and Society* 5 (3).

Roscigno, Vincent J. 2000. Family/School Inequality for African American/Hispanic American Achievement. *Social Problems* 47: 266–90.

Rosen, Christine. 2002. Three Cheers for Patriarchy! *Women's Quarterly,* Spring.

Rosen, Jeffrey. 2001. Twelve Thoughtful Men: A Review of *Not Guilty: Twelve Black Men Speak Out on Law, Justice, and Life,* ed. J. Asim. *Washington Post,* 5 November.

Rosenfeld, Megan. 1985. Brmmm! Time for Baby Talk! Dr. T. Berry Brazelton and the Working Parent's Write of Passage. *Washington Post,* 6 November.

———. 1995. Games Girls Play: A Toy Chest Full of Stereotypes. *Washington Post,* 22 December.

Ross, Catherine E., and John Mirowsky. 2001. Neighborhood Disadvantage, Disorder, and Health. *Journal of Health and Social Behavior* 42: 258–76.

Rosser, Sue V. 1992. *Biology and Feminism: A Dynamic Interaction.* New York: Twayne Publishers.

Rossi, Alice S. 1985. Gender and Parenthood. In *Gender and the Life Course,* ed. A. S. Rossi. New York: Aldine Publishing Co.

———. 1987. Parenthood in Transition: From Lineage to Child to Self-Orientation. In *Parenting across the Lifespan,* ed. J. B. Lancaster, Jeanne Altmann, Alice S. Rossi and Lonnie R. Sherrod. New York: Aldine de Gruyter.

———. 1995. A Plea for Less Attention to Monkeys and Apes, and More to Human Biology and Evolutionary Psychology. *Politics and the Life Sciences,* August: 185–88.

———. 1997. The Impact of Family Structure and Social Change. *Children and Youth Services Review* 19 (5/6): 369–400.

Rothman, Stanley. 1995. Was There Ever a Backlash against Women? In *The Presentation of Gender in the Mass Media: Neither Victim nor Enemy, Women's Freedom Network Looks at Gender in America,* ed. Rita J. Simon. Lanham, MD: University Press of America.

Rountree, Pamela Wilcox, and Barbara D. Warner. 1999. Social Ties and Crime: Is the Relationship Gendered? *Criminology* 37 (4): 789–813.

Rovner, Sandy. 1983. Health Talk: Heart Attacks and Wives. *Washington Post.* 1 July.

Rowe, David C. 1994. *The Limits of Family Influence: Genes, Experience, and Behavior.* New York: The Guilford Press.

Rumbelow, Helen. 2002. Study Looks at Women, Marriage and Divorce. *Washington Post,* 25 July.

Rushton, J. P. 2002. Evolution of Social Responsibility: A Twin Study. Paper presented at 14th Annual Meeting of the Human Behavior and Evolution Society, New Brunswick, NJ, 19–23 June.

Russek, L. G., G. E. Schwartz, I. R. Bell and C. M. Baldwin. 1998. Positive Perceptions of Parental Caring Are Associated with Reduced Psychiatric and Somatic Symptoms. *Psychosomatic Medicine* 60: 654–57.

Russell, Christine. 1999. Only 10 Percent of Day Care Is Rated Excellent. *Washington Post,* 23 February.

Ruth, Sheila. 2000. *Issues in Feminism: An Introduction to Women's Studies.* 5th ed. Mountain View, CA: Mayfield Publishing Co.

Ryan, Alan S., and Gilbert A. Martinez. 1989. Breast-Feeding and the Working Mother: A Profile. *Pediatrics* 83 (4).

Salasky, Julia. 2001. A Review of *Cosmopolitan,* August 2000 (v.229, i.2) –July 2001 (v.231, i.1). In *Research Assistant Report* for Steven Rhoads, Department of Politics, University of Virginia, Charlottesville.

———. 2002. Hookup Memo to Steven E. Rhoads, Department of Politics, University of Virginia, Charlottesville.

Samiei, Haleh, V. 2002. Working Late into a Pregnancy May Prompt Pre-Eclampsia. *Washington Post,* 23 April.

Samuelson, Robert. 1999. The Stealth Power Brokers. *Newsweek,* 13 December: 59.

Sandman, Curt A., Pathik D. Wadhwa, Christine Killingsworth Rini and Christine Dunkel-Schetter. 1999. Psychological Adaptation and Birth Outcomes: The Role of Personal Resources, Stress, and Sociocultural Context in Pregnancy. *Health Psychology* 18 (4): 333–45.

Sapolsky, Robert M. 1997. *The Trouble with Testosterone.* New York: Scribner.

Sargent, James. 2000. Should All Mothers Breast-Feed? *Effective Clinical Practice* 3: 141–43.

Sargent, Stephanie, Dolf Zillmann and James Weaver. 1998. The Gender Gap in the Enjoyment of Televised Sports. *Journal of Sport and Social Issues* 22 (1).

Sawhill, Isabel V. 2002. The Perils of Early Motherhood. *Public Interest* 146: 74–84.

Schaefer, Naomi. 2000. Burning Both Ends. *American Enterprise,* March.

Schaub, Diana. 1997. From Boys to Men. *Public Interest,* Spring.

———. 1998. Gen X Is OK (part II). *American Enterprise,* January/February: 42–45.

Scheck, Anne. 1996. UNC's Anson Dorrance Got On-the-Job Gender Education. *Southern Soccer Scene,* April.

Schlessinger, Laura. 1994. *Ten Stupid Things Women Do to Mess Up Their Lives.* New York: HarperCollins.

Schmitt, David P. 2003. Universal Sex Differences in the Desire for Sexual Variety: Tests from 52 Nations, 6 Continents, and 13 Islands. *Journal of Personality and Social Psychology* 85 (1): 85–104.

Schmitt, David, Todd Shackelford and David Buss. 2001. Are Men Really More "Oriented" toward Short-Term Mating Than Women? *Psychology, Evolution and Gender:* 211–239.

Scholer, Seth J., Jr., Edward F. Mitchel Jr. and Wayne A. Ray. 1997. Predictors of Injury Mortality in Early Childhood. *Pediatrics* 100: 342–47.

Schwartz, Felice. 1989. Management Women. *Harvard Business Review,* January/February: 65–76.

Schwartz, Pepper. 1994. Peer Marriage. *Family Therapy Networker,* September/October: 93–97.

Schwartz, Pepper, and Virginia Rutter. 1998. *The Gender of Sexuality.* Thousand Oaks, CA: Pine Forges Press.

Science Notebook: Mating and the Immune System. 2000. *Washington Post,* 13 November.

Science Notebook: The Pill's Olfactory Effect. 2001. *Washington Post,* 29 October.

Scrapbook. 1999. *Weekly Standard,* 15 February.

See, Carolyn. 1999. Review of *Waiting for Truffaut* (film). *Washington Post,* 7 May.

Selmi, Michael. 2000. Family Leave and the Gender Wage Gap. *North Carolina Law Review* 178 (3): 707–82.

Sephton, Sandra E., Robert M. Sapolsky, Helena C. Kraemer and David Spiegel. 2000. Diurnal Cortisol Rhythm as a Predictor of Breast Cancer Survival. *Journal of the National Cancer Institute* 92 (12): 994.

Shalit, Wendy. 1997. Daughters of the (Sexual) Revolution. *Commentary* 104 (6).

———. 1999. *A Return to Modesty.* New York: Simon and Schuster.

Shapiro, Laura. 1997. The Myth of Quality Time. *Newsweek,* 12 May.

Shapiro, Leonard, and Thomas Heath. 2000. Leaving It All on the Football Field. *Washington Post,* 7 February.

Sharbutt, Jay. 1990. Connie Chung Puts Series on Hold, Wants Baby. Associated Press, 30 July.

Sheets, Virgil. 2002. Patterns of Jealousy in Russia. Paper presented at 14th Annual Meeting of the Human Behavior and Evolution Society, New Brunswick, NJ, 19–23 June.

Sherwin, Barbara B. 1988. A Comparative Analysis of the Role of Androgen in Human Male and Female Sexual Behavior: Behavioral

Specificity, Critical Thresholds, and Sensitivity. *Psychobiology* 16 (4): 416–25.

Shields, Julie. 2002. *How to Avoid the Mommy Trap: A Roadmap for Sharing Parenting and Making It Work.* Sterling, VA: Capital Books.

———. 2003. More U.S. Dads Balance Laptops, Kids on Lap. *Women's ENews.* Available via e-mail: womensnewstoday@womensenews.org.

Shirley, Louisa J., and Anne Campbell. 2000. Same-Sex Preference in Infancy. *Psychology, Evolution and Gender* 2 (1): 3.

Shreve, Anita. 1987. *Remaking Motherhood: How Working Mothers Are Shaping Our Children's Futures.* New York: Viking Press.

Sidak, Melinda Ledden. 2000. Why Paul McCartney Is the Sexiest Man Alive. *Women's Quarterly,* Winter.

Signorella, Margaret L., and Wesley Jamison. 1986. Masculinity, Femininity, Androgyny, and Cognitive Performance: A Meta-Analysis. *Psychological Bulletin* 100 (2): 207–28.

Sileo, Chi Chi. 1995. Studies Put Genetic Twist on Theories about Sex and Love. *Insight,* 3–10 July: 36–37.

Simeone, Roseann. 2001. Charlottesville Planned Parenthood Memo.

Smith, Carolyn A. 1997. Factors Associated with Early Sexual Activity among Urban Adolescents. *Social Work* 42 (2/3): 334–46.

Smith, Jeffrey. 2000. Modern Times Erode an Israeli Institution. *Washington Post,* 24 April.

Smock, Pamela J. 2000. Cohabitation in the United States: An Appraisal of Research Themes, Findings, and Implications. *Annual Review of Sociology* 26: 1–20.

Smock, Pamela J., and Wendy D. Manning. 1997. Cohabiting Partners' Economic Circumstances and Marriage. *Demography* 34 (3): 331–41.

Smoking, Breast-Feeding Connected to SIDS (compiled from reports by the Associated Press). 2001. *Washington Post,* 24 April.

Smuts, Barbara. 1996. Male Aggression against Women. In *Sex, Power, Conflict: Evolutionary and Feminist Perspectives*, ed. D. M. Buss and N. M. Malamuth. Oxford: Oxford University Press.

Sneed, Elizabeth. 1992. Fonda Basks in Luxury of Staying Home. *USA Today,* 3 September.

Sociobiology: A Beauty Contest. 1998. *Economist,* 28 November.

Solomon, Alisa. 2003. Playing Games: Title IX Was Always about More Than Sports; So Is the Fight. *Village Voice,* 9–15 April.

Sommers, Christina Hoff. 1994. *Who Stole Feminism?* New York: Simon and Schuster.

———. 1996. Feminism Is Not the Story of Their Lives. *Heterodoxy,* May/June.

———. 1999. Social Science in Denial: Sex Differences in the Hard Wiring. *ExFemina* Special Edition.

———. 2000. *The War against Boys.* New York: Simon and Schuster.
———. 2001. E-mail to the author.
South, Scott J. 1993. Racial and Ethnic Differences in the Desire to Marry. *Journal of Marriage and the Family* 55 (2): 357–70.
———. 2001. Time Dependent Effects of Wives' Employment on Marital Dissolution. *American Sociological Review* 66 (2): 226–45.
Spake, Amanda. 1999. Brownie Wise Had One Word for You: Plastics. *U.S. News and World Report,* 18 October.
Span, Paula. 1996. Women's Rites Champion. *Washington Post,* 19 November.
———. 1997. It's a Girl's World. *Washington Post Magazine,* 22 June.
———. 1999. Television Tunes In to the Real Differences between the Sexes. *Washington Post,* 16 March.
Sporting Goods Manufacturers Association. 1998. Trends in Female Participation in Sports 1987–1997, Percentage of Frequent Participation in Sports. *Gaining Ground:* 310–11.
Sprecher, Susan, Quintin Sullivan and Elaine Hatfield. 1994. Mate Selection Preferences: Gender Differences Examined in a National Sample. *Journal of Personality and Social Psychology* 66 (6): 1074–80.
Squires, Sally. 1999. Early Breast Milk Linked to Reduced Allergies. *Washington Post,* 29 September.
———. 2000. Mom's Milk: Just Add D. *Washington Post,* 29 May, Health section, 7.
Steil, Janice M. 1997. *Marital Equality: Its Relationship to the Well-Being of Husbands and Wives.* Thousand Oaks, CA: Sage Publications.
Stein, Harry. 1993. The Making of an Anti-Feminist. *GQ,* May: 188–92.
Stein, Rob. 2002. Do Men Have Anger in Mind? *Washington Post,* 30 September.
———. 2003a. More Parents Bring Baby to Bed. *Washington Post,* 14 January.
———. 2003b. Theory Says Disease Tendencies Begin in Womb. *Washington Post,* 7 July.
Steinem, Gloria. 1992. *Revolution from Within: A Book of Self-Esteem.* Boston: Little, Brown and Co.
———. 1995. Steinem Skewers Gender Blinders at Commencement. *Smith Alumnae Quarterly.*
Stepp, Laura Sessions. 1999a. Parents Are Alarmed by an Unsettling New Fad in Middle Schools: Oral Sex. *Washington Post,* 8 July.
———. 1999b. When "Good Girls" Get a Bad Rep. *Washington Post,* 24 August.
———. 2002. From the Classroom to the Mall, Girls' Fashions Are Long on Skin, Short on Modesty. *Washington Post,* 3 June.
Stewart, Susan D., Wendy D. Manning and Pamela J. Smock. 2003.

Union Formation among Men in the U.S.: Does Having Prior Children Matter? *Journal of Marriage and the Family* 65: 90–104.

Stolba, Christine. 1999. Ms. on Estrogen. *Women's Quarterly,* Summer: 13.

Stolzenberg, Ross M. 2001. It's about Time and Gender: Spousal Employment and Health. *American Journal of Sociology* 107 (1): 61–100.

Storey, Anne E., Carolyn J. Walsh, Roma L. Quinton and Katherine E. Wynne-Edwards. 2000. Hormonal Correlates of Paternal Responsiveness in New and Expectant Fathers. *Evolution and Human Behavior* 21: 79–95.

Stossel, John. *The Ugly Truth about Beauty.* ABC News.com. http://abcnews.go.com/sections/2020/DailyNews/2020_lookism_020823.html (accessed 23 August 2002).

Strauss, Evelyn. 1998. The Female Orgasm. *Scientific American,* July.

Strauss, Valerie. 2001. Child Care Worries Adding Up. *Washington Post,* 30 April.

Streeter, Sybil A., and Donald H. McBurney. 2003. Waist-Hip Ratio and Attractiveness: New Evidence and a Critique of "a Critical Test." *Evolution and Human Behavior* 24 (2): 88–98.

Sunstein, Emily. 1975. *A Different Face: The Life of Mary Wollstonecraft.* New York: Harper and Row.

Sweeney, Megan. 2002. Two Decades of Family Change: The Shifting Economic Foundations of Marriage. *American Sociological Review* 67: 132–47.

Sweney, Jennifer Foote. 2001. *Jay Belsky Doesn't Play Well with Others.* http://dir.salon.com/mwt/feature/2001/04/26/belsky/index.html (accessed 26 April 2001).

Symons, Donald. 1981. Interview with Donald Symons on Men, Women and Sex. *Washington Post,* 22 March.

Tanenbaum, Leora. 1999. *Slut!* New York: Seven Stories Press.

Tannen, Deborah. 1990. *You Just Don't Understand: Women and Men in Conversation.* New York: William Morrow.

———. 1994. *Talking from 9 to 5: Women and Men in the Workplace: Language, Sex and Power.* New York: Avon.

———. 2001. *You Just Don't Understand: Women and Men in Conversation.* New York: Quill.

Tasker, Fred. 1995. X Marks the Fantasy. *Washington Post,* 27 July.

Tassinary, Louis G., and Kristi A. Hansen. 1998. A Critical Test of the Waist-to-Hip-Ratio Hypothesis of Female Physical Attractiveness. *Psychological Science* 9 (2).

Tavris, Carol. 1992. *The Mismeasure of Woman.* New York: Simon and Schuster.

———. 1998. Beware Biological Head Games. *Gazette,* 1 August.

Taylor, Shelly E., Laura Cousino Klein, Brian P. Lewis, Tara L. Gruenewald, Regan A. R. Gurung and John A. Updegraff. 2000. Biobehavioral Responses to Stress in Females: Tend-and-Befriend, Not Fight-or-Flight. *Psychological Review* 107 (3): 411–29.

Thiers, Naomi. 1986. Modern Parenting. *Washington Post,* 14 November.

Thompson, Linda, and Alexis J. Walker. 1989. Gender in Families: Women and Men in Marriage, Work and Parenthood. *Journal of Marriage and the Family* 51: 845–71.

Thompson, Tracy. 1998. A War inside Your Head. *Washington Post Magazine,* 15 February.

Thomson, Elizabeth. 1997. Couple Childbearing Desires, Intentions, and Births. *Demography* 34 (3).

Thrane, Nana, et al. 2001. Influence of Day Care Attendance on the Use of Systemic Antibiotics in 1- to 2-Year-Old Children. *Pediatrics* 107.

Tierney, John. 2003. Why Don't Women Watch Sports? *New York Times,* 15 June.

Tiger, Lionel. 1987. Alienated from the Meanings of Reproduction? In *Masculinity/Femininity: Basic Perspectives*, ed. J. M. Reinisch, Leonard Rosenblum and Stephanie Sanders. Oxford: Oxford University Press.

———. 1999. *The Decline of Males.* New York: Golden Books.

———. 2003. The Human Nature Project. Bradley Lecture at the American Enterprise Institute in Washington, D.C.

Tiger, Lionel, and Joseph Shepher. 1975. *Women in the Kibbutz.* New York: Harcourt Brace Jovanovich.

Todd, Janet. 2000. *Mary Wollstonecraft: A Revolutionary Life.* New York: Columbia University Press.

Toner, Robin. 2002. Two Parents Not Always Best for Children, Study Finds. 21 February.

Tooley, James. 2002. *The Miseducation of Women.* London: Continuum Publishing Group.

Toto, Christine. 2002. Basic Body Types. *Washington Times,* 2 July.

Tough, Suzanne C., et al. 2002. Delayed Chilbearing and Its Impact on Population Rate Changes in Lower Birth Weight, Multiple Birth, and Preterm Delivery. *Pediatrics* 109: 399–403.

Tousignant, Marylou. 1996. Hoops and Hollers without the Hype. *Washington Post,* 13 February.

Tout, Kathryn, Michelle de Hann, Elizabeth Kipp Campbell and Megan R. Gunnar. 1998. Social Behavior Correlates of Cortisol Activity in Child Care: Gender Differences and Time-of-Day Effects. *Child Development* 69 (5): 1247–62.

Townsend, Bickley, and Kathleen O'Neil. 1990. American Women Get Mad. *American Demographics* 12 (8): 26–31.

Townsend, John Marshall. 1995. Sex without Emotional Involvement: An Evolutionary Interpretation of Sex Differences. *Archives of Sexual Behavior* 24 (2): 173–206.

———. 1998. *What Women Want—What Men Want*. New York: Oxford University Press.

Townsend, John Marshall, Jeffrey Kline and Timothy H. Wasserman. 1995. Low-Investment Copulation: Sex Differences in Motivations and Emotional Reactions. *Ethology and Sociobiology* 16: 25–51.

Trafford, Abigail. 1996. Having Another Child. *Washington Post,* 11 June.

———. 1997. What's Good for the Baby May Guilt-Trip the Mother. *Washington Post,* 9 December, Health section.

———. 2002. Women Can't Beat the Clock. *Washington Post,* 16 April.

Travis, Cheryl Brown, and C. P. Yeager. 1991. Sexual Selection. Parental Investments and Sexism. *Journal of Social Issues* 47 (3): 117–29.

Treistman, Ann. 1999. Ring Anxiety. *Glamour,* October: 158–61.

Trevathan, Wenda R. 1987. *Human Birth: An Evolutionary Perspective.* New York: Aldine de Gruyter.

Trollope, Anthony. 1991. *The Duke's Children.* Oxford: Oxford University Press.

Tuggle, C. A., and Anne Owen. 1999. A Descriptive Analysis of NBC's Coverage of the Centennial Olympics: "The Games of the Woman"? *Journal of Sport and Social Issues* 23 (2).

Twenge, Jean M. 2000. The Age of Anxiety: Birth Cohort Change in Anxiety and Neuroticism, 1952–1993. *Journal of Personality and Social Psychology* 79 (6): 1007–21.

Tyre, Peg, and Daniel McGinn. 2003. She Works, He Doesn't. *Newsweek,* 12 May: 42–54.

Udry, J. Richard. 1988. Biological Predispositions and Social Control in Adolescent Sexual Behavior. *American Sociological Review* 53 (5): 709–22.

———. 1994. The Nature of Gender. *Demography* 31 (4): 561–73.

———. 2000. Biological Limits of Gender Construction. *American Sociological Review* 65: 443–57.

Udry, J. Richard, and John O. G. Billy. 1985. Patterns of Adolescent Friendship and Effects on Sexual Behavior. *Social Psychological Quarterly* 48: 27–41.

Udry, J. Richard, John O. G. Billy, Naomi M. Morris, Terry R. Groff and Madhwa H. Raj. 1985. Serum Androgenic Hormones Motivate Sexual Behavior in Adolescent Boys. *Fertility and Sterility* 43 (1): 90.

Udry, J. Richard, and John O. G. Billy. 1987. Initiation of Coitus in Early Adolescence. *American Sociological Review* 52: 841–55.

Udry, J. Richard, Naomi M. Morris and Judith Kovenock. 1995. Androgen Effects on Women's Gendered Behavior. *Journal of Biosocial Science* 27: 359–68.

Udry, J. Richard, Luther M. Talbert and Naomi M. Morris. 1986. Biosocial Foundations for Adolescent Female Sexuality. *Demography* 23 (2): 217.

Unger, Rhoda, and Mary Crawford. 1996. *Women and Gender: A Feminist Psychology.* New York: McGraw-Hill.

Upton, Rebecca L. 2000. The Next One Changes Everything: Parental Adjustment to the Second Child among Middle-Class American Families. University of Michigan Microfilms.

U.S. Census Bureau. 1964. *1960 Decennial Census: Characteristics of the Population, Part 1, U.S. Summary.* Vol. 1. Washington, D.C.: U.S. Government Printing Office.

———. 2002. *2002 Population Estimates.* Washington, D.C.: U.S. Government Printing Office.

U.S. Department of Education, National Center for Education Statistics. 2002.

U.S. Department of Education, Secretary's Commission for Opportunity in Athletics. 2003. Open to All: Title IX at Thirty. Washington, D.C.

U.S. Department of Health and Human Services. 1997. Vital and Health Statistics. Hyattsville, MD: DHHS Publication.

U.S. Department of Justice. 1997. Uniform Crime Reports for the United States: 1965–1997. Washington D.C.: Federal Bureau of Investigation.

Uvnas-Moberg et al. 1990. *Journal of Psychosomatic Obstetrics and Gynecology* 11: 270–72.

Uzych, Leo. 1992. Anabolic-Androgenic Steroids and Psychiatric-Related Effects: A Review. *Canadian Journal of Psychiatry* 37.

Valian, Virginia. 1998. *Why So Slow? The Advancement of Women.* Cambridge, MA: Harvard University Press.

Van Creveld, Martin. 2000. A Woman's Place: Reflections on the Origins of Violence. *Social Research* 67 (3): 825–47.

Vedantam, Shankar. 2001. Child Aggressiveness Study Cites Child Care. *Washington Post,* 19 April.

———. 2002a. No One Way to Keep Love in Bloom, Experts Say. *Washington Post,* 11 February.

———. 2002b. Study Reassesses Risk in Pre-term Births; Mild Developmental Delays Found Likely. *Washington Post,* 15 January.

———. 2003. Does a Ring Bring Happiness, or Vice Versa? *Washington Post,* 21 April.

Vernon-Feagans, Lynne, et al. 1996. Otitis Media and Social Behavior of Day Care Attending Children. *Child Development* 67: 1528–39.

Veroff, Joseph, Elizabeth Douvan, Terri L. Orbuch and Linda K. Acitelli. 1998. Happiness in Stable Marriages: The Early Years. In *The Developmental Course of Marital Dysfunction,* ed. T. N. Bradbury. Cambridge: Cambridge University Press.

Veysey, Bonita M., and Steven F. Messner. 1999. Further Testing of Social Disorganization Theory: An Elaboration of Sampson and Groves's "Community Structure and Crime." *Journal of Research in Crime and Delinquency* 36: 156–74.

Vobejda, Barbara. 1997. Who's Minding the Children. *Washington Post,* 22 October.

Voss, Kimberly Wilmot. 2002. Colleges Train Students to Press for Equal Wages. *Women's ENews.* Available via e-mail: womensnewstoday@womensenews.org.

Waite, Linda J. 1999/2000. The Negative Effects of Cohabitation. *The Responsive Community,* Winter: 31–38.

Waite, Linda J., and Kara Joyner. 2001. Emotional and Physical Satisfaction with Sex in Married, Cohabiting, and Dating Sexual Unions: Do Men and Women Differ? In *Sex, Love, and Health in America,* ed. E. O. Laumann and R. T. Michael. Chicago: University of Chicago Press.

Waite, Linda, and Ye Luo. 2002. Marital Happiness and Marital Stability: Consequences for Psychological Well-Being. Paper presented at 97th Annual Meeting of the American Sociological Association, August 2002.

Waite, Linda, Barbara Dafoe Whitehead and David Popenoe. 2000. *The State of Our Unions 2000: The Social Health of Marriage in America.* The National Marriage Project. New Brunswick, NJ: Rutgers, The State University of New Jersey.

Wald, E. R., et al. 1988. Frequency and Severity of Infections in Day Care. *Journal of Pediatrics,* April: 540–46.

Walker, Lorraine O., and Mary Ann Best. 1991. Well-Being of Mothers with Infant Children: A Preliminary Comparison of Employed Women and Homemakers. *Women and Health* 17 (1).

Walker, Susan P., Micheal Permezel, Shaun P. Brennecke, Antony M. Ugoni and John R. Higgins. 2001. Blood Pressure in Late Pregnancy and Work outside the Home. *Obstetrics and Gynecology* 97 (3).

Walsh, Elsa. 1994. The Long Recovery from Motherhood. *Washington Post,* 3 April.

Walsh, Mary Roth, ed. 1997. *Women, Men, and Gender: Ongoing Debates.* New Haven: Yale University Press.

Watamura, Sarah E., Bonny Donzella, Jan Alwin and Megan R. Gunmar. 2003. Morning-to-Afternoon Increases in Cortisol Concentrations for Infants and Toddlers at Child Care: Age Differences and Behavioral Correlates. *Child Development* 74 (4): 1006–20.

Watts, Graham F., Sr., and Stephen Nagy. 2000. Sociodemographic Factors, Attitudes, and Expectations towards Adolescent Coitus. *American Journal of Health Behaviors* 24: 309–17.

Waxman, Sharon. 1998. Mother Knows Best. *Washington Post,* 19 September.

Weaver, Courtney. 1999a. Review of *Slut!* by Leora Tanenbaum. *Washington Post,* 23 May.

———. 1999b. *Unzipped.* New York: Doubleday.

Webb, Rose Mary, David Lubinski and Camilla P. Benbow. 2002. Mathematically Facile Adolescents. *Journal of Educational Psychology* 94 (4): 785–94.

Weeks, Linton. 1999. Sex and Seniors. *Washington Post,* 19 October.

———. 2001. A Writer Who Takes the Prize. *Washington Post,* 3 November.

Weisfeld, Glenn E., R. J. H. Russel, C. C. Weisfeld and P. A. Wells. 1992. Correlates of Satisfaction in British Marriages. *Ethology and Sociobiology* 13: 125–45.

Weisfeld, Glenn E., Sally A. Bloch and Joseph W. Ivers. 1983. A Factor Analytic Study of Peer-Perceived Dominance in Adolescent Boys. *Adolescence* 18 (70).

Weisfeld, Glenn E., Denise M. Muczenski, Carol C. Weisfeld and Donald R. Omark. 1987. Stability of Boys' Social Success among Peers over an Eleven-Year Period. In *Interpersonal Relations: Family, Peers, Friends,* ed. J. A. Meacham, vol. 18 in Contributions to Human Development Monograph Series. New York: Karger.

Weiss, Rick. 1995. The Racer's Edge: Do Men Have It? *Washington Post,* 28 February.

———. 2002. Infertility Campaign Can't Get Ad Space. *Washington Post,* 28 August.

Weitoft, Gunilla Ringbäch, Anders Hjern, Bengt Haglund and Mans Rosen. 2002. Mortality, Severe Morbidity, and Injury in Children Living with Single Parent in Sweden: A Population-Based Study. *Lancet* 361 (9354): 289–95.

Welch, Patrick. 1998. The Cult of the Super-Girl. *Washington Post,* 18 December.

West, Robin L. 1987. The Difference in Women's Hedonic Lives: A Phenomenological Critique of Feminist Legal Theory. *Wisconsin Women's Law Journal* 3 (59): 81–145.

West, Thomas G. 1997. *Vindicating the Founders.* Lanham, MD: Rowman and Littlefield.

Whitehead, Barbara Dafoe. 1999. The Plight of the High-Status Woman. *Atlantic Monthly,* December.

———. 2003. *Why There Are No Good Men Left.* New York: Broadway Books.

Whitehead, Barbara Dafoe, and David Popenoe. 2000. Social Indicators of Marital Health and Wellbeing. In *The National Marriage Project, Annual Report: The Social Health of Marriage in*

America. New Brunswick, NJ: Rutgers, The State University of New Jersey.

Whitehead, Barbara Dafoe, and David Popenoe. 2002. Why Men Won't Commit. Paper presented at The National Marriage Project: The State of Our Unions 2002, at New Brunswick, NJ: Rutgers, The State University of New Jersey.

Whitehead, Barbara Dafoe, and Christina Hoff Sommers. 1998. The Girls of Gen X. *American Enterprise,* January/February: 54–60.

Whiteman, M. C., I. J. Deary, A. J. Lee and F. G. R. Fowkes. 1997. Submissiveness and Protection from Coronary Heart Disease in the General Population: Edinburgh Artery Study. *Lancet* 350: 541–45.

Whiteside, Kelly. 2001. Potential Bush Nominee under Fire over Title IX. *USA Today,* 17 July.

Whiting, Beatrice, and Carolyn Pope Edwards. 1973. A Cross-Cultural Analysis of Sex Differences in the Behavior of Children Aged Three through Eleven. *Journal of Social Psychology* 91: 171–88.

Who's Minding the Children. 1998. *Washington Post,* 12 May.

Widiger, Thomas A. 2000. Gender Bias in the Diagnosis of Personality Disorders. *Harvard Mental Health Letter.*

Wiederman, Michael W., and Elizabeth Rice Allgeier. 1992. Gender Differences in Mate Selection Criteria: Sociobiological or Socioeconomic Explanation? *Ethology and Sociobiology* 13: 115–24.

Wiesenfeld, Alan R., Carol Zander Malatesta and Linda L. DeLoach. 1981. Differential Parental Response to Familiar and Unfamiliar Infant Distress Signals. *Infant Behavior and Development* 4: 281–95.

Wilcox, W. Bradford. 2002a. E-mail to author. 5 November.

———. 2002b. The Ironies of Conservative Protestant Male Familial Involvement. In *National Survey of Families and Households.*

———. 2004. *Soft Patriarchs, New Men: How Christianity Shapes Fathers and Husbands.* Chicago: University of Chicago Press.

———. Forthcoming. *The Importance of Fatherhood for the Healthy Development of Children.* Child Abuse and Neglect User Manual Series. Washington, D.C.: U.S. Department of Health and Human Services.

Williams, Joan C. 1989. Deconstructing Gender. *Michigan Law Review* 87: 797–845.

———. 1992. Deconstructing Gender. In *Feminist Jurisprudence,* ed. L. F. Goldstein. Lanham, MD: Rowman and Littlefield.

Williams, John E., and Deborah L. Best. 1990a. *Measuring Sex Stereotypes: A Multination Study.* Rev. ed. Newbury Park, CA: Sage Publications.

———. 1990b. *Sex and Psyche: Gender and Self Viewed Cross-Culturally.* Newbury Park, CA: Sage Publications.

Williams, Marjorie. 1988. The Ms. Mystique: Feminism Puts on a Pretty Face. *Washington Post,* 3 August.

———. 2001. Mommy at her Desk. *Washington Post,* 25 April.

Williamson, Penelope. 1992. By Honor Bound. In *Dangerous Men and Adventurous Women,* ed. Jayne Anne Krentz. Philadelphia: University of Pennsylvania Press.

Willingham, Warren W., and Nancy S. Cole. 1997. *Gender and Fair Assessment.* Mahwah, NJ: Lawrence Erlbaum Associates.

Wilmouth, Janet, and Gregor Koso. 2002. Does Marital History Matter? Marital Status and Wealth Outcomes among Preretirement Adults. *Journal of Marriage and the Family* 64: 254–68.

Wilson, James Q. 1993. The Family-Values Debate. *Commentary* 95 (4): 24–28.

———. 2002. *The Marriage Problem: How Our Culture Has Weakened Families.* New York: HarperCollins.

Winkler, Claudia. 2000. Review of *As Nature Made Him,* by John Colapinto. *Weekly Standard,* 19 May.

Wisensale, Steven K. 2001. *Family Leave Policy: The Political Economy of Work and Family in America.* Armonk, NY: M. E. Sharpe.

Wolf, Naomi. 2002. *Misconceptions.* New York: Doubleday.

Wolfe, Alan. 1991. *Whose Keeper? Social Science and Moral Obligation.* Berkeley, CA: University of California Press.

———. 1998. Scholarship on Family Values: Weighing Competing Claims. *Chronicle of Higher Education* 44 (20): B7–8.

Women's Sports Foundation. 2002. Report of National Coalition for Women and Girls in Education—Title IX Athletics Policies: Issues and Data for Education Decision Makers.

Wright, Robert. 1994. Feminists Meet Mr. Darwin: The Evolutionary Psychology of the Female Mind. *New Republic,* 28 November: 34–46.

Yalom, Irvin D., Richard Green and Norman Fisk. 1973. Prenatal Exposure to Female Hormones. *Archives of General Psychiatry* 28.

Yang, John E. 1996. Rep. Lincoln Offers Barbour Maternal Insight. *Washington Post,* 9 June.

Yardley, Jonathan. 1999. Been There, Done That. *Washington Post,* 26 September.

———. 2002. Review of *The Fall of Berlin,* by Antony Beevor. *Washington Post,* 19 May.

Yoest, Charmaine. 1998. What Do Parents Want? *American Enterprise,* May.

———. 2003. Empowering Shakespeare's Sister: Parental Leave and the Level Playing Field. Paper presented at Annual Meeting of the American Political Science Association, August 28–31. http://www.faculty.virginia.edu/familyandtenure/apsapaper.pdf.

Young, Cathy. 1999. *Ceasefire!* New York: The Free Press.

Zeisel, Susan, et al. 1995. Prospective Surveillance for Otitis Media with Effusion among Black Infants in Group Child Care. *Journal of Pediatrics* 127: 875–80.

Zengerle, Jason Gray. 1997. Back to Boys' School. *American Prospect,* July: 85.

Zhang, Cui-Xia, and J. E. Farley. 1995. Gender and the Distribution of Household Work: A Comparison of Self-Reports by Female College Faculty in the United States and China. *Journal of Comparative Family Studies* 26: 195–205

Zheng, Tongzhang, Li Duan, Yi Liu, Bing Zhang, Yan Wang, Yongxiang Chen, Yawei Zhang and Patricia H. Owens. 2000. Lactation Reduces Breast Cancer Risk in Shandong Province, China. *Journal of Epidemiology* 152 (12): 1129–34.

Zorpette, Glenn. 1999. Extreme Sports, Sensation Seeking and the Brain. *Scientific American* 10 (2): 56–59.

Zuckerman, Diana. 1998. Institute for Women's Policy Research. *Washington Post,* 6 January.

INDEX